D1538302

"*A Woman's Guide to Cycling* . . . gives us easy-to-find, co.
cycling information . . . [while] personal experience vignettes in each chapter
make the information come alive. This book fills the void left by all-too-often
macho cycling books that focus on training charts, schedules, and lists. . . ."

–Phyllis Cohen, Race Across AMerica record-setter, women's 50+ team

"At last, an intelligent and accurate guide to cycling written by a woman
for women. . . .This book educates, motivates and inspires. . . ."

–Deborah Cronin, competitive cyclist, for *Cooking Light*

"This summer we met a new rider . . . who seemed to have an astounding
knowledge of all things a new cyclist should know but usually doesn't. When
asked how she became so informed, she showed us a book called *A Woman's
Guide to Cycling*. We borrowed it for a few days and were amazed to find that
it covered the necessities better than anything else we've ever seen. If you
know someone (regardless of gender) who is just starting out or who needs to
learn a little more about the sport, we highly recommend this book."

–Ann and John McKinley, Dayton Cycling Club's *Spoke 'N' Link*

"This excellent book is the most readable and appealing I have seen on
bicycling in recent years. The level of thought and detail that went into all
areas is evident. *A Woman's Guide to Cycling* includes many topics and insights
rarely found in modern cycling books."

–Dan Burden, Bicycle Coordinator for the State of Florida

A Woman's Guide to Cycling

A Woman's Guide to Cycling

Revised Edition

by SUSAN WEAVER

Illustrated by SALLY ONOPA
with a Foreword by SUSAN DeMATTEI

TEN SPEED PRESS
BERKELEY, CALIFORNIA

© 1990, 1991, 1998 by Susan Weaver
Line drawings © 1990, 1998 by Sally Onopa
Forward © 1998 by Susan DeMattei

All rights reserved. No part of this book may be reproduced in any form, except brief
excerpts for the purpose of review, without written permission of the publisher.

Carlotta Cuerdon's account of the 24 Hours of Canaan is excerpted from the June 1995
issue of *Mountain Bike* magazine, by permission of Rodale Press, Inc., © 1995.

"Nine Special Months of Cycling" is reprinted in condensed form from the March 1981
issue of *Bicycling* magazine, by permission of Rodale Press, Inc., ©1981.

Ten Speed Press
P.O. Box 7123
Berkeley, California 94707

Distributed in Australia by Simon and Schuster Australia, in Canada by Publishers Group
West, in New Zealand by Tandem Press, in South Africa by Real Books, in Southeast Asia
by Berkeley Books, and in the United Kingdom and Europe by Airlift Books.

Cover design by Gary Bernal
Interior design by Laura Lind Design
Photo credits: Dennis Coello: front cover, color insert (1–3, 5–9, 11–16), back cover
(all but author photo); Bob Houser: color insert (4); Donna Chiarelli (10).

Library of Congress Cataloging-in-Publication Data

Weaver, Susan.
   A woman's guide to cycling / by Susan Weaver ; illustrated by
  Sally Onopa. -- Rev. ed.
       p. cm.
   Includes bibliographical references (p.) and index.
   ISBN 0-89815-982-2
    1. Cycling for women. I. Title.
  GV1057.W33 1998
  796.6' 082--dc21   98-18006
                                CIP

First printing this edition 1998
Printed in Canada

1 2 3 4 5 6 7 8 9 10 — 02 01 00 99 98

*To my husband and mountain biking partner, Joseph Skrapits,
and to my parents, who early on taught me to love the outdoors.*

Contents

Illustrations

Acknowledgments

I want to thank those who helped make this revised edition possible, beginning with the folks at Ten Speed Press who believed in the book and furthered the process, including publisher Kirsty Melville; production editors Kathryn Bear and Aaron Wehner; developmental editor cum bike messenger Rebecca Davenport, who read the original book and offered helpful suggestions for updating; and Wade Fox for his perceptive copy edit. I would also like to thank Laura Lind for her wonderful design work on the new edition.

For reviewing manuscript for the revision prior to publication, thanks to: Susan I. Barr, Ph.D.; Susan DeMattei; Michael Koenig; Mel Kornbluh; Patrick McDonough; Brian Savercool; Denise Simons-Morton, M.D., Ph.D.; and my husband Joseph Skrapits. Chapters for the original book were reviewed by: John S. Allen; Curt Bond; Katherine Brubaker, M.D.; Edward F. Coyle, Ph.D.; Jennifer Dodd; Ellen Dorsey; William Farrell; Ann Grandjean, Ed.D.; Nancy Kaiser; Barbara and Mel Kornbluh; John Kukoda; Everett L. Smith, Ph.D. In addition to experts in a variety of fields named and quoted in this book, I thank exercise physiologist Diane Fowler, M.Ed., who consulted on stretching exercises.

I appreciate the technical support of Bikeline bike shop (Allentown, Pennsylvania), and especially Papo Aquino; as well as that of Curt Miller of Curt's Cyclery (Nazareth, Pennsylvania).

Nichols Expeditions of Moab, Utah, expanded my off-road travel horizons by hosting me on a delightful five-day tour of the White Rim Trail in Canyonlands National Park (Utah).

Thanks to *Bicycling* magazine and its staff, which enabled my survey of North American women cyclists and helped me in many other ways. My sincere appreciation goes to all the women who completed these surveys, many of whom wrote at length about their cycling experiences. Their essays help give this book its special flavor.

Foreword

When the first edition of *A Woman's Guide to Cycling* hit the bookshelves, I was just beginning to discover what it means to be a cyclist. Friends of mine in the bike-friendly town of Chico, California, had extolled the virtues of gorgeous, challenging rides through the foothills of northern California, and I finally succumbed to their pleas to try something new by putting away my running shoes and buying a road bike. For me, the attraction to cycling was immediate and overwhelming. Were all of these beautiful destinations really within pedaling distance of downtown? You mean I get to coast down those hills if I want to? The people I met out on the roads, coupled with the fun of exploring every one of these roads within a fifty-mile radius of town, combined to hook me on a sport that continues to change my life.

As my enthusiasm for cycling continued, I began accruing all the necessary "tools of the trade" to increase my comfort while in the saddle: two or three extra pairs of Lycra shorts (which at that time were not cut for women), a well-fitting, semi-lightweight helmet, some gloves, and a pair of shoes specifically designed for cycling. It wasn't long before I found myself shopping for another bike, only this one was something new to the two-wheeled world—a mountain bike.

The advent of the mountain bike enabled people to enjoy cycling in less populated and, in many instances, more scenic locales than ever. I loved both varieties of cycling, and still do, but the mountain bike was to be my ticket to see the world, in more ways than one. Mountain biking was finding its way into the mainstream, slowly but surely, and national and local races were cropping up in many a nearby city. Friends convinced me that I ought to sign up for a race, just for the fun of it. I thought, "Why not?" and took my place on the starting line, along with a handful of other eager women. I had a great time making my way through the course, thanks to a woman named Jacquie Phelan (pioneer of women's mountain biking), who rode behind me the entire race to cheer me on and provide some sorely needed tips on how to handle a bike on the dirt. Soon I was juggling my work schedule at the hospital to ensure I had time off to participate in as many races as possible. I had the cycling bug in a big way!

Every year the racing calendar would expand, both nationally and internationally. I found myself mountain biking in Italy, Switzerland, Germany, Holland, and Spain, in awe of the cultures and scenery that I was suddenly privy to, thanks to my affiliation with the race scene and cycling in general. My good fortune as a mountain bike racer culminated in 1996, when I was selected to compete in the Atlanta games as a member of the first U.S. Olympic mountain biking team. The Olympic race was unlike any other. A palpable energy surrounded the race venue.

Family, friends, and my fiancé were all in attendance, along with 40,000-plus fans. I thought back to my first race ten years earlier, when hopes of an Olympic berth for the sport were unheard of, and a handful of women were trying to make names for themselves among a sea of men. Now, women are commonplace on starting lines, roads, and trails all over the world.

I came away from the games with a bronze medal, something I never dreamed I'd be holding during my lifetime, but that memorable day was only one of a countless number that I've experienced over a twelve-year (and counting) period.

Now that I'm no longer racing, one of my goals is to facilitate other women in reaping the benefits of a lifestyle that includes cycling. I recommend *A Woman's Guide to Cycling* as a part of that process. Susan Weaver has captured what it means to be a cyclist, no matter whether you're a beginner or a veteran, and she conveys to the reader the reasons why women are getting—and staying—involved in this incredible sport.

People have often asked me, "What is it you love about cycling?" It's all I can do to keep my response down to ten minutes. Can I describe to them how I love to immerse myself in the sights and sounds of the terrain around me; how I love to socialize with my girlfriends who also thrive on the challenge of a ride that pushes us beyond what we thought we could accomplish, no matter what the speed; how I've gained self-confidence in all aspects of my life through the obstacles I've had to overcome (both literally and figuratively) while on the roads and trails? Or should I just respond with my old favorite: "I love cycling because it's so much fun!"

In this book, Susan Weaver will give you another hundred reasons—if you don't already have your own—to incorporate cycling into your life. Women everywhere are indebted to her for sharing her expertise and experiences with us. *A Woman's Guide to Cycling* covers all the bases, giving helpful tips on every aspect of cycling—not an easy feat! If only I had found this book earlier . . .

Susan DeMattei

Introduction

On a loamy trail through woods only five miles away from my home in the center of the city, I toil uphill, through soggy leaves, on my mountain bike. Pleased to make it to the top without stopping, I stand on the pedals and slide way back on my saddle—second nature now. Catching my breath on the fly, I descend to creekside. In the water near the far bank I spy a great blue heron, motionless, gray-blue like the winter trees beyond, well camouflaged. Then it launches itself on expansive wings, surely the biggest heron I've ever seen . . . This moment seems so distant from my busy street, my house, my computer, and the day's writing.

Isn't it amazing how far, literally and figuratively, a bicycle can take you? Or is it, how far you can take a bicycle? If you're a seasoned cyclist, you know how the bike transports you toward new horizons: You discover yourself and what you're capable of accomplishing. You build friendships based on shared sweat and private confidences. You see your surroundings with fresh eyes or travel beyond your usual boundaries.

When I wrote *A Woman's Guide to Cycling* almost ten years ago, I didn't dream I'd ever be given the opportunity to update it. My goal then was to make the world of bicycling as accessible as possible to new and intermediate cyclists. I aimed to write a woman-friendly book, addressing all of the points routinely overlooked in the cycling magazines. Besides, in our male-dominated sport, I thought, we need more female "roll models." Let's show women doing it and sharing their feelings about it. I hoped to connect with you, and to enliven the necessary how-to, by sharing my experiences and those of dozens of other women cyclists. There is a cycling sisterhood out there, and I wanted to tap into it with interviews and surveys.

Now, a decade later, the spirit of what these women shared about our sport— a celebration of their discovered strength, competence, independence, rejuvenation—still speaks to us. But cycling itself has undergone a metamorphosis, and thus the need to revise the book.

More than ever, there truly are different spokes for different folks. For a woman who pedals the pavement, the market offers more options in road bikes that really fit, and hill-shrinking gearing to empower us on the steeps. If we don't want to bend over those dropped handlebars, we have hybrids and comfort bikes, spawned by the fat tire revolution. Recumbents (the La-Z-Boys of bicycles) and tandems (the great equalizers for pairs) are more affordable and more widely available than before. Meanwhile, mountain biking has redefined the kinds of turf we can explore on two wheels and the fun we can have doing it.

Just as we have more bikes to choose from, we now have more equipment and information to suit a woman's needs. More saddles and other components engineered for female comfort. An explosion of riding opportunities—off-road and on. More cyclewear designed with women in mind. Additional equipment choices for riding with the family. Better guidelines for cycling during pregnancy and afterward. Improved ride-fuel and new nutrition info. The latest insights from doctors about cycling and our sexuality. More good news about how our activity promotes our health. And more!

To help you sort through this wealth of choices (and get past some inevitable hype), I've completely updated *A Woman's Guide to Cycling*. In these pages, I pass along the information you need to make a start or to progress further in whichever aspects of cycling you choose. Again, since our abilities and our goals and our sensibilities vary, it won't be just my voice you hear, but the encouragement, advice, and rich experiences of women at every level of cycling. They welcome you, and I welcome you, to the vast horizons of this two-wheeled world.

Bikes Let the Good Times Roll

Since I'm a cycling journalist, keeping tabs on the latest in new bicycles, I often get phone calls from friends thinking of getting into the sport. Typically they want to know what sort of bike they should buy or what brand I recommend.

To help someone toward that answer, I fire back some inquiries of my own: What sort of cycling suits your style, your idea of a good time, your way of building fitness? Are you considering biking for basic transportation? What don't you want to do?

I ask because no other sport offers more variety, one reason why bicycling continues to grow in popularity as lifelong recreation for adults. Nor can any other sport so well suit evolving interests, goals, and moods from year to year or day to day. Perhaps today you need to be relaxed, tomorrow you want to be stimulated. One day you want to ride alone or with a friend, another you'd enjoy a group to talk and joke with. This month you appreciate the reassurance of a familiar route, next month you're ready to tackle new trails or sign up for a bike tour vacation. And that's just a hint of the options!

Your bike can get you out into the woods (a mountain bike can go almost anywhere that feet can go, but faster) or take you back and forth to work. Cycling can help you meet new friends and explore new horizons, in the next county or in your dream destination in Europe. The only thing you can't change is that you're getting fitter while having all that fun.

At this moment you don't have to map out your cycling goals far into the future. You and bicycling will grow with each other. Some of us know at the outset we are eager for high adventure. Others of us will surprise ourselves: Things we think we could never do will become accomplishments to remember proudly. And some of us may find such satisfaction in the cycling we're doing now that we feel no desire to move beyond those pleasant, familiar rides.

In any case, it's exciting to mull over the possibilities. And it's an important first step for getting started. Ask yourself:

- What sort of riding will I do immediately?
- What direction would I like to take in the near future? Which cycling activities would be a natural extension of things I'm already doing?
- What would be pleasurable, fun, satisfying, crazy, wild, irresistible, the ultimate? Imagine something you'd really like to do, even if you're not sure it's possible. There'll be plenty of time later, as you keep reading, to answer practical questions and examine the obstacles.

If you don't know all the answers right now, that's OK. Just think about it. And keep an open mind as you hear what other women, perhaps not unlike yourself, have to say about the cycling experiences they enjoy most. Whose cycling shoes would you like to step into?

RECREATIONAL RIDER

Faith West Sherry, 43, a court reporter in Dakota County, Minnesota, is an active cyclist who enjoys club outings and weekend and longer tours. She hops on her bicycle to do errands and rides a stationary bike indoors to stay fit during the snowy Minnesota winters. For her it's a big change from her former sedentary self. But aside from whatever else she looks for in cycling, she values the day-to-day pleasures of her local rides.

The more regularly she rides, the more she appreciates how cycling helps her feel good about herself and about life in general. The fresh air and sense of freedom on a bike ease tension and raise spirits. This is especially true if, like Faith, we find scenic, lightly trafficked routes easily accessible from home. They're worth searching out, even worth putting the bike in a car and driving to, if need be. Here Faith describes the rewards.

Bad weather had started early that year in Minnesota, but then in late November there was a break. A few temperate days seemed a last blessing before the long, hard winter would set in.

I felt really blue (who knows why this time!), but I forced myself to go out since it might be my last chance before it would snow. I rode twelve miles to a natural preserve in a county park that has seven miles of paved trail through beautiful country. I'd been there many times before, but this time the leaves in the woods had fallen, and the tall grass was yellow. I could see farther through the marshes and the trees than ever before. I was gawking at hundreds of white egrets, perched on the naked trees in a swampy lake. Suddenly I realized I felt nothing from the waist down. Were my legs really moving? I couldn't hear my tires on the trail. I was floating! And I was no longer blue.

BACKCOUNTRY BIKER

When Anita Paul, 26, of Pasadena, California, won a mountain bike vacation as a magazine sweepstakes prize last year, she had no cycling experience and had never even been camping. But she was game for adventure and in shape from aerobics and other fitness activities, so she and her husband Matthew signed on. The tour operator helped them to select a trip with a minimum of climbing, a maximum of views, and a riding surface they could handle. Solar showers and the guides' good cooking made the camping as enjoyable as the riding; a truck carried all the gear. Of their five-day trip through Utah, from Capitol Reef National Park to Lake Powell, Anita says:

It was an absolute blast. Neither of us had ever been to Utah, so its natural beauty enthralled us—the clean air, the fluttering yellow aspens on Hell's Backbone, the seas of wildflowers in the desert, greener than usual from recent rain. Everywhere in canyon country, the kaleidoscope of colors and textures of rock formations created a feast for our eyes and souls.

At first we felt intimidated by our ultra-fit guides and the other, more experienced participants, but they quickly assured us that this was not a race and that we were there to have fun. Everyone—and I mean every single one— offered great encouragement. Someone was always helping me to familiarize myself with my bike and the riding techniques—a true learning experience.

Mountain biking is definitely one of the more underrated activities. Discovering an exhilarating and quite rewarding new sport made this trip special to me. And being in the backcountry on a bike, you see much more than if you hiked or even drove through in a car. Definitely the only way to go.

TRIATHLETE

Each year Shari Klarich of Bonner's Ferry, Idaho, sets a personal goal. During her second year of riding, that goal was to complete a triathlon. To many who haven't tried it, this triple-threat event sounds out of reach. But what Shari accomplished at age thirty-nine in just one summer shows the difference conditioning can make. Shari says:

Up to that point, my most pleasurable, challenging, and rewarding experience was that triathlon—a 1-mile swim, 25-mile bike, and 6.2-mile run, held in July. When I started training in May, I was already a year-round runner, but I could barely swim one lap of a pool or ride my bike for forty-five minutes. My goal during training was just to finish.

I enjoyed the training, and by race day I felt a bit more ambitious: My goal was not to finish last. I met it by placing third from last. My friends told me I smiled all the way. I loved it!

BICYCLE COMMUTER

"I do it primarily because I enjoy it," says Marty Carnes of her bike commute over the last eleven years. "This is a wonderful way to start the day." A physical education teacher from St. Simons Island, Georgia, Marty lives near the ocean and rides her hybrid bike ten miles each way to and from school. For four miles, her route takes her over a causeway through a marsh:

It's home to thousands of red-wing blackbirds. The sun is just coming up, and as I climb the bridge over the intercoastal waterway, I can see out to the other islands and the glittering Atlantic. The marsh changes with the seasons, and the birds change, too. When I drive my car over the causeway, which I do when it's too cold to bicycle, I'm caught up in traffic. When I ride my bike, I'm more relaxed. And anticipating the bike ride home gets me through the more stressful days of teaching.

Marty, 49, also likes setting an example for her students. "I want to show them a person my age still being active. I'm just ancient to them," she says with a laugh. "And I have this goal of wanting to be fitter than ever when I turn fifty."

In fact, the commute provides good training for BRAG (the seven-day, 400-mile Bicycle Ride Across Georgia), which she's ridden with friends (and 3,000 other cyclists of all ages) in mid-June for the last eight years. To train for the events, she supplements the commute mileage with weight training and speed work on the bike.

"The main thing to me about bicycling is the freedom. I hate getting old," she admits. "I can't run anymore because of my knees, but I can still bicycle."

MOUNTAIN BIKER

"I didn't have a bike as a kid, and even after getting a road bike, I never considered myself much of a bicyclist," admits Carol Stickles, 43, of Bath, Pennsylvania. "With the awkward drop handlebars I felt out of control in traffic."

But a few years ago Carol and her husband Gene were intrigued when friends in their ski club began mountain biking the local trails. "Gene tried it first and told me the bike would be more comfortable," says Carol. "We figured off-road riding would be good cross-training for our ski racing."

They started on a converted rail-trail to get used to the gears. Then they tackled singletrack with their ski-club buddies. The first time she rode narrow trails with the trees tight around her, she "felt kind of scared," but the pristine surroundings—the trail follows a meandering stream, woods open occasionally to wildflower meadows—appealed to her love of nature. "It's been fun encountering deer on the trail and seeing the flowers, the mushrooms, the leaves change with the seasons," she says.

How quickly she got the hang of singletrack surprised her. She found that she could ride within her ability level, walking the parts that seemed too difficult and gradually gaining mastery:

There's always some new and different challenge. I like that. Last week I managed to ride over a log I always had to dismount and step over before. I never thought I could dodge rocks, roll over tree roots, and negotiate the off-camber trails the way I do now. Some technical climbs still give me trouble, but lately I seem to get farther up each time!

TWO-WHEEL TRAVELER

Erica Springstead from Saratoga, California, had been cycling less than a year when, at forty, she took her first bicycle vacation—in her words, "an unbelievable experience!" The setting for her tour was Tuscany, Italy's magnificent green hill country where umbrella pines and cypresses punctuate the undulating landscape, where olive groves and vineyards surround medieval towns and villages, and where Florence and Siena are truly worthy destinations.

On this professionally organized trip, the tour operator took care of all the fuss, like booking hotels, planning routes, and providing a vehicle to carry luggage, leaving the group free to enjoy pedaling their road bikes through this rustic landscape. Erica suggests why this sort of travel has grown more popular—not so much because it's inexpensive, in fact it isn't always—but because it gives an intimate view of the region. She writes:

> *It was very challenging biking because I opted to go with the "goats" rather than the rest of the group, but I found my fellow cyclists to be fabulous people, the countryside beautiful, and the wines wonderful. The villas and hotels we stayed in were great.*

> *Bicycling through the countryside gives you a far better view of things than whizzing by in a car. You get a much better sense of how people live. I loved cycling through a forest and seeing some of the local folk emerge from the trees, carrying shopping bags full of wild porcini mushrooms they had just picked. I got a kick out of the astonishment and delight on the faces of some Italian male cyclists as another woman and I hopped on their paceline and stuck with them for ten miles. A very positive and memorable first tour!*

CLUB RIDER

Hilary Brooke from York, England, raves about club riding. Hilary, who hated sports in school, began cycling in her mid-twenties when her brother invited her to go for a ride with his bike club. "I went out of curiosity," she says, "and I've been hooked on cycling ever since."

Why join a club? For many of us it makes cycling more sociable. A club ride to a firehouse breakfast or a picnic-and-twenty-five-miler is a terrific way to spend time with old friends and make new ones. Riding together, we learn from each other, motivate each other. Miles go by faster if we're part of a group that can laugh at the hills or hunker down in a headwind on a paceline, or "chain-gang," as it's called in the United Kingdom.

Hilary particularly emphasizes the fun you can have with a club. Now a racer herself, she says:

Most people think cycling clubs are only for men who race every week and have legs of iron. But even if you do join a racing club, you can have a real laugh and enjoy yourself. Many clubs, however, are general cycling clubs that cater to everyone from schoolchildren up to seventy-year-olds. And the clubs organize a lot of social events.

FAMILY CYCLIST AND TANDEM PARTNER

Having three children never held Rita Menet and her husband back. When the kids were youngsters they rode regularly as a family in and around Appleton, Wisconsin—the older ones, Luke and Peter, on their own bikes and daughter Joy, at five, getting a free ride in a Cannondale Bugger trailer, often pulled by Dad on his bike.

"I liked the Bugger," says Rita, "because when I rode behind, Joy faced me. I'd talk to her and sing songs to her, throw her candy from my bike bag. She had some toys to play with. And we'd make a point of stopping about every ten miles to do something the whole family enjoys—take a swim, visit the zoo, or feed ducks in the park. That let her move around, too.

"We got the kids into bikes with gears as soon as possible," she adds. "We had a 22-inch wheeled five-speed bike that each of them rode as soon as they were big enough." Once you buy the equipment, Rita notes, bicycling costs less than many other things families do together.

As their children grew, the family's cycling evolved. "Now my husband and I do a lot of riding on our tandem, often just the two of us, since we're each other's best company. The tandem is the only way I can keep up with him, and I have his undivided ear."

One by one, the children developed their own interests. "You have to let them have their wings," she says. Still, their oldest son Luke remains a keen cyclist at nineteen. The family cheers him on at road races. Last summer he taught mountain-biking skills at a YMCA camp in northern Wisconsin; each week a new group of kids would learn the basics and then go on an overnight bike trip with Luke as leader. "He enjoyed it tremendously," says Rita, proud her son can pass on what the family has shared together.

"Here in Wisconsin we are fortunate to have safe, scenic off-road bike trails which were once railroad beds. One crosses a marsh over a tramway; others traverse beautiful farmlands. Our kids loved a thirty-mile trail we'd ride as a weekend camping trip. The trail goes through three tunnels, where it's so cool inside. In fact, it 'rains' in the tunnel from condensation." To the children, it was sort of magic.

NOVICE RACER

Susan King from Orangevale, California, worked as a clerk/mechanic for five years at a bike shop, Shaw's Lightweight Cycles, in Santa Clara. That's when she got bit by the racing bug. At twenty, a college student, she'd been riding for just a few years.

"My first criterium race was scary, but exciting," says Susan, referring to those crowd-pleasing, mass-start bike races where riders whiz many laps around a course that's less than a mile long. Racers try to stay in a pack or string out in a paceline, one behind another, for shelter from the wind. They zip through the corners, a dizzying blur of bright jerseys and humming wheels.

Susan remembers she felt less nervous than she might have otherwise been because a friend was also racing for the first time:

> Right after the start, the pack left us behind. We couldn't keep up, but that didn't bother me! The guys at the shop said I'd probably last only three or four laps. Once we were dropped, my friend and I and a third girl worked together, taking turns at the lead. I loved the feeling of flying around the corners, especially one S curve that was narrow and dangerous. I liked speeding by the crowd as my companions and I would call out to each other, "OK, take over" or "Let's go, work hard!" I felt very professional.
>
> The pack caught us after our seventh lap, and we had to drop out, but I sure felt powerful when we stopped. I couldn't help talking about it all the way home! I was proud I'd managed to avoid a near accident early in the race when riders closed in on either side of me. Somehow I missed locking wheels with both of them.

As for the guys at the bike shop, she couldn't wait to tell them. "I lasted twice as long as those guys thought I would!"

In these snippets of women's cycling lives, the common thread running through each is enjoyment. That's why they make time for riding in their busy schedules. Cycling has also helped each one with weight control and keeping fit; these things have followed naturally, but they aren't the be-all and end-all of their cycling. Pleasure is the reason these women still ride. No matter what other goals you set for yourself in cycling, have fun with it.

In the chapters that follow, you'll find all you need to know to step into the shoes of these women and to try still other aspects of the sport.

Ready to get on with it? Then you might skip the next few chapters and pick up with chapter 5, "So You Want to Buy a Bike?"

Or are you feeling some hesitations? We talk about surmounting some beginners' hang-ups in the next chapter.

Obstacle or Excuse?   2

The best advice is: If you don't cycle, you should. And if you do, then cycle more! –Katrina O'Doherty, Brighton, Sussex, England

This chapter is for anyone who's hesitating. Frankly, it's a pep talk. If you don't need one right now, skip over this chapter for the present, or read it simply to see what some of your cycling sisters have accomplished.

"I'M NOT THE ATHLETIC TYPE"

Is that what you say? Take heart. Studies show that those who are least active and most out of shape make the greatest fitness improvement when they take up an activity like bicycling, if they just stay with it. In later chapters, we'll talk about conditioning to build endurance and cycling strength. Meanwhile, meet Janet Lewis of Huntington Beach, California.

Growing up, Janet wasn't fond of sports. Yet at forty-something, there's nothing she'd rather do on a sunny day than cycle twenty miles along the bike path near the ocean, watching the waves and the surfers as she goes.

It took a severe shock to make Janet change. She was only twenty-three when a pain in her knee turned out to be osteogenic sarcoma, a bone cancer. It required chemotherapy and removal of her left leg up to the hip joint. There was nothing for a prosthesis to hold on to, so a sort of plastic bucket with straps that fit around her hip was devised to allow use of an artificial limb, though it was uncomfortable and Janet had to walk with a cane.

She survived the cancer and continued to work as a teacher in Michigan, where she lived at the time. One day a friend banged on her door at eight in the morning, waving a newspaper. In it was a photograph of a one-legged cyclist who was riding coast-to-coast. "Janet," her friend urged, "if he can ride across the United States, you can certainly ride around Ann Arbor!"

The cyclist's name was Bruce Jennings. When Janet eventually contacted him at his home in California, he encouraged her, told her how to compensate for the missing leg and what equipment to buy. She followed his instructions, but then the bike sat in her living room for weeks.

"I was scared to death of crashing. Finally a neighbor said, 'I'm coming over and we're going to take your bike to a parking lot and try it out.'"

Shaking, she managed to sit on the saddle with his help. Visions of herself bloody and bruised made her stomach turn over. But as she coasted down a slight incline, she found the missing leg made little difference. The balance was in her arms. Then she tried pedaling, using a toeclip. She could do it, but her leg muscles tired quickly.

Gradually her leg strengthened and her endurance improved. Eventually she mastered cycling. Then she gave in to a long-time urge to move to California, where she could really be outdoors. She started a new life with her own apartment near the ocean, convenient for her favorite rides.

What does cycling mean to Janet Lewis? Off the bike she depends on crutches, since years ago she abandoned the painful prosthesis. "The prosthesis was worse, but I still feel earthbound on crutches," she says. "Bicycling makes me feel free and in control. Independence is so important to me, probably most important!"

And she enjoys meeting other riders on the bike path and making friends. Sometimes they'll go for miles without noticing she has only one leg. "Other times people will notice, and they'll say 'Good luck' or 'Keep up the good work.' Or they'll tell their friends about me, so when their friends see me, they point and say, 'There she is!'"

Many people stop and tell her she inspires them, and that always makes her feel good. To anyone who asks, her advice is "Go for it!"

"I'M PUT OFF BY THE MACHINERY"

Years ago I hopped on a borrowed ten-speed to join friends on a bike hike. Nobody explained how the gears operated, and I twiddled the two shift levers but couldn't do anything except spin the pedals aimlessly around and go nowhere. Or else suddenly I was in such a high gear I could scarcely turn the cranks. I eventually blundered into the right combination and managed to catch up and stick with the group. Luckily we stayed on fairly level ground, because I had no idea what I was doing.

Later when I bought my own bike, I discovered how simple gearing really is, once you learn how. If you've been put off by gear-fear, stop worrying. We'll deal with it in chapter 6, "On Your Bike!"

Maybe your problem is "fear of buying"; with so many bikes out there, how do you choose the right one? (See chapter 5, "So You Want to Buy a Bike?")

And if you're concerned about keeping your bike in good repair, mending the inevitable puncture, and so on, you aren't alone. In my own survey, handling bike repair and maintenance proved to be the second most serious concern of the women who responded. They said they needed articles and books written in terms they could understand.

In this book we'll start with the basics of maintenance, covering the things that most frequently go wrong and how to take care of them. You'll also find a bike safety checkup you can do yourself to get your bike rolling.

"I'M TOO FAT"

With the current thinness fetish it's easy for any woman with more padding than a hat rack to feel self-conscious about her figure. Sadly enough, this self-consciousness not only makes us feel bad about ourselves, but it may keep us from going out and getting exercise that we'd probably enjoy and that would help keep our metabolisms perking along and burning calories.

Self-consciousness didn't keep Sherry Black from making a comeback, however. Now a secretary at Tompkins Cortland (New York) Community College, Sherry captured a cycling bronze medal back in 1979 in the Empire State Games, a mini Olympics for New York state residents. Later came marriage, a business, raising two children, and sixty-five additional pounds. Five years ago, she decided to shape up and return to racing.

At first she tired easily but found that as she shed pounds, she gained staying power. "Cycling raises your energy level. Once you become used to the idea of riding, it's easier to get out there," she learned. "It's a reward in itself and really rejuvenates me. I come back from a bike ride feeling like a new person."

And she is. At age forty-five she returned to the Empire State Games and triumphed in the ten-mile time trial and the Masters 45–54 road race. She had trimmed down, thanks to cycling, cutting fat from her diet, and eating lots of vegetables. "But I don't go overboard. I think moderation is important. I have a sweet tooth, so I eat candy sometimes and dessert. If you always deprive yourself, you might binge," she cautions. "Eating low-calorie veggies and carbohydrates instead of fat lets me eat a lot of food. That's one reason I like to ride—I can eat a lot."

To overcome feeling uncomfortable at first, find a friend to ride with—someone who will keep a compatible pace—on off-road trails or scenic, lightly trafficked roads, and you'll be having too good a time to worry much about what others think. Remember, anyone who knows the least bit about fitness and exercise will admire you for your efforts. Also recognize that we are probably our own toughest critics, since being dissatisfied with our bodies is a pervasive attitude among women. In a *Glamour* magazine survey of 33,000 women, 75 percent said they felt "too fat," while in fact only 25 percent of the respondents were overweight according to fairly rigorous life insurance height/weight tables. And 45 percent of the underweight women believed themselves "too fat." We'll talk more about body image and weight loss in a later chapter.

Meanwhile, getting started is the key. Sherry Black found that even brief rides dropped pounds. Divorced and a single mom, she'd arrive home from work at four and have to retrieve her son from day care by five-thirty. "So I don't have much time to train," she says. "But even forty minutes of cycling can help you lose weight if you go hard."

"I'M TOO BUSY"

Sherry's story leads us right into the next bugaboo. If you haven't muttered "I'm too busy" to yourself, you're a rare individual. Any exercise program takes time, and cycling is no exception.

What to do? Life is short, why not play first?

Schedule time for your riding, says mountain biker Naomi Bloom of Cupertino, California:

> *About three days a week, I get up at five-thirty so I'll have time for a fourteen-mile training loop into the foothills. When everything's working in sync, I'll make five out of six green lights, there won't be any gravel trucks going out to the quarry, and commuter traffic will be light. That's when I feel on top of the world, charging up Mount Eden, swooping back down the other side, making every second count in a personal time trial. What a great way to start the day!*

Are the early morning hours too cruel? Try using the bike for shopping and other errands. And bicycle to work. It may well be quicker than driving or taking public transportation, or it might take a little longer, but there's a lot going for it. You are not polluting, and you automatically build cycling time into your schedule.

Some top racers have told me they do much of their training on long commuting rides to and from work. At thirty-two, Karen Kurreck of Cupertino, California, won the 1994 women's time trial world championship while working full-time as a senior software engineer; she did it by cramming workouts into five slots in her day: before work, the morning commute, lunch, return commute, and evening. One day, for example, she might cycle eight miles to the job, ride during lunch hour, and bike home.

Time management experts tell us to find time to do things we want to do, not by working harder, but by working smarter. The idea: Eliminate some of the unnecessary things we're doing now by delegating them to others or realizing they can be left undone. But it isn't always easy to let go.

In her early twenties, Susan Krueger was married, working at a pro bike shop in Augusta, Maine, and had recently taken up racing. She was in a bind for lack of time. "Since I started riding, I haven't had time to work, ride, and clean house, so I gave up cleaning the house. This has been a great source of frustration."

Nevertheless, relaxing our standards may be the happiest and healthiest way to do the things we really find fulfilling. Saying no more frequently to requests for our time, persuading family members to be more self-sufficient and to assume more responsibilities at home—these changes take thought and effort on our part and cooperation from the people who share our lives, but eventually they pay off by saving us time.

"WHAT ABOUT ALL THOSE CRAZY DRIVERS?"

In my survey of women cyclists, out of a dozen things that might create problems, "the inconsiderate motorist" was ranked most troublesome by more respondents than any other item. This is the driver who unnerves you by passing to close or by making a turn right in front of you so you have to brake to a halt or turn quickly even though you hadn't intended to. Sooner or later we all meet this driver, and we are wary.

Fortunately, we have coping strategies. One of my favorites is to take up riding off-road, where cars cannot go and I can concentrate my full attention on the trail and the great outdoors surrounding me. Chapter 15, "Fat Tire Freedom," tells what you need to know.

On-road most cyclists seem to find, as I have, that the truly rude driver constitutes a tiny minority. My survey respondents cited "fear of riding in moderate traffic" much less frequently as a concern. In our experience, traffic generally operates in an orderly flow, and the cyclist can learn to become a part of that flow while riding defensively. As accident studies have shown, poor riding skills and cyclists' errors in judgment are the biggest risk factors in bike accidents.

In later chapters we'll talk about:

- Choosing the best roads
- Making yourself visible during day- and night-time riding
- Taking your rightful place on the road
- Recognizing and avoiding road hazards
- Communicating your intentions clearly to motorists
- Defensive precautions to cut the chances of accidents
- Emergency maneuvers
- Handling harassment

Don't forget, you increase your protection by wearing a good helmet—traffic or no traffic.

"MY LIFE IS TOO MIXED UP RIGHT NOW"

When something goes terribly wrong—a marriage ends, you lose your job, a parent dies, a transfer forces you to move—it's natural to feel overwhelmed. "At such a time," says Jane Jackel of Montreal, Canada, "I think physical activity is one of the best things you can do. Something where you work hard and take your mind off your feelings."

Admittedly, a completely new pursuit might seem too daunting. You may feel too depressed—as if you're already walking underwater just trying to make it through the day. Luckily, cycling isn't new to most of us. If we haven't been on a bike in years, at least we learned in childhood. Remember the cool wind rushing against your face as you coasted down a hill? Can you recall the thrill of going very fast under your own power? Reliving those girlhood sensations might help you cope with the current upheaval.

"After my marriage broke up, cycling was one of the ways I not only kept a grip on my sanity, but also recovered," says Jane Jackel, who was thirty-three at the time.

> The most important thing I did after my life fell apart was to go for counseling, but bicycling played a role in my recovery. I had joined a bicycling club and was able to practice some of the things I learned during my counseling sessions—for instance, being able to trust other people and learning to relax both with myself and with others.
>
> The rhythmic motion of pedaling, especially out in the country, frees your mind to think more clearly and raises your spirits. I can't frown on a bike ride! Not only that, but the improvement in fitness makes you feel powerful and confident.

If a major disruption has taken place in your life, you might follow Jane's lead and reach out for help. At the same time you'll probably survey your own resources to discover how to make yourself feel better in a healthful way. Interestingly, recent psychological research shows that regular exercise can be a catalyst for healing the spirit. And in my own survey, 85.6 percent of all women who responded said that cycling usually lifts them out of a blue mood; another 12.9 percent said that it sometimes does. In a later chapter we'll delve deeper into why this is so.

"I'M TOO OLD TO START NOW"

"We all have our aches and pains, but when we are active they seem to diminish or we haven't time to think about them," says Nora Young of Toronto, Canada. At eighty, Nora is vibrant proof that no matter when you start exercising, you can actually reverse the effects of aging. As recent studies show, you can improve the functioning of heart and lungs, build muscle strength, quicken reaction times, become more flexible, and feel more energetic.

Always a natural athlete and an "all-rounder," Nora first raced bicycles in Exhibition Park in Toronto in the thirties. But after the Second World War she dropped out of cycling and didn't take it up again until 1978, when she was sixty-one. As she puts it, she "started slowly, going on a couple of tours."

Several years later, when her city hosted the first World Masters Games in 1985, Nora contacted some riders she'd known in the early days and in a few months got in "reasonably fair shape." Her competitive spirit also rekindled.

> The 45-kilometer [28-mile] road race was tough—very hilly, with the temperature over ninety degrees. I was dropped on the first hill but plugged along, and about a mile or so from the finish I looked ahead and saw a rider.

She appeared to be tiring, so I drew on my reserve, caught up going down the hill, raced to the finish, and she nipped me at the line. They gave us both the same time: one hour and forty-two minutes. Boy, were my legs aching, but it was a wonderful feeling!

Since then she's been racing in Masters events across North America. "I can do things today I would have had a hard time doing eleven years ago," she told me when I first interviewed her in 1988. She was seventy-one at the time. "Competing just gives you a nice feeling—you are trying to better yourself, trying to stay on top when someone else is trying to beat you. I like that sense of improvement."

I talked with Nora again recently, the day after her eightieth birthday. She reported that she won silver medals in all her cycling events at the '97 Senior Classic in Tucson—two road races and two time trials—and that everyone was eager for her to turn eighty so that they wouldn't have to compete in her age group for a while. Clearly, Nora Young still lives up to her name.

So what about you? If you truly have been sedentary, that's even more reason to take up cycling; you should begin to see benefits fairly quickly. Bear in mind, you can ride at quite a leisurely pace if you choose. And bicycling is easier on the joints than, say, jogging, since cycling is not a weight-bearing activity. In fact, women who've been troubled by arthritis often remark that riding a bike helps them overcome stiffness and keep mobile.

If you've been inactive, you may be wondering whether you need your doctor's OK before you start riding. Most people don't, according to the American Heart Association, because a gradual, sensible bicycling program poses little risk. Sedentary women who are fifty-plus (or inactive men over forty), however, should confer with their health practitioners if they plan to push themselves hard from the start, says the AHA. Also, if you have or are at risk for a chronic condition like cardiovascular disease, insulin-dependent diabetes, or obesity, talk to your doctor first. Once you do get the go-ahead, cycling can benefit you. (See chapter 4, "A Long and Healthy Life.")

A last thought: Along with the pleasures and rewards of cycling, it does offer challenges. Ultimately, however, it's the very challenges that provide some of the sport's great benefits. In overcoming the difficulties, we build confidence and competence that enrich both our cycling and our entire lives. As Connie Carpenter Phinney, America's first female Olympic gold medalist in cycling, has said, "To accept the challenge of the road is to take a journey within yourself."

To Your Health—Cycling and the Psyche

There has never been a time when I haven't felt better after a ride, even when I felt great to start with! –Cathy Nestor, Honolulu, Hawaii

I certainly feel much happier in general whenever I exercise—it's the best way of diffusing stress. I also feel stronger, fitter, and more energetic and "firm" body-wise. –Cynthia Scott, London, England

I was looking for a vote of confidence that cycling promotes good health, and I received it with the hundreds of survey questionnaires women cyclists returned to me from all over the United States, Canada, and the United Kingdom. Their enthusiastic responses confirmed the results of medical studies and the findings of health professionals about the benefits of regular exercise. In instance after instance, women told how cycling enhanced already active lives or contributed to the creation of a healthy, new self. By their own accounts these women are excited, uplifted, strengthened, fulfilled, contented, and energized by their riding and what it has helped them to discover and develop within themselves. They—we—have found a way to build fitness, improve our health, and set our minds and bodies in tune with each other—happy side effects of having a good time on a bicycle.

RIDING BACK FROM DEPRESSION

Medicine has begun to recognize the mind's power to help heal the body, as well as the body's ability to strongly influence our state of mind. Especially exciting among recent research is evidence that exercise can assist in safeguarding or even improving mental health.

Jane Stockwell of Julian, California, proved that to herself. She was in her late twenties and relatively new to cycling when she tackled her first 100-mile ride. She explains why it served as a barometer for the emotional struggles in her life:

I rode alone on my first century though I had my family to see me off and receive me at the finish. To them, I was attempting a cycling milestone, but to me, it was more. It was my way of celebrating life, health, and happiness after a particularly difficult two years spent coping with serious depression. The ride was a way of convincing myself that I had done more than survive. I had rallied to new heights.

Through my riding I had found new reserves of physical and emotional strength. The miles had tallied up into a greater sense of self-respect. I had learned to relate to myself with a new, more gentle persistence. Cycling had offered me a sense of achievement and a metaphoric pathway through many of my life's obstacles by allowing me to learn a skill or tactic on the road and then apply it to the broader scheme of my life. I had so much to be thankful for when I crossed that finish line, for I sensed this was just the beginning of a new, wonderful life.

Depression is a major health concern in our society, especially for women. According to Dr. Donald F. Klein and Dr. Paul H. Wender, psychiatrists and authors of *Understanding Depression* (New York: Oxford University Press, 1993), one woman in five will experience depression at some point in her life. Symptoms can include feelings of gloom and worthlessness; lowered energy or activity levels; poor concentration and muddled thinking; disturbances in eating, sleeping, and sexual patterns; and thoughts of death and suicide. Depression may mask itself in physical symptoms like chronic fatigue or headaches. For this reason, depression often goes undiagnosed or is improperly treated.

Among the good news in depression research (along with advances in drug treatments) is recent experimentation with exercise as therapy—of interest to anyone who ever wondered why we always feel so good after a ride.

In a study involving 561 university students, researchers identified 101 as clinically depressed, and 460 as nondepressed. Each group was divided equally: into an experimental group that would participate in a ten-week, regular exercise program and a control group that would not exercise. After ten weeks, all were reevaluated. The exercising groups—both depressed and nondepressed students—showed real improvement in their mood state. Those classified as depressed felt more cheerful and energetic at the end of the ten-week program. The nonexercising groups did not improve in mood.

In another study, exercise outperformed psychotherapy. Twenty-eight patients with mild or moderate depression were divided into three groups. Two groups would have psychotherapy. A third group would not but would follow a regular routine of jogging at least three times a week. In three weeks most of the exercising patients were "virtually well," according to the psychiatrist heading the study, Dr. John H. Greist of the University of Wisconsin.

How does he explain it? Dr. Greist views depression as a person's response to loss of control. "People who are able to stick with a regular [exercise] routine . . . get a sense of success and mastery from it," he observes. "When people find they're able to do something they didn't know they could do, they begin to realize they also can make other changes in their lives for the better."

In addition, according to Dr. Greist, regular doses of exercise like running or cycling that use large muscle masses in regular rhythm appear to produce chemical and physiological changes in the body and brain that affect mood. The precise nature of these changes is still undergoing study. Nevertheless, regular aerobic exercise is clearly one of the things we can do, along with good nutrition, to promote *homeostasis,* the body's natural propensity to balance its own chemistry.

A cautionary word: A depression sufferer may need more than an exercise program to resolve her problems, and proper diagnosis is important. But more conventional therapy might well be given a boost by the addition of regular, pleasurable aerobic activity.

Other depressions to which we're vulnerable—like the depression often associated with PMS (premenstrual syndrome)—are complex and not fully understood either. Much controversy surrounds the more than seventy different treatments currently used for PMS, many of which are contradictory, untested, or expensive. But one treatment that probably can't hurt—and which many women find helpful—is exercise.

Exercise is one of the first things recommended by Dr. Sally K. Severino, a psychiatry professor at the University of New Mexico Health Sciences Center, author of *Premenstrual Syndrome: A Clinician's Guide* (New York: The Guilford Press, 1989), and co-editor of *Premenstrual Dysphorias: Myths and Realities* (Washington, DC: American Psychiatric Press, 1994). Women may be willing to put up with the bloating, breast tenderness, and constipation that many experience with PMS, she notes. But when they develop emotional symptoms—irritability, anger, depression, or anxiety—they often seek help. "And when they do," says Dr. Severino, "I feel it's sensible to advocate exercise for most patients. First, it may help relieve symptoms related to bloating; second, many women find that regular physical exercise improves their self-esteem, especially in our fitness-oriented culture; and third, depression and anxiety may be relieved."

Gloria Knoll of Appleton, Wisconsin, found this to be true when, as a mother of five in her early forties, she "experienced the tension and depression of PMS." A bike ride, she says, would help take the edge off it.

> *I so looked forward to an hour or two on my bike each day. Usually I'd ride before picking my kids up from school or after supper. It was my quiet time and a tension release. Cycling helped me keep things in perspective, and the bouts with depression weren't nearly as severe.*

As for how to go about it, consider what Jane Stockwell discovered for herself:

> *I need to remember to ride to please myself because if I ride too fast, too hard, or too far, the magic goes out of the ride and I'm ready for the bike-toss. If I'm riding to please another, I return depleted and resentful. Yet if I ride with respect for my own desires and limitations, I return exhilarated and eager to ride again. To avoid "bad rides," I plan rides that are challenging and yet well within my grasp. Success breeds success.*

DE-STRESSING

Responsibilities of job, family, home—no wonder today's woman may be stressed. If we typically do for others first and ourselves last, our personal time goes down the drain. Often the fun things, including our cycling, are what we give up.

If so, we're making a big mistake. One of the best antidotes for stress is exercise, as many women cyclists know. Charlotte Vasey of Devon, England, has called her bicycle commute a "time to unwind. Leaving work after a long, oppressive day in the office, having plenty of time to spare and heading for the cycle path . . . There are few places prettier on a hot summer evening, and the long ride home is so relaxing."

Studies validate this experience. In research with both men and women, psychologist Richard Dienstbier, Ph.D., at the University of Nebraska, found that people become "more stress-tolerant after taking up a regular program of aerobic exercise than they were before." Measuring reactions to stress such as heartbeat and skin conductance, as well as hormonal responses, he tested subjects before and after a few months of aerobic training. They showed striking improvement in their ability to handle tension, a process he calls "toughening."

Dr. Dienstbier explains:

I think regular exercise changes the hormonal balance of the body so that if you face psychological stressors after you've been in a training program, you generate more energy and less tension. Energy tends to be associated with adrenaline and noradrenaline. Adrenaline particularly is associated with blood glucose, and glucose is the fuel of the nervous system—the only fuel the nervous system can burn. Exercise increases our ability to generate those hormones.

OVERCOMING SUBSTANCE ABUSE

"When I started participating in sports, I came to know once again how it felt to be healthy," says Elaine Fisher of Stockport, Cheshire, England. "In my mid-twenties, three years previous to my cycling, I had fallen into the habit of drinking every night. It seemed almost normal to be hungover."

Elaine, a cocktail waitress and a student at the time, discovered how easy it is to abuse alcohol. It's readily available, legal, and no prescription is needed. Drinking is socially acceptable and, in some lifestyles, almost unavoidable, as it was for Elaine working in a bar.

Previously an active cyclist, she was lucky enough, she says, to meet someone who rekindled her interest in the sport:

When I started riding, as well as lifting weights and playing tennis, I gradually began drinking less. One of the problems of tapering off is that on the nights when you don't drink, you can't sleep. But I found the tired feeling from cycling far more effective than a drink-induced sleep, especially the next morning, as you don't wake up depressed and hungover.

Drinking had also caused her to put on about nine pounds, but "with less drinking and more exercise, this problem solved itself."

This account describes what Judy Myers, Ph.D., says medical experts have been discovering: That fitness is "indeed a key to recovery." In *Staying Sober: A Nutrition and Exercise Program for the Recovering Alcoholic* (New York: Pocket Books, 1987), Dr. Myers writes of her own battle with alcoholism: "In fact, fitness was not merely a key. It was the missing link."

Judy Myers had hit bottom, dried out at a detox facility, and had relocated to a recovery house, attempting to rebuild her life. Sober but suffering bouts of depression, she did not yet feel "healthy or happy. What was missing?" As the recovery house offered no nutritional counseling nor fitness program, this former health and physical education teacher decided to develop her own regime by studying nutrition and jogging in a local park. In one month, as her conditioning improved, she began to regain a sense of control over her life. Other women at the center asked her to help them, too. Some weeks later they entered the Alcoholic Olympics and as a team earned a silver medal.

Maintaining her sobriety, Dr. Myers eventually became a fitness and nutrition consultant to alcohol and drug treatment centers, corporations, hospitals, and health resorts where she has instituted fitness and wellness programs.

Surely there is no health problem in which the mind and body are more connected than in substance abuse, now recognized as a genuine health issue for women. In complexity it exceeds the scope of this short chapter, but the role exercise has begun to play in treatment is encouraging to observe.

Putting the Pieces Back Together

One Christmas, Jennifer Shea's life began falling apart. She was twenty-five. Her vivid account expresses the kind of healing we've been talking about:

Most people would be glad to replace an old bike with a new one, but I cried when my boyfriend gave me a shiny, new Trek touring bike. Why? This bike symbolized the end of our relationship. I had given him an option: All I wanted for Christmas was a commitment from him; if not, my only request was a Trek, just like his.

I kept the bike; I left him.

In January my bicycle and I returned home to care for my ailing grandmother. She was not just another grandmother, but much more. When I was five, my father had abandoned my mother, older brother, sister, and me. My grandmother raised us from then on, while my mother watched in an alcoholic state.

On Fourth of July I became a holiday statistic. A drunk driver ran a red light and totaled me and my car. A fractured sternum, ribs, and right ankle laid me up the rest of the summer. When I returned to my job, I found I'd been demoted. I then quit.

That October my grandmother had to be put in a convalescent home, and that was when she gave up the will to live. In May the next year I sat with my grandmother and watched her die. I never felt such pain in my life. I cannot even express it on paper.

I moved in with a girlfriend for the summer, out in the country. I had reached the bottom, and I did not have the inner strength to climb back up. All life was pain; I did not want to go on.

But one Saturday in June I woke with the sun and felt my survival strength returning, something I learned about as a child. I took out my Trek and hit the country back roads. On this ride I felt every emotion possible, except perhaps joy. I cried as I rode, I felt anger inside as I pumped up the hills, I felt inner strength, I felt drive. "I've got to make it up this hill!" I competed with the hill—and with myself—and made it to the top.

I flew down the hill, pedaling faster and faster. I couldn't stop my legs but just kept going. I passed some horses and smiled at them. I waved to an old farmer on a plow and talked to his cows as I flew by. I looked up to the sun and the crisp blue sky. I talked to my grandmother and cried again. I talked to my inner self, and I yelled out loud on that deserted country road.

I stood on the pedals and pumped up another hill. My body felt strong. Sweat ran down my face, mixed with my tears. I splashed my face and drank water from my water bottle as I kept going and could not stop. I felt one with nature, with my bike, with myself. I was in control of my life and destiny. I wanted to fight again . . . and to live again.

The rest of that summer I did not trust people or life, but I did trust myself and my Trek. My bike could not hurt me. Together my Trek and I got through the hardest time in my life. I did belong here and I was not alone.

A year later I live in my own home in the country where I was cycling. Recently I've been riding those roads, but it isn't the same now. I feel contentment and inner peace. I'm learning how to love myself for the first time in my life, and I'm thankful my bike guided me down the right road and gave me strength to go on.

A Long and Healthy Life   4

Cycling puts us on the road to better physical health and, possibly, longer life.

"I'm a walking health story," Sherry Denny says with a chuckle. Before she started cycling for real, Sherry, at twenty-seven, had high blood pressure and soaring cholesterol. Back then she owned a cheap, heavy bike that rarely left the garage because "it wasn't much fun to ride." There were no other fitness activities she liked. There never had been.

But she became involved with a bike club when somebody asked Sherry and her husband to drive the sag wagon and pick up stragglers at a club event. "I saw how much fun everybody was having and how fit they were," she says. She wanted that for herself.

She and her husband ordered good bikes, and while she waited for hers to arrive, she began chugging around on the old one. She aimed to be prepared for the club's hilly rides in the area of El Paso, Texas, where she lived at the time.

When the new bike came, shiny and full of promise, Sherry felt primed for a challenge. Eight miles from her front door loomed the top of a mountain. The five-mile stretch of road going up gained 1,350 feet in elevation. Torn between hope and self-doubt, she set out to pedal to the summit. And she did it.

> Here I was forty pounds overweight, and I bicycled up this mountain. Looking back, that was as much a psychological mountain as a physical one. It inspired me to stick with it.
>
> In the past eight years I've lost about thirty pounds. I eat better, my blood pressure is down to normal, and my cholesterol level has dropped by forty-six points. I've discovered cycling as a life-sport, and it has changed me.

If we're looking for a long and healthy life, cycling can help us distance ourselves from many of the medical problems that plague our deskbound, convenience-food car-culture. If we're already suffering from some of these ailments, we can work for our own cure. We can add quality to our years and years to our lives.

That's a fact, confirmed by the Institute for Aerobics Research and the Cooper Clinic in Dallas, Texas. Their study followed more than 13,000 men and women for an average of eight years, correlating fitness to death rates. Based on treadmill testing, participants were divided into five groups, from least fit to most fit.

The good news for anyone just starting to exercise: The greatest drop in the death rates from one group to the next occurred among those just one step above the least fit. Women and men who take up regular, moderate exercise can increase their fitness for dramatic gains in health benefits, especially in lower rates of heart disease and cancer—proof that just breaking out of those sit-on-your-butt habits makes a big difference.

Death rates continued to drop among the fitter groups, indicating that the fit and the fittest do earn better health by their efforts.

Here's a look at some ways aerobic exercise like cycling works to benefit your body.

FOR A HEALTHIER HEART

Coronary heart disease is the number one killer of American females. Surprised? Because men have more heart attacks than women and tend to have them earlier in life, women may be lulled into thinking we have nothing to worry about. That's how it seems in our early adult years when estrogen works in our defense to help keep blood cholesterol levels low. But time starts to catch up with us. From age thirty-five to fifty there's often a steady increase in our cholesterol level, especially after menopause. In the United States, at about age fifty a woman's cholesterol level typically surpasses the level in men, putting her into the high-risk category.

To beat that high-risk curve, medical research tells us that women should start exercising prior to menopause to keep down that steep rise in cholesterol as they age. They should consider lowering their intake of *saturated fats* (found mainly in animal products like fatty meats, and many dairy items), trans-fatty acids, and dietary cholesterol.

Women should also have their total cholesterol level checked. A reading below 200 (mg/dl) is desirable; 200–239 is considered borderline to high; and 240 and above is high. If your level is in the desirable range, you want to know how to keep it there. If you test above 200, you can do something about it, as you'll see. Also talk to your doctor, who may recommend a more complete cholesterol test showing the amount of LDL (the "bad" cholesterol) and HDL (the "good" cholesterol).

You've heard plenty about how that disagreeable sludge called *cholesterol* can build up in the main arteries of the heart and its network of lesser, connecting arteries—a condition known as *arteriosclerosis,* a thickening of the artery walls that may eventually cause clogging. People with high levels of cholesterol in the blood have a greater chance of developing coronary disease.

You may already have improved your diet, which is all to the good. What you ought to know is that the body fights its own "street war" against cholesterol. Here's how exercise can help in that fight.

What happens to fat from the food we eat—say, an ice cream cone or a cheeseburger? After being broken down into its component *lipids* by the small intestine, the fat from food is absorbed into *lymph,* the watery fluid flowing between the cells of the intestine. The fat-laden lymph moves through tiny lymph vessels and finally enters the bloodstream. The insoluble fat can travel in

the watery lymph and blood because the lipids have combined with protein to create *lipoprotein particles,* which form a suspension in water.

At their destinations, these lipoprotein particles are broken down by enzymes. Some of the lipids are stored in body cells as fat. Leftover lipids are recombined into smaller lipoprotein particles containing cholesterol and other lipids.

These smaller lipoprotein particles vary in size and weight, and scientists classify them accordingly. Lightweight ones, called *LDL cholesterol,* tend to stick to the walls of the arteries like snow on a city street. A few snowflakes don't make much difference, but if they continue to accumulate, the street (artery) eventually could become impassable. If a clogged artery impedes the flow of blood, that may cause a heart attack.

In the healthy body, before that can happen, heavier lipoprotein particles, called *HDL cholesterol,* plow their way through, taking some of the LDL "flakes" with them. In sufficient number, HDL particles can make the "streets" more passable, maybe even clear them. The more HDL you have compared to LDL, the better.

Here's where exercise helps. It cuts down the amount of total cholesterol and increases the percentage of the beneficial HDL. How exercise does this is still debated. Some studies indicate a relationship to weight loss, which often occurs when sedentary people become more active.

How much exercise is required? If you're not already fit from other sports, cycling three times a week for a half hour to an hour at a time can prove beneficial at the start. The important thing is to increase your level of activity. How strenuous should it be? With a moderate pace you are more likely to enjoy cycling and stick with it than if you try to become Wonder Woman overnight. And it's safer for your heart. If you are already athletic, or as you get into shape, you may want to exercise more.

Do you need your doctor's OK before you start? Most people don't, since a gradual, sensible program has minimal health risks. But inactive women over fifty (and sedentary men over forty) should consult a physician if they intend to embark on a relatively vigorous regime—say, biking up a mountain á la Sherry Denny. Also, if you have or are at risk for a chronic condition such as cardiovascular disease, insulin-dependent diabetes, or obesity, consult your doctor first.

Meanwhile give your eating habits a quick review. Could you improve them by:

• Cutting down on fat from animal sources like butter and lard?
• Choosing unsaturated oils for cooking and salad oil? These include the *polyunsaturated* oils like safflower, sunflower, corn, soybean, and sesame oils; and *monounsaturated* oils like olive, peanut, and canola (rapeseed) oil. For years nutritionists have urged us to replace saturated fats in our diets with polyunsaturates. Now experts tell us that olive oil and other monounsaturates might benefit you even more because they actually increase your level of "good" HDL cholesterol.

- Checking the labels on commercial baked goods for "tropical" oils? Coconut oil, palm kernel oil, and palm oil are highly saturated.
- Avoiding *hydrogenated* oils (trans-fatty acids) when possible? Some of the unsaturated fats in (normally beneficial) vegetable oils are made more saturated by *hydrogenation* (a process which combines heat and hydrogen) to firm texture and lengthen shelf life. Stick margarines are more hydrogenated than tub margarines, for example. Again, read those labels.
- Cutting back on red meat and eating more fish and fowl? Tip: Most of the fat in chicken, turkey, and other fowl lurks in the skin, so you can reduce the fat in poultry by eating it skinless.
- Cooking the low-fat way? Thumbs down to deep-fat frying. Thumbs up to roasting, baking, broiling, and simmering meat, poultry, or fish. Stir-frying uses little fat and lets you play up the vegetables. Defat meat and poultry juices and liquids left from stewing: Just chill them in the freezer until fat becomes solid, then spoon it off.
- Adding more whole grains, rice, and dried peas and beans to your menus? These can replace meat as a source of protein in some meals and at lower cost. Vegetarian dishes can give delicious variety to meals.
- Eating more fresh fruits and green and yellow vegetables? Try to get your "five-a-day."
- Upping fiber intake with bran or whole grains, like brown rice or whole wheat?

For a healthier heart and all-around better nutrition, the accompanying chart suggests substitutions that require no calorie counting. These changes could gradually be incorporated into meals for an entire family, as they are recommended for anyone over age two. If your family has favorite dishes you eat again and again, try modifying them to increase nutrition without sacrificing taste. Or select several new good-for-you meals to make standards. Remember, if you don't want to give up something—like your favorite cheeses—you could choose to cut down on portion size. More information should be available from your local heart association.

TAKING THE PRESSURE OFF

Another bonus of regular exercise is the role it plays in helping to prevent high blood pressure (*hypertension*) and even lowering blood pressure that exceeds normal healthy levels. Often undiagnosed, this "silent killer" can contribute to heart disease or cause stroke or kidney failure. A blood pressure of 140/90 mm Hg or greater is generally classified as high, and requiring treatment.

The desirable blood pressure for a healthy adult is about 120/80 mm Hg. Here's what those numbers mean and a simple trick for remembering. When your heart beats, blood *surges* from the heart, and pressure in the arteries rises.

What's to Eat? Tips for Lowering Dietary Cholesterol and Saturated Fat

If you need to make changes in eating habits, do so gradually. Try one or two of the following tips at a time and get used to it. And talk it over with your health-care provider or a nutritionist before you start. You may already be eating a fairly wholesome diet, full of nutritious fruits, vegetables, and whole grains. Radical and unnecessary dieting can be harmful.

Low-fat processed foods are not necessarily low in calories. For example, low-fat frozen yogurt, sherbet, and the like contain far less fat than regular or premium ice creams, but not necessarily less sugar. In fact, one way manufacturers substitute for the rich taste of fat in a product is to pour in extra sugar. Therefore, we still need to read labels as we decide whether certain foods should be occasional indulgences or dietary mainstays.

Eat This	Instead of This
Olive, canola, safflower, or sunflower oil or other unsaturated oils	Hard shortening, lard, or bacon grease
Tub margarine	Butter or stick margarine
Fish, shellfish, skinless poultry, or lean cuts of meat; tofu (soybean curd) and dried beans for vegetable protein	Fatty cuts of beef, lamb, pork
Turkey breast, tuna packed in water, natural unhydrogenated peanut butter	Luncheon meats
Low-fat and part-skim cheeses	Cheeses containing more than 2–6 grams of fat per ounce
Skim or 1 percent milk	2 percent or whole milk, nondairy creamers
Fruit ices, sorbets, sherbet, low-fat frozen yogurt, ice milk	Ice cream, especially the richest specialty ice creams
Nonfat sour cream	Sour cream or imitation sour cream
Raisin, whole wheat, or pumpernickel bagels	Doughnuts or pastries
Gingersnaps, graham crackers, or fig bars (made with corn, sunflower, or safflower oil)	Chocolate chip and other high-fat cookies
Low-fat whole grain crackers, soda crackers, or bread sticks	High-fat crackers (including unsalted versions)
Unbuttered popcorn or pretzels	Commercial chips and cheese puffs

This is the *systolic* pressure, the first number in the fraction (remember, "surge" and "systolic"). Between beats the heart rests, no blood is pumped, and pressure *decreases*. This is the second number, the *diastolic* pressure. Both pressures are measured in millimeters (mm) of mercury (Hg). Keep in mind, 120/80 is the average for a range of healthy blood pressures.

If your blood pressure has begun to creep up—for example, if it measures above 130/85 mm Hg, the threshold for "high-normal"—discuss the options with your doctor. If you've been inactive, changes in diet (including cutting down on salt) and cycling regularly might be enough therapy to avoid taking medication. If medication is recommended immediately, discuss also the advisability of exercise and other lifestyle changes.

PROTECTION AGAINST CANCER?

Numerous studies have linked lower cancer rates and higher levels of exercise. In 1985 the American Cancer Society began recommending exercise to protect against cancer.

A pioneering study first reported that year surveyed over 5,000 female college graduates, ranging in age from twenty-one to eighty. Women who were active in sports or other regular athletic pursuits in college had a markedly lower lifetime occurrence rate of breast or reproductive-organ cancer than the alumnae who had not been athletic in college. Although family histories of cancer for the two groups were statistically similar, the former nonathletes had nearly twice the risk of breast cancer and two-and-a-half times the risk of cancer of the reproductive system, compared to the former athletes. The study's authors, Rose E. Frisch, Ph.D., and colleagues, sum up: "Long-term athletic training establishes a lifestyle that somehow lowers the risk of breast cancer and cancers of the reproductive system."

Of the former college athletes, 82.4 percent had taken part in sports in high school or earlier, compared to only 24.9 percent of the nonathletes. And 73.5 percent were still exercising regularly at the time of the survey, compared to 57 percent of the former nonathletes.

How does long-term participation in athletics affect a woman's body? At all ages in the study, the athlete group had a lower percentage of body fat and a higher percentage of lean muscle mass, compared to the nonathlete group. And the athletes had a later onset of menstruation and earlier menopause, suggesting lower levels of estrogen in the athletes that may in turn be related to the lower cancer rate.

Based on this study, Dr. Frisch stresses the need for early physical activity:

Regular, moderate activity is very important. You're leaner for the rest of your life. Body fat makes estrogen by converting androgens to estrogen. Also, if you are leaner, you make a less potent metabolite of estrogen, causing fewer cells in the breast and uterus to divide, and therefore there is less risk of a mistake leading to cancer. These may be the mechanisms at work.

This is strong evidence for sharing our active lifestyle with our daughters and granddaughters. Meanwhile, there's good news for us, too. Follow-up studies seem to confirm a protective effect for women who become active (at work or through sport) during their adult years.

DODGING DIABETES

Dr. Frisch and her colleagues also found startling news about late onset, non-insulin-dependent diabetes. Prevalence of the disease among former college athletes was much lower than that of their nonathletic classmates. Including all cases of diabetes beginning at age twenty and older, researchers found that "0.5 percent of the former college athletes had diabetes compared to 1.2 percent of the nonathletes"—a marked difference despite basically similar family histories of the disease.

Along with proper diet, the benefits of regular exercise in managing all types of diabetes have been well demonstrated. Mild or moderate exercise assists by taking some glucose out of the blood to use for energy, which lowers blood glucose levels closer to normal. Being physically active also helps protect against cardiovascular disease, the leading killer of diabetics.

As one enthusiastic cyclist/diabetic, Charlotte Versagi, says:

With diabetes it is extremely important to maintain an even, consistent level of exercise. Cycling allows for the sustained kind of exertion that is best for the disorder. And I can do it nine months out of the year! It is easy to monitor by my physical responses the food intake I need, and people are usually nearby in case I should get into blood-sugar trouble. But that hasn't happened yet.

Charlotte is an adult-onset, noninsulin-dependent diabetic who believes that "there really isn't a better way to see the country, meet people, and be kind to your body while having a wonderful workout."

She did just that, at thirty-something, on a solo tour across her state of Michigan, cycling about sixty to seventy miles a day and camping at night. She'd start each day with a good breakfast—bread, fruit, granola, and juice—and then ride most of the day except for snack breaks. About three or four P.M., just before arriving at her campsite, she'd stop for a big meal. "I'd be in camp by five or six, shower, set up camp, and read or talk to folks until around nine or ten and then just die!" She adds:

People were, without exception, kind and curious and helpful. Once during a horrible rainstorm in the middle of a country road, a big bearded guy, whom I called St. Joseph, stopped his pickup and lifted my bike and all its packs into the back of the truck and invited me, dripping wet, into the cab. There he turned on the heat to try to dry me off and drove me the last ten miles to my campsite.

Obviously, Charlotte cycles as much for recreation as to control her diabetes. But even six miles a day could make a difference.

FREEDOM FROM SMOKING

There's little doubt about the link between smoking and (1) heart disease, (2) lung cancer (now the biggest cancer killer among American women), (3) emphysema, (4) complications during pregnancy, (5) high blood pressure, and (6) circulatory problems that complicate diabetes. If you smoke, you already know that you could do your health the greatest favor by quitting.

A range of stop-smoking aids—"the patch," nicotine gum, hypnosis and self-hypnosis, acupuncture—may help. Also recognize that smoking is a physical, psychological, and even social dependency, and find coping behaviors to address these three types of needs. Cycling can assist you.

"Exercise is one of your greatest allies in fighting off cravings," says the American Lung Association (ALA) in its self-help program manual, *Freedom from Smoking*. Give yourself a psychological boost: Look on cycling as a positive habit to replace a bad one and as a reward you will have earned by quitting. If you share cycling with friends or find new friends who enjoy it, it becomes a social coping technique—something to do besides sitting together over coffee and a cigarette. And there's never a worry about what to do with your hands.

John Williams, speaking for the ALA, suggests:

- *Giving up cigarettes is plenty stressful. Regular exercise like cycling can help reduce overall tension.* When really bad jitters strike, perhaps you can escape for a short ride.
- *People often smoke from boredom. Find something to do if you have time on your hands.* Go for a bike ride, or call a friend and plan one for later. Read another chapter in this book. Lube your chain. Do something to interrupt that smoking urge.
- *Cycling can help to prevent weight gain, often a worry after kicking the habit.*

Once you're caught up in the pleasure of cycling, it becomes a reward in itself. After quitting smoking, one couple took off for a two-week holiday on their new bikes to ride in the hills and along the coast in California. Despite "sore back ends," they discovered "how much fun cycling can be." Another former smoker remarks, "As I've become fitter, the urge to smoke has vanished. Besides, I need all my vital capacity!"

It's seldom too late to quit and benefit from it. Clarissa Gerhardt and her husband began their retirement years by giving up smoking. She was forty-three; he was sixty-four. They bought new touring bikes and spent four months in Florida, riding every day. Back home in Ohio with the warm weather, they set off to see their state . . . on their bikes. The tour was especially wonderful "because of our pleasure in knowing we'd recaptured our health," she exults. "We built up our tired bodies so we could cycle those back roads that most people our age would see only from their camper vehicles."

You can quit smoking, and you don't have to do it alone. Your local ALA chapter offers copies of *Freedom from Smoking* as well as a ten-day program book for pregnant women, *Freedom from Smoking for You and Your Baby.*

If you've tried to quit smoking before and failed, don't be afraid to try again. Often it takes as many as four to ten attempts to quit and stay quit. Phyllis Cohen of Santa Monica, California, had stopped smoking many times, but not for long. Serious about fitness, she did aerobics and played racquetball for years, then took up weight training and the studio cycling program called Spinning. But she still lacked the right incentive to quit smoking forever. About the time she turned fifty, a cycling coach encouraged her to train for the Race Across AMerica (RAAM). With the help of a three-month supply of NicoDerm patches, Phyllis did quit on Christmas 1994 and set about recruiting three more fifty-plus women to ride the relay division of the race. After two-and-a-half years of organizing and training, they competed in the nonstop, 2,905-mile road race, which, in 1997, started in Irvine, California. Seven days, seventeen hours, and fifty minutes later they finished in Savannah, Georgia, the first fifty-plus women's team to complete the race, and thus record-setters. As of this writing, Phyllis's personal record of three-and-a-half years smoke-free still stands.

EASING ARTHRITIS

If you don't use it, you lose it, says the Arthritis Foundation. Accordingly, the big movement in treatment of arthritis is a comprehensive approach including joint protection, medication, and exercise or physical therapy.

"We recommend that everyone get involved in recreational exercise," says Annette Myarick of Philadelphia, speaking for the foundation, "though we don't mean to suggest that it should replace prescribed physical therapy. But exercise is a good supplement to therapy."

The Arthritis Foundation recommends exercise that promotes stretching (to increase range of motion), muscle strengthening, and endurance. In fact, if you have arthritis and your own doctor discourages exercise as treatment, the foundation suggests you seek a second opinion. As their booklet *Exercise and Your Arthritis* notes, "If you have already lost the function of some joints, a regular exercise program can help prevent further loss. It may also help you to regain function."

Cycling, as Iva Oshaunesy of Albuquerque, New Mexico, has discovered, can work wonders. She says:

Life begins at fifty!

At age forty-seven I developed arthritis from a rubella vaccination. Anger and depression were consuming my energy the following June, when I met a man who told me his arthritis decreased after he started cycling regularly.

The very next week I bought a heavy six-speed bike and started learning to ride. No one can imagine how little I knew about cycling, but I blundered along, and by August of that year I was able to backpack!

The following summer after reading up and asking advice from a cycling female co-worker, I bought a new, good-quality road bike. I had a lot to learn about handling it, but I didn't let that stop me. Six weeks later, without any idea what I was doing, I signed up to ride 200 miles in three days. It was really too much, but pride kept me going through those 200 miles.

A year later I celebrated turning fifty by going on the same 200-mile ride and enjoying it. A year of cycling regularly had strengthened my legs, built up my endurance, and let me surround myself with healthy, happy, active friends.

The following year I rode more than 5,000 miles. Now I have a new custom bike and am more healthy mentally and physically than at any other time in my life."

A Cyclist's Love Story

It would be foolish to imply that athletic people don't get cancer. Sometimes they do. In those cases, is bicycling or other regular exercise good therapy during recovery? Can cycling help to keep cancer in remission? Does it somehow help the body to marshal its own defenses? Or aid the spirit to rally a greater will to live?

We don't know, but in Carlyn Hove Roedell's life, cycling has made a difference. Carlyn, 46, a teacher in Seahurst, Washington, writes:

My husband had cancer in 1985, a year after our 1,000-mile bike tour in France. His ability to ride was greatly diminished, as was his entire being.

Although I wasn't sure I could do it, I completed a ride for the American Cancer Society, a ninety-mile day up a mountain pass by Mount St. Helens. It happened I won a prize on the ride (not for finishing first!), which was a Klein custom bicycle frame.

I gave it to my husband as a get-well present. It worked! He's back riding, stronger than ever. The following year he cycled the entire 200-mile "Hel'en Gone" ride around Mount St. Helens in one day, while I did the two-day version. We had a great time. It makes one love biking and life all the more!

PS Thirteen years after his illness, we're both healthy and still cycling.

So You Want to Buy a Bike?

If you're planning to start out fresh with a new bike, you have the opportunity to buy just the one to meet your needs—to suit your style of riding and to fit your proportions, which, because you are a woman, may differ from those of a man.

But you need to be a savvy consumer. Many women tell me they were quite naive when they bought their first adult bike. So was I. In this chapter you'll learn how to avoid the mistakes we made and buy the bike you want the first time around. After all, bicycles can be as different from one another as a Jeep is from a Jaguar. And you wouldn't flip a coin over that decision. Even if you buy a used bicycle, it pays to be well informed. And if you're an experienced cyclist buying your second (third, whatever) bike, you can find tips here on features, bike types, or fit that you should probably consider.

If I mention bike parts you're unfamiliar with, see figures 1, 4, 6, and 9. Furthermore, though we'll look at bikes available at this writing, the market continues to change. So we'll also talk about fundamental needs and how to meet them. That basic understanding will never go out of style.

These questions often come up when buying.

1. WHAT KIND OF A BIKE SHOULD I BUY?

Lucky you! Today's market offers a huge range of choices in the variety of bicycle types available. The right choice depends on what kind of riding you want to do.

- Which of the cycling goals in chapter 1 appeals most?
- Where's the best riding? Have you miles of paved country lanes or other scenic roads with little traffic? Is there a network of off-road paths or wilderness trails beckoning to be explored? Have you a velodrome in your area? Do you intend to commute between home and work, perhaps connecting with mass transit?

Among the following categories, you'll likely find one bike type that best fits your answers. You'll see that some bikes are highly versatile. Others suit one particular purpose, which is why many avid cyclists own more than one bicycle. For example, in recent years so many people bought a mountain bike as their first purchase that road bike sales plummeted. Now as some dirt riders discover the conditioning value of training on pavement, they're adding road bikes to their stables.

Here's a look at eleven types of bikes, what each can do, and some features to look for:

Mountain Bike (MTB). In recent memory MTBs have been the biggest sellers for riding both off-road and on.

Want to get away from it all? This fat-tired bike with flat or riser handlebars was originally designed for rock-studded hilly descents and trail climbing. Is there a stream in your path? A log? You can splash through it or bump over it. OK, there's some technique involved, but it's easily learned and fun (see chapter 15, "Fat Tire Freedom"). Besides, who says you can't get off and walk the tough spots?

But you can also use a mountain machine in a less spine-tingling fashion, gliding along a cinder path, a fire road, or a converted railroad bed, communing with nature. Stop and watch the butterflies in a mountain meadow or lunch by a waterfall. Whichever style of riding gives you renewal, you can escape to the wild places in your area on an MTB.

Or take it on the country lanes or in town. In fact, if you have to thread your way through broken glass and rough pavement, these durable tires may be just what you're looking for. Ditto the handlebars: Many women who don't like drop bars on a road bike prefer this more upright position for seeing traffic and greater back comfort.

A true dirt rig will have twenty-one or twenty-four speeds, with gearing that ranges from super-low for climbing hilly trails while seated, all the way up to high gears that go plenty fast. You'll need a frame built to take abuse and, of course, fat knobby tires; wheels 26 inches in diameter are standard. Until recently, you could expect a quick-release seatpost, but now better MTBs may just have a binder bolt at the top of the seat tube (since experienced riders don't raise and lower the saddle in the course of a ride). If a more aggressive style of trail riding appeals to you, invest in a reasonably lightweight bike with suspension forks. These shock-eating front forks boost comfort and control by softening bumps and helping to keep wheels on the ground. Front suspension comes standard now on all serious mountain bikes; a suspension adds weight, but these are ounces well spent.

You may be wondering about rear suspension. It came to us from the warp-speed world of downhill racing. If you're not into that, you might still appreciate dual-suspension if you typically hammer rough trails for several hours at a time on your hardtail bike and think a cushier ride would extend your staying power. Rear suspension will add weight—one reason why some who could afford the cost haven't sprung for a dualie.

Also plush, but a less expensive alternative (or an aftermarket item) is the suspension seatpost.

Tell the salesperson what sort of off-road riding you intend to do and ask for a bike with appropriate handling characteristics.

If you plan to ride your MTB mostly on-road, be aware that the more upright seating position and wide, knobby, relatively low-pressure tires make for a slower pace than you'd have with a road bike; ask about treadless tires to reduce rolling resistance. As a matter of fact, a new category, the "comfort" bike, has already emerged with this modification. Look also at hybrids and utility/cruiser bikes.

Factoid: A mountain bike is usually several pounds heavier than a comparably priced road bike.

Hybrid Bike. For some uses a mountain bike is overkill, so somebody crossed a road bike with a mountain bike to get (ta-da!) the cross bike, or hybrid. You still have lots of gears—usually twenty-one speeds but sometimes eighteen. This machine's lighter tubing and medium-width, higher-pressure tires deliver a faster, more responsive ride on pavement than you get with a mountain bike. Yet a hybrid's tires are more durable and cushier on rough roads than a touring/sport bike's. The hybrid bike's high-rise stem and upswept, swept-back, or flat handlebars give a fairly upright seating position that many new cyclists favor over drop handlebars. Experienced riders whose backs aren't as limber as they once were may also like sitting up more.

Getting a good fit, even for shorties like me (I'm five-foot-two), is fairly easy on a hybrid. I discovered that several years ago when cycling in the south of France with a tour company that provided me with a hybrid bike. Especially compared to ill-fitting road bikes of previous tours, the hybrid bike's higher handlebars allowed a comfortable reach, and the more upright seating was ideal for enjoying the views of vineyards and old hill-towns. Low gears on the triple chainring took me up those hills more easily.

For someone who piles on the miles, a hybrid's handlebar may seem constraining, with only one hand position. If you plan rides upwards of thirty-five miles, bar ends (which can be added) would be a bonus since they let you vary your grip and are handy to pull on when climbing.

Just plan to pedal pavement? Select smoother street tires for less rolling resistance. To ride dirt roads as well, look for tires with a dual-purpose tread. Off-road, some hybrids are more aggressive than others. All can handle packed dirt trails, gravel roads, and modest climbs, to let you keep going when the pavement stops. But don't expect a hybrid's lighter frame to take rattling and bouncing like an MTB or to give you the same control.

Suspension forks and seatposts are showing up on some hybrid bikes, and I've tested one with a suspension stem. If you ride a lot of rough pavement, maybe these goodies would make a difference. Road-test and compare to no-frills models to be sure.

Utility Bike/Cruiser. Inspired by European utility bikes (see figure 7), these rigs evolved for tooling around a summer resort or for city riding—for cruising through potholes without damaging the wheel rims and, with that upright position, keeping an eye on traffic. Generally, their easily-maintained gearing can be either very basic (a one-speed) or *internal-hub,* with up to seven speeds. Just to

Anatomy of a Smart Buy: Mountain Bike

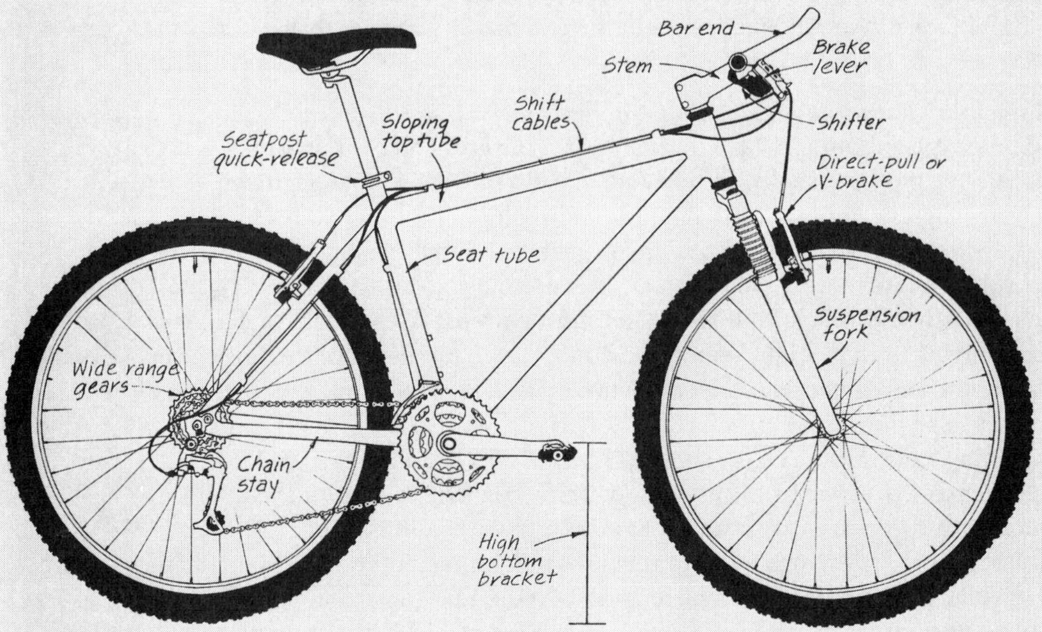

Fig. 1: Anatomy of a smart buy: mountain bike

Currently, there are more mountain bikes and mountain bike look-alikes in the shops than any other bike type. How do you sort through them all to meet the rigors of off-road biking? From stem to stern, here's what to look for in a trailworthy rig.

Frame size. Corresponds with seat tube length. An MTB frame should give at least three or four inches of clearance over the top tube so you don't hit it when you put a foot down quickly to steady yourself. Comfortable reach to the handlebars is also essential.

Weight. Less is more. An MTB can tip the scales at over thirty pounds, or weigh as little as twenty-three. As the price goes up, the weight of the frame and components goes down. In an unsuspended bike, a weight of twenty-five or twenty-six pounds suggests decent quality. A front suspension out-weighs a rigid fork, however, so make allowances. If you want to compare weights, take your bathroom scale along (really). Bike weights in catalogs may be more optimistic than realistic.

Front suspension. Do you need it? You'll probably appreciate it if you're riding moderate to rough terrain, bumping over rocks, roots, and the like. Suspension soaks up the impacts, cuts fatigue, and provides more steering control. Try your friends' front-suspended rigs if you can and read the latest product reviews to choose the best suspension fork for you. One school of thought is that you should learn technical skills on an unsuspended bike, and then move up to a suspension bike; others would say this is hopelessly old-fashioned and that with suspension you'll have fewer falls and more fun riding from the beginning.

Before test-riding one from a shop, ask to have the fork's preload set for your weight and riding style. As you encounter obstacles, the fork should move freely. Each of four companies—RockShox, Answer/Manitou, Marzocchi, and RST—makes shock forks at a range of price points that appear on many different brands of bikes. Bike manufacturer Cannondale has its own HeadShok. If you don't want to buy front-suspension now but think you might add one later, choose a good-quality rigid bike that is "suspension-ready."

Sloping top tube. Gives more stand-over height in case of a quick dismount when trail riding; not a gender-specific feature.

Shift cables. Run along the top tube to keep mud from clogging them.

Wheels. Rims should be a light but strong aluminum alloy. Quick-release hubs are convenient. Name-brand hubs such as Shimano and stainless steel spokes signify durability.

Tires. For all-purpose use, a combination tread has a continuous center section with a surrounding knobby pattern for smooth pedaling on pavement and traction on easy trails. For best off-road performance, get full knobbies.

Gearing. Indexed shifting and triple chainrings are standard.

Brakes. Cantilever brakes have proved very trailworthy over recent years. Now the direct-pull (or linear-pull) brake—so called because the cable goes directly to the brake arm instead of through a hanger—puts more muscle into stopping; go easy on 'em.

Handlebars. For off-road, buy flat bars for best leverage and control.

Stem. Some stems raise the bars higher than others. Less stem rise favors more aggressive trail riding and climbing; more rise suits recreational riders who want to sit more upright.

Bar ends. Let you vary hand position; especially efficient for climbing. Available as add-ons.

Seatpost. The quick-release lets you raise and lower the saddle, but experienced riders have other ways of shifting their weight. Some seatposts (mostly aftermarket) have shock-absorbing bumpers inside.

Shifters. Both the trigger style from Shimano and Grip Shift's twist type let you keep hands on the bars when shifting. Test-ride fully to determine your preference, shifting up and down with each derailleur.

Brake levers. Are angled down so wrists can be kept straight, not cocked. Levers with adjustable reach are desirable.

Grips. Firm ones fatigue your hands less than squishy ones.

Pedals. Ask whether pedals will accept toeclips and straps. Conventional pedals have a gripping surface on both sides. Clipless pedals can be stepped into on either side.

Bottom bracket. Houses the axle that connects the crank arms; higher than on road bikes to let you clear obstacles on the trail.

Chain stays. Other things being equal, bikes with shorter chain stays (17 inches or less) make climbing easier, especially when standing.

ride a few blocks to the beach or to buy the morning paper, you could econo-
mize on a single-speed. For longer forays on flat terrain, a couple of extra speeds
come in handy for gearing down in a headwind.

You'll often find street treads on the ballooner tires, which may be a little
skinnier than on an MTB; other bikes in this category sport knobbies for easy
trails. Handlebars are likely to rise higher for greater comfort.

Some frame styles with gracefully curving tubes, and maybe even a horn
tank, hark back to the classic cruisers of the 1950s. These retro rigs have "beach
bike" and "seashore boardwalk" written all over them; just try to keep sand out
of the components and don't leave your cruiser at the shore year-round, as salt
air can rust a bike. If you intend to stay on-road with your city bike, consider
mudguards and a chainguard (to keep chain grease off clothing), especially if
you cycle-commute in work attire. A word of warning: Some of these cruisers
weigh a ton.

For town use, see also the folding bike, below.

Comfort Bike. What do you have when you take a mountain bike frame, change
the tires to street treads, and add some shock-absorption features like suspension seatpost and stem? A comfort bike—which might be just what you're looking for to ride in the neighborhood with your kids or cruise easy local trails.
Recently introduced by a number of manufacturers, they come in a range of
price points. The bike's weight and the quality of frame and components will
vary accordingly. If you like the idea but find limited selection, ask the retailer
about other models in the manufacturers' lines, which might be ordered for you.

Why not just buy a hybrid? The comfort bike's selling point is that later you
could change the tires to knobbies, tackle gnarlier trails, and bounce around some
on this bike. Its rims and frame are built to take it. Usually a hybrid's are not.

If you opt for a comfort bike, discuss with the salesperson whether the *elastomers* (compressible elastic polymer "bumpers") in the suspension components
have been chosen with your body weight in mind. Too stiff an elastomer will not
have the intended cushioning effect.

Road-Racing Bike. You don't have to be a racer to enjoy a road-racing bike—simply a cyclist with some experience who wants a little more speed in your life. In
the future, if you decide to graduate from recreational riding to competition,
you'll have the steed to do it.

These days racers come with narrow, high-pressure *clincher* tires, so called
because they have a wire bead that "clinches" the tire to the rim. These skinny
tires have more durability and nearly as low rolling resistance as the tubular tire,
or *sew-up,* which racers used to swear by. Many cyclists stick with clinchers for
racing and training. If you think you might make a switch, however, keep your
options open by selecting 700C rims (instead of 27-inch rims). If later you want
to buy an extra set of rims with lightweight, *tubular* racing tires (which always
come in 700C), they'll be interchangeable.

Compared to a touring or touring/sport bike, a racer will be geared higher for speed—with sixteen and eighteen closely spaced gears—and won't have the lower range of gears needed by the average rider for hills. Gearing can be modified, however, if you determine that these bikes are for you.

In handling, these speed machines differ according to intended use. As a general rule, buy only as much maneuverability as you need. A road-racing bike should be fairly maneuverable but still not require constant correction just to keep it rolling in a straight line. By contrast, a criterium bike is designed for quick cornering in the many turns in such races. An opposite extreme, a time trial bike's main mission is usually to ride a straight course; it might handle more like a touring/sport or even a touring bike.

Touring/Sport Bike. This versatile drop-handlebar/derailleur bike was the original "ten-speed." These days it often has twenty-one speeds (if not twenty-four or twenty-seven)—thanks to seven, eight, or nine cogs on the rear wheel and a triple chainring. Some bikes in this category come with a double chainring, however. Given a choice, I'd choose a triple if you anticipate any hill climbing.

What distinguishes a touring/sport bike? This road bike handles corners with sufficient agility for pleasure and fitness riding, and it's well suited for pace-line training sessions and century rides. The relatively narrow tires and light wheels, along with the aerodynamic riding position possible on the drop bars, give you speed advantages over hybrid and mountain bikes on the road. Add a rack to make the touring/sport bike a travel vehicle for light touring (carrying clothes, but not camping gear). This bike could be very serviceable for a beginning triathlete or time trialist, since neither type of racing usually involves much cornering. Standard wheels on this bike are 27-inch diameter or 700C.

Touring Bike. Are you looking for a beast of burden for a long bicycle camping trip? The touring bike is designed for stability when carrying over twenty-five pounds of gear. You may not see much difference between this and the touring/sport bike, but you'll feel it on a test ride. The loaded touring bike has longer chain stays and a longer *wheelbase* (distance between the center of the front axle and the rear axle), assuring a safer, more comfortable ride for long days in the saddle. Its shallower head angle (about seventy-one to seventy-two degrees on a bike with standard size wheels), also contributes to the comfort.

Features to look for include *cantilever* brakes, which give extra stopping power—desirable when descending long hills with all your camping gear accelerating your speed. Cantis also allow the easy addition of fenders for wet-weather riding. A triple chainring provides extra-low gears for climbing hills with a load. These bikes, if not already fitted out with racks, should have eyelets for mounting them, as well as "braze-on" mountings for water bottle cages (see chapter 22, "Planning Your Own Tour").

Recumbent. Almost as comfortable as your favorite recliner, a recumbent features a chairlike seat for full back support and no bending over—relief for cyclists with back pain or saddle problems, or anyone else who wants laid-back seating and no weight on their hands. Or maybe you like the idea of going faster on the flats and downhill, thanks to the streamlined, lower position with legs extending forward to the pedals (ask about a racing recumbent). You could really go space-age and select one with a fairing to cut through the wind. These bikes have been around for years, but they're growing in popularity as prices have lowered, more models have become available, and word gets around.

A few drawbacks: Recumbents weigh more than regular bikes and climb slower (no out-of-the saddle on hills). Transporting one in your car might be trickier, although some models fold for storage or mounting on a car rack. Also, recumbents are lower to the ground, possibly making the rider less visible to motorists.

To learn more about these bikes, you might subscribe to the newsletter *Recumbent Cyclist News* (see appendix).

Tandem. Are you part of a twosome with different fitness levels? Or a pair that just likes to work closely together? Better than drafting, a tandem can be a great equalizer. It's perfect for inseparables who like to talk as they ride, and it's one possible answer for including a child too young to pedal her or his own bike very far (see chapter 16, "Cycling with the Family"). You'll find tandems in road, hybrid, recumbent, and mountain versions; the latter take well to fire roads but not to technical singletrack. You can expect to travel faster generally on a "twicer" than on a single bike, but climb more slowly. A good tandem with a stiff, strong frame of quality tubing isn't cheap, but their prices are becoming more reasonable.

Talk to other tandem owners and try before you buy. Because both partners' cranksets are connected to each other, tandemists must pedal in unison. The *captain* (in front) controls steering, shifting, and most braking. Thus good communication and trust on the part of the *stoker* (rear partner) are essential for happy tandeming. Fit tip: The frame must have low enough standover height to allow straddling the top tube. The captain especially needs to be able to dismount and control the bike at traffic signals.

Folding Bikes. Probably not a first-bike pick, these ingenious rigs fold up (no tools needed) for carrying on a bus or the subway. Some even fit into a suitcase which can be slid under an airline seat. With folders a test ride is especially important, as some do better than others at delivering "real bike" performance. (Green Gear's Air Friday has even been raced in the Iron Man Triathlon.) In addition, run through assembly and disassembly yourself to see how long it takes and what it involves. Some brands to ask about: Brompton, Dahon, Gaerlan's Jeep Renegade, Green Gear Cycling, Montague, and Swift.

Track Bikes. Specially designed for velodrome racing, a track bike has a single *fixed gear* (no coasting), no brakes, and tubular tires. If you want to be a trackie, contact the nearest velodrome and ask about development classes; bikes may be available for loan to participants at the 'drome. When you're ready, your coach can refer you to the best pro shop in the area.

2. HOW MUCH SHOULD I SPEND?

There is no single "right price" to pay for a bike. Keep an open mind about cost and look for the hallmarks of quality discussed here. Just how far adult bikes have come since the toys we rode as kids may surprise you—we're talking aircraft technology and space-age materials. The very best bikes (costing thousands of dollars) are on the cutting edge, but a trickle-down effect benefits the rest of the bicycle market. A good bike will be more pleasurable to ride, will motivate you to progress further in the sport, and will be easier to keep in good repair than a bargain-basement cheapie.

3. WHERE SHOULD I BUY MY BIKE?

At a bike shop, you're more likely to find knowledgeable salespeople to answer your questions and personalized service from a skilled mechanic to help you maintain your bike and get the most out of riding it. Prices are usually lower at a department store, but so is the quality. And most department stores don't repair bikes. Bike shops generally offer a far wider range of quality levels and will allow you to test-ride.

Study this chapter and you'll know much more than the sales personnel will expect you to know. So don't feel embarrassed if you don't understand some point or term in the sales rap. Ask questions where you have to. If a dealer is impatient or unhelpful, go elsewhere. Bike shopping is a learning process. Don't let anybody rush you.

Should you find little selection locally, go to a nearby city with a number of shops. To find the closest retailer who carries a brand mentioned in this book, check the appendix. Regardless, it's wise to shop around. There are many good bicycle manufacturers, but some may offer a greater variety of models in your frame size or the bike type you prefer. Some brands will have special sizing programs to better fit women's proportions. You may find the same bike at a lower price in another shop or a dealer willing to throw in a woman's saddle or other accessories to make the sale. Likewise, once you find a frame that fits, don't be shy about asking to change the saddle, toeclips, tires, or even gearing. Do bear in mind that the profit margin on bike sales is often quite low, even in bike shops. Some changes justify a charge to cover labor or the upgrade.

Bike shops often have a Fit Kit or some other sizing system. Many cyclists find the cost of such a service well worth it.

If the salesperson doesn't volunteer the information, ask whether the shop offers a free, thirty-day tune-up after you've purchased. During the initial month of cycling, your bike's cables, bearings, spokes, nuts, and bolts tend to stretch or loosen and should be adjusted. Take advantage of this checkup to ensure performance.

And save your sales receipt. Frames and forks are typically guaranteed for life against failure caused by defects in materials or workmanship. Components are generally guaranteed for six months to a year.

4. DO I NEED A "WOMAN'S BIKE"?

Those bicycles we traditionally thought of as "girls' bikes"—the kind you step astride without swinging your leg over a high top tube—were originally designed in the 1880s, when ladies pedaled in long skirts. The *step-through frame* is still practical for this purpose, and I've observed in England and the Netherlands, for example, that many women in skirts do commute to work and do errands on bikes like this with upright bars (see figure 7).

In the 1970s, however, bikes from the racing world began to impact recreational use. Ten-speeds, drop-handlebar road bicycles, designed for the traditionally male world of racing and club riding, suddenly became the rage. Basically sized to fit men, some models were offered with lowered top tubes and called "women's bikes" (see figures 2 and 3). Of these, the stronger *mixte* (pronounced MIX-tee) frame was preferable for riding any extended distance or for carrying a load.

The trouble was, nobody seemed to recognize another dimension needing change: These bikes were too long for many females who tried to ride them. Just because a purchaser could straddle the bicycle didn't mean it was her size. Some

Fig. 2: Step-through or "ladies" frame

Fig. 3: Mixte frame: twin lateral tubes attached at the seat tube and running back to connect with the seatstays and chainstays make the mixte stronger than a step-through frame.

women had to strain to reach the handlebars and use the brakes. That sort of "girl's bike" didn't solve every female's fit problems.

At the same time, women wearing pants discovered they could throw a leg over a horizontal top tube as easily as a guy. So we no longer called this bike a "men's bike" but a *diamond frame,* because of the shape taken by the main tubes, including the chainstays. Women took enthusiastically to the diamond frame, partly because it gave them lots more choice in bicycles. Unfortunately, lengthwise, it didn't fit some of the women who tried to ride it.

5. WHAT'S THE PROBLEM WITH FEMALE PROPORTIONS?

Stand a woman and a man of the same height side by side, and the woman will usually have shorter arms and a shorter torso, longer legs, smaller hands and feet, narrower shoulders, and a wider pelvis. We certainly aren't built like men, but for a long time the bicycle industry ignored those differences.

Untold numbers of women went through the bike-buying experience that Ann Counts, of Euless, Texas, describes:

When I bought my first bicycle, I knew nothing about bikes and depended on the salesperson. Thus I wound up with a bike that was never comfortable because it didn't fit. I had no top-tube clearance. Too-big brake levers made it tough for me to stop. My arms ached as the handlebars were much too wide, and I always hurt from having to reach too far.

I had too much money in the bike to start over, so I slowly changed items, trying to make the bike more comfortable. I replaced the brake levers and handlebars, shortened the stem, and switched saddles three times. Even so, the bicycle wasn't as comfortable for my build, at five-foot-one, as a bike can and should be.

Ultimately I found a different bike shop. I made an effort to know the personnel. This shop gives fabulous service and honest answers to their customers. Following their advice, I went through a complete Fit Kit before buying a new bike which I am truly pleased with.

Although a bike shop is your best bet for well-informed sales help, as Jean Welch, of Van Nuys, California, points out, you cannot simply throw yourself at the shop's mercy. "I had to research bike fit for myself," she says. "Bike shops usually wanted to sell me whichever bicycle they had that came the closest."

Even now, you must be aware of these sizing problems and assert your need for proper fit, especially if you are a woman shorter than five-foot-five. Otherwise, the painful result can be shoulder, neck, and back strain, plus a bicycle that doesn't feel as much a part of you or handle as well as one that fits properly. In extreme cases of poor fit, a bicycle can be really crash-prone.

6. HOW CAN I FIND A BIKE THAT FITS?

- *Take a long enough test ride to sense any discomfort poor fit would cause.* Not around the block, but several miles or so. You should be able to ride with your elbows slightly bent to keep your upper body relaxed. Don't expect to sit on a bike like a pro if you're a fairly new rider; that takes time. However, you can suspect poor bike fit if you suffer neck and shoulder pain despite stretching exercises or if you're sliding too far forward on the saddle even though it's level.
- *Be aware of bike types where fit is most problematic.* The biggie: drop-handlebar bikes. Mountain bike performance on demanding off-road trails also depends on good fit; both men and women often seem to buy their first off-road rig too large.
- *Seek out proportional models if you need a shorter reach to the bars.* A proportional bike has a shorter-than-standard top tube that may slope for greater standover clearance. Such a bicycle usually also features components that better suit our anatomy, such as smaller brake levers, shorter crankarms, and narrower handlebars—plus a woman's saddle. Ask to be sure.

Proportional bikes were first offered as production line bicycles when one very independent framebuilder from New York state named Georgena Terry introduced Terry Precision Bicycles for Women in 1985.

Now several fine quality drop-handlebar bicycles for the road, plus some well-thought-out mountain bikes are available. At this writing, the following manufacturers offer proportional road bikes: REI (the Novara line), Terry Precision Cycling for Women, R + E Cycles (the "Stellar"), Cannondale (compact model), Aegis (racer/triathlon bike), Green Gear (folding bicycles made to custom specifications). Proportional mountain bike makers include Battle Mountain Bikes, Fat City Cycles ("Yo, Betty!"), Giant, Green Gear, Jamis, Kona, and REI. For phone numbers to locate a retailer near you or to obtain ordering information, see the appendix.

- *Splurge on a professional bike fit.* Many shops offer this for an additional fee.
- *Having a bicycle custom-made remains an option.* It's not always so pricey as you might think. Many racers, certainly the elite, have their bicycles custom-made. So do other cyclists who simply relish the idea of a well-made cycle uniquely their own. And custom builders have always received a fair amount of business from the very tall and the very short.

Many women ride bikes they only *think* fit. I did. For a magazine assignment some years ago, I test-rode a Terry proportional bike for most of the summer and liked it so much I eventually bought it. I didn't mind the small front wheel at all. Later on I took a spin on my old bike, and it felt big, awkward, and unruly. Until you ride a machine that really fits, it's impossible to know how good it can feel.

7. HOW DO I CHECK FOR BIKE FIT?

Frame size. Lack of standardization in the bike industry make this a little confusing to talk about, but bear with me. A bike's frame size equals the seat tube height, which is usually measured from the center of the bottom bracket to the top of the seat tube, although some makers measure from the bottom bracket center to the center of the top tube. But that's not all. Some companies measure frames in inches, while others use centimeters. Refer to the Frame Sizing Conversion Chart if unsure how the two measuring systems compare. To make your own conversions, remember: 1 inch = 2.54 centimeters.

Comparing frame sizes can get really complicated with mountain bikes because sloping top tubes can make for relatively short seat tubes. To try to simplify matters, some firms now size frames as small, medium, large, and extra-large.

So numbers are a starting point, but trying is believing.

To get fitted vertically, check *standover*—the clearance between your crotch and the top tube when you straddle the bike. The blush-proof way to do this is to straddle the bike's top tube and then lift the bicycle with one hand in front of you and the other hand behind. Anyone assisting you can see how far the bike lifts off the ground and thus how much clearance you have.

For a road or track bike, as you stand flat-footed, you want at least one or two inches of clearance between your crotch and the top tube. For off-road use, a mountain bike frame should give you three to four inches at least; a sloping top tube may give you more, a benefit. Look for comparable clearance in a comfort bike if you ever expect to take it off-road. Clearance for a hybrid or cruiser should be at least two inches.

Hypothetically speaking, if you could ride two different frame sizes in a particular model, the smaller is usually the better choice: It will be lighter, stiffer, and handle better. Just don't choose such a small one that the seatpost must be raised beyond its maximum extension line.

Frame Sizing Conversion Chart

Inches	12	13	14	15	16	17	18	19	20	21	22	23	24	25	26	27
Centimeters	30	32	34	36	38	40	42	44	46	48	50	52	54	56	58	60	62	64	66	68

Saddle height. Sit on the saddle with heels on the pedals and backpedal without rocking from side to side. The salesperson should adjust the saddle so that with the pedal at the bottom of the stroke, your knee is slightly bent; when observed from behind, your hips should not rock when you pedal. (This is an approximation. Some riders, especially those who use clipless pedals, prefer their saddles about 1 cm higher.) Note that there is a maximum extension line above which the seatpost must not be raised.

Saddle tilt. For comfort, the saddle should be level, since tilting the saddle nose downward makes you lean too much weight on your hands. (Men usually prefer their saddles tilted up, but this can be painful for women.)

Reach. This is a critical measurement for finding your frame size. Aim for a loose, relaxed upper body. On your test ride, note whether you have the requisite bend in your elbows. Experienced riders are usually comfortable riding with their backs at a forty-five-degree angle to the top tube. Some tourists and new riders are more happy at a fifty-degree angle. (If you want to sit bolt upright, some cruisers, hybrids, and comfort bikes will let you. Be forewarned, though, that you may have saddle problems because of too much weight on your sit-bones. See chapter 12, "Ouch-less Riding.")

Remember, the reach is determined by top tube length and the stem extension (see figure 4). A bike with the right length top tube can still feel too rangy if the stem is disproportionately long. You can have the stem changed, but radical changes in stem length can affect bike handling, so talk it over with the salesperson.

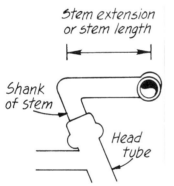

Fig. 4: The extension of the stem, or stem length, is measured as shown. A longer stem puts the handlebars farther away from a rider than a shorter one would. The portion of the stem which inserts into the head tube is called the shank of the stem. Sometimes a stem with an extra long shank is desirable to bring handlebars up higher and thus closer to the cyclist.

If your upper arms and shoulders tire quickly because you are too cramped—as can occur, especially with tall riders—you may require a longer stem or a frame with a longer top tube.

Handlebar sweep. Some MTB-type bars have more rearward sweep than others, which can affect your reach to the bars. You may also find that your wrists feel more comfortable with one type than with another. Test-ride to find out.

Stem height and rise angle. For climbing control during off-road riding, an MTB handlebar should be placed one to three inches below the top of the saddle, provided you don't feel too stretched in this position. Mountain bikes intended for less technical cycling often have a steeper rise on the stem, which positions the bars higher to let the rider sit more upright. If the bike has a threadless headset, little or no change can be made in stem height, but a stem with a different rise could be substituted to raise or lower the bars as desired.

Note the maximum extension line on any handlebar stem. For safety's sake, don't raise it any higher. Special stems with extra-long shanks can be purchased if needed (see figure 4).

Fore/aft saddle position. A saddle can be moved forward or back. Ideally, we don't do this to adjust reach to the bars (that's what the different stem lengths are for), but to position the knee properly over the pedal. Check this while you're sitting comfortably on the saddle, with the pedals at three and six o'clock: A plumb bob dropped from the bump below your forward kneecap should bisect the pedal axle. Adjust the saddle forward or back to accomplish this (see figure 5). You now have a neutral saddle position, which may suit your riding style perfectly. Or you may wish to experiment slightly: Moving the saddle 1 to 2 cm to the rear favors a powerful pedaling style for climbing or time trialing. Moving it 1 cm forward facilitates spinning and sprinting.

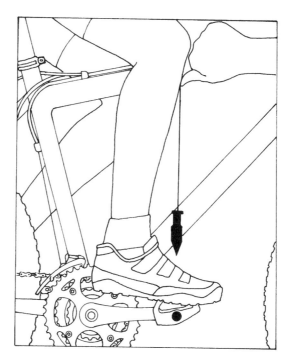

Fig. 5: Establishing a neutral fore/aft saddle position.

Handlebar size. Does the bar width feel natural with your hands on the grips? MTB bars generally range in width from 21 to 24 inches. If, like most women, you have narrower shoulders than a man, the 21-inch width would probably be comfortable yet wide enough for good control at slow speed. (As a rule, the narrower the bar, the quicker the steering.) If you think you'd like narrower bars, you can remove the grips and cut off the ends with a hacksaw, but first test-ride with the controls moved in to make sure the new width won't mess up your steering. Don't forget to leave a little extra length at each end if you use bar ends or wish to add them.

For drop handlebars, bar width should equal shoulder width. Racers, however, may want a slightly wider position for easier breathing.

Crank length. You need two numbers—crank size, usually marked on the back of the crank, and your inseam (measured from your crotch to the floor, with bare feet). The same rider typically uses cranks 5 mm longer on a mountain bike— for better climbing leverage—than on a road bike. On an MTB, for an inseam less than 29 inches, use 170 mm cranks. For 29 to 32 inches, go with 175 mm; 33 to 34 inches, 177.5 mm; longer than 34 inches, 180 mm.

Brakes. With hands smaller than men's, some women have difficulty gripping standard-sized brake levers. On a mountain bike you should be able to comfortably reach the brake levers with your hands resting on the grips, and you should be able to brake with two fingers. If your hands feel too stretched during either motion, your levers are too far away. Many mountain bike levers come with adjustment screws that let you position the levers closer to the bar, a plus.

On a road bike try braking while riding with your hands on the rubber brake hoods (see figure 6). If you can't exert enough grip to brake efficiently to a full stop, the levers aren't sized for you and will not only be uncomfortable but unsafe. At this writing, the hot setup is dual-control levers, which integrate shifters and brake levers for easy shifting from atop the brake hoods. Some women like this convenience because they never have to take their hands off the bar. Others complain of sore wrists after forty miles—their hands lack the size and strength needed for frequent shifts to the big chainring. Bar-end shifters are a good alternative, and short-reach brake levers for road bikes are available.

Saddle. For discussion of the many options, see chapter 12. If you're interested in a new bike, but its saddle doesn't suit you, ask to trade the saddle for one of your choice (at reduced or no cost) when you buy.

Toeclips/clipless pedals. Toeclips come in sizes. Try them using the shoes you intend to wear cycling. The right size for you places the ball of your foot just slightly in front of the pedal spindle, with almost a quarter-inch to spare between the tip of your shoe and the clip. To get the same orientation with a clipless system, position the cleat on your shoe so that the cleat is 1 cm or so behind the pedal axle. (See the shoe section in chapter 8, "Clothes with Wheel Appeal.")

8. HOW CAN I PREDICT HOW A BIKE WILL HANDLE?

As noted above in describing road bikes, some machines are designed to be highly stable; that is, they tend to travel straight down the road and take corners wide, like a truck. Other bicycles are designed to be extremely maneuverable, taking corners easily and with a shorter turning radius, but they require a little more effort to keep in a straight line. And many bicycles fall somewhere in between. We call such performance differences a bicycle's *handling characteristics.*

No one way of handling is "best"—unless it happens to be appropriate for the way you intend to use the bicycle. A good rule of thumb: Don't buy more maneuverability than you need. And don't just guess how a bike will handle. Road-test it.

9. HOW CAN I JUDGE QUALITY?

All the bikes on the showroom floor may look shiny and beautiful, but good quality is more than skin deep. To be a savvy consumer, look for these indicators:

Weight. With bicycles, the more you pay, the less weight you get in tubing and components. A reasonably lightweight bike is the object if you have hills to climb. For quick acceleration, for example, when training with a group, lighter wheels are important. Just how light a machine you need depends on your goals and the type of bike. A racer will invest more than many of the rest of us to shed ounces and grams from her machine. But all of us deserve a bicycle of a certain quality level to maximize our own performance—attainable even on a budget.

Consider tubing. The least expensive bicycles are made of low carbon steel, also called *"high tensile"* (hi-ten) steel, which sounds good but has a low strength-to-weight ratio. The result is thicker, heavier tubing with a sort of dead feel when you ride it. High carbon steel alloyed with chromium and molybdenum can be drawn thinner for a resilient, lightweight tubing which delivers a lively, fun ride. Frames and forks made completely of *chro-moly steel* have become so reasonable in recent years that one minimum requirement I would make (if you choose steel) is to insist on an all chro-moly frame. Be aware that, to shave cost, some machines have hi-ten forks and/or chainstays, with only the "main triangle" of chro-moly. If you decide to compromise, fine—but don't do so unwittingly. Ask.

Any drawbacks to chro-moly? Technically, it could rust if you scratch the paint, but that's pretty easy to prevent with application of WD-40 or bike frame cleaner/wax (see chapter 18, "Nothing Flat—And More Repairs You Can Do Yourself").

Alternatives to steel include aluminum, which is a little lighter and often stiffer. Aluminum frames are increasingly popular, especially in mountain bikes. They never rust and have become quite affordable in recent years. Aluminum can take a roughing up, but if the tubing is damaged, it's not so easily straightened or repaired as steel. Test to compare the riding properties of aluminum versus chro-moly.

Folks with fatter wallets can consider two more options. Composite frames, such as carbon fiber, will not corrode and are known for delivering a smooth ride (dampening vibration). Carbon bikes have come down in cost in recent years, which could account for their increasing share of the market.

Titanium frames are known for resiliency, strength, lightness, and their resistance to impact dents. They're corrosion-proof. A relative few can afford to buy them, but those who do love the ride.

Butting. Butting is a technology that allows frame tubing to be made thicker-walled where it gets the most stress (usually tube ends and joints) and thinner in the middle. Double-butted or triple-butted tubing is a sign of quality.

The word on wheels. Aluminum alloy rims are a must for lightness and for better braking in rainy conditions. Double-wall rims are strong; if you want extra strength, look for ones with eyelets for the spokes. Quick-release levers are now standard on front and rear wheels.

Components. The name-brand parts that get added to a bicycle frame are manufactured in component groups (or *gruppos*) which the maker—such as Shimano, Sachs, or Campagnolo—offers to bike manufacturers in a hierarchy of quality levels/price points. Each component group has a name, such as Shimano's Ultegra, so if a salesperson simply says that a bike has "Shimano parts," you aren't being told much. Ask the group name or ask to see the *specs* (specifications) in the bike manufacturer's catalog. Usually the higher-priced groups offer weight savings and better finish, rather than superior durability. Better groups may shift a little smoother, and the levers feel nicer in your hand.

Some bikes will feature one complete component group, while other bikes may mix parts from two groups. Either approach has its justifications. It's just smart for you to know what you're paying for. Any salesperson should be able to rattle off the component gruppos on the current market from most expensive to least expensive; if you write them down, then you can compare.

10. WHAT ABOUT GEARING?

Selecting a bike that's not geared low enough used to be one of the most common mistakes made by newcomers to the sport. The same hills that put variety and exhilaration into a ride on a bicycle with the right gearing are drudgery on a bike geared too high.

Now that so many bicycles—hybrids, comfort bikes, touring bikes, some touring/sport bikes, and of course mountain bikes—come with triple chainings, that wonderful smallest chainring lets us keep pedaling up a challenging grade instead of dismounting and walking. Most people buying these kinds of rigs can assume that simply selecting a bicycle with a triple chainring will answer all their gearing needs.

Nevertheless, in some situations you may want to be able to compare gearing on two bicycles. Say you plan to tour with camping gear, and you anticipate some significant climbing; which of the touring bikes you're pondering has the lowest gearing? Perhaps you're replacing an old three-speed bike because you're tired of walking hills with it; how can you be sure the new bike you buy will be markedly better? Or you may want to modify the gearing on a bike you already own. Perhaps, like many racers, you want to make a temporary change in gearing for a particular event.

In any of these situations, speaking the language of gear ratios and gear inches will let you make these decisions intelligently. Have your pocket calculator handy, and you'll sail through this introduction to gear speak.

A bit of cycling history will help to explain this measuring system. It goes back more than a century, to the introduction of chain-driven bikes with equal-size wheels (which, by the way, made cycling far more accessible to women, still trapped in long skirts). These new "safety bikes," which were safer for riders of both sexes, had to compete with the highwheelers then in popular use. Also called "ordinaries," these older-style bikes had the pedal cranks attached directly to their huge front wheel, the size of which was dictated by the length of the cyclist's legs. "The bigger the front wheel, the further the cyclist went for each revolution, though the harder the effort," as John Forester says in *Effective Cycling*. "Naturally, people bought bicycles as big as they could straddle, specifying them by the wheel diameter in inches—such as 54 inches or 60 inches." The front wheel would go around once with one turn of the pedals.

The chain on the newer bikes turned their rear wheel more than once for each pedal revolution. To compare their efficiency to the old direct-drive cycles, a system of gearing inches was created. A 54-inch gear on a safety bike would feel like the effort of pedaling a 54-inch front wheel and travel as far, Forester explains.

Gearing can still be talked about in gear inches. The higher the number, the farther a bike travels with one pedal rotation, and the more effort it takes. The lower the number, the easier the gear, and the shorter the distance traveled.

You can use a simple formula or a gear chart to figure gear inches for any chainring/sprocket combination, or *gear ratio,* on a bicycle with derailleur gearing. Here's how:

To determine the low gear on a mountain bike with 26-inch wheels, for example, you need to know the number of teeth on the small chainring; it's typically engraved on the chainring. Let's say it's 24. And you need to know how many teeth the biggest rear sprocket has; you count 30. (If you're figuring gearing on a new bike in a shop, the dealer can easily look up the sprocket tooth numbers in a catalog.) You can use the following formula and your calculator:

$$\frac{\text{teeth in front chainring}}{\text{teeth in rear sprocket}} \times \text{wheel diameter} = \text{gear inches}$$

Here it's:

$$\frac{24}{30} \times 26 \text{ inches} = 20.8 \text{ gear inches}$$

Or turn to the gear charts on page 261 at the back of the book. Use the chart for 26-inch wheels and find the number, rounded off to 21. For a bike with 700C wheels, use the 27-inch chart.

To figure the gearing on a three-speed bicycle, begin by calculating the *normal gear,* the middle, direct-drive gear. Check the wheel size on the tire sidewall if you are unsure of this measurement. Let's say this bike has 700C wheels, with a 46T (46-tooth) chainring and an 18T rear sprocket. Using the formula gives us the answer of 68.9 gear inches; the gear chart rounds it off to 69 inches.

To find low for the three-speed, multiply the gear inches (69) for normal gear by .75. We get 51.75 inches. (If anybody's wondering why that three-speed's dogging it on hills, compare this low gear to the mountain bike's above.)

To calculate high gear, multiply the number for normal gear (69) by 1.33. We get 91.77 gear inches.

You Can Modify That Three-Speed

Do you have a three-speed bike you're generally happy with, except for the gearing? You can have it modified to some extent. The simplest thing would be to replace the sprocket with one that has more teeth. For example, the three-speed described above had a normal gear of 69 inches, low gear of 52 inches, and high gear of 92 inches (with the numbers rounded off).

Suppose you change the rear sprocket to 22T (which ought to be available; ask at your bike shop). You'd have a normal gear of 56 inches, a more forgiving low gear of 42 inches, and a high gear of 74.48 (75) inches. You still can't climb "The Wall" with this baby, but it's better. Admittedly, high gear is now lower, too. But a leisurely rider who usually coasts down hills won't mind.

A bike shop mechanic might have other suggestions. Maybe you'll end up with a three-speed town bike you can lock up and leave to do errands without too much worry of theft. (With all that money you saved, you can splurge on a true mountain bike to ride the trails. Uh-oh, the devil made me say that.)

On Your Bike!

Let's get rolling.

For many of you, taking up cycling may not require a new bike. It simply means going to the garage or the cellar and moving aside the butterfly net and the broken snowshoes that are stacked in front of a bike you already own. Maybe you haven't been on it since your teens. Or maybe it's one you bought more recently, but it never felt right. Whatever its history, a bicycle that you may be able to resurrect languishes underneath those cobwebs. So drag it out and dust it off.

I'd love to tell you to just hop on and ride down the street, glorying in the fresh spring air. But the tires are bound to be flat, and you want to make sure the bike is safe to ride and as comfortable as possible.

You have two alternatives: You can take it to a local bike shop and ask them to inspect it and put air in the tires, or you can start now on the road to independence by giving the bike a safety check yourself. If discomfort was the reason you stopped riding the bicycle, you'd best evaluate the bike for fit and whether you can make inexpensive modifications to solve any problems. (See "How Do I Check for Bike Fit?" in chapter 5.)

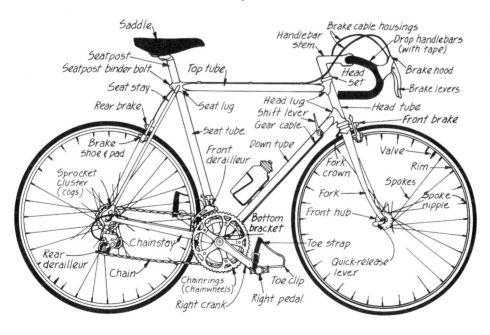

Fig. 6: Do you have a road bike in your garage?

OPTION 1: BIKE SHOP TUNE-UP

You can simply tell the shop to go over the bike and make sure it's safe to ride, properly lubricated, with the gears adjusted and the tires fully pumped up. Also ask the mechanic to check the saddle height for you, adjust it if necessary, and make sure the saddle is level.

By the way, if that saddle has been uncomfortable for you, replace it. To keep the price competitive, millions of bikes have been sold over the years with cheap, hard, narrow saddles that would have made great medieval torture devices. Ask to be shown "anatomic" or "women's" saddles; you may be able to take one on a test ride, or if there's a bike in the shop with one on it, sit on it and see how it feels. Talk it over with the salesperson at the shop. (See also chapter 12, "Ouch-less Riding.")

As with any request for work at a shop, before you leave your bike inquire what the inspection will cost. And ask to be phoned with an estimate in advance of any unanticipated repairs. Nobody likes surprises when it comes to paying bills.

While at the shop buy a cycling helmet. If you ever have an accident, your

Should You Consider a New Bike?

How old is "old"? Here's the short answer: If you have an aging drop-handlebar road bike—what we used to call a ten-speed—and it doesn't have indexed-shifting and aluminum alloy rims, a lightweight new bike of your choice would be more inviting to ride. Especially if you didn't like bending over those handlebars anyway.

But let's say you don't mind the drop bars, and it isn't going to cost much to put your present bike on the road. Assuming the bicycle will give you a pleasurable ride once you fix it up, then you might be smart to do it, especially if you're not sure what sort of riding you want to take up. You can have fun getting out on that bike, and meanwhile, ponder your options and familiarize yourself with what's available by visiting shops and test-riding new bicycles. Then you'll know whether you're missing something just because you have a vintage model.

On the other hand, if your old bike would be expensive to rehabilitate, you risk investing beaucoup bucks in a bike that doesn't perform well and may have a limited life expectancy. Plus, whole new categories of bikes have come on the market since your antique was manufactured: mountain bikes, hybrids, cruisers, comfort bikes, and road bikes in proportional sizing to better fit women. This is your chance to learn what constitutes good quality and choose a bike with less hefty components, a responsive well-fitted frame, and lighter tires and wheels. These things mean a bicycle that handles better, has less weight to take up hills, and a faster pickup when you accelerate. (Is this starting to sound like a sports car?) Not only that, but these days the gearing is more intelligently selected, with hill-shrinking low gears even on road bikes. (See chapter 5, "So You Want to Buy a Bike?")

brain will thank you for wearing it; almost two-thirds of all bicycle accident deaths are caused by head injury. Look for a helmet with a sticker or tag certifying approval by one of the institutes licensed to test bicycle helmets: ANSI, ASTM, and Snell.

If the bicycle has rusted parts or is quite old, you may be told that it's impossible or impractical to try to return it to working condition.

OPTION 2: YOUR OWN SAFETY CHECKUP

You can do your own inspection if you're willing to take a little time to do it. In many ways a bike is quite a simple machine. As one instructor jokes in her bike maintenance classes for women, "You can tell it's wrong if there are parts left over on the floor!"

You'll find the checkup at the start of chapter 18, "Nothing Flat." The "bike anatomy" charts (figures 1, 4, 6, and 9) will help you with names of any bike parts you're unfamiliar with. For this checkup, you scarcely have to take anything apart. Just read the steps and follow them. If you find something that seems worn or broken, you can take the bike to the shop with the advantage of knowing more about your bicycle than if you hadn't inspected it yourself.

As suggested above, when you go to the shop for service, ask for a cost estimate before you leave your bike. And don't forget the cycling helmet.

ON THE ROAD

Once you have your bike ready to ride, you'll probably be heading out into traffic, even if it's just a short distance on your way to the off-road trails in a local park.

Let's take a few minutes to sharpen up your street smarts. These tips will help you avoid the most dangerous mistakes cyclists make, and greatly reduce your chances of an accident. Bear in mind that a bicycle is regarded by law and for practical purposes as a vehicle. Generally, when cycling you should think as a vehicle operator, not as a pedestrian.

•For example, cycle with the flow of traffic, not against it. In the United States and Canada, of course, that means on the right, and in the United Kingdom on the left. This is the most predictable and thus the safest place for a cyclist. Studies of bicycle/motor vehicle accidents indicate that riding against traffic causes more accidents than any other cyclist error.

You may be worried about rear-end collisions and believe, therefore, that you should ride facing the flow of traffic. It's human nature to distrust what we don't know or can't see, and many riders, at least beginners, fear this type of accident. Actually, rear-end collisions account for a tiny percentage of all car-bike collisions, some of which are caused by the error of the cyclist.

What sort of bicycle do you have? If you don't have a mountain bike and your bike's been around a while, maybe you have one of these.

Fig. 7: The single-speed is the draft horse of cycling—heavy, sturdy, with wide balloon tires and coaster brakes. You have to walk it up hills, but it's fine on level ground. In the United States these bikes, with some updating, have made a comeback as beach bikes. In Europe I've seen this bike, with its upright bars, widely used for errands. In England some folks call it a "sit-up-and-beg."

Fig. 8: The internally geared bicycle, which includes all three-speed bikes and some five-speeds, was called an "English racer" in the United States in the 1950s. A single lever on the handle-bar activates gear changes inside the hub of the rear wheel. Hand brakes provide stopping power; tires are narrow. These bikes are geared for moderately hilly terrain at best.

Fig. 9: On the road bike, which for years was commonly called the ten-speed, gear changers lift (or "derail") the chain from the teeth of one sprocket to another in full sight. How many speeds the bike has depends on the number of sprockets and chainwheels (also called "chainrings"). A ten-speed has a cluster of five sprockets on the rear wheel and two chainrings at the cranks; 2 chainrings x 5 sprockets = 10 speeds. These multispeed derailleur bikes have more gearing options and the capability of lower gearing than the internally geared bicycle.

Some five-speed bikes have a rear derailleur but no front derailleur, as there is only one chainwheel at the cranks.

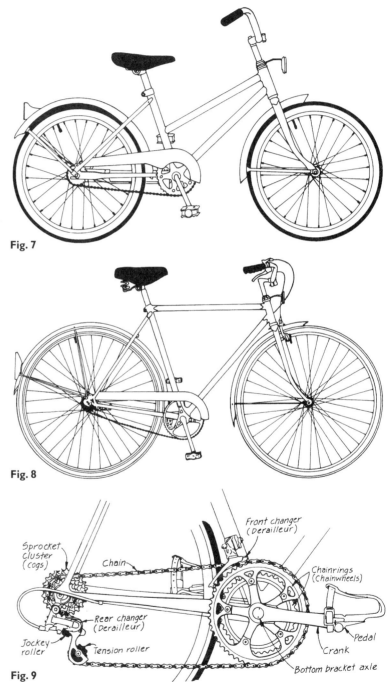

Fig. 7

Fig. 8

Sprocket Cluster (cogs)

Chain

Front changer (Derailleur)

Chainrings (Chainwheels)

Rear changer (Derailleur)

Jockey roller

Tension roller

Pedal

Crank

Bottom bracket axle

Fig. 9

- Obey "one-way" street signs like a motorist. Often a driver won't think to look both ways crossing or turning onto a one-way street, so a wrong-way bicyclist can easily be hit.
- Obey traffic signals. Maybe you could get away with doing otherwise, but in traffic, following the rules of the road is the safest thing. You're also doing your bit for better relations with motorists.
- No traffic signals? Yield to cross traffic at intersections with larger roads.
- Be predictable. Riding in a straight line on the road makes it easier for drivers to pass you safely. Don't try to weave in and out among parked vehicles. Leave enough space between yourself and parked cars so that a door can't be opened in your path.
- Signal. Use right- and left-hand signals for turning, to let motorists or other cyclists know your intentions. You'll be treated with greater respect.
- Choose lightly traveled streets rather than busier, arterial routes while you're still developing your cycling-in-traffic skills and practicing bike handling.
- Be seen. Being conspicuous may not usually be your style, but on a bike you want to be seen by motorists. A shirt in bright, wild colors is a good choice. Tests show that, in broad daylight, hot pink is spotted easily at a distance, dark blue is not. On a gray, rainy day, bright yellow commands attention. If you ride at night, wear light colors and be flashy with lots of reflectors and proper front and rear lights.
- Be aware. Look back before changing lanes or pulling out into traffic. Cycling mirrors are handy for keeping an eye on who's coming up behind you, but they have a blind spot and shouldn't be depended on in this situation. And don't rely on your ears to tell you whether there's a car or other traffic behind you.

That doesn't mean sound cues aren't important. They can alert you to approaching traffic, and if you have a riding partner, you want to be able to communicate. So leave your headphones at home for entertainment when riding your stationary bike; in many states headphones are illegal in traffic because they handicap you. That's what Maxine Killasch of Northville, Michigan, tried to tell a friend who almost had more scent than sense. Maxine says:

My friend Jane and I were out for a leisurely ride along the orchards in rural Cañon City, Colorado, where we both lived. Jane, wearing headphones despite my protests, pedaled ahead of me. It was near dusk, usually a peaceful time there. But this was Fourth of July, and the booms and crackles of fireworks made the road seem like a war zone.

Then a sudden blur of movement caught my eye. A near-hog-size skunk had darted through the ditch and was charging down the road in fast pursuit.

"Skunk!" I yelled to Jane, who didn't hear, and I shot past her at a speed I'd never attained before. I looked back. The skunk had closed the gap to about twenty-five feet. Jane looked back and was soon sprinting down the road with me. We reached home in record time, unnerved and, fortunately, unscented.

Don't wear headphones on the trail either; communication there is still important. And if you use a personal stereo while exercising indoors, keep the volume way down. As you pedal away, blood goes to the working muscles, lessening the blood supply to the ears. Music-triggered adrenaline increases that effect, says audiologist Dr. Richard Navarro, so ears are vulnerable to damage from normally safe sound levels.

PREVENT BIKE THEFT

Now that you have that bike all fixed up, don't "give it away" to a bike thief. If you must leave it where you can't keep an eye on it, lock it to be sure. And lock it properly. These quick-releases that many bikes have—often on both front and rear wheels, as well as on the seatpost—are handy for us but they also make stealing easier.

A large U-shaped lock is most reliable and lets you enclose the bike's seat tube and rear wheel; you should remove the quick-release front wheel and lock it up as well, since it's especially easy to take out. Some cyclists prefer to thread a thick cable through the wheels and into the lock—an easy and cheap theft-deterrent. Secure the bike to a strong, stationary object, like a parking meter or wrought-iron fence. And consider taking that quick-release seatpost and saddle with you.

BEGINNING BASICS

Riding with a more experienced friend or partner can help you improve your riding technique quickly. That's one reason for joining a cycling club. However, experienced cyclists often forget to tell beginners some things because, by now, these habits have become second nature. Not long ago I was helping a college-student friend, and I couldn't figure out why she was losing her balance when stopping and dismounting from her new mountain bike. Finally she noticed I was getting up off my saddle before putting my foot on the ground. I hadn't mentioned it. No wonder she was toppling over! Once we straightened that out, we tried some off-road riding, and she was climbing and descending singletrack like a veteran that same afternoon.

If you haven't been on a bike in years, these tips should help you avoid having to learn the hard way.

Clothing. Don't ride in blue jeans; those thick seams in the crotch can mean agony. If you don't have cycling clothing yet, you can manage for a few miles in running shorts or sweatpants if the seams don't irritate you. Sneakers or running shoes will do for now. And wear that helmet.

Check your shoelaces. Long loops can catch on your chainring—grinding you to a shockingly quick halt! I double-knot my laces or tuck in the loops.

Braking. If you haven't ridden since you were a kid using coaster brakes, mentally review how your new hand caliper brakes work. You don't want to be spinning your feet wildly backward, unable to stop as you're heading toward an intersection. At the beginning use equal pressure on both brake levers. As you stop, if you feel the back wheel begin to skid, ease up slightly on the brake levers.

Mounting and dismounting. Since I hate getting chainring marks on my calf—and those chainring teeth can bite, too—I always mount and dismount from the left side of the bike, as if getting on a horse. I also walk my bike from the left.

To saddle up, I squeeze the brakes and straddle the top tube, putting my right foot on a pedal, raised in the *power position*. I step down, releasing the brake. That propels the bike forward, and the momentum makes balancing easier as I then sit on the saddle and settle my left foot on the other pedal. Do the reverse to dismount, sliding forward off the saddle and putting your weight on the low pedal before braking to a stop and touching down.

GEAR SHIFTING, CADENCE, AND HILLS

OK, let's take this class on the road. We'll go for a ride in the parkway. It's a sunny morning with a light breeze, and there's never much traffic there.

We'll spin along at an easy pace and let our muscles loosen up for five minutes or so. Pretty place to ride, isn't it, with the willows lining the creek? Would you believe, I've written haiku poetry while cycling along here? The first time I thought of it, I was lucky and found a pen and an old brochure in my bike bag to write on.

New-green willow
with winter-gray brothers,
do they envy your spring dress?

Caterpillar, I inch up this hill.
Down the other side,
butterfly!

Road blurs beneath my wheels,
wind rushes to meet me—
freedom machine.

Well, down to business. Try experimenting with your shifters. Keep pedaling lightly and move your left shifter with your left hand. Notice that it operates the front derailleur to move the chain on the chainrings located between the pedals. Try it in the various positions. You'll feel the most resistance with the chain on the big ring—"high" gear—and moderate resistance on the middle ring—"medium" gear. There's very little resistance on the small ring, a "low" gear useful for climbing or pedaling into a strong headwind.

If your bike has only two chainrings—a *double*—then you have "high" and "medium." With both double and triple chainrings, you can feel that shifts on the front rings are sort of macro shifts, big changes from one ring to another. We can use these chainrings to get into the ballpark, so to speak, for the gear we want. For now, leave the chain on the medium chainring. You'll probably use this chainring most, as I do.

Play with the right shifter, which operates the rear derailleur. This moves the chain from one cog to another on the rear freewheel, more subtle changes than shifts on the chainrings. Note which direction you move the shifter for lower (easier) gears and which direction for higher (harder-to-pedal) gears. Shift one gear at a time; ripping through several gears in a single shift dramatically shortens the life of your drivetrain. While in the lowest gear, look down at the freewheel briefly; note that the chain is on the biggest cog (see figure 10). In the highest gear, the chain is on the smallest cog (see figure 11). If you think checking this out while riding might throw your balance off, stop and dismount to observe.

We fine-tune with the right shifter. Try doing that—finding a gear that feels comfortable on this straightaway. You don't want to struggle too hard turning the pedals; it's tough on the knees. Hit a happy medium between having to push too hard and spinning so fast you waste energy just moving your legs. We call this pedaling rate *cadence,* the number of revolutions per minute (rpm) one foot makes going around on the pedal.

I'm using a fairly brisk cadence, about 90 rpm. Try to match it. An easy way is to say under your breath: "One potato, two potato, three potato, four potato,

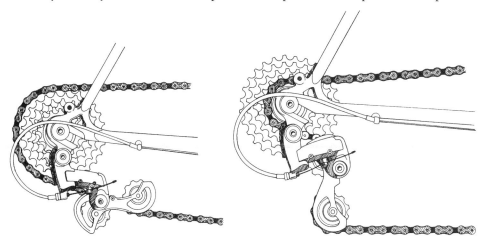

Fig. 10: Chain on the largest sprocket = low gear   **Fig. 11:** Chain on the smallest sprocket = high gear

Tips for Non-Click Shifting

If your gearing system predates indexed shifting, here's how you, too, can shift like a pro. Perform the same shifting exercises as above, beginning with the left shifter and front derailleur. As you pedal, move the lever and listen to the sound. You should hear the chain rattle a little and then a definite ka-chunk as it settles into the new gear, followed by fairly quiet chain movement. If the chain keeps rattling, that's a sign the gear hasn't quite meshed: Try a slight adjustment with the left shifter and listen for a change to a smooth-running sound. Still rattling? Tweak the right shifter slightly and see if the sound subsides. This slight manual adjustment is called *trimming your gears*. Use these same sound cues when shifting the right lever/rear derailleur, and similarly adjust slightly to trim the gears. Your shifting may be noisy at first, but you'll quickly improve.

one potato . . ." As you say "one potato," one foot should make a complete pedal revolution at about 80 or 90 rpm. You'll quickly get a feel for it. Got it? Great! If it gets difficult, shift to a lower gear but keep your cadence up.

You might notice your heart rate has picked up. This is the way to get a good workout without causing overuse injury to your knees. Keep your upper body relaxed, with a little bend in your elbows, and don't cock your wrists.

There's a hill just around the bend. Shift into low before we start climbing (either your smallest chainring, remember, or one of your bigger rear cogs) so that you don't miss the shift or put unnecessary strain on the gear system. Keep your cadence up as much as possible and stay on the saddle if you like. Or stand on the pedals and let your body weight give more of a down-thrust to each pedal, swaying the bike slightly from side to side. You can climb in a little bit bigger gear if you stand.

The first time I tried standing to climb a hill, I wasn't sure I had the balance and the strength in my legs to do it! But I didn't fall over, and in a short time it felt natural.

Made it to the top, good job! As you catch your breath, shift into high gear so that you can pedal on the way down or as you level off, to take advantage of your momentum. If you must brake on the descent, *feather* your brakes to avoid overheating the wheel rims and possibly causing a blowout; that is, lightly squeeze and release, squeeze and release both brakes simultaneously, as needed, instead of keeping the brakes on all the time. Continuing on the level, settle into the gear you want to maintain.

More rolling hills are coming up—good practice for getting the most out of your gears. I imagine by now you've learned which way to move your shifters to gear up or down. Some systems have numbers to jog the memory. If yours doesn't and you need a reminder, you could put a piece of masking tape on your handlebar near each shifter and mark it.

With today's indexed shifting (shifters that click into place), you should get nice, clean shifts. If you hear the chain rubbing, check to see if you've put the chain on the big front chainring and the big rear cog, or the small chainring and small cog; we avoid those combinations because they put the chain at too sharp an angle, causing rubbing and wear on the derailleur. If you get a real meatgrinder sound, it means your indexed-shifting needs adjustment without delay!

For better balance as you ride and shift, keep your cadence and your speed up.

MORE SKILLS EXERCISES

Riding one-handed. This important balancing skill enables you to signal for turns or to reach for a water bottle while riding. Unless you're passing over a bumpy surface, taking a hand off the bars of a mountain bike or hybrid shouldn't put you off balance because of the fairly upright cycling position. Just keep the rest of your body weight centered.

On a drop-handlebar road bike, however, you could easily be supporting about 40 percent of your body weight on the handlebars; leaning heavily on one off-center hand can make you lose your balance. To prevent that, here's how to stabilize yourself. Say you're riding with both hands on the tops of the bars, several inches apart, and you want to shift or signal a turn. Slide both hands in toward the stem to balance your weight. Then remove one hand to shift or signal, while you keep your weight centered over the other hand.

Suppose you're riding with both hands resting on the rubber brake hoods—a position that gives immediate access to the brakes, and a steady one as long as both hands are on the bars. Until you develop really good balance, though, when you want to take a hand off the bars, do as above: Move both in toward the center first. Likewise when riding the drops: Sit up a little, slip your hands onto the tops of the bars and toward the center before taking one hand off the bars.

Remember, balancing is easier when you are moving. Signal well before you reach your corner and keep your arm extended as long as you can. If you feel wobbly as you slow for a light or to make the turn, return your hand to the bars.

The backward scan. Perhaps if human beings keep cycling for a few millennia, we'll evolve with eyes in the backs of our heads. Until then, we must learn to look back while still traveling straight ahead. To check for motor vehicle or bicycle traffic behind us before changing lanes or moving farther out into the lane we're in, there is no substitute for a backward scan. Don't depend on a cycling mirror, as mirrors have a blind spot, nor (excepting tandemists) should you depend on a cycling partner to do the looking for you.

The exercise simply involves cycling in a straight line and looking back over your shoulder. Practice turning your head without wobbling the handlebars or drifting in the direction you're looking. Choose an empty parking lot to work on this if you want to avoid traffic completely for now.

Steadier riders will want to practice this on a quiet street. Ride parallel to the curb but well enough away so that you have room to pass any parked cars. Pedal along at a normal speed. At a point where there are no parked cars, moving vehicles, or intersections, turn your head to look behind you. Then turn your head forward again. Are you still on course and parallel to the curb? Did the bicycle feel steady? Great! Continue on and practice again at the next opportunity. Work toward being able to look directly behind you long enough to see a car one block back.

Also practice this exercise in situations where you would look to the opposite side—say, on a one-way street where you might ride on the other side of the road.

Practice the backward scan on your next several rides. Soon you'll be using it naturally each time you ride.

Cornering. Good cornering technique makes riding more fun, helps us negotiate roads in traffic, and is one of the differences between a raw recruit and an experienced cyclist. Everybody needs cornering skills. I once saw a woman lean into a turn with the wrong pedal down. It scraped the pavement, and she went flying off her bike—youch!

Leaning, not turning the handlebars, is the key to cornering. Here are the steps. On a drop handlebar bike, your hands should be on the brake hoods or, as racers do, on the drops, to keep the center of gravity low and hold the bike steady. If you need to slow for the corner, squeeze and release the brakes *before* you start the turn; braking during a turn can cause the rear wheel to lose traction and you could crash. Entering the turn, stop pedaling and raise the inside pedal so it can't scrape; extend your outside leg and put some weight on it. Lean your bike in the direction of your turn, and it will pilot itself around the corner.

An empty road and a turn less than ninety degrees are ideal for practice. Before entering the turn, visualize the arc you want to follow and stick to it by leaning into the turn; trying to alter your line in midturn could cause your tires to slip. As you gain skill, you can make faster and sharper turns.

Watch out for road hazards at corners. Sand or gravel or a bump at the spot where you intend to turn can cause you to lose traction; slow way down in these situations by braking before you encounter the hazard. Don't try an extreme lean here. Likewise, on wet roads, use less lean.

Knobby tires won't handle as much of a lean as road treads, so go easier on corners on a mountain bike. Of course, in traffic all riders must moderate the turns to avoid veering into the path of another vehicle.

Dodging. At times it pays to be an artful dodger—around potholes, rocks, or broken glass. Imagine yourself pedaling along with a car beside you, without much room to maneuver. Immediately ahead you see a pothole. You can avoid it with the dodge: You turn the handlebars quickly but without leaning, and your front wheel travels around the rock. As the rear wheel follows, your bicycle starts to tip in the direction you steered, so you must steer rather sharply back in the

Fig. 12: Dodging

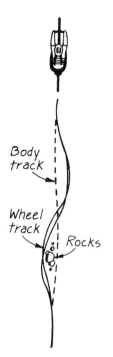

Body track

Wheel track

Rocks

opposite direction. You and your bike have avoided the pothole while scarcely moving from your position in the lane.

The only way to feel confident with this maneuver is to practice it. As John Forester advises in *Effective Cycling* (Cambridge, MA: MIT Press, 1984), you can try the dodge with a sponge in an empty parking lot. Throw the sponge on the ground and try dodging around it. Begin cautiously, with slight turns of the handlebars to accustom yourself to oversteering and correcting. Gradually exaggerate the movements as you learn.

You should definitely be rolling by now. Don't worry if you don't pick up everything with the first few tries. You'll develop the skills over time. Just stick with it and have fun.

Accessories

One cyclist I know calls them "the necessories"—those things you need, besides a bike, for riding comfortably, safely, and hassle-free. So important are they that you ought to budget at least $150 for accessories at the start. You could spend more, and you could find more goodies that would be nice to have. By the way, cycling magazines regularly review products of many types. Reviews based on actual-use evaluation or laboratory tests can help you find the best value for your money.

DON'T LEAVE HOME WITHOUT A . . .

Helmet. One cyclist I know says that in three years of riding her funniest experience was being hit on the head with a golf ball while pedaling past a golf course. She wouldn't have been laughing, she adds, if she hadn't been wearing a helmet.

Mountain bikers discover on their first trail ride in the woods that a helmet guards them from low-hanging branches that clunk them on the head as they duck under. For extra protection many helmets now come with an add-on visor, or you can purchase one separately. The visor also works like the bill of a baseball cap to help shield your eyes from sun or rain.

But most importantly, a helmet protects you in a crash. A study, published in the *Journal of the American Medical Association,* showed head injury was involved in 62 percent of all bicycle-related deaths over a recent four-year period in the United States. So I repeat: Along with a bicycle, a helmet is the first thing a new cyclist should buy. And if your helmet is several years old, consider replacing it. According to manufacturers, the expanded-polystyrene (EPS) foam that provides protection degrades over time, losing ability to absorb impact. Ditto if you've crashed on yours. (Talk to your bicycle dealer; your helmet's maker may have an accident replacement program.)

When shopping, look for a helmet with a sticker certifying it's met the safety requirements of ANSI, ASTM, or the Snell Foundation. And wear your brain bucket on every ride, whether on-road or off-road. I do, even when cycling just a few blocks, because I feel naked without one. It's not that I lack confidence riding in traffic, but I feel much better protected in a helmet.

In fact, I'll admit that each of the several times I've crashed on my road bike it's been my own fault, no car involved. All it takes is a moment's inattentiveness, an off-balance move at low speed, or a collision with another cyclist I didn't hear approaching from behind. The same kinds of errors can cause an accident on the smoothest of bike paths or off-road trails. Accident statistics bear this out: The great majority of bicycle accidents causing injury do not involve motor vehicles.

Many riders who are in the helmet habit also believe that motorists treat them with more respect because they're wearing one. It makes us look like vehicle users who follow the rules of the road.

Speaking of looks, the current generation of helmets appears more streamlined and stylish, with plenty of selection in design and colors if you shop around. Vanity still bothering you? Listen to this cycle commuter whose friend suffered a serious head injury in a bike accident: "These helmets are so dorky, but at the same time," she reasons, "how stupid am I going to look after a brain injury, with my whole left side paralyzed, not able to make facial expressions or hold a pen or something!"

Think a helmet will be too heavy or too hot? A study funded by the U.S. Cycling Federation and the U.S. Olympic Committee determined that donning a helmet causes no significant rise in internal body temperature, skin temperature, sweat production, heart rate, or general discomfort. Thanks to considerable scientific research, today's helmets weigh a mere eight ounces or so and are well ventilated to maximize cooling airflow.

Lightweight stabilizer "locking" systems, extending from the back to hug your head, help to keep the helmet comfortably and safely in place, provided you select one that fits securely. Usually some self-adhesive pads come with a helmet for customizing the fit. If you wear a ponytail to ride, you may need to look for a ponytail-compatible design, available from a number of manufacturers.

All of this is to no avail if, like some cyclists I see, you don't wear the helmet correctly. Position it low on your forehead. A profile view in a mirror should show the lower edge of that thin plastic outer shell to be level, parallel with the floor when you stand. Adjust the straps accordingly: On each side the two straps coming down make a V where they are joined by an adjustable plastic slide. Add or remove slack until the slide rests just below your earlobe and the straps in the V are taut. Then tighten the chin strap so you can just slip a finger under it to avoid pinching your skin as you fasten the buckle. Now try pulling off the helmet from the front and then from the back. If it slides around, it needs a little more tightening so it will stay put if you have a close encounter with road or trail.

Water bottle and cage or hydration system. "Drink before you're thirsty," as the saying goes in bicycling. Anyone riding more than a couple of miles needs to carry water in a water bottle or a hydration system, as cycling makes you perspire in any weather. Especially in the heat, dehydration can endanger you and hamper performance.

Most quality bikes have braze-on fittings (called "bosses"), for attaching two bottle cages. For bikes lacking braze-ons, there are cages that attach with clips or hook-and-loop straps. I find the bottle easy to reach on the down tube; usually a second cage can be added on the seat tube.

Two bottles are a must for long rides. Some cyclists like to put sport drink in one, water in the other—handy for a cool squirt on the back of the neck.

Commuters who think of their morning coffee as high-test often put their joe in one of those bottles.

For hot-weather riding, a widemouth water bottle lets you fill up with ice cubes before you add water or sport drink. Even better, an insulated bottle keeps everything colder longer.

You'll quickly get the knack of using a water bottle. Reach for a drink when you're spinning smoothly along, not when approaching an intersection or other situation that might require both hands on the bars, as Chris Drillsam of Grafton, Wisconsin, observes:

> One time I was riding in a large pack, and the guy next to me pulled out his water bottle as the light ahead of us turned red. He grabbed his brake to stop, with water bottle in hand. Trying to balance, he proceeded to spray everyone around him, yelling, "Oh, sorry, sorry, excuse me, sorry!"

Give that guy a hydration system! Seriously, these strap-on-your-back water bladders with the no-hands-needed drinking tubes offer a good alternative to the water bottle. All kinds of cyclists love them, especially off-roadies. On the trail an unexpected bounce could make you crash if you have a hand off the bar to drink. On a recent fat tire tour in the desert conditions of Utah's Canyonlands, I found myself guzzling water like never before. Usually I'd stop to drink because, on the Jeep road we were riding, we never knew when a patch of drifted sand or a rocky section might catch us off guard. One of the women kept saying her new Camelbak was the best investment she could have made; I wished I had one, too.

When buying, try the bladder or pack on for comfortable fit. Women often prefer a model without a chest strap. Also look for a system with an insulated reservoir to keep your drink at the desired temperature in any season. Your body absorbs cool liquids more quickly than warm ones, and they taste more refreshing under a sizzling sun.

Camelbak, the originator of these fluid delivery systems, has been joined by a number of other makers. One of them, Z-Kreation, now offers a bladder that straps on the bike.

Emergency repair kit. A flat tire is not such a deflating experience if you are prepared. For the inevitable (and I hope infrequent) puncture or pinch flat, carry a spare tube. Buy one when you pick up your bike, and the salesperson can help you select the right size and valve type (see figure 35).

Lightweight plastic tire levers, which come in sets of two or preferably three, won't drive you crazy by jingling in your bike bag. As an alternative I like the V-shaped plastic VAR lever (see appendix for sources) for high-pressure road tires, which can be persnickety to get back on the rim with just your hands as purists recommend. The VAR lever does the job without pinching or puncturing the inner tube. A smaller lever nests inside the V-shaped one, and you use both of them when removing a tire from the rim. I've also successfully used the No

Pinch Tyre Changer (distributed by ABS Sports) to remove and reinstall mountain bike tires; this odd-looking tool is mostly handle and resembles a sawed-off screwdriver.

To put the air back in your tires, a full-size frame-fit pump will prove more efficient than a mini pump. (Those little pumps are cute, but they can be frustrating to those of us who haven't been doing our push-ups.) Bear in mind the valve type when you buy and check that the length accommodates your frame.

The patch kit may see more at-home use for tube repairs, but it's good to have along on a ride in case bad karma strikes and you have a second puncture.

Once you've made your purchases, practice changing a tube once or twice at home so that it will be easy when you need to do it on a ride. (See chapter 18, "Nothing Flat—And More Repairs You Can Do Yourself.")

Bike bag. OK, I admit in my beginner days I did the occasional ride with a bag of bagels in one hand. But it compromised my braking and confused drivers when I tried to signal. Quickly I found safer ways to carry stuff. Usually I prefer a bike bag, since riding with a day pack makes my back sweat underneath. Plus I have to remove the pack to get to its contents. However, if I'm going to be off and on the bike a lot, a day pack seems more convenient, since I needn't remove it from the bike every time. For just a few items, I favor a cycling jersey with those convenient rear pockets. If you like to ride in a T-shirt, a fanny pack may work for you.

You don't need my help picking out day packs and fanny packs, except for the observation that hydration systems often have cargo pockets and some fanny packs feature compartments to carry water bottles—that very practical two-birds-with-one-stone concept.

As for bike bags, they come in many types for many purposes. Cruising to the beach? An insulated rack pack totes a sixer of your favorite cold beverage. Commuting? When I did it, I was partial to front panniers mounted on a rear carrier to hold a change of clothing and sometimes groceries when I shopped on the way home from work, plus the inevitable file of papers. You'll also find briefcase-shaped bags that mount on a rear rack, as well as courier bags.

But for a first purchase I'd pass those by and select instead a seat bag or handlebar bag. Either will carry your spare tube, levers and patch kit, as well as your snacks, keys, money, I.D., lightweight jacket, etc.

Seat bags have become the hot setup in recent years as cyclists and the industry recognized that carrying weight in a seat pack doesn't compromise steering the way an overloaded handlebar bag does. Improved design has provided for secure mounting under the saddle. Typically wedge-shaped, the bag attaches both to the seatpost and to the saddle rails to minimize annoying sway. Check out seat packs that clip on, as well as those that use hook-and-loop straps. You'll find a choice of bag sizes, from teeny to large. Some seat bags expand with a zipper, opening a pleat to carry bigger loads when you want to. If you might cycle after dark, consider a model with a mounting plate for a rear light.

For trail riding where a load on the handlebars can really mess up bike handling and obscure your view of the front wheel and the ground around it, a seat bag is usually more suitable. Road riders concerned with aerodynamics will also prefer the seat bag.

One thing seat bags lack, though, is that handy top map pocket. Maps get mutilated quickly when they're just tossed in a bag or shoved in a jersey pocket, and then you have to pull them out to read them. To solve that problem, you could buy a handlebar-mount map case to use only when needed. Typically these feature a narrow map window when folded; a large-view window, unfolded; and a small inside pocket for your energy bars—without the heft of a handlebar bag.

If you still prefer the at-your-fingertips convenience of a handlebar bag, these often have a transparent map case on top. You'll find bags that fit hybrid and mountain bike handlebars, and others made for drop bars. A bag with a single compartment requires less labor to produce and costs less than a bag with multiple compartments; and it may be less tempting to overload.

Other desirable features include a detachable shoulder strap for carrying the bag when off the bike. Reflectors or reflective striping on a bag are a plus for after-dark riding, to complement (not replace) a lighting system. By the way, don't expect bike bags to be waterproof, as zippers can leak even if fabric is water-resistant. If rain threatens, I tuck a plastic bag inside to hold items that need protecting.

An exception to the above, however, are waterproof bags by Ortlieb featuring coated, heavy-duty Cordura nylon; overlapped welded seams; and special closure systems.

Lock. As discussed in chapter 6, you need a lock if you ever plan to ride your bike to the pool or gym, pedal to the drugstore or library, take your bike on tour and park it while you visit a museum, or . . . you get the idea. Assess the amount of risk and choose accordingly: The U-lock is most durable but heavy; a cable with padlock or combination lock works in low-risk areas and doesn't require front wheel removal.

MAINTENANCE MUSTS

To take proper care of your bike from the start, these are the essentials.

Chain lubricant. Regular lubrication of your chain, your bike's most exposed moving part, is among the easiest things you can do to prolong the life of your machine and assure smooth shifting. Ask at your bike shop about the best lubricant for your riding conditions, and buy bike lube rather than making do with some all-purpose spritz. Generally speaking, in a dry environment, dry lube works and picks up less dirt. A stickier wet lube washes off less quickly in wet conditions. Use a rag to wipe excess lubricant from the chain so it doesn't become a dirt magnet.

Floor pump. You may have gotten away with inflating your bike tires with a gas station air hose, but the air flow is hard to control and you could easily blow a tube. Invest in a good floor pump. It will put air in your tires much faster than your portable frame pump and will save wear and tear on it and on you. Select a floor pump with a pressure gauge with easy-to-read numbers. Inquire about an adapter for your valve type if needed.

WISH LIST

Some of the following items are a bit of a splurge, and it's possible to start without them. On the other hand, you may quickly find use for this equipment, and you might get a bargain if you pick up some of it used from other cyclists. Club newsletters often carry notices.

Panniers and carrier rack. What a suitcase is to the ordinary traveler, bicycle panniers are to the cycle tourist. The word *pannier* goes back to medieval times and, coming from the French, literally meant "bread basket." As a rule, they were used in pairs, slung one on each side across the back of a pack animal. Today when a bike becomes our beast of burden, these paired bags come into service.

Even on van-supported tours when I'm not hauling my own luggage, small panniers on a rear rack have provided handy cargo space for my camera, windbreaker, rain gear, snacks, and any unexpected purchases made during the day—like the bottle of grappa my husband and I once bought from an Italian woman who'd given us coffee and conversation on a farm outside Verona one serendipitous afternoon.

If you have more than one bike in your stable, you can buy panniers and racks that will fit most bike sizes and frame types. The bags designed for off-road riding's tougher demands should meet any cycle tourist's needs. Panniers typically feature heavy nylon fabric to withstand abrasion and extra-secure locking systems to keep them on your rack when you're bouncing along. Ortlieb panniers convert to backpacks, a versatile feature if you're biking and hiking.

For on-road use only, traditional mounting systems work very well. Usually these consist of hooks to fasten to the rack, and a spring, strap, or elastic cord to fasten the bottom of the bag to the eyelet near the rear dropout.

For carrying off the bike, look for panniers that have handles and either snap or strap together, plus an attachable shoulder strap.

It's tempting to try to save money by selecting a gargantuan pair of rear bags and carrying all your gear in them and a large handlebar pack; however, this can be a recipe for instability and front wheel shimmy. The bike will handle far better with the load distributed mostly between front and rear panniers, with no more than 5 percent of the total weight in a small handlebar bag.

The front rack of choice centers these front bags low on the forks at the center of the wheel for optimum steering. Select a welded rack; those which bolt together (so they can be folded for cheaper shipping) are vulnerable to fatigue and sway. They're OK for kids carrying a few books home from school, but unacceptable for touring.

Bicycle computer. Today's cyclocomputers—especially those with heart monitors—are very useful training devices and just plain fun to use. At the push of a button the computer's LCD numerals will display, in turn, such things as current speed, average speed, cadence, elapsed time, trip distance, and total distance. Make certain you buy a computer with a cadence monitor if you want to polish your pedaling technique; many computers lack that function.

Want to get fit faster? Consider a computer that includes a heart monitor (see chapter 10, "Building Fitness"). Look for a model with a chest belt; its electrode pads detect your heartbeat by picking up the mild electrical activity of the heart muscle. Chest belt transmitters have proved more reliable than monitors that measure pulse with fingertip or earlobe sensors; these tend to lose accuracy at higher heart rates.

In a particularly female-friendly move, Polar Electro Inc. recently introduced a sports bra that accommodates their chest transmitter. I tried it and liked the way it positioned the transmitter comfortably and securely for fail-proof readings—no more feeling as if the chest belt and the bra are fighting for the same space on my body!

Milestone

Having been biking for only a little over a year, I had my best moment when I saw 1,000 miles pop up on my cyclocomputer. We were riding through hilly southern Indiana on a September day, and I was watching the miles go by. At last, 1,000! It was exhilarating to believe that I did all those miles! We celebrated that night with a delicious dinner and a wonderful bottle of wine that I still have the cork from.

–Linda Chandler, Toledo, Ohio

Bike rack. In some parts of the country, if the best rides in your area don't start at your door, a good mass-transit system with bike-access can whisk you and your bike where you want to go. But for many of us these options don't exist, and a good car rack makes life a lot simpler.

This year I was between bike racks—our old bike rack didn't fit on our current car—and we were hauling two mountain bikes back and forth to our favorite riding spots in the back of the station wagon, hassling with piling one bike on top of another, worrying about chipping paint or bending a derailleur. What a relief to get a new bike rack!

In the selection process I considered the pros and cons of the various racks now available. I eliminated roof racks based on previous experience. At a statuesque five-foot-two, I've found mounting a bike on a roof rack difficult at best; some guys I know admit the same thing. I once bounced off a road into a parking lot and saw my shiny new mountain bike fly off the roof rack onto the ground, fortunately sustaining only scratches. Obviously I hadn't fully secured it.

But for tall folks who can manage better, roof racks do offer some advantages. Mounted bikes can't possibly obstruct your rear view when driving, or your turn signals and brake lights, either. And bikes look cool on a roof rack. "I am a cyclist," they proclaim to all who see you on the road. For the multisport individual, roof racks can accommodate your skis, kayak, surfboard, etc., with the appropriate additional components; plan before you buy. The down side? Beware of a tendency, as some roof rack owners will admit, to forget that you have bikes up there. Don't dart unthinkingly into a car wash.

Another choice, for you sports utility vehicle drivers and any others with trailer hitches on your cars, is the hitch rack. Consider one that folds down for easy access to the rear of your vehicle, handy for those inevitable times when you have bikes loaded and then want to get into the hatchback one more time. Select a rack that carries the bikes high enough that they can't be damaged if you back into a curb or drive into a dip. And check to see that your car's rear signals and your rear view aren't obscured by mounted bicycles.

For my car, lacking a trailer hitch, I chose a rear/trunk rack, the Bones, made by Saris. Lightweight and easy to install, it securely carries our two bikes (three with a little finagling), and I can mount them myself without any strain. With the rack in place, I can't open the tailgate of my car, but since it's a four-door wagon I'm not inconvenienced. As with the hitch rack, it's important to check for obstruction of the vehicle's brake lights and turn signals and for a clear view in the rear-view mirror. While driving I do see the bikes in the mirror and through the rear window, reminding me not to back into anything.

There are also racks that mount on a spare-tire carrier, bumper racks (requiring solid metal bumpers), and for pickup owners, racks for the back of your truck.

Whatever your need, the rack manufacturers' catalogs have extensive vehicle-compatibility charts to help you get a perfect match. Give thought also to the security system you'll use if you expect to leave your rigs on the rack when out of your sight. As you mount bikes on your rack, position them so they can't rattle against each other or, if need be, use padding. With any rack, stop periodically on long trips to check that neither the bikes nor the rack itself have worked loose.

Oops!

I drove into my garage, completely forgetting my brand new mountain bike on the roof rack. Fortunately the garage door made contact with the strongest point of the handlebars, and the fork mount on the rack exploded before the bike did, so the bike was thrown off the back of the car. Aside from a few scratches to the car roof, a kink in the bike's brake cable, and my extreme embarrassment, we all survived to share the story with others who have done the same thing! –Susie Short, Vista, California

Clothes with Wheel Appeal

New recruits to cycling may wonder why we dress as we do. Comfort and ease of motion are the big motivators. Think about the sensitivity of the parts of your anatomy that make contact with the bike—your hands, your feet, and your nether regions. Putting thick-seamed shorts or blue jeans between you and the saddle, for example, will literally rub you the wrong way. If your goal is to enjoy riding and increase fitness, you don't want your clothing holding you back.

I'll save my breath and try not to talk too much about the bad old days, when a cycling jersey would fit a woman only if she had a build like a bicycle pump—or a man. Now it's possible to find garments sized for you. With an understanding of what fosters cycling comfort and what's available on the market, you can make your own decision about what to wear.

FUNCTIONAL FASHIONS

Balloon-bright colors, billboard lettering, and stretchy nylon/Lycra that follows every curve of the body—that's the bike racer's look. Racers dress for aerodynamics, comfort, and flash.

Like bicycles, clothing for competition is no longer just designed, it's engineered. Wind tunnel tests have shown that an outfit that billows, wrinkles, or even has rough-textured fabric disrupts smooth airflow and increases wind resistance, slowing a racer down. In events where hundredths of a second count, these factors make a difference. And I don't need to explain that team sponsors necessitate advertising—hence the eye-grabbing colors and names emblazoned everywhere. As for comfort, the many hours racers spend competing and training not only require it, they also make these riders potential testers for new fabrics and designs in cycling apparel. So, as it has for decades, competition-wear continues to influence designs and fabric choices for recreational cyclists as well.

When bike shorts came out in nylon/Lycra, it seemed a real improvement over the then-standard wool. In these clingy spandex shorts it was easier for us females to find a fit in the men's and unisex sizes that were available then. Not long after that, mass-produced cyclewear began to offer sizes cut specifically for our gender. I was thrilled to be able to buy cycling jerseys and jackets that didn't hang down below my butt. And the sleeves actually started at my shoulder line.

Since then I've watched the selection in cycling clothing for women grow as the market attempts to meet our needs (as well it should, since over half of all adult bicyclists are female). Now bikewear manufacturers big and small have women's lines. Some of these companies were started by female cyclists with an entrepreneurial bent who saw a niche needing to be filled. And there's been plenty of adaptation going on, with racing-inspired designs reinterpreted in a range of fabric types and looser fits for more general appeal.

So take these women-specific garments seriously, as they include many fine products among them and all kinds of looks—fabric prints ranging from feminine to funny to ferocious; mix 'n' match solids; a take-your-pick palette of pastels, brights, earth tones, and basic black; garments styled for on-road, off-road, or casual pedaling; pieces that say cycling; and others closer to traditional clothing.

But you gotta shop around. No one store could possibly carry all the women's lines now available. In fact, if you visited a half dozen shops and each one stocked completely different brands, you still couldn't see everything on the market. A retailer who takes apparel seriously, however, should offer a good selection and creative displays of each brand carried, with enough choices to let you put together an attractive, functional cycling wardrobe. To try all this great stuff on, the store should have a dressing room with a full-length mirror.

As always, a good consumer is discriminating. Don't blindly trust all makers who claim to cater to our gender. Check the garments themselves as well as the labels. Anomalies like huge arm holes on sleeveless jerseys suggest that a manufacturer has merely offered you a downsized version of a men's cut instead of a true women's design. The guidelines that follow will help you shop.

What? The bike stores in your area are clueless? Then get on the phone or the Internet and check out the brands with women's lines listed in the appendix. Makers can help you locate a retailer or provide mail order information.

DUDS THAT AREN'T DUDS

First, consider the various items of cyclewear and their function. What do you really need, and what's fashionable to complete the outfit?

Cycling shorts. A can't-do-without piece, cycling-specific shorts are designed to minimize bulk and prevent irritation. The cling of spandex keeps shorts from riding up and exposing your thighs to chafing against the saddle—the reason why shorts should extend at least midway to the knee. DuPont, who created Lycra-brand spandex, now claims that garments made of LYCRAPOWER fabric can enhance performance, too. According to a Penn State Center for Sports Medicine study, specially designed garments compress the muscles, reducing vibration and thus fatigue by an average of 12 percent. If you want to see for yourself, look for the LYCRAPOWER hangtag. At this writing, Cantina's Dirt! short is one of the licensed garments in femme sizing.

If you dislike the glossiest racer looks, you can find suitably clingy spandex/cotton or spandex with other blends. This style short works well both on- and off-road, and some models for mountain biking have extra-durable panels of Spandura or Cordura in case you should biff on the trail. These shorts are cut in four-, six-, and eight-panel constructions, with the eight-panel models priced highest but giving the best fit.

If the skin tight look bothers you, go the camouflage route: relaxed-cut shorts with built-in, lined spandex shorts. These "double shorts" have gained popularity for about-town cycling and trail use. Although they do compromise comfort for megamile rides, these double-shorts make a versatile garment for recreational cyclists.

What's inside both types of shorts counts for a lot. There should be a center liner, or *chamois*, that pads and protects your crotch from friction. The name "chamois" comes from traditional leather liners, but more supple, synthetic materials make up the modern ones. Don't buy any shorts with a seam running through the center of the chamois; this can irritate tender tissues. Most women prefer a molded, one-piece chamois or a liner with two curved seams—what we call "baseball stitching"—that keeps the center smooth. Shorts for women now typically feature one or the other. Many liners have antibacterial treatment, so check labels for this if you're prone to boils. Under-the-liner padding may be fleece, gel, or a liquid-filled bladder.

The shape of the liner and the amount of padding will vary from one brand to another. Experiment to see what feels best to you. Once you find the perfect combination you'll probably be loathe to change brands. For my taste, some shorts have too much padding or too wide a chamois, which feels as if I'm wearing a diaper when I walk and causes bunching and discomfort when I ride. With a good women's saddle I find I don't need a lot of padding in shorts. (At this writing, Koulius Zaard and SporTobin both make shorts with narrower liners.) Buying the correct size shorts also helps to alleviate bunching; shorts should fit skintight, so try on before you buy.

For larger sizes cut for women, Terry Precision Cycling and Koulius Zaard offer several styles each. Also Performance has the Fuller Form short; Bike Nashbar, the Sure-Fit short. Cycling for two? Terry has introduced a maternity short. Or try the relaxed waistline of a bib short or a one-piece, a size larger than normal.

Don't ride in unlined shorts. If you want to don a pair of non-cycling baggies or other street shorts, make them more comfy by wearing a thigh-length padded cycling brief underneath, available in women's sizes from a number of makers.

A few points on hygiene: Starting each ride with a clean pair of shorts helps protect against developing skin irritations. To cut down on laundry, some women get away with wearing light underwear with minimal seams. Cycling shorts are meant to be worn *sans* underwear, however. I've worn them that way ever since the twenty-five-mile point on my first century when I ripped off some annoying panties in a porta-john.

As soon as possible after a ride, change out of cycling shorts into dry, more breathable attire to avoid any chance of yeast infection. While today's shorts liners dry more quickly than a leather chamois and wick moisture more effectively, they still create a warm moist environment—better not to prolong it.

Most cycling shorts can be machine washed; line drying will prolong the life of spandex and elastic.

Finally, let's talk about color preferences. Plain black cycling shorts have a reason for being. As Sandy von Allmen of Norfolk, New York, observes, "You never have to worry about color coordination or about where to wipe your hands after putting a chain back on." Black doesn't show grass stains, blood stains, or dark smudges from your saddle, as pale colors will. "Besides," Sandy adds, "when I'm out cycling alone, I prefer to dress in a way that's functional to the sport but unrevealing as to gender."

Sunglasses. These are a must for cutting ultraviolet rays and glare, plus shielding your eyes from dive-bombing insects. I've had some healthy-sized bugs bounce off my specs, and they were going fast enough to have done some serious damage.

Cycling-specific sunglasses come in a range of prices. They often have a wraparound lens design, helpful for cutting wind that can cause tearing. Wraparounds also work better, contact lens wearers tell me, for keeping dust out of the eyes. Look for polycarbonate lenses, which resist impact and filter out all UV rays, and insist on flexible, forgiving nylon polymide frames. I learned this the hard way once while in-line skating in a pair of fashion sunglasses: I fell and broke their hard plastic frame; a sharp edge of it cut my face. The cost of my emergency room treatment would have paid for a very good pair of sport glasses.

When shopping, try glasses on to ensure that enough lens extends above your eyes to shield them as you bend over the handlebars; check that earpieces don't obscure peripheral vision. And make sure that the glasses are the right size for your head and won't slip. Some one-size-fits-all glasses fit (you guessed it) men better. For that reason, I recently tested two brands of sport glasses that hug a woman's smaller face. Thumbs up to Trixie Spex for Women from Performance and Sliders by Smith. Another plus, both come with interchangeable lenses: a dark lens for sunny days, an amber lens for overcast conditions, and an untinted lens for dusk and night riding.

Gloves. Not just a fashion item, cycling gloves prevent blisters and help dampen vibration that might otherwise cause numbness. They give a more secure grip on the bars when sweaty hands might be slippery. And they protect hands in a crash, as I was reminded last autumn after a mountain bike maneuver that was more embarrassing than painful—thanks to gloves that kept road grit out of my palms.

In selecting gloves, concern yourself with correct size and comfort first, then colors and materials. You want a snug fit but freedom of movement. When trying them on, grip a handlebar in various positions to see how the gloves feel. Check for seams in any awkward spots where you expect to put pressure on your hands.

Several manufacturers make women's sizes in the standard gloves designed for road riding in warm weather. These are cut way short on the fingers and may or may not have that opening on the back of the hand that gives you a cyclist's tan. Gloves come in a variety of materials, with backs of stretchy nylon mesh or poly/cotton/Lycra or the traditional crocheted cotton. Palms are often of leather-like, machine-washable Amara or genuine leather, which may also be washable (check the label). Underneath should be gel or foam padding or a water-filled bladder to give added protection. A terry-cloth thumb, a frequent feature, comes in handy to wipe a damp brow.

Standard road gloves suffice for many mountain bikers, as they do for me on the typical two- or three-hour rides I do at home. But day after day on tour last fall, I began to wish for more thumb coverage. The industry may have admitted by now that women also ride the trails, but off-road gloves I see come only in men's sizes at present. Typically these mitts have a full thumb and first two fingers, to save wear and tear from several hours' use of twist-shift and to protect those two braking fingers. Another design features a full thumb and three-quarter length on all fingers. Look for the smallest men's or unisex size and clamor for women's sizing. It will surely emerge on the market soon.

The easiest way to remove gloves that fit snugly is to peel them off inside out. They'll last longer.

Shoes. If you're just starting out and you already have a pair of running shoes, they may work just fine for riding. Since I was a runner, I had scads of old running shoes and found that some—the ones with a narrow profile—sufficed for cycling, even with toe clips. Or you could choose to pedal off-road in hiking shoes or cross-trainers. The key question is whether the soles are stiff enough to protect the thick ligament under the sole of your foot (the *plantar fascia*) from the constant pressure of your foot on the pedal. A shoe that flexes in the middle of the sole puts too much stress on this ligament, causing discomfort. That's why sneakers just don't make it for cycling.

At some point you may want something made for cycling. Clipless pedals, for example, require shoes that accommodate the system's cleat.

For road riding these shoes have extremely stiff soles for the most efficient transfer of energy to the pedals. The cleat mates with a step-in binding. Not only racers, but also many other roadies love the clipless pedals for the feeling of oneness with the bike and the energy saved, especially on hills. Even for day rides and touring, clipless pedals are an option if the shoes have a recess for the cleat, making them "walkable." Most of these shoes come in unisex sizes, which may fit you. However, Diadora makes the Women's Classico road shoe, and Performance sells the Women's Chronos shoe under its own label. The conversion chart below should help you make sense of the various sizing systems.

Experienced mountain bikers are also going clipless off-road. Check out uni-sex sizes as well as women's models from Cannondale, Performance, and Lake.

Whether you choose clipless or toeclips, for trail riding you need shoes with an aggressive tread for traction, just as you require knobby tires: If you dismount in a hurry, you want to land on your feet and stay upright. The soles will have a little flex for comfort while walking. When selecting a clipless shoe, look for one with a recess for the cleat.

Today's clipless pedal systems usually have float built into either the pedal or the cleat, allowing your foot to angle naturally on the pedals. To minimize knee stress, choose a system with at least 6 degrees of float. Position the cleat on your shoe so that the cleat is 1 cm or so behind the pedal axle, thus putting the ball of your foot a little in front of the axle; this setup usually facilitates efficient pedaling while preventing numbness or tingling in your toes. Position the cleat laterally so that your anklebone passes close to the crankarm without hitting it while pedaling.

If you should decide on a fixed cleat (no float), ask the bike shop for assistance with correct lateral placement of the cleats, or you could be flirting with injury.

Shoe size conversion chart – European Metric to U.S.

Metric	36	37	38	39	40	41	42	43	44	45	46	47
Women	5	5½-6	6½-7	7½-8	8-8½	9	9½-10					
Men			5-5½	6-6½	7-7½	8-8½	8½-9	9½	10	10½	11	11½-12

Cycling jersey or other top. You can do without a jersey at first—perhaps forever. I love the rear pockets, though, for stashing keys, sunscreen, a handkerchief, and granola bars. On tour I've carried a small 35mm camera in a pocket for quick photo stops. And a jersey's extra length in back keeps you from exposing bare skin to the sun as you lean forward toward the bars.

These days cycling jerseys, in cuts and sizes made especially for our proportions, offer women more choices than ever. You'll find a range of necklines, sleeve types, and other styling options. You can open some jerseys to the breeze with a long vent zipper—and show off your coordinating sport bra underneath. You'll see polo shirt collars and tee neck jerseys. There are breezy crop tops. Tank tops and to-the-waist T-back tops with built-in bras still provide air conditioning while cutting back on the wolf whistles. Some have a handy pocket in the back.

For good fit, as you're standing, a jersey or other full-length top should come down about midway on your hips. Or if it has elastic in the hem it may ride closer to your waist, depending on how tight the elastic is; try bending over to be sure it won't ride up too far and give you a burn on a scorching day. Most sport riders wear jerseys looser than racers do; suit your own taste.

Regarding color choice, for the road I recommend bright colors so motorists can see you more easily. On the trail, many riders favor earth colors as sympatico with the surroundings, but during hunting season it's wise to advertise your human nature by wearing the closest thing you have to blaze orange.

Shiny nylon/spandex is not the only choice in jersey fabrics these days. Since many women want less shine or less cling, the industry offers jerseys in cotton/Lycra, CoolMax, and cotton/poly blends. These "technical" fabrics wick away moisture for greater comfort. You'll find plenty of 100 percent cotton T-shirts and sleeveless T-shirts if you want to go all-natural.

You still prefer your own tee or polo shirt? Wear it. You'll have plenty of company.

Sport bra. You know what you need in this department. Just a reminder here about Polar's heart monitor sport bra, mentioned in the previous chapter.

Knickers and warmers. Shorts might take you comfortably through the warmer months, but knickers offer a change of pace with some practical applications. When it's just a little too cold for shorts (below 65°F) and you don't feel like donning tights—knickers can warm those knees and provide off-roadies with extra protection from trail bramble.

For changeable early- and late-season days, arm and leg warmers with cuddly fleece on the inside slip on easily when you want a little insulation; stash them in a jersey pocket when temps rise. Koulius Zaard makes them in women's sizes.

Other looks. Short, kicky skirts are hot fashion right now, so if you want one for on and off your bike, why not? Zoic makes the Skort and the Coolotte.

ALL-WEATHER GEAR

The go-for-it garb above should outfit you for cycling on warm, fair days. If you want to be a woman for all seasons, you'll need to add to your wardrobe from the following.

Rain gear. In drizzle or deluge you need to keep dry because body heat escapes quickly from wet skin and clothing, possibly leading to hypothermia, even in fifty-degree weather.

A lightweight, waterproof nylon rain jacket and a pair of rain pants ward off wind and wetness for me; underarm zips and back vents in the jacket help control temperature and reduce moisture buildup inside. This rain suit, with appropriate layers underneath, has kept me happy on many occasions, most recently during a spring tour in the Netherlands with rain, headwinds, and even a bit of hail blowing in from the North Sea. On warm days in a light rain, instead of pulling rain pants on over shorts, I prefer cycling tights because they shed the raindrops and allow more freedom of movement.

A simple coated-nylon rain jacket or rain suit like mine, which makes no claims of breathability, may suit your needs too, depending on the climate of your area and how often/how long you might expect to ride in the rain. Inexpensively priced, these outfits come in cycling-specific designs. Or you might prefer a waterproof rain cape or poncho, which is likely to blow about, but there's minimal heat buildup underneath to cause condensation.

Alternatively, you could choose a pricier rain suit in one of the water-proof/breathable (WPB) fabrics or *laminates* now available under a host of brand names. The earliest among these, Gore-Tex, sandwiches a moisture-barrier membrane between inner and outer fabrics; other companies have since followed suit with their own WPB laminates, such as Sympatex. In another approach, *microporous coatings,* such as Ultrex, have tiny pores that allow a material to breathe. Admittedly, there is a trade-off in water-resistance; how much is sacrificed will vary with the fabric of the garment and the amount of coating. And there are *microfibers,* very fine fibers which can be tightly woven to create fabrics that are water-repellent, if not waterproof.

These technologies continue to evolve. Discuss your needs with your retailer and look for product reviews to steer you toward the best choice for you. Whatever option you choose, select a garment with good venting—even if its fabric is supposed to be breathable. Why? If you're sweating up a storm inside, even breathable fabrics may not be able to manage the moisture.

Underarm vents provide the best ventilation, as they admit wind to dry perspiration without chilling your chest; a front-facing flap over the zipper helps to keep rain from leaking in. Back vents let wind escape the jacket to cut down on billowing. Less effective, chest vents tend to be blown closed by the wind. Other features to consider: The jacket should be cut shorter in front than in back, with a tail long enough to keep rear-wheel spray off your rear. A drawstring at the hem prevents flapping. With the jacket on, sit on a bike in cycling position to check fit before buying: Sleeves should extend to cover your wrists while riding. Look for a close fit at the collar and construction that avoids shoulder seams (notorious for leaking). Yellow—easy to spot on gray days—makes the best color for road riders' rainwear. Reflective striping on the jacket back improves visibility after dark.

Next to your skin wear a layer that will wick perspiration away from your body—not an all-cotton T-shirt. If you find that you're overheating in your jacket in spite of opening the vents, stop in a sheltered spot and remove an under layer if you can.

Do you have rain gear that's lost its water-repellency? Want to waterproof a favorite windshell? Wash-in waterproofers have recently been improved to provide a more durable waterproof finish. Reportedly it does not compromise the garment's breathability and should last through several launderings. Ask your local outdoor retailer about such brands as Nikwax and Granger's Extreme.

Debut in a Downpour

On a Sunday in spring I'm doing three things I've never done before—taking part in an organized ride, doing it in foot-numbing rain, and pedaling a brand-new mountain bike. It's raining steadily at the starting point. "I've paid my money," I say to myself, "and I'm going to ride."

Wearing my sailing rain gear and thus protected except for my feet, I set out, uncertain, even apprehensive. I see few other riders on the twenty-mile route, and I'm only the eighth person to reach the food stop by noon. On numb feet I stand, munching absolutely the very best cookies in the world. Then a miracle: The feeling returns to my feet. Heartened, I tuck extra cookies and a banana into a pannier and pedal on, water streaming over my sunglasses.

A bridge beckons me to stop and watch swallows skim the rain-dotted Huron River. From time to time the air hangs heavy with the sweet scent of new spring blossoms. The road is slick, but I feel safe on those fat, knobby tires. Apprehension vanishes like rain down a culvert, and I begin to feel good, damn good, even proud, damn proud.

"Then the ride is over—and so, of course, is the rain. Back at the pavilion I pull on my new, long-sleeved ride T-shirt, feeling no less a winner than those who earn the right to wear the yellow jersey in the Tour de France. Victory—any kind—is sweet indeed!

–Suzanne Vannell, Troy, Michigan

Jacket or long-sleeved jersey. A lightweight shell that folds to slip into your seat pack or jersey pocket can save you from shivering if a ride turns cold. Features to look for: zippered pockets for items you want handy, a front-closure zipper that's easy to operate one-handed, comfortable elastic in cuffs to keep sleeves where you want 'em, and a tail long enough to cover you when riding. A shell should be breathable and/or vented so you don't create your own shower inside.

Could you ask for more? Trail riders will appreciate durability in the jacket's fabric. Pavement pedalers should consider conspicuity: Jackets often come in dark colors, practical for not showing dirt; a large, bright graphic or band of color on front and back improves visibility on the road. After the sun goes down, the ultimate insurance is a fabric called illumiNite, a Supplex nylon with thousands of microscopic reflective dishes embedded in it to reflect in a car's headlights at night.

Retro and very useful, long-sleeved cycling jerseys have made a comeback in all-wool and wool-blend. I can see why. Last year I brought a long-sleeved, wool/acrylic jersey out of retirement and wore it on those just-starting-to-get-cool fall days with only a sport bra underneath. The jersey proved warm enough but not too hot, thanks to its highly breathable weave. In colder, rainy spring weather I wore a wool long-sleeved jersey as an insulating middle layer over a short-sleeve jersey and under a windbreaker and eventually my rain jacket; layering let me stay dry and just warm enough.

Base layer. Successful layering begins with a foundation garment that transports perspiration from your body to the next layer of clothing. As I did, you might wear a short-sleeve jersey with good wicking properties. Or you could buy a silky-soft base-layer shirt, available at this writing in women's cuts from Sugoi and Pearl Izumi. Don't start with a cotton T-shirt as your foundation, because cotton grabs onto sweat and absorbs body heat into the garment, making you colder.

Tights. A versatile choice for a first purchase, unlined nylon/spandex tights don't need washing after every ride, and you can use them for noncycling activities, too. Racers and other experienced cyclists generally slip a pair of unlined tights on over their regular cycling shorts when temperatures drop below sixty-five degrees, mainly to keep knees warm and lessen any chance of injury from cold, stiff muscles. Nylon/spandex tights are ideal for those days when it's just a little too cool for shorts. If the weather warms during your ride, just slip off the tights, roll 'em up, and stow 'em in a jersey pocket or your bike bag.

Purchase pointers: Tights cut lower in front and higher in back fit your on-bike body best. While you're trying on tights, sit on a bicycle in riding position. Tights that seem too generous in the knees or derriere when you're standing could be perfect on the bike.

Should you decide later that you want a warmer tight with a chamois liner, several companies—including Terry Precision Cycling, Bouré, Koulius Zaard—make these in women's sizes. Toasty unlined tights are also available from Cannondale, SporTobin, and GLD. InSport offers women considerable choice in both types of tight. Or a unisex tight might do it for you—Giordana's popular Roubaix bib tight stays up nicely but leaves you unrestricted at the waist.

Fingers and toes. When there's a nip in the air, hands and feet seem to notice it first. For starters, you'll probably find suitable full-finger cycling gloves at your local bike shop. On really cold days, consider layering. For example, two versatile chill-chasers from InSport give lots of options. Their lightweight Max Glove, made of Thermax/Lycra, is thin enough to serve as a liner under other full-finger gloves or under their L.L.A.P. (Live Long and Prosper) Mitten, which is split to allow two-finger braking for mountain biking. These ripstop nylon mitts don't take much room in your seat bag. Sometimes I wear them on top of full-finger gloves as a wind barrier.

Speaking of wind barriers, check out Madden's monster-size Bullwinkles, made of heavy-duty Cordura nylon. These slip over the ends of straight handlebars on a mountain bike (over your shifters and brake levers, too) to keep hands toasty and let you operate the controls. All you need in there is a thin glove.

As for toes, cold is uncomfortable; cold and wet is worse. Now there are waterproof socks, some insulated. To wear over shoes, neoprene toe covers are available.

Women's clothing options will continue to improve as manufacturers and retailers recognize the purchasing power of woman cyclists. So don't be a stranger at your bike shop. Express your wishes and look for retailers who try to meet them.

Shaping Up and Body Shape

Since I've cycled regularly I feel more confident about myself and my body. I feel fitter and more able to cope generally. I've lost seven pounds without dieting and don't seem to feel as hungry or as bothered about eating.
−Judith Stuuter, Wymondham, Norfolk, England

With cycling I can accomplish many things, like long rides, that I never dreamed I could do. And it's fun. But most rewarding for me is that I've lost forty-five pounds without dieting. The pounds more or less "fell" off; I didn't even realize I was losing weight until all my clothes started getting baggy. I'm smaller and in better shape than before I had my children. I feel great. I'd like to lose ten more pounds, but I'm not on a diet per se. I know, as I continue riding, the weight will eventually come off. Biking has given me a new, younger body! −Carol Nelson, Chino Hills, California

I was amazed at the effect cycling had on my body in such a short time. My legs got very strong and had better muscle definition. Cycling three miles each way to work and on weekends, I keep my weight very stable. And my circulation has improved tremendously. I also found that I became interested in other sports and outside activities.
−Maura Thornton, Clifford Park, Coventry, England

I eat as much as possible so I can train as hard as possible. This keeps the weight off! −Eve Wildi Hawkins, Webster, New York

I now have more stamina and no longer "give up." I eat as much as I used to and weigh as much, but people say I look better.
−Yvonne Fallows, Whitburn, West Lothian, England

When I went through a depression and lost my appetite, vigorous cycling was all I could think of to try and stimulate it. It worked and I quickly put weight back on. Now my weight has stabilized since three months after I began cycling. −D. Hamilton, Abingdon, Oxfordshire, England

If weight control is one of your goals, can cycling help?

Possibly. Certainly we know that significant calorie-cutting without exercise can be frustrating. After some pounds are shed, the body—responding to eons of evolutionary influences—thinks it is being starved. As a protective measure, metabolism drops, and the body burns calories more slowly. Determined not to give in, the dieter continues the calorie deprivation. Craving food, she finds herself easily distracted, agitated, depressed. She may deny her hunger frequently enough that eventually she loses touch with how it feels to be hungry. Then when temptation overpowers her and she dives into one of her "forbidden" foods, she may binge beyond the point of satisfying hunger. She thinks, "I've already broken my diet for today, so what's the difference?" Researchers Janet Polivy and C. Peter Herman, in their book *Breaking the Diet Habit* (New York: Basic Books, 1983), call this the "what-the-hell effect." They point out that dieting generally precedes episodes of binge eating, often by many months.

MOVING IN THE RIGHT DIRECTION

By contrast, becoming more active is a much safer way to try to initiate weight loss. Why?

Exercise, as we've seen in chapters 3 and 4, is often the body's great regulator and, generally, a promoter of better health. Here, too, in the matter of weight control, exercise can start an individual rolling in the right direction.

Everybody knows that physical activity burns calories. It also gradually helps to build muscle, not only toning the body but also raising metabolism. The body's fat cells are basically inert storage tissue, but muscle is working tissue, always burning calories to maintain itself. An improved muscle-mass-to-body-weight ratio means more calories burned.

An increase in the level of physical activity also seems to foster the growth of fat-burning enzymes, some researchers tell us. In *The New Fit or Fat* (Boston, MA: Houghton Mifflin, 1991), Covert Bailey calls this process of developing lean body mass "building a better butter burner."

Over time, even a small change in the metabolic rate can influence weight control. (Interestingly, for individuals whose basal metabolic rate tends to be too high, a condition often associated with tension, exercise can help to lower the metabolic rate.)

DO IT

But don't overdo. A desperation attempt at a quick-fix is doomed to failure. One hot summer Saturday, as I pedaled toward the local parkway, with its tree-shaded paths, I observed a red-faced, roly-poly man lumbering along the street, sealed up in a plastic suit like a turkey in a roasting bag. Was he enjoying himself? Was he likely to stick with this program of exercise? No. He was working too hard, feeling painfully out of breath. And he was asking for trouble, courting heat exhaustion by preventing his body from cooling itself. How much smarter he'd have been to drive to the parkway and take a walk or an easy bike ride under the trees (minus the plastic suit, of course). Discovering pleasure in the activity is a better way to start. Gradually he would begin to feel satisfaction in a sense of mastery.

And satisfaction is just what Judith, Carol, and others quoted above have found—joy in what their bodies can now do. Judith has more body confidence and feels "less bothered about food." Maura has developed an interest in other sports and thinks she has become more outgoing. All seem more self-accepting. By adapting cycling to suit their various lifestyles, they succeeded by trusting their bodies and by taking charge, just as Diane Epstein and Kathleen Thompson recommend in *Feeding on Dreams: Why America's Diet Industry Doesn't Work and What Will Work for You* (Old Tappan, NJ: Macmillan Publishing Company, 1994): "You take control and you make the choices that fit into your life."

In my survey of North American women cyclists, 83.3 percent of the respondents indicated that the exercise of cycling (and other sports, for some), along with a balanced diet, suffices to maintain a weight that satisfies them. Inherent in a balanced diet may be some calorie restriction, as 23.8 percent said they restrict calories moderately. Only a tiny percentage uses more extreme methods of weight control.

In our diet-conscious society, these findings testify to both the beneficial effects of cycling for regulating weight and a strong level of self-confidence in these women.

Survey Findings: Cycling and Weight Control

Total sample size for this question was 583 women.

Q. Do you find that a combination of the exercise of cycling and eating nutritious, balanced meals is sufficient for you to maintain a weight you are satisfied with?

A. 78.7% Yes

16.6% No

4.6% Yes, when combined with other exercise

Q. Do you use other measures of weight control?

A. 23.8% Moderate calorie restriction

1.4% Fasting

1.2% Crash diets

1.0% Diet pills or related aids

0.3% Liquid diets

0.3% Weight Watchers

0.3% Overeaters Anonymous

Note: 1.4% Indicated they don't try to lose weight and that they must watch out for excess weight loss.

The question remains: Do we take up our sport because we happen to be confident, positive types, or do we feel better about ourselves and our bodies as a result of our cycling? While I don't exclude the first theory, clearly most of my survey respondents credit bicycling for promoting body confidence. The majority (57.6 percent) feel "much happier" about their bodies since starting to ride; another 27.9 percent feel "somewhat happier"; and 13.8 percent feel "about the same as before."

Survey Findings: Cycling and Body Image

The vast majority of women participating in my survey stated that they are happier with their bodies since taking up cycling: Of the total, 57.6 percent are "much happier," 27.9 percent are "somewhat happier," and 13.8 percent feel "about the same." Women indicating no change in feelings may nevertheless be quite happy with their bodies, as a number did, in fact, comment. Only 0.5 percent expressed dissatisfaction, saying that their legs had grown bigger or the muscles became more defined than desired.

The women who grew up with the least athletic experience showed, as a group, the most improvement in their feelings about their bodies after taking up cycling.

With the following question, respondents were asked to describe their background:

Q. How did you feel about sport activities before you began cycling?
  • "I grew up enthusiastic about sports."
  • "I hated organized sports and gym class in school."
  • "I'd been pretty inactive until taking up cycling."
  • Other (Write-in answers turned this category into:)
    "I'd become active previously in recent years."

A fifth group emerged, of women who both "hated organized sports and gym class in school" and had "been pretty inactive until taking up cycling." This group indicated the most improvement in body image: 90 percent felt "much happier" with their bodies. It was as if these women had really found themselves. The responses for all five groups appear below.

	Much Happier	Somewhat Happier	Same	Less
Hated Organized Sports/Pretty Inactive	90%	6.6%	3.3%	—
Hated Organized Sports	71%	21.7%	7.2%	—
Pretty Inactive	63.2%	27.5%	9.1%	—
Grew Up Enthusiastic	52.2%	30.5%	16.3%	0.9%
Previously Active in Recent Years	48.5%	32.3%	19.1%	—

MEETING YOUR GOALS

If, after a realistic assessment, your goals include weight control, here are some answers to questions you've probably been asking.

What about cutting calories? Should you (along with cycling) cut calories, if your goal is weight loss? That's for you to decide. If you choose to, your smartest bet for good health is to draw on a great variety of foods to create satisfying, well-balanced meals that cut fat consumption and especially saturated fats and trans (hydrogenated) fats. Feature "lots of fruits and vegetables and more beans and fish in place of meat," says Dr. William Connor of Oregon Health Sciences University in Portland. Compared to higher-fat foods, fruits and veggies pack in fewer calories for the same amount of food, and their nutrients help protect you from cancer and heart disease. Likewise, the fats in fish, he notes, appear to fight these diseases. (See the chart "What's to Eat?" on pg. 29; also chapter 11, "Fueling the Engine.")

In cutting total daily fat calories, don't overcompensate with too many low-fat/high-sugar cookies, frozen yogurt, and other sweet treats. (Dessert is not at the bottom of the food pyramid.) Too many folks eat so much of this sort of thing that they increase their total calorie consumption and so sabotage their efforts at weight reduction.

How much do our genes come into play? Much as the diet industry might want us to believe otherwise, losing weight is not so simple an equation as "fewer calories in + more calories burned = thinner."

Research supports the theory that each person has a setpoint, or "natural weight range," below which weight loss is extremely difficult because of many natural defenses of the body. Studies of identical twins raised separately appear to indicate that the setpoint regulating fatness or thinness "is as much as 75 percent heritable. Roughly translated, this means that when two people have different amounts of fat, at least three-quarters of the difference has been caused by their dissimilar genes; the remainder is the result of differences in experience, environment, or habits," say William Bennett, M.D. and Joel Gurin in *The Dieter's Dilemma: Eating Less and Weighing More* (New York: Basic Books, 1982).

Exercise appears to alter the setpoint, the authors note. "If a person is truly sedentary—as most Americans probably are unless they make a special effort— then the setpoint adjusts to an abnormally high level. Regular activity can bring it back down." While one jog or bike ride burns a relatively few extra calories, the effects of doing it regularly are long-lasting. "An active body is 'set' to be thinner than an inactive one."

How hard should I ride? Dr. Bennett and Mr. Gurin are referring to endurance, or aerobic, exercise. Bear in mind that for beginners, more pain means less gain, since making the activity unpleasant ups the likelihood of quitting. Chapter 10, "Building Fitness," discusses how to ease into successful riding habits.

Cyclists who've developed an endurance base may choose to vary the pace from ride to ride, doing interval training one day, long steady mileage another, a time-trial pace later in the week, and so on. Is one of these workouts more conducive to fat burning than another? It's popularly thought that low-intensity cycling does this best, because fat serves as the chief fuel for such exercise done at less than 70 percent of maximum effort. Yes, fat is the main energy source for easy-pace exercise; while above 70 percent of maximum effort we burn more carbohydrates. (See also chapter 11, "Fueling the Engine.")

However, according to *Bicycling* magazine's nutrition columnist, Susan I. Barr, Ph.D., "a recent Georgia State University study shows that weight loss depends on the total number of calories burned during a workout, not whether those calories came from carbohydrate or fat."

Dr. Barr offers the example of two cyclists as an illustration. One pedals easily for two hours and burns 600 calories, over half coming from fat. During other activities that day, though, she draws more on carbohydrates "because carbohydrate isn't easily stored by the body, so the amount eaten is generally used as an energy source on the same day," says Dr. Barr. The second bicyclist also expends 600 calories, but mostly carbohydrate, by riding hard for an hour. This more or less depletes her stored carbs, so her off-bike activities that day will draw on fat for fuel. Both women burn fat, though in different ways. What counts for weight loss is the total calories burned per day—which, in this example, should be the same for both riders if all other things are equal.

So set your pace based on your mood or your training goals. Enjoy your ride and let the fat burning take care of itself.

My clothes fit looser but my scales don't show much progress; what's happening? Don't equate fat with weight. While you are burning fat, you're also building muscle, which is denser and thus heavier than fat. As noted, adding muscle not only strengthens you as a cyclist but also improves your metabolism. If you have lost some weight and trimmed down, you are moving in the right direction.

How fast should I lose? Be patient. A loss of one-half to two pounds a week will favor retention of valuable muscle while fat melts away. Dr. Barr recommends that, after a ten-pound loss, you "maintain the new weight for six months before attempting further weight loss. This may help your body recognize the new weight as its usual weight and prevent subsequent gain."

REALISTIC EXPECTATIONS

Now, a word about expectations. If you take up cycling to lose weight or shape up your shape, what can you expect?

Lou Hotton is five-foot-two worth of cycling muscle and drive. Her strong legs (in pink leopard-print tights) have stoked the tandem she shares with captain Patti Brehler to two impressive records.

On September 19, 1986, the Pink Leopard Cycling Team set a world record for the women's twenty-four-hour tandem event, clocking 422.518 miles. That means they powered their custom-made "bicycle-built-for-two" round and round a sixteen-mile course over rolling hills and through a night veiled in patches of heavy fog. As the hours wore on, the same hills seemed to steepen, and Patti and Lou's speed slipped from their initial 22 mph to an overall average of 17.6 mph. But that was anticipated, and they outperformed even their own goal of 400 miles.

About a year later, the Pink Leopards took on another challenge, cycling's best known "recreational" marathon event, the 750-mile Paris-Brest-Paris. Originating in 1891 and now held every four years, P-B-P is a bike race from Paris to the coast of Brittany and back. Thousands participate, and the clock runs nonstop.

The difficult route rises and falls with an estimated 1,250 climbs (especially challenging for tandems), but the French love a bicycle race, and even in the middle of the night onlookers cheer by the roadside. Lou and Patti, shown on TV and featured in French newspapers as the only women's tandem team, garnered special attention from spectators. Even the press described Patti and Lou as exuberant, despite managing a mere four hours' sleep over three days. Understandably the event remains Lou's favorite. They finished in seventy-nine hours, forty-three minutes, and were greeted with kisses and a huge bouquet as the first women's tandem team ever to complete P-B-P. At this writing, their record still stands.

A former marathon runner turned cyclist, Lou Hotton is in shape. She not only bikes; she runs, swims, plays soccer, skis in winter, and works out with weights. With all that exercise, if anybody can sculpt the perfect athletic body, it ought to be Lou. So how does she feel about the results?

Her answer surprised me. To my survey question about whether cycling exercise and nutritious, balanced meals suffice for maintaining a satisfactory weight, the forty-something ultra-distance cyclist and mother of two checked "yes." In the margin she added, "Pretty much—although sometimes my expectations are unrealistic."

OK, let's talk about expectations. We're in this sport for the exhilaration of riding out in the fresh air and the companionship that goes along with it. We like to see what we can do—maybe not on Lou's level, but we enjoy meeting our own challenges and noting our progress. No doubt we expect certain health benefits. And inevitably some of us expect to work some change in our appearance. Usually that means losing weight and firming up.

But expectations, as Lou pointed out, aren't always realistic. And sometimes as little as five or ten pounds mean the difference between liking our bodies and feeling that they are somehow unacceptable.

WOMEN AND BODY IMAGE

My point is not simply that one woman might have unrealistic expectations. The expectations of an entire society regarding women and body image have become distorted. We now have a mass obsession among women with food and thinness.

In a consumer age in which women's bodies are constantly being utilized to sell goods and girls are weaned on MTV, we are pressured from early in life to regard appearance as currency for getting what we want. It's a world of mixed images: A female can be anything she wants, a female must look perfect. Advertising holds every part of the body up to scrutiny and dictates the image—an insidious campaign to make us feel bad and encourage us, product by product, to buy back our sagging confidence. And one body image only is sold to us as if body size and type were a hemline we could raise or lower at will.

The notion of an ideal body type is nothing new. The flat-chested flapper shaped the image of the 1920s. From the thirties through the fifties, we needed voluptuousness and curves á la Marilyn Monroe.

Then the modern ideal began to shrink. The sixties brought us Twiggy in the fashion world and the youth rebellion. Advertising capitalized, pairing thinness with the struggle against aging. In the seventies, as women demanded a larger role in the workplace and comparable pay, fashion demanded that we shrink further.

Then fitness boomed: The perfect body needed muscles, definition. Before implants became clearly dangerous, models sprouted breasts on super slim bodies. Now as we near the turn of the century, models look waiflike again, and the average model weighs 23 percent less than the average woman, compared to 8 percent less a generation ago.

With these images ever more pervasive, we've seen a disturbing increase in anorexia and bulimia among young women, some of them on their way toward a death wish revealed in a mid-nineties *Esquire* poll: Half of the eighteen- to twenty-five-year-old women polled said they'd rather be dead than fat. Meanwhile, normal-weight adolescent and preadolescent girls, suffering a crisis in self-confidence, take up crash dieting and purging.

A SANER PERSPECTIVE, PLEASE

In this short space it's easy to oversimplify the issue. But expectations about weight control need to be put into perspective. If you want to lose weight and firm up while cycling, that may happen. And if it does, I hope you will feel as good about it as the women whose comments introduced the chapter.

At the same time, why not accept that a range of body types can be healthy and attractive? Let us find joy in our sport, improve our fitness level, feel better, and generate more energy for the things we want to do throughout the day. These more realistic and worthwhile aims seem to be shared by many of the women who take up cycling and stick with it, my survey suggests.

Survey Findings: Reasons for Involvement with Cycling

Respondents were asked to check off their reasons for taking up cycling and keeping it up. "Fitness," chosen by 84.7 percent of the women, ranked highest. "Weight control," selected by 45.8 percent, ranked only fourth.

84.7%	Fitness
73.7%	Recreation, seeing the countryside
46.5%	An activity to enjoy with friends or club
45.8%	Weight control
36.1%	Cycle touring
25.3%	Because spouse or significant other rides
24.1%	Local transportation, commuting
12.8%	Racing

"As women we need to move away from what a sport can do for our appearance and into a pure appreciation for how our preferred activity makes us feel," writes one very perceptive cyclist. "Only if we accept that form follows function will we have the freedom to search for and discover the sport that is uniquely right for us as an individual."

A point well made. And Karen Dowie from Des Moines, Iowa, illustrates it beautifully. "The best part of biking is my self-confidence," she writes. "All my life I've had a short, stocky body—very muscular. I've always hated my build. Finally I found a sport I'm built for! My large, powerful legs are great for passing all kinds of cyclists on hills," she observes, and she should know, after having ridden the popular cross-Iowa ride (known as RAGBRAI) with about 10,000 other cyclists. And Iowa does have hills.

"I love hills," Karen goes on. "The best part of my ride is hills, the bigger the better. If my muscles aren't burning at the top of a hill, it wasn't challenging enough.

"Biking has done wonders for my self-concept. I've finally found a sport that 'fits' me and I'm good at!"

Building Fitness

By now you've familiarized yourself with your new bike or one languishing in your garage, you've established the beginnings of good technique and refreshed your memory on the rules of the road. To continue to progress quickly, it's time to add some structure to your program.

GO-FOR-IT GOALS

A satisfying goal, in cycling as in anything else, is one you think you can meet but that requires stretching yourself a little to accomplish. It should be performance-related and specific, so you know when you've met it. And it should fit your idea of cycling fun and accomplishment. So be creative: You don't have to center on speed or on competing with anyone else. Consider, for example, Amy Hubbard's goal in her first year of riding near Syracuse, New York:

Last year I promised myself I'd cycle to Pratt's Falls, a local park, and back before summer's end. Though only twenty-six miles, it would be my longest ride and a new destination. There's something a little scary about riding to a new place. But then bicycling in general is a real adventure—on a small scale, with small delights and surprises. Afterward I feel I've really accomplished something.

On this early Sunday morning a storm threatened, but I decided to go anyway, telling myself I could always turn back or find shelter.

Leaving town, I bought bagels at a drugstore that opens early on weekends. On Woodchuck Road I passed three deer who were as startled to see me as I was to see them. I came upon a deserted green field canopied with brightly striped tents (the site, I later learned, of a fair about to take place).

At last at the falls, I ate a bagel and then headed home. En route I had a dazzling view of a local lake as I sped down a steep hill.

Considered singly, these things might not seem like much, but it was all new to me. This sense of being able to try something new and succeed spills over into other parts of my life. It's great!

Many cyclists like having a big goal to climax the riding season—something to work toward. I do. Typically I'll sign up early in the season for a big group ride, a week-long bicycle tour, or even a triathlon set to run in August or September. It's no coincidence that, in the United States, September is Century Month, with many clubs holding these 100-mile challenge rides.

Meanwhile, you need a series of goals to meet throughout the season, for a regular success "fix" and a gauge of improvement. These short-term goals should be compatible with a gradual increase in mileage, so that your endurance builds naturally and you don't ask too much of yourself too soon. The year I trained for my first European cycle tour, one of my intermediate goals was to ride alone from my city to another (about fifty-five miles) on a Saturday, carrying clothes I needed for a weekend visit with my parents; they had indulgently promised to drive me and my bicycle home afterwards. Like Amy I enjoyed the adventure. It involved map reading and finding my way along surprisingly scenic back roads. I didn't even mind that it rained most of the way; I got to try out my new rain suit.

Elite cyclists also confirm the importance of intermediate goals. Coach and former racer Connie Carpenter Phinney says that as she came up through the ranks, she set goals a week or a month ahead. Not until she neared the top in 1982 did she let herself dream of the gold medal, which she won in the '84 Olympics.

Having well-thought-out goals needn't rule out spontaneity, though, as Toni's example proves. Toni Childs-Gray of Sacramento, California, had just been introduced to a "terrific guy," a keen cyclist like herself. He asked her to join him for a ride and picked a devilishly hilly route. Toni says:

I think I surprised him by being able to keep up until the last killer hill. I really struggled but made it.

A week later he asked me to ride again on the same course. This time I was prepared. I'd worked on hills all week. You should have seen the look on his face as I called, "On your left," and passed him near the top! From then on it was a sweet ride downhill to the jacuzzi.

I suggest you set a goal for each month of this season. For new cyclists here are a few ideas:

- First month: Explore your area and develop three different routes you like. Cycle at least twice a week. Invite a friend to share some rides with you.
- Second month: Find a local cycling club or other group that welcomes new cyclists on short rides and join them on one.
- Third month: Treat yourself to a biking weekend in some area you'd enjoy discovering. Pick an organized tour with pleasant lodgings and low daily mileage, no more than thirty-five miles on the road or twenty off-road.
- Fourth month: Select a challenging organized ride that strikes your fancy. Prove what you can do.

INCREASING YOUR AEROBIC CAPACITY

A few principles lay the foundation for any conditioning program. Once you understand them, you can tailor the suggestions that follow to meet your needs. If, for example, your interests are divided between cycling and other sports, you may decide to substitute other aerobic activities for some cycling sessions.

All cycling training programs begin with *aerobic* conditioning. That is, you set a moderate pace at which your muscles can be fueled by the oxygen you're burning. Racers resuming training after a brief winter layoff start with many miles of steady, aerobic riding in low-to-medium gears before they sharpen up with more demanding speedwork. For non-competitive cyclists as well, such conditioning develops endurance while it strengthens muscles and joints.

Finding your heart rate. To ride aerobically, you want to spin a brisk cadence at a steady pace, raising your heart rate high enough to create a training effect but not so high that you wear yourself out too quickly.

How fast is that? After a while you'll be able to tell simply by how you feel. You should sense your rate of breathing increase, but you shouldn't feel so breathless that you can't talk. Casual cyclists may find this "talk test" a sufficient guideline and not concern themselves with formulas or pulse taking.

However, many people prefer to have some numbers to go by. There are numerous formulas for estimating a *target heart-rate zone*. No one system works for everybody, but for folks who have been inactive and need safe guidelines for improving fitness, here's one that the American Heart Association and the National Heart, Lung, and Blood Institute suggest in their booklet, *Exercise and Your Heart: A Guide to Physical Activity* (1993).

To figure your *maximum heart rate (MHR)*, the fastest your heart can beat, subtract your age from 220. To attain fitness benefits without overstressing your cardiovascular system, plan to exercise between 50 to 75 percent of MHR. Early on, don't push yourself much above the 50 percent level. As your conditioning improves, work up gradually toward the 75 percent level. After six months or so of regular cycling, extend the upper limit of your target heart zone to 85 percent of MHR if you feel ready and comfortable to do so. (This 85 percent figure does not appear on the chart below, but you can easily calculate it.)

For anyone on medication for hypertension, experts warn that some of these medicines reduce MHR; thus, your target heart zone may need to be lowered. Check with your health-care practitioner to be sure.

Exercise and Your Heart provides this chart for convenience:

Age	Target HR Zone 50–75%	Average Maximum Heart Rate 100%
20 years	100–150 beats per min.	200
25 years	98–146 beats per min.	195
30 years	95–142 beats per min.	190
35 years	93–138 beats per min.	185
40 years	90–135 beats per min.	180
45 years	88–131 beats per min.	175
50 years	85–127 beats per min.	170
55 years	83–123 beats per min.	165
60 years	80–120 beats per min.	160
65 years	78–116 beats per min.	155
70 years	75–113 beats per min.	150

Reproduced with permission. *Exercise and Your Heart,* 1993 ©American Heart Association

Individuals already fit from other forms of aerobic activity will probably find those figures too low for efficient conditioning. Depending on your perceived exertion, you could begin training at the higher end of the target heart zone given above for your age group. Or you might prefer to calculate your target zone based on a guideline that exercise physiologists call the *Karvonen formula.* This formula, like any other, is an approximation.

You'll notice that the suggested lower end of the target heart zone in this formula is 60 percent of MHR, a safe minimum level that should provide conditioning benefits.

Step 1. Subtract your age from 220 to compute your maximum heart rate (MHR).

Step 2. Subtract your resting pulse (see box) from your MHR.

Step 3. Multiply that figure by .60, then add your resting pulse rate, to calculate the lower limit of your target heart zone.

Step 4. Multiply that same figure from step 2 by .85, then add your resting pulse rate, to calculate the upper limit of your target heart zone.

220 – your age = MHR
MHR – resting pulse x .60 + resting pulse = lower limit
MHR – resting pulse x .85 + resting pulse = upper limit

Learn to Take Your Resting Pulse

Your resting pulse is one indicator of your fitness. Racers typically take their resting pulse each morning and record it in their training diaries. You can, too. Over time you should see a gradual lowering of your resting pulse as your fitness improves.

Resting pulse is usually taken just after waking in the morning while still lying quietly in bed. Take your pulse for fifteen seconds and multiply by four to determine your resting pulse for one minute.

For example, let's say Jennifer, 30, has a resting pulse of 77.

220 − 30 = 190 (Jennifer's MHR)
190 − 77 x .60 + 77 = 145 bpm (beats per minute)
190 − 77 x .85 + 77 = 173 bpm

Jennifer's target heart zone is between 145 and 175 bpm. She should achieve training benefits if she keeps her heart rate within that range as she rides. Theoretically, she'd improve more quickly if she trains in the upper portion of that range on some of her rides. However, she must also be guided by which level of exertion feels comfortable to maintain.

If both of these formulas seem way off, another way to arrive at a maximum heart rate—aside from being tested at a sports-medicine facility—is to note the highest heart rate you reach when maxing out on a long climb. However, don't try this if you have been sedentary.

How do you know your heart rate when riding? Many racers—like America's Olympic bronze medalist Susan DeMattei—train with a heart-rate monitor. Preparing for mountain bike racing season, Susan would typically do two medium-hard endurance workouts a week, one on the road and one on the trail. She'd wear her heart monitor to keep her pace constant. "If cross-training," she adds, "you can wear your monitor and run your workout, or cross-country ski it in the off-season." Many recreational cyclists also use cycle computers with a heart monitor.

Some riders manage instead by taking an exercise pulse. If you can ride no-handed, you can take a pulse at your wrist, which is preferable, or, keeping one hand on the bar, take a pulse at your neck while coasting briefly during a workout. Press your neck lightly, just enough to feel the pulsations. Use your fingers, as the thumb has a pulse of its own. Take the pulse for six seconds only, then multiply by ten to obtain your rate per minute.

If you feel shaky trying it while moving, stop your bike and immediately take your pulse at your wrist for six seconds.

Quickening your cadence (rpm). You've been working on cadence, so by now you shouldn't look as if you're pedaling in slow motion. A lively cadence raises your heart rate, makes your legs more supple, and helps you avoid sore knees that can result from pushing too big a gear. On-road, try for a cadence of 80 rpm, or 90 if you can manage it; off-road, aim for 60 to 80 rpm for cruising.

If you haven't treated yourself to a computer with a cadence function yet, you might want to: it lets you check your rpm frequently. You'd be surprised how your pedal speed can lag when you aren't thinking about it. Or wear a watch that shows the seconds. Count revolutions of one pedal for fifteen seconds and multiply by four to get your rpm.

Do you ride with a friend? From time to time, on the call of "count," both of you count your cadence for fifteen seconds. Don't cheat by suddenly speeding it up; you want to know what you're habitually doing. If her cadence tends to be closer to the desired rpm than yours, then watch her and try to match her cadence.

Such practice goes best on level terrain or gently rolling hills. On bigger climbs your cadence will drop as you run out of low gears to shift into. Remember to choose gears that will allow the desired cadence. If you feel the need to coast on level terrain to rest your legs, gear down.

A fast pedaling rate may feel unnatural at first. If you have difficulty keeping your upper body still as you spin your legs, make a conscious effort not to bounce around.

Now, about a few other equipment matters that can affect cadence: First, if your legs rub the sides of your saddle as you pedal, your saddle may be too wide and need replacing.

Second, if you don't have toeclips and straps or clipless pedals, think about adding them because they make pedaling more efficient. Good cyclists pedal "round," but without a system to fasten your shoe on the pedal, you can only push away and down. In cycle speak we call that "pedaling squares." Efficient riders also pull up on their pedals. To have a brisk and smooth pedaling cadence, you must be able to pedal "round." Once you get toeclips or clipless pedals, you will delight in a new sense of oneness with your bike and discover you have new power on the hills.

Admittedly, the thought of fastening your feet onto the pedals may cause you some concern about falling over because you can't get your feet free. And it seems to happen to everybody once—sooner or later. Usually you bruise your ego and that's about it.

On the other hand, holding the shoe on the pedal prevents another possible mishap—having your foot slip off the pedal, with the painful result that the pedal catches you in the back of the heel as it comes around. This might even make you lose it and crash.

Racers absolutely require pedal binding systems. Otherwise, for example, a road or track racer couldn't keep her feet on the pedals in a sprint, since she's spinning anywhere from 120 to 180 rpm. Even as a nonracer, I can't imagine riding with nothing securing my feet to the pedals. Most experienced cyclists say the same thing.

If you choose to start out with toeclips and straps, which are inexpensive, you can wear the straps loose enough to pull your foot out, until you learn to remember you're wearing them. Experienced cycle-commuters who use toeclips often keep the straps loose for stop-and-go riding in town. Off-road, I routinely wear my straps loose for a quick exit on a tricky section of trail; I recommend this approach for newbies. You can graduate to clipless later as your skills improve.

It Happens . . .

Some accidents are just funny. After a long ride a friend and I reached an intersection controlled by a traffic light. It was red for us. We stopped and did track stands, waiting for our arrow. Then boom! My friend fell over. He just lay there like a turtle on his back, both feet still fastened into his clipless pedals and his bike salvaged in the air. I laughed so hard I fell right on top of him. And there we both lay in the middle of a busy intersection on our backs, laughing hysterically! —Maripat Boland, Norman, Oklahoma

---

Here's the secret for slipping into your toeclips or clipping in without wobbling as you start out. Before mounting up, put one foot in, then step down on the pedal as you always do. Seat yourself on the saddle and pedal a few revolutions before trying to engage the other foot. Having this momentum helps you keep your balance.

Now to pedal "round," visualize this: At the top of the pedal stroke, extend your leg forward from the knee. As your foot moves down, gradually add power from the thigh. Keep pressure smooth and even. Just before the bottom of the stroke, start bending your leg at the knee and pull back on the pedal; the movement is like scraping mud off your shoe on an old-fashioned boot scraper. As the pedal travels upward, you don't have to pull up very hard (except ascending a hill). Let your leg float up in a smooth motion.

Begin gradually. What this means in terms of miles and pace will vary with each person. Start with short distances and in moderate terrain so you don't feel wrung out and discouraged at the end of a ride. Allow your body, and especially your knees, to become accustomed to this new activity by using moderate gearing and gradually increasing in mileage. A good rule of thumb is to add to your weekly mileage by no more than 10 percent each week.

If you're new to cycling, begin with rides every other day at first, or three times a week. Commuting, if feasible, is an ideal way to work in some bike miles on a regular basis. After a week or so, you should feel ready to take at least a short ride five or six days a week if you want to. Allow yourself no less than one rest day per week.

Easy day/hard day. A widely accepted rule for everyone who rides almost daily is to alternate "hard" workout days with "easy" days, which let your body rest. In the beginning stages of conditioning, "hard" means longer distances. (Later on, it could also refer to efforts of higher intensity.) Take shorter rides on "easy" days.

For example, if you do your longest mileage over the weekend, then Monday and Friday are good choices for easy days. If you want to cycle a somewhat longer distance during the week, schedule it midweek. You'll build endurance more quickly if you vary the lengths of your rides this way. In fact, as soon as you feel up to it, make your long one twice the length of your regular training sessions.

Following such a plan, you can start with very low mileage and increase surprisingly quickly, as in this sample schedule for a new cyclist. This suits most purposes—fitness and recreational riding as well as conditioning for touring.

	Miles/ Week-Day	Miles/ 5-day Week	Miles/ Weekend	Maximum Total/Week
April				
(Week 1)	2–5	10–25	6–12	37
(Week 2)	*	*	*	40
(Week 3)	*	*	*	45
(Week 4)	*	*	*	50
May				
(Week 1)	4–7	20–35	10–20	55
(Week 2)	*	*	*	60
(Week 3)	*	*	*	67
(Week 4)	*	*	*	73
June				
(Week 1)	6–9	30–40	20–40	80
(Week 2)	*	*	*	88
(Week 3)	*	*	*	97
(Week 4)	*	*	*	100
July				
(Week 1)	8–11	40–55	40–60	105
(Week 2)	*	*	*	115
(Week 3)	*	*	*	125
(Week 4)	*	*	*	137

*Increase mileage according to your preference within the established pattern to meet the week's total.

You don't have to increase every week if it seems like too much effort. You might hit a comfortable plateau that suits the time you have available.

Consider this schedule an illustration. Following these principles, you could base your training program on time rather than miles. This works especially well for cyclists who ride in hills one day and on the flats another. In this case, effort is more easily gauged if you measure it by the clock.

As noted earlier, should you wish to substitute some other aerobic workouts on easy cycling days—you and your friends also enjoy in-line skating, for example—do it. By using slightly different muscle groups you give your bike muscles a rest.

HOW TO STICK WITH IT

Look for scenic routes. And experiment with your daily schedule to find the time when you most enjoy riding. For some cyclists, like Vivien Turnbull of Harwich, Essex, England, that's while others are sleeping.

> *I ride in the early morning when few people are about, along country lanes where wildlife abounds or down to the beach, sparkling with the rising sun. On such a morning in late spring, I met a horseman. As we passed, he called out to me, "Look at that! Over there! The first swallow of summer!" I followed his gaze and there it was, swooping low over the glistening meadow.*

A moment like that can make your whole day.

Tell someone else your goal. When that person shares your expectations, you'll have two reasons to live up to them. Gail Johnson of Fergins Falls, Minnesota, took this idea a step further by involving her entire family:

> *During my first summer of serious cycling I would ride once a week to my parents' house, twenty-seven miles away, and take my younger brothers swimming. It would take two-and-a-half hours each way, quite a feat for me. It made for a rather full day, and I really felt good about myself. Nobody else in my family exercised at the time, so they were rather impressed. They also thought I was nuts, but they're coming around now.*

Keep a training diary. It's satisfying to see the miles add up. More important, your diary shows you how your body responds to training—the reason most racers keep one. Use a simple format and record the date, miles (or hours) ridden, and the weather. Add where you rode and with whom, and how you felt. If you time a workout to judge your progress, record that, too. Your very first entry for each day will probably be your resting pulse. You may want to add more details to describe special rides.

What can you learn from your diary? You'll see patterns. You may discover that an increase by several beats in your resting pulse means you're coming down with something, a cold perhaps, or the elevated pulse may correlate with a sudden increase in training mileage and a feeling of tiredness a few days later.

You may be surprised how much you can learn about your body from such a diary. Review it from time to time to see what seems to benefit your cycling most. And if one these days you suddenly feel as if you have cement in your tires, check your diary to see what might have you dragging.

Find a riding partner or partners. For most of us, myself included, cycling is more fun with company. Even if you're a self-starter, it's great to have somebody else to suggest meeting for a ride. You have extra motivation knowing you don't want to disappoint your partner by wimping out at the last minute. And on- or off-road, there's safety in numbers. Certainly out on a trail where you might otherwise be completely alone, a buddy comes in handy if you take a spill and need assistance.

Given a choice of companions to divide your training time with, you could do well to ride one day with someone a little faster than you so that you work harder. And, training with more experienced cyclists, you pick up better technique almost by osmosis. On another day train with someone at your own level. Unless you're the highly competitive type, playing catch-up all the time can be discouraging.

Adapting in the off-season. Especially as it gets dark earlier, many of us say the same thing: "But I can't ride three or four days during the week." There are ways around this obstacle.

We've talked about using commuting hours for cycling, which you can continue to do in the off-season by adding appropriate front and rear lights to your bike—required in all states in the United States after dark. Mount a good rechargeable headlight plus a battery-powered, flashing red taillight on your rig, as well as some reflective tape on your helmet, bike frame, crankarms, and rims. Add a reflective vest or jacket for extra insurance.

Or pedal indoors on a stationary bike, trainer, or rollers at home. Unless you can turn the heat way down, set up a big fan to blow air on you for cooling. Build strength and beat boredom by doing intervals (see chapter 17, "Fitter and Faster"). Motor to your favorite music or watch a cycling video; if you use headphones, keep the decibels down to avoid damaging your ears. You may be surprised how intense a workout like this can be, without tailwinds or hills to coast down. So don't automatically expect to spend as much time on an indoor trainer as you do on your outdoor rides. Listen to your body.

If you want to tap into some group energy, join a Spinning or other studio cycling class, where peer enthusiasm, the music, and the motivation of the instructor can rev up an indoor workout like you never thought possible. If you have access to a gym, you might want to pedal an exercise bike and then lift weights for strength training.

Especially in winter, many busy cyclists run during their lunch hours or before or after work instead of riding. Running doesn't use precisely the same muscles as cycling, but you'd get a good aerobic workout nonetheless. If this is your choice, begin with low running mileage—for example, two miles—and gradually increase to avoid overuse injury. Figure one mile of running is roughly equivalent to three miles on your bicycle. Some people prefer in-line skating, or walking briskly, swinging your arms.

Many bike racers pursue other sports, such as speed-skating or cross-country skiing, during the winter to give them a mental break from the intensity of cycling competition.

Get to know what motivates you. What puts me off might bring out the best in you. Consider the case of Karen Bell of Mystic, Connecticut:

After I took up cycling I began riding with competitive women in the area. Because of my pride, I seemed always to be in so much pain just to keep up, and sometimes I couldn't even do that. I read cycling magazines, dropped ten pounds, cross-trained with swimming, and developed a better attitude. A male cycling friend convinced me to try a time trial so I could gauge my improvement.

On time trial day I was only a little nervous. I'd been doing pretty well on the road for the last month, so I expected to fare OK. As it turned out, I took first place in the women's division. I even beat the two who used to drop me only four months before! As a full-time working mother, I felt well rewarded to be competitive with women who train all the time and are responsible only for themselves.

When a ride gets tough, remind yourself that you will improve. And find ways to measure your progress. Don't race against a stopwatch every session; that's too much pressure. But you might time yourself once a week or every other week on the same route and keep a record of it. Or take a gamble and enter the club's time trial. Who knows what you can do until you try?

Fueling the Engine

About seventy-five miles into a century, all my technique and form just fell apart. I'd been riding with a small group in a paceline, and then a couple of us were dropped. The least little hill was an ordeal, my cadence was slowing. No matter how hard I tried, I had no power, so I was shifting to lower and lower gears. I kept losing ground even to the friend who was riding with me—he'd wait for me from time to time at the top of a hill.

I was starting to wonder whether I could complete the 100 miles. Then I fished a cookie out of my pocket and ate it. In a few minutes things came together for me, and I finished strongly. –Ellen Dorsey, Bethlehem, Pennsylvania

Success in a challenging ride depends not only on training and comfort on your bike, but on something so seemingly simple as what and when you eat and drink. Here Ellen Dorsey has described the draining experience endurance athletes call "hitting the wall." In a way, it's like running out of gas. But savvy riders like Ellen know how to pick themselves up out of an energy slump—better yet, how to prevent one—and so will you. And this doesn't apply just to 100-mile efforts. For some, a challenging ride might be considerably shorter.

To continue the automobile analogy, not only must we fuel our muscles, but we have to be mindful of our cooling systems. We need to drink plenty to keep our fluid levels up. In this chapter we'll talk about these aspects of nutrition and the way training and exercise intensity affect how energy is burned, or *metabolized*.

FUNDAMENTALS OF GOOD NUTRITION

Properly fueling your engine begins with a well-balanced diet—the basis for good nutrition for sport and for promoting heart health and warding off cancer—a diet in which carbohydrates provide the majority of calories, with dietary fat kept reasonably low. This is also the smartest way to curb calories for weight loss.

While on the fundamentals, let's let the air out of a couple of myths about protein.

Myth 1: High-protein/low-carbohydrate diets are the path toward weight-loss. Among the problems posed by high-protein diets, protein in food is hard to get without taking in fat at the same time. Fat packs twice the calories of carbohydrates (9 calories per gram compared to 4).

Myth 2: Eating more protein enhances performance. True, athletes do need more protein than nonathletes. Active folks should take in 1.2 to 1.5 grams of protein daily per kilogram (2.2 pounds) of body weight. But the typical Western diet, even that of vegetarians if they eat nutrient-dense, complex carbohydrates, includes ample protein to build and repair muscles. And protein provides little energy during exercise. But a diet low in carbo robs us of energy needed for daily activities and for cycling.

Therefore, the first of three fundamentals for eating right is that almost half of the calories we take in must come from complex carbohydrates. Second, we ought to base our meals on whole foods as much as possible. Third, we should eat according to a food group plan, such as The Basic Five, that meets our needs for vitamins, minerals, fiber, and other good things.

According to sports nutritionist Ann Grandjean, Ed.D., a healthful regimen for the average person would break down as follows:

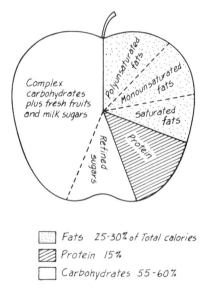

Fig. 13: Bite into this regime for good daily nutrition.

Complex carbohydrates plus fresh fruits and milk sugars

polyunsaturated fats
Monounsaturated fats
saturated fats
Protein
Refined sugars

Fats   25-30% of Total calories
Protein   15%
Carbohydrates   55-60%

•At least 55 percent carbohydrates, of which no more than 10 percent comes from refined sugars (table sugar, honey, jellies, etc.) and the remaining 45 percent or more comes from complex carbohydrates plus the sugars in milk and fresh fruits.

•15 percent protein.

•A maximum of 30 percent fat, of which 10 percent is polyunsaturated, 10 percent is monounsaturated, and 10 percent is saturated. Even better, limit dietary fat to 25 percent by eliminating half of the saturated fats. (In this case, total carbohydrate consumption would rise to 60 percent.)

The following definitions should clarify things:

Complex carbohydrates. These include the "starchy" foods—whole grain breads, cereals, pasta, dried beans of all kinds, rice, potatoes—plus vegetables. Rich in vitamins and minerals and good sources of fiber, these foods fill us up and help us feel satisfied. They're a great energy source for exercise, and they are not fattening—until we slather butter or margarine on our bread or make our potatoes into french fries. Well-planned vegetarian meals (which provide excellent nutrition) draw heavily on complex carbohydrates.

Simple sugars. *Monosaccharides* occur naturally in fruits and honey; the slightly more complex *disaccharides* include table sugar. They're easily consumed and can provide athletes with a quick burst of energy to stretch performance, as Ellen did during her century ride.

During the noncycling parts of your day, concentrate on complex carbohydrates for healthful meals and snacks.

Whole foods. Along with structuring your food plan in the above proportions, nutritionists urge us to eat mostly *whole foods*—foods as fresh from the garden as possible—to make the most of the vitamins, minerals, and fiber they supply. For example, lightly steamed fresh asparagus is more nutritious and appealing than the same vegetable out of a can.

OK, if you're like me, you don't grow your own broccoli, green beans, and asparagus for good reasons, like lack of space and time. But you can buy veggies and fruits fresh from a farmers' market or grocery produce section and find a few quick, easy ways to prepare them that you enjoy. That doesn't mean it's criminal to open a can of something once in a while (canned, whole tomatoes for cooking are a regular staple on my pantry shelf), but a daily regimen of supermarket microwavable entrées, canned veggies, and fast food on the run can provide us with fewer nutrients and more fats than do fresh fruits and vegetables and our own home cooking.

The Basic Five. Variety is the soul of good nutrition. If you build your meals from the five food groups of the Food Guide Pyramid, you'll select foods of sufficient variety to provide the vitamins and minerals, proteins and carbohydrates you need. The U.S. Department of Agriculture's Center for Nutrition Policy and Promotion recommends these guidelines as "a pattern for daily food choices" for individuals who regularly eat foods from each group.

Their suggested serving sizes are included; note that some may be smaller than your normal portions. For example, those six to eleven servings of grain products sound like a lot, until you consider that a half cup of cooked pasta counts as a serving. If you like pasta as I do, you probably don't stop at a mere half cup. When counting servings, credit yourself with the number of servings that reflects your portion sizes at mealtime.

For the average woman (I don't presume to advise the diabetic or hypoglycemic individual), the following comprise a balanced diet:

- *Grain Products Group (bread, cereal, pasta, rice)*. Six to eleven servings daily, counting as a single serving 1 slice of bread; half of a bagel; 1 ounce of ready-to-eat cereal; or ½ cup of cooked cereal, rice, or pasta. These are the complex carbohydrates you need. Select whole-grain bread (rich in fiber and B vitamins); for a spread, a little jam is no sin. You can serve pasta with low-fat sauces that win raves. This group isn't fattening unless you make it that way with butter, gravy, or other high-fat toppings.
- *Vegetable Group*. Three to five servings daily, e.g., 1 cup of raw leafy vegetables; ½ cup of other vegetables, cooked or chopped raw; or ¾ cup vegetable juice. Veggies provide valuable fiber. Dark green, leafy ones provide nutrients—like vitamin A, folacin (a B vitamin that helps to make red blood cells and hemoglobin), iron, and magnesium—that tend to be low in most diets. Deep yellow vegetables also are rich in vitamin A and beta-carotene.

Starchy vegetables, like potatoes, corn, green peas, and dried peas and beans, offer B6, folacin, iron, and magnesium.

•*Fruit Group.* Two to four servings per day, e.g., 1 medium apple, banana, or orange; ½ cup of chopped, cooked, or canned fruit; or ¾ cup of fruit juice. Fruits are high in fiber and vitamins C and A. For a good start on the day, top a bowl of whole-grain cereal with sliced bananas, peaches, or berries and pour on skim milk; it tastes so good I don't even add sugar.

•*Milk Group (milk, cheese, and yogurt).* Two to three servings a day, e.g., 1 cup of milk or cottage cheese, 8 ounces of yogurt, 1½ ounces of natural cheese, 2 ounces of processed cheese. This group provides much of the calcium most of us take in. Skim milk and skim milk products—cottage cheeses and low- or nonfat yogurt—are lowest in fat and thus most highly recommended; extra servings of skim milk and fat-free yogurt are an excellent way to up your calcium intake without adding fat to your diet, says the U.S.D.A. The vitamin D typically added to milk enhances calcium absorption. Dairy products provide an important, but not the only, source of calcium, an essential nutrient for healthy bones, discussed later in this chapter.

•*Meat and Beans Group (meat, poultry, fish, dry beans, eggs, and nuts).* Two to three servings daily, e.g., 2 to 3 ounces of cooked lean meat, poultry, or fish; ½ cup of cooked dry beans or 1 egg counts as 1 ounce of lean meat; two tablespoons of peanut butter or ⅓ cup of nuts is equivalent to 1 ounce of meat. This group provides protein to build and repair muscle. To minimize saturated fats, choose lean cuts of meat and skinless poultry. Some fish— tuna (canned, in water), cod, haddock, flounder, red snapper, halibut, rainbow trout—are as lean or leaner. *Legumes* (dried peas, beans, and lentils) have even less fat, and the fat in legumes is unsaturated. If legumes are new to you, a good vegetarian cookbook will show how to turn dried peas and beans into flavorful, inexpensive dishes that diversify menus.

The U.S.D.A. recognizes a sixth group, *Fats, Sweets, and Alcoholic Beverages,* which provides little nutrition and should be consumed in moderation. (For further information on the dietary guidelines, write to: The Center for Nutrition Policy and Promotion, 1120 20th St. N.W., North Lobby Suite 200, Washington, DC 20036, for a copy of *Nutrition and Your Health—Dietary Guidelines for Americans.*)

Now that we've laid out the basics of good nutrition, let's move on to what cyclists need to know to enhance performance.

EXERCISE AND YOUR ENERGY SYSTEMS

Just how are our human engines fueled for cycling? By now you've learned that you can ride all out for a relatively short distance or cycle farther at a slower speed. In pacing yourself like this you call on the appropriate energy system for the type of effort you've chosen to make.

Any exercise lasting more than about two minutes draws on two fuels for the muscles, *glucose* and *free fatty acids*, both of which require *oxygen*, brought to the muscle via the bloodstream, for the fuel to be utilized. Where do these fuels come from?

Glucose comes mainly from *glycogen*, which is stored carbohydrate. At most our bodies hold about three to four pounds of this fuel in reserve, most of it in the muscles, with about ¾ of a pound stored in the liver. The precise amount of glycogen stockpiled in the body depends on how much carbohydrate we eat. Cutting down on carbohydrate in the diet reduces the amount of this precious fuel we have to draw on.

By contrast, free fatty acids come from the body's fat stores—which we could never deplete, no matter how long we exercise. We needn't try to increase the fat content in our diets because we have plenty to meet energy needs. If only we could burn enough fatty acids to fuel the entire effort, our endurance would greatly increase. But it doesn't work that way.

Exercise intensity—how hard you're working—figures into fuel selection. At or below 50 percent of maximum effort (measured in terms of oxygen consumption or VO_2max), fat serves as the chief source of fuel, with glycogen used in lesser proportion. As this leisurely pace is increased to above 70 percent of VO_2max—for example, in a training ride or a race—glycogen becomes the main fuel.

If you ride about an hour and a half at this faster pace, glycogen is gradually depleted and the body has only fat for fuel. However, because fatty acids require more oxygen for metabolizing than glycogen does, the transition is not easily made. Fatigue sets in, muscles stiffen, and thinking may get hazy as even the brain runs out of glucose.

STAYING POWER

Here's how the informed cyclist can fight fatigue during endurance efforts and boost output during hard-paced events as short as one hour.

Conditioning. A gradual conditioning program that includes long rides, as recommended in chapter 10, "Building Fitness," helps muscles improve their ability to use free fatty acids as fuel. The body slowly adapts so that the trained cyclist can burn fat for energy at a higher work intensity than an untrained rider. As the season progresses, you should notice enhanced endurance as fat metabolism becomes easier.

Energy in your pocket. Ellen's well-timed cookie, a bunch of grapes, or other carbo-containing snacks can give a boost as your energy starts to flag, after you've ridden for an hour or so. During her 100-mile event Ellen probably should have been nibbling regularly all along, following the maxim in cycling: "Eat before you are hungry; drink before you are thirsty."

This is why cycling jerseys have pockets. In a racing tradition that goes back decades, a rider's support crew would hand up a *musette,* a cloth bag with a long strap containing fruit, cookies, sometimes bite-size sandwiches; the racer would slow to grab the musette, sling its strap over a shoulder, and pedal on, stuffing the carbo-rich snacks in the back jersey pockets.

The food in today's musette, however, comes as much from the lab as from the kitchen. Though more expensive than cookies and fruit, a racer's favorite carbo gels and energy bars require no advance peeling and wrapping and are sold in carefully measured single-serving packets and lots of flavors. All these goos and bars require is to be washed down with several gulps of water so the body can utilize them efficiently. Riders can also imbibe liquid energy in the form of a sports drink.

Whether you decide to buy your pocket fuel at the grocery store or get the engineered products at your bike shop, a little math can help you figure how much carbohydrate you should take in per hour to prolong performance in an endurance event. According to cyclist and nutritionist Susan I. Barr, Ph.D., the guideline is ⅓ gram of carbo per pound of your body weight per hour. For a 120-pound cyclist, that's 40 grams per hour. Figure in both energy drink, if you use one, and snacks. To see how this works for you, consider starting with a lesser amount; observe how your body responds and increase until you find the optimum level. If you go the fat-free cookies and fruit route, see the "Fresh Fruit as Fuel" list for carbo grams and check prepared foods' labels.

Fresh Fruit as Fuel

Fruit	Grams of Carbohydrate
Apple, 2½-inch diam.	15.3
Banana, large, 9¾-inch by 1⁷⁄₁₆-inch diam.	30.2
Kiwifruit, 1	9.0
Navel orange, 2⅘-inch diam.	15.5
Pear, 3-inch x 2½-inch diam.	25.4
Raisins, ¼ cup	33.0
Seedless grapes, ½ cup	14.5
Sweet cherries, whole, ½ cup	10.2
Tangerine, 2⅜-inch diam.	10.0

How do you know what to eat or drink and when? It depends on what will digest well for you. During a hard-paced event, carbohydrates (energy drinks, gels, and fruits) probably work better, says former pro Davis Phinney. For a quick boost when you're feeling wasted, try an energy gel; all-carbo, it contains both simple and complex carbohydrates for fast-acting and long-lasting energy. By contrast, the bars have lots of carbohydrates plus added nutrients such as protein and fat, which can slow the metabolic process for up to an hour.

During events when the exertion level fluctuates, like on hilly or fast group rides, you might munch an energy bar for sustenance when the pace slackens. Three or four PowerBars plus some fruit and drink fueled Davis on long race days, he says, when he was one of the 7-Eleven team that introduced the new energy bars to the peloton during the '86 Tour de France.

Even if you don't race or ride centuries, like the pros you will learn from experience when to eat and which foods taste best while riding and deliver needed energy. If you start off on what is, for you, a long ride, pop one of these snacks in your bike bag. Or have in mind a spot where you can buy something when you might need it.

One of my friends, Reg Tauke of Bath, Pennsylvania, remembers reaching the sixty-mile point of a ride in need of something to perk her up. "With only ten more miles to go," she recalls, "I probably would have made it OK. But I said to myself, 'I'm not enjoying this. I just don't have the energy to turn the pedals.' So I went into a gas station convenience store and bought a thirty-two-ounce cola—one of those mini-mart specials—and drank it. In a few minutes I was fine."

The caffeine/sugar combo in her cola is an old pro's trick often used near the end of a race to coax extra performance from tiring legs. Studies have shown that caffeine not only stimulates alertness but also shuttles more fatty acids into the bloodstream. This favors fat burning, which spares glucose and glycogen, and lengthens the amount of time a cyclist can ride before hitting the wall.

Beware, however, that caffeine's *diuretic effect* (increased urination) may require a pit stop and could hasten dehydration. Reg's timing, toward the end of her long event, avoided those potential problems. Another way to experiment with more modest amounts of caffeine is to try an energy gel, bar, or drink that lists caffeine, cola nut, or guarana among the ingredients. If, on the other hand, you wish to avoid caffeine, you should also be checking labels.

To sum up, when you're riding all day, you'll digest frequent, small snacks more easily than one or two belly-buster meals. If you choose energy gels or bars, drink water with them. Avoid high-fat foods, which take longer to digest. Experiment to see what works best for you.

More miles to the gallon. The most important ingredient you can put in your water bottle is water. As noted above, however, you can add a little sugar, in one form or another, to that water for rides when you think your glycogen might run low. I like to fill my water bottle halfway with orange juice, add ice cubes, and top off with water for an inexpensive, pleasant-tasting homemade energy drink. Or you can buy a commercially prepared sports drink. Look for one with a 6 to 8 percent concentration of carbohydrate. Although there are drinks with higher concentrations, the extra carbo may cause nausea for some riders. Even within the 6 to 8 percent range, you might discover that you tolerate a 6 percent drink better.

The type of carbohydrate used may also affect how your body handles it. Writing for *Bicycling* magazine, Susan Barr points out that a sports drink should provide mainly glucose, since that is the fuel your muscles utilize. "Starch, maltodextrins, glucose polymers, and glucose provide 100 percent glucose, while sucrose and high-fructose corn syrup, often included to improve palatability, provide about 50 percent glucose." A formulation that has fructose as the first ingredient may cause digestive problems because the fructose is absorbed slowly and pulls water into the gastrointestinal tract. Experiment with the drink when training, rather than during an important event. You may want to try several different drinks in order to find the one that agrees with you and tastes best.

As noted earlier, you can figure your sport drink needs based on a simple formula (⅓ gram of carbohydrate per pound of body weight per hour), adjusted for any snacks you consume. Begin sipping your drink immediately before the event and continue regularly throughout.

Another tip: Don't mistake these sports fluids for "health" drinks to slurp down any time of day under any circumstances, especially if you're counting calories. These drinks are designed for use while exercising to prolong endurance. If you just want to sip something healthy, how about carrot juice or water?

Fueling short, hard efforts. Until recently we were advised to save our energy drinks for events stretching ninety minutes or longer. Now experts tell us that we can boost performance in hour-long events if they climax with a finishing sprint or otherwise require intermittent spurts of high-intensity effort.

Writing in *VeloNews,* sports nutritionist/bike racer Monique Ryan, R.D., cites new studies that simulate shorter race conditions—research by Ed Coyle, Ph.D., and another study by exercise physiologists at Springfield College in Massachusetts. For sprinting we draw on our fast-twitch muscle fibers, which can become glycogen-depleted even though our slow-twitch endurance fibers might still have plenty, she reminds us. "Fast-twitch fibers . . . primarily use muscle glycogen, produce lactic acid rapidly, and fatigue quickly. But fast-twitch fibers can also synthesize muscle glycogen more rapidly. You just have to give them some glucose to work with." In these studies trained cyclists rode hard for fifty minutes (at 80 percent of VO_2max); in a simulated sprint finish, those who'd been hydrating with a carbohydrate-electrolyte drink outperformed those who'd drunk water.

Monique Ryan sums up: "Consider using [sports drinks] for short, high-intensity training and racing. They're relatively inexpensive, legal, safe, and convenient—and you already know how to use them."

Carbo loading. Cyclists preparing for endurance events can store extra glycogen by *carbo loading*—increasing carbohydrate intake up to 75 percent of total calorie-intake for three days just prior to competition. By emphasizing grains, starchy vegetables, fruits, and low-fat milk you can meet protein and other nutrient needs while loading in the needed complex carbohydrates. A few extra slices of toast with jam would also be in the spirit of things.

The usual approach is to do a fairly strenuous ride five to seven days before the endurance event. Ride hard in the time allotted (even a good, intense hour could be enough) so that toward the end your legs feel pretty tired. Your last hard training session before the big event uses most of your existing glycogen stores so that during the three days of loading, your muscles hunger for glycogen and really pack it in.

On the days after this ride, but before you begin loading, train moderately and eat normally. Then during those three carbo-loading days limit cycling to a few easy miles. Drink plenty of water during this time, as glycogen production requires water. In fact, it causes water to be stored in the body, for release later as glycogen is broken down during your endurance event. Don't be disturbed to notice yourself several pounds heavier as a result of loading; it is the water weight. (If you don't gain some weight, you're probably not storing glycogen.)

An hour or two before your event, top off your energy stores with something easily digested like a banana or an energy bar.

When should you carbo load? Don't bother for an event shorter than one hour because normal glycogen supplies should be ample. In contrast, century riders often carbo load, as do marathon runners.

Post-event. Once over the finish line, while you're collecting congratulations and slipping into your warmup jacket, pop the top on a recovery drink like Nitro Fuel or Boost Nutritional Energy Drink. The big ride has emptied your glycogen stores, and your muscles and liver are clamoring for a refill. You could just guzzle more of your on-bike-energy drink, but recovery drinks make better fuel at this point because they blend in some protein and fat. The protein starts repairing muscle while the glycogen gets packed away. Stage racers, bike tourists, or anyone else with day-after-day long rides should especially take advantage of this window of opportunity for restocking energy stores.

Rather sink your teeth into something? Chomp on an energy bar that includes some modest amounts of protein and fat, and down a cup or so of water with it.

BEATING DEHYDRATION

Whether you drink plain water or rely on the water in a sports drink, wet, wonderful water is the main thing a cyclist needs to avoid dehydration. That's especially true if weather is hot or, worse, hot and humid, as humidity makes us perspire even more. In both conditions the body can lose a great deal of water in sweat—as much as a couple of quarts or more per hour. We may not feel the perspiration on a bicycle because wind dries it as we ride. And thirst won't warn us in time. Wait until you feel thirsty, and you're already on the way to dehydration.

That can be dangerous. "I could have died if a motorist hadn't found me," says Janet Noll, speaking of the day the heat got her on a training ride. A Californian living in Palm Springs and an experienced cyclist, Janet knew the importance of staying hydrated and carried two water bottles on her bike. On this June day they weren't enough.

With temperatures routinely above 100 degrees that summer, Janet tried to start early on her rides—often by seven-thirty A.M. but always by nine.

That morning I started late for my two-hour ride and foolishly left my helmet behind. Several miles before the end I felt fatigued and stopped to refill my water bottles. I remember little after that, except that about a mile from my house a man found me lying in the street. I'd passed out on my bike. As he helped me up, my thinking was fuzzy. He offered to drive me home, but we had an awful time finding it although it wasn't far away. Even as we pulled up to the house, I wasn't sure I recognized it!

Janet was lucky. She had a good bit of road rash and a gash in her head that required twelve stitches in the emergency room, but she's here to tell the tale and to remind us to drink up.

Research shows that dehydration resulting in a 2 percent loss of body weight hampers the body's ability to regulate temperature and reduces aerobic endurance. Water losses of 5 percent of body weight cut the muscles' capacity for work by 20 to 30 percent. A dangerous rise in body heat can cause heatstroke and even death.

As a journalist covering cycling events with five-hour road-race stages, I've seen highly conditioned racers pass out on their bikes from heat exhaustion. I've stood around outside the "drug control" van, notebook in hand, for a half-hour and longer, while the parched stage winner inside drank glass after glass of water, still unable to urinate for the required drug test before being interviewed by the press.

These racers were men, whose events are longer than women's typically are. Nevertheless, it's possible to feel the effects of dehydration within ninety minutes of exercise on a hot day. Seasoned women racers know they, too, must make an effort to remain hydrated by drinking throughout the race.

"Even so," says Susan DeMattei, 1996 Olympic bronze medalist on the mountain bike, "during a tough event you can get caught up in not wanting to take your hands off the bars, so I make a point to do it. I have two bottle cages on my bike, and in a race I carry one bottle of water and have someone hand me another bottle partway through that contains flat Coke because that's palatable to me."

Like Susan, drink plenty and pay attention to what works for you. Remember, your body probably needs plain water in addition to an energy drink. Figure the amount of sport drink per hour you want to take in, then slurp enough water in addition to equal somewhere between 1 and 2½ standard (twenty ounce) water bottles per hour, depending on riding conditions. And start out well hydrated. If you do notice you've lost weight on a ride, from perspiration, weigh yourself before and after long rides to figure your personal sweat rate and increase your fluid intake to accommodate it.

Under a sizzling sun, if you use an energy drink and you don't seem to be hydrating as well as you think you should, check on the type of carbohydrate in your drink, as noted earlier. If switching brands doesn't fix it, dilute the drink with water and see if you have better results. If you choose plain water instead, when riding several hours in the heat, you could add a ⅛ to ¼ teaspoon of table salt (no more) to a large water bottle. This replaces salt lost in sweat, the most important of the electrolytes that sports drinks replenish. For shorter rides don't worry about salt; our normal diets contain plenty. Furthermore, with training, our bodies acclimatize and lose less salt in perspiration.

Don't take salt tablets, even for long days in the saddle. They deliver a much bigger dose of salt than anyone needs. If taken without water, salt tablets can hasten dehydration dangerously.

Know the signs of dehydration and *heat exhaustion* and take them seriously: If you feel confused, dizzy, as if you might faint, head-achey, or nauseous, or even (despite the heat) chills and goose bumps, you need lots of water and a cool place to sit or lie down.

If you don't drink water, body temperature can rise dramatically causing *heat stroke*. Sweating will stop even though you feel thirsty, and your muscles may cramp. You'll have trouble thinking and speaking clearly, and may lose consciousness. Heat stroke is life threatening. Should you observe these symptoms in yourself or a companion, get immediate emergency help.

Heat stroke need never happen, however. If you are sensitive to heat, ride in the cool, early part of the day. Wear lightweight clothing that breathes. And drink, drink, drink water—throughout the day—before, during, and after riding. If you do, it could help prevent other complaints women sometimes experience, such as bladder infections, which may be related to problems of dehydration.

Some riders need to take extra care. Cyclists who use blood pressure medication (which causes frequent urination) or diuretics may already be slightly dehydrated. Overweight riders should be aware that their bodies have less efficient cooling systems—fat works to keep heat in. Discuss any problems or questions with your doctor.

MEETING A WOMAN'S NEED FOR CALCIUM

A well-balanced diet of nutritious foods provides a good supply of most vitamins and minerals needed for athletic performance. Even with a good diet, however, calcium, necessary for muscle contraction as well as for building strong bones, may be in short supply. Many Americans, especially teens and women on reduced-calorie diets, don't take in enough of this essential mineral. As a result, calcium needed for daily activity is taken from their bones.

That's why insufficient calcium intake can put us at risk for osteoporosis, or bone-thinning. Current standards recommend 1,000 mg or more of calcium for women, or the equivalent of at least 3½ eight-ounce glasses of milk per day.

Other factors can increase loss of bone mass density:

- High caffeine consumption. Five to eight cups of coffee (or the caffeine equivalent in diet colas and tea) will increase the amount of calcium excreted in urine.
- Phosphoric acid in some cola.
- Using prescription medication. If taken for longer than one week, certain medicines may affect calcium balance, including some sedatives, antibiotics, steroids, some cardiovascular therapies, muscle relaxants, and oral antidiabetic drugs.
- High protein intake appears to increase bone loss.
- Excess alcohol consumption reduces calcium absorption.
- Cigarette smoking has been related to earlier menopause, when the protective effect of estrogen is lost.
- Genetic influences.
- Thin bone structure.
- Race. People of European or Asian descent have a significantly higher incidence of osteoporosis.

Calcium consumption is important during the teen years, when we accumulate about half of our adult bone mass. By about age twenty, our bones have attained mature size; however, they can still become denser and stronger if we provide sufficient calcium for them to absorb. Otherwise, bones can start thinning even before age forty.

Recognizing calcium's critical role, the Institute of Medicine at the National Academy of Sciences, which establishes the Recommended Dietary Allowances

High Marks for Calcium: A Sampling

Milligrams of Calcium

Milk, 8 oz. or 1 cup		Leafy Greens (cooked)	
Skim	302	Bok choy (from fresh), ½ cup	126
1% low-fat	300	Collards (from fresh), ½ cup	179
2% low-fat	297	Collards (from frozen), ½ cup	149
Whole	291	Kale (from fresh), ½ cup	103
Yogurt, low-fat, 8 oz. or 1 cup		Kale (from frozen), ½ cup	79
Plain	415	Turnip greens (from fresh), ½ cup	126
Fruit	345	Turnip greens (from frozen), ½ cup	98
Flavored	389	**Fish and Other Protein**	
Cheeses		Oysters, raw, 7–9	113
American, pasteurized, processed, 1 oz.	174	Salmon, with bones, 3 oz.	167
Cheddar, 1 oz.	204	Sardines, with bones, 3 oz.	372
Colby, 1 oz.	194	Shrimp, canned, 3 oz.	99
Monterey jack, 1 oz.	212	Dried beans, cooked, 1 cup	90
Mozzarella, 1 oz.	183	Bean curd (tofu)*, 4 oz.	145
Swiss, 1 oz.	272		
Cottage, 2% low-fat, 1 cup	154		

Source: National Dairy Council (U.S.A.)
*Only if processed with calcium sulfate

(RDAs), has set new, higher standards for females' calcium intake as follows:

- Ages 9–18:   1,300 mg
- Ages 19–50:   1,000 mg
- Ages 51–70+:   1,200 mg

These Dietary Reference Intakes (DRIs), created in 1997 to replace the old RDAs, are intended to promote bone strength at the different stages of life. Note that no distinctions have been made for women who are pregnant or breast-feeding. Drawing on new research, the panel of nutritionists refutes the conventional wisdom that pregnant and lactating women need extra calcium. Thanks to their better absorption of the mineral, the DRI for their age-group should provide enough, the experts say.

To meet our requirements, nutritionists recommend calcium-rich foods, rather than pills, as the best sources of calcium because absorption rates are higher (see p. 121, "High Marks for Calcium"). Providing you draw generously on the dairy group, getting your daily calcium from food should not be too difficult. (For those who need them, lactose-free dairy products are now available.) Other foods in this list, like those good-for-you greens, contain lesser amounts of calcium, but they can help you top off your daily total. Don't overlook calcium-fortified foods such as fruit juices or cereals. Read their labels carefully to see how much calcium they provide.

Supplements may be advisable. If you're taking one, a simple test will show whether yours is likely to disintegrate in time to be effective: Put your calcium tablet in six ounces of room-temperature vinegar. Within a half hour, the tablet should break up into small particles. Calcium from supplements is best absorbed when taken in doses of 500 mg or less.

Don't go overboard with calcium tablets. Excess intake could cause adverse effects, such as kidney stone formation. The Institute of Medicine panel has set 2,500 mg as an upper limit for total daily calcium intake, including calcium from food and from pills.

If you are forty-five or older and want to know your risk for osteoporosis, discuss a baseline screening with your health-care provider. New, less complicated diagnostic procedures make testing more affordable than in the past.

IRON WOMAN

Some women suffer from iron deficiency—about 10 percent of the premenopausal women in this country (mostly those who menstruate heavily or are pregnant) and about 6 percent of postmenopausal women. Female endurance athletes are at somewhat greater risk for iron deficiency, especially those in high-impact, endurance sports like marathon running, because during long, strenuous exercise, iron is lost in perspiration. Such movement can also break down red blood cells and cause tiny intestinal ruptures that allow minor bleeding and iron loss, compounding a tendency toward anemia if the diet is routinely low in iron. With anemia comes a reduction in *hemoglobin*, the oxygen-carrying pigment in red blood cells. This impairment results in that characteristic slow, draggy feeling and a possible drop in athletic performance. In women, hemoglobin values below 12 mg/dl indicate anemia.

While this "sports anemia" affects cyclists less frequently, it does sometimes occur, with pro and long-distance riders the most likely candidates. Ann Grandjean, Ed.D., a sports nutritionist who has worked closely with elite American athletes, encourages competitive cyclists who are menstruating to have their hemoglobin and their hematocrit evaluated twice a year.

She adds that female recreational cyclists—if they are going to their gynecologists for their annual pelvic exam and Pap smear, as they should—are probably already being screened through routine blood work. If you are unsure whether these blood tests are being done, ask. For the casual cyclist, whose performance is unlikely to suffer from low *ferritin* (the main form in which iron is stored in the body), an annual check should suffice.

For racers, ultramarathoners, or women who tour, the annual check may suffice also. But if a high-mileage cyclist experiences persistent fatigue or if performance seems unaccountably below par, she should inquire about further testing for a deficiency.

Nutritionists warn that we ought not take iron supplements without previous testing indicating a need. Growing evidence shows that taking in too much iron may harm our health more than not getting enough. Some studies have linked iron overload to cancer, heart disease, diabetes, and arthritis, for example. Thus, supplementation should be monitored by your doctor.

Meanwhile, with results from your ferritin tests, you can consider whether you're eating enough iron-rich food in your daily diet—or too much. The RDA is 15 mg for nonpregnant females ages eleven to fifty years, including nursing women; 30 mg for those who are pregnant; and 10 mg for females over fifty.

A varied, balanced diet is our best bet for getting enough of this nutrient. Iron from animal sources (such as red meat, poultry, and fish), called *heme* iron, is easier to absorb than *non-heme* iron (from vegetable sources such as peas, beans, and some dark-green leafy vegetables). Combining the two types—as in chile con carne—enhances absorption of the non-heme iron. Simmer it in a cast-iron skillet for three hours and the iron content should increase thirtyfold. Other sources of iron include fortified breads and cereals, sweet potatoes, prune juice, figs, raisins, pineapple, dates, cherries, and sesame seeds. Breakfast can be a good time to boost intake by means of a cereal enriched with iron. Since accompanying iron-rich foods with something high in vitamin C increases iron absorption, enjoy a glass of orange juice or a slice of cantaloupe along with your meal.

If you think you need to reduce your iron stores, you could cut back on the red meat, up your cycling mileage, and/or give a pint of blood. Discuss with your health care practitioner.

ANTIOXIDANTS FOR ACTIVE PEOPLE

The biggest nutrition news in recent years is the benefits we get from *antioxidants* and their role in taming *free radicals*—important to athletic folks like us. While research continues, here's the current understanding.

Our bodies naturally produce free radicals, chemicals which perform some useful functions, like killing bacteria and fighting inflammation. But when too many free radicals form, they can cause damage (*oxidation*) to healthy cells, opening the door to advanced aging, heart disease, cancer, and degenerative diseases like arthritis. Your body has its own antioxidation mechanism that protects you from most of this harm.

But certain factors can accelerate free radical production—tobacco smoke, car exhaust, radiation, excessive sunlight, certain drugs, and stress. And, would you believe, our healthy habit of exercising.

What can you do about it? Eat more plants, for starters. Fruits and vegetables are rich in the known antioxidants, especially vitamin C and beta-carotene. According to the *University of California at Berkeley Wellness Letter,* these same plants

> *contain countless other phytochemicals that act as antioxidants, many of which haven't even been identified yet. Scientists believe that each of these compounds plays its own special role in the body and that many work together. Thus the benefits of these foods go way beyond the conventional measurement of known nutrients.*

Chow down daily on three to five servings of veggies, and two to four of fruits from the accompanying chart, and you should get enough vitamin C and beta-carotene to be protected, along with a bonus of other phytochemical benefits. If you want a little extra insurance, pop a one-a-day containing antioxidants—in the neighborhood of 250 mg of C and 5 to 6 mg of beta-carotene.

Vitamin E is more elusive, especially if you've lowered your fat intake and are trying to avoid foods rich in vegetable oils. See the chart; if you aren't getting these "good fats," up your intake or consider a daily supplement of 100 to 400 mg of vitamin E.

Antioxidant All-Stars

Beta-Carotene	Vitamin C	Vitamin E
Carrots, sweet potatoes, pumpkin, yellow squash, spinach, broccoli, dark leafy green vegetables, cantaloupe, apricots, papayas, mangoes, nectarines, peaches, red peppers	Apples and apple juice, citrus fruits, cantaloupe, honeydew, watermelon, mangoes, papayas, kiwifruit, strawberries, green and red sweet peppers, cabbage, Brussels sprouts, cauliflower, kale, potato, kohlrabi, snowpeas, asparagus, tomato juice, tomato-vegetable juice	Nuts (especially almonds and hazelnuts), peanut butter, sunflower and other seeds, raw wheat germ, fish liver oils, shrimp, unsaturated vegetable oils

Ouch-less Riding

Long training sessions build endurance, but it's hard to stay in the saddle if you're falling victim to the ouch factor. A tender butt, sore neck, and numb hands are among potential cycling discomforts, but you don't have to suffer from them. If you feel an ache or pain, find the cause and fix it. Better yet, avoid it altogether. This chapter tells how.

ELIMINATING NECK AND SHOULDER PAIN

After a ride, if you have the feeling someone's just stabbed an icepick into your neck and shoulders, check your position on the bike, says Tricia Liggett. She ought to know. As masseuse/trainer and team manager, Tricia has accompanied some of Britain's best women racers to numerous Tours de France, where day after day she would help racers cope with the grueling strains of racing hard and then driving in a cramped car to the start of the next day's stage. Comfort, training advice, and a good rub-down are her specialties.

If you were to complain of pain, Tricia would take an inventory: Are you on the right size frame? Is the reach to the handlebars too long (or, less likely, too short)? Would a handlebar stem with a shorter extension fix the problem, or do you need a new bike, perhaps even a custom frame? (See chapter 5, "So You Want to Buy a Bike?")

You should be able to reach the bars with a bend in your elbows, she notes. Straight arms are stiff arms, and tension travels up the arms to your neck. Try to keep arms and shoulders relaxed while riding.

Even with a properly fitting bicycle, the strain of a long ride tightens muscles. Try these on-bike stretches from time to time while cycling. Don't wait until you start to stiffen. As with any stretches, do them smoothly and slowly. Don't jerk or push to the point of pain.

- Stretch 1: Roll your head slowly to each side—but not back beyond the shoulder. You could pull a muscle.
- Stretch 2: To loosen shoulders, with your left hand on the handlebar near the stem, put your right hand behind your head. Move your right elbow up and backward and hold the position for a few moments. Switch hands and stretch your left side, too.

Fig. 14: Stretch 3

If you take a break off the bike, stretch.

- Stretch 3: Stand with your feet shoulder-width apart, bend your knees a little, and tuck your hips under. Pull your belly button toward your spine while you reach overhead with your arms, and hold for several seconds. Then lower your arms and reach out in front of you. Hold for thirty seconds.
- Stretch 4: While you're still off your bike, work your fingers into the muscle that covers the back of your neck and the shoulder, as well as the inside of the shoulder blade, while you move your shoulder at the same time. Repeat on other side.

BREATHING AND PERFORMANCE

The way you breathe can also make a difference. When a cyclist climbs or labors to stay with a group of riders, she tends to catch her breath, trying to take more air in quickly. "You tend to shallow-breathe," Tricia says, "and shallow breathing takes place in the upper thoracic area and lung area. That in itself causes tightness in your shoulders and chest. You then get a stitch and lose power."

Tricia advocates deep, relaxed breathing with the diaphragm. Regulate your breathing by counting a certain number of pedal revolutions on the in-breath and the same number of revolutions on the out-breath. When working hard breathe deeper, not faster.

It should be no surprise that breathing can affect overall riding performance, since breathing delivers oxygen that fuels the muscles. To give the out-breath equal time, Tricia often tells riders to concentrate more on it than on the in-breath. "It helps anyone who is asthmatic or suffers from stress-induced or exercise-induced asthma, which is quite common," she adds.

Another interesting thing may happen when you think about your breathing: You may discover that you unconsciously hold your breath during intense effort, a habit to break.

To facilitate deep breathing, again consider your position on the bike. As a cyclist assumes an aerodynamic position on a road bike, bending low over the bars to reduce wind resistance, she should be careful not to scrunch up her chest and hamper breathing. Holding the elbows too close to the body and humping the back will crowd the diaphragm. Regarding fit on a road bike, the bony tops of the shoulders and the handlebar width should be the same. And for a racer (who typically has her saddle higher relative to the handlebars than other riders), the tops of the bars still should be no more than two inches below the saddle.

Other cyclists would probably be more comfortable with handlebars only one inch below the saddle or possibly even with it. If needed, the stem on many bikes can be safely raised, to a point. (Look for the minimum insertion mark; for safety, two inches must remain in the steerer tube.) If that's not high enough because your frame is too small, the solution may be to have your bike shop install a stem with a longer shank, such as the Terry T-Stem, available for road and mountain bikes.

As you know, when hill climbing you crave as much oxygen as you can get. That's why top road racers sit up to climb, with their hands on the brake hoods or on the handlebar tops, not on the drops. Or they stand on the pedals with hands on the brake hoods for optimum balance. Either way, to breathe freely, as Olympic gold medalist Connie Carpenter Phinney advises, "Never climb in the drops; hold your head high, and keep your shoulders wide."

HANDS-ON ADVICE

I remember the thrill of switching from my touring bike to a new racer years ago. It was like trading in a pickup truck for a sports car—so much more responsive on the corners, and the lighter wheels helped me keep up on training rides. But compared to my touring bike, with its laidback frame angles and the fat, foam rubber handlebar padding, my sporty racing bike transmitted more road shock up the frame, through the handlebars, and straight to my elbows. Without ever lifting a racquet I soon had tennis elbow in both arms.

Riding drop bars, hands and arms bear a good portion of the cyclist's weight. But they don't have to suffer. I solved my elbow woes with some of the tips above. I substituted a stem with a shorter extension to bring the handlebars a little closer, which made it easier to bend my elbows. And I relaxed as I grew accustomed to riding with a faster crowd.

Wrists, hands, and fingers are vulnerable, also. Two different conditions can cause symptoms: *Carpal tunnel syndrome,* a nerve compression at the wrist, can result in tingling, numbness, or weakness in fingers and thumb. *Ulnar neuropathy, or cyclist's palsy,* often caused by pressure on the heel of the hand, involves one or both branches of the ulnar nerve. A surface branch extends from the wrist to the little finger side of the hand. A deeper branch of the ulnar nerve goes to the small hand muscles attached to the fourth and fifth fingers. Compression of these nerves can lead to tingling, numbness, and possibly loss of movement in those fingers. If you experience either condition and don't get relief from the tips below, consult your medical practitioner.

Here's how savvy cyclists avoid these problems:

•Wear cycling gloves.
•Now and then during a long ride, take one hand off the bar and shake it to stimulate circulation; then shake the other.
•Avoid riding with your wrists cocked.
•Change hand positions often to relax muscles and avoid numbness.

Drop bars. Unlike other handlebar types, drop handlebars offer a variety of places for your hands to rest. Make use of them.

•When riding the drops, keep wrists straight and hold the curved, not the flat, part of the bars.
•The brake hoods offer several options. The most obvious choice is riding with thumbs on one side of the rubber hoods and fingers on the other. You can also rest your palms on the bend of the bars just above the hoods. I prefer those two positions, but try also riding with three fingers on the outside of the hood, with index finger and thumb inside or, if you have large hands, you may like a position with two fingers on either side of the brake hoods.
•On the tops of the bars keep wrists relaxed and straight.

Fig. 15: On the drops, riding with hands on the curved portion of the bars helps you to keep wrists straight.

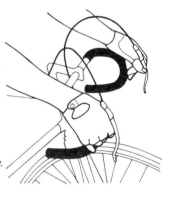

Fig. 16: This frequently used position on the brake hoods gives easy access to brakes and stability for climbing out of the saddle, and it is a position comfortable for your upper body.

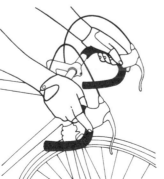

Fig. 17: A variation, with palms on the bars just above the hoods.

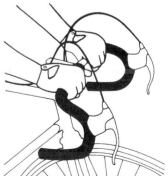

Fig. 18: Hands on the tops of the bars provide the greatest stability for one-handed maneuvers like signaling.

If, despite good hand positioning, you experience symptoms, equip drop bars with handlebar padding. Buy cycling gloves with extra cushioning to help absorb vibration. Or get the pressure off by adding aero bars, favored by triathletes and ultramarathon cyclists.

Other bars. On other types of bikes some of the above tips apply: Wear padded cycling gloves; don't put a lot of pressure on wrists or ride with wrists cocked. On some mountain bikes and hybrids, bar ends let you change hand positions for cruising; they're also intended as the ideal handhold for pulling on the bars for efficient climbing. If you typically ride more than twenty-five miles at a time on a bike with straight handlebars, consider retrofitting bar ends.

Check the grips on your bike. Some off-road bikes and mountain-bike look-alikes have squishy foam grips, which seem to offer comfort on the showroom floor, but firmer, less compressible grips actually tire your hands less. When riding on rough terrain, hold the grips firmly to pass vibration on to your arms; soak it up by keeping your elbows bent. A light grasp permits the bar to vibrate against your hands, resulting in stinging or numbness.

For pedaling pavement and smooth bike paths, some combination of the above changes should alleviate discomfort. If you feel the need to do something more—or if you simply like trick components—you could add a suspension stem to your handlebar. For the ultimate in off-road cush, a suspension fork helps soak up bumps for trail riding; maybe it's time to upgrade.

If you have front suspension but aren't getting enough boing out of it, quite possibly the factory set it up for a man's heavier weight. Check to see whether there's a preload adjustment you can make to soften the suspension. Put it at the easiest setting and test-ride; if you bottom out, set it progressively harder until you get it right.

Not cushy enough yet? Don't blame your imagination. It could still be that factory-setup-for-guys thing. Ask at the shop whether your fork can be tuned further—for example, by swapping elastomers or springs for softer ones that are available in tuning kits from the manufacturer.

SOLVING SADDLE SORENESS

Posted on America Online: "You know you've ridden too much when . . . getting out of the saddle actually hurts worse than sitting! On BRAG (Bicycle Ride Across Georgia) last year a bunch of us found that when sitting, after the initial shock of fanny meets seat, we went kinda numb. When we'd stand up to climb, all the blood would rush back and OUCH! . . ."

Uncomfortable in the saddle? Frequent Internet postings from women cyclists on this sore subject indicate that you're not alone. Their cycling chat-room correspondence reinforces two points: One, individual differences matter—what suits my anatomy may not suit yours. Two, you need to look at a combination of factors to solve the problem. But the good news is that several suggestions can probably head you in the right direction, and after that, experimentation should let you find the correct saddle. The payback should be a less tender tush and better cycling performance.

Starting with your present seat, check to make sure it's level. A saddle tilted up in front will cause you to put pressure on the genitals, and that hurts. A recent saddle change reminded me that what a male mechanic thinks is level may not feel level to me, and just a tiny lowering of the saddle nose can make a big difference.

Second, check bike fit yourself or have it evaluated at a good pro shop.

- Correct seat height is crucial: You should have a slight bend in your knee with the pedal in the six o'clock position. If while sitting and pedaling you rock from side to side even a little, the friction will cause rubbing and discomfort.
- Proper fore/aft adjustment of the saddle affects pedaling efficiency and making the best use of the strength of your leg and hip muscles. Use the plumb line test (see figure 5).
- With saddle height and fore/aft position properly adjusted, check overall bike fit. A too-long top tube will make you bend too far forward or sit too close to the saddle nose, with genital crunching the result in either case.

The shorts you wear matter. (See chapter 8, "Clothes with Wheel Appeal"). Seams in the wrong places, shorts that wrinkle in the crotch because they fit badly, too much padding that bunches—these irritants can cause discomfort despite the best of saddles. Invest in a couple pairs of quality spandex shorts that fit.

Saddle type also matters. Long ago I tested a bicycle and, though I remember nothing else about it, I'll never forget the seat. Stylishly narrow and covered with an elegant midnight-blue suede, it had me in agony because my *sit-bones,* the part of the pelvic bones we sit on called the "ischial tuberosities," hung over the edges of that saddle, as would most women's, because of our slightly wider pelvises. Without my sit-bones supporting me, my body weight was crushing some rather tender tissues against that blue suede implement of torture.

Many women need a saddle slightly wider in the back than a man requires. I said *slightly.* "Not one of those really wide saddles," cautions exercise physiologist and cyclist Christine Wells, Ph.D.

Since my blue suede experience, "anatomic" saddles have come into being. A woman's anatomic saddle—a little wider in back and a little shorter than a man's saddle—provides a padded area to cushion the ischial tuberosities. Some anatomic saddles have nylon foam inserts that form bumps of padding near the back of the saddle; other versions use gel or a liquid-filled bladder for cushioning. Both women's and men's models exist for a range of cycling applications—touring, racing, mountain biking, and so on. And they come in varying widths and with differing amounts of cushioning. Avocet offers a series of saddles ranging from soft to firm, as more experienced women cyclists often like firmer support.

In recent years many women's saddles have another refinement, a hole cut in the hard subsurface of the saddle nose, or through the entire saddle so as to be visible. Other saddles dip in the critical spot. The idea is to alleviate pressure on tender genitals when leaning forward toward the handlebars. Otherwise you can rub them swollen and raw, a condition Race Across AMerica legend Susan Notorangelo calls "smash."

Trying to avoid that genital discomfort, many women sit too upright. This cuts down on aerodynamic efficiency, overworks the legs, and underutilizes the powerful gluteus muscles in the buttocks. Ideally, the gluteus maximus should provide much of the power as you push the pedals away from you. A saddle that both supports the sit-bones and lets you comfortably adopt a more forward-reaching position will favor maximum performance.

Many women, including myself, find something suitable among the women's/anatomic saddles. If you don't have one and need a change, try one. Brands to consider include Avocet, Terry, San Marco, InMotion, Trico, and WRS. Find a bike shop with a wide selection and arrange to test-ride them. Probably you'll need to buy several (save your receipt), with an agreement that you can exchange or return any that don't work out.

If none of these suit, maybe you're a candidate for a good leather saddle (women's models are available) or a men's anatomic. Not every female is enamored of the hole in the saddle, or of women's saddles in general. A good quality leather saddle, which some women swear by, will conform to your shape after about 500 miles or so of riding and occasional applications of a leather dressing to the underside of the saddle. Don't buy a cheap, poor quality leather saddle because it will never break in and feel comfortable.

For selecting and using your saddle Dr. Wells suggests:

- Some beginners make the mistake of rolling forward on their saddle so that they're not supported on their sit-bones. To feel what it's like to perch on your ischial tuberosities, sit on a curb. Those bones you sit on are the sit-bones.
- Again, check bike fit. If the reach to the handlebars is too long, you will tend to sit forward on the seat and not where the sit-bones have good support.
- It's OK if the flesh of our buttocks hangs over the saddle so long as our sit-bones perch comfortably.
- Don't think of your weight as being fully supported by the saddle and your arms. Think of yourself as straddling the saddle and putting some weight on the pedals as you spin them.

Regardless of your choice of saddle, getting up off of it once in awhile relieves pressure entirely, stretches your legs, and allows a cooling breeze. Every half hour, at least, stand up and pedal for thirty seconds or so. One reason many of us have fewer seat problems while trail riding is that we stand on the pedals more.

Many cyclists of both genders, especially megamile riders, lubricate their

No Longer Rubbed the Wrong Way

Herewith, more online tips from our sisters:

"Get a fit check from a pro shop. It costs, but I'm glad I did. I discovered that one leg is 3 mm longer than the other, not a big deal but just enough to rub me wrong on longer rides. The correction was a shim beneath my shoe cleat. Also, after the fit check the pros properly adjust your bike and recommend proper stem length and saddle choice. It may be worth it—no ifs, ands, or butts!" –Ann Martha, Cheltenham, Pennsylvania

"A hard saddle with a dip in the middle, like the Avocet 02, can support the pubic bone and sit bones in a sort of tripod. The dip means you don't squash your labia. The other approach many women like is a soft-nosed saddle; the weight is supported on the sit bones and you can lean forward without squashing. What I don't recommend to my women customers—I have a mobile bike shop in a van—is a big squishy saddle or one of those squishy seat covers that people buy, trying to make the wrong saddle feel better." –Linda Gryczan, Alice B. Toeclips Cyclery, Clancy, Montana

" . . .I have found the larger heart-shaped saddles very hard to utilize on mountain bikes. I can't seem to spread my legs wide enough to lean off the back while descending. I live next to the Blue Ridge Mountains and there is lots of descending going on . . ." –Char St. Laurent, Charlottesville, Virginia

shorts' liners to reduce friction. Among the products to try: Bag Balm, Vaseline, Noxzema, Desitin, and made specifically for this purpose, Chamois Butt'r from Paceline Products. At a rest stop on a long ride, clean up with a moist wipe and reapply the lubricant.

As for the BRAG rider's complaint that opened this section, take to heart this response: "Training, training, and training—the first longer rides after a layoff always make me sore, so I try to work up gradually to the longer distances." (See also "No Longer Rubbed the Wrong Way.")

WHAT YOUR KNEES NEED

Among female athletes knee problems crop up as a common complaint—usually a result of overuse, caused by forces applied in a repeated movement such as running or pedaling.

Because it's not a weight-bearing activity, cycling, by comparison, is much kinder to knees than jogging. The many runners who take up bicycling while sidelined by pavement-pounding injuries can tell you that. In fact, some will credit biking with helping them strengthen legs and knees during recovery.

Nevertheless, women cyclists must take care to avoid injury to this vulnerable joint. Our wider pelvic bone, compared to a man's, directs the stresses of exercise toward the kneecap at an angle. So there may be an uneven distribution

1

Like these mountain bikers in Alaska's Chugach Mountains, allow a safety gap on the trail between riders in case one of you should have to stop suddenly.

3

A mother and daughter explore the carriage roads of Acadia National Park in Maine. Riding with your child is the best way to share healthful exercise and teach bike safety.

2 On a training ride near Grand Teton National Park in Wyoming, this racer reduces wind resistance by riding the drops, taking advantage of the road bike's potential for speed. Her bent elbows help absorb road shock.

4

The cruiser is all about relaxed fun.

5 On an organized tour in south China, a cyclist finds the pace perfect for discovering another culture.

7

The telltale tube shows us this smart cyclist knows to drink plenty, especially in hot weather. Her hydration system with fluid delivery tube lets her keep her hands free.

6 To be a safe participant in the traffic mix, obey traffic signals, ride with the flow of traffic, and wear your helmet.

8

What a difference a century has made, in bicycles and in women's lives! In the 1880's the safety bike, with cushy, air-filled tires and two equal-sized wheels, opened cycling to the masses and was a catalyst for the emancipation of women.

9 These Salt Lake City police officers know their mountain bikes can often reach a crime scene faster than a patrol car, and sometimes unnoticed—decided advantages, along with the exercise these officers get from daily cycling.

10

At the Lehigh County Velodrome in Pennsylvania, two nationally ranked racers, Becky Quinn and Nicole Reinhart, duke it out in the match sprint, a cat-and-mouse game of tactics, nerves, and speed.

11

Compared to toting panniers, a bike with a trailer handles more like an unloaded bike. When you stand up to climb, the pivot on the trailer lets you sway the bike from side to side as you pedal. You can't put the same body English into climbing with loaded bike bags.

12 Anyone planning to put more than twenty pounds in a pair of rear panniers should consider adding a low-rider front rack and small front panniers, like this well-equipped tourist has done. This setup makes for the safest bike handling. Limit weight in the handlebar bag to 5 percent of the total.

13 Whatever the weather, cyclists can adapt, prevail, and have fun—as this Italian rider is doing on a tour of California's wine country.

14 Along with drinking, dousing is a good way to stay cool when on the road in Bali (or elsewhere).

15 On tour, take time to stop and meet the locals or share a hee-haw with a friendly mule (as here, on Whidbey Island off the coast of Washington). These will be some of your best (beast?) memories.

16 For road riding, a hybrid serves many women well. The triple chainring (lots of gears) handles the hills, and the more upright seating gives a great view and requires less bending over. For a long day in the saddle—as on Maine's Sunday River to the Sea benefit ride—bar ends provide additional hand positions, a plus.

of weight, more pull and tension on the ligaments and muscles around the knee, and more potential for wear and tear on our knees.

Whether or not women are more prone to "cyclist's knee," riders of both sexes experience it. The first symptom is often a stinging sensation during or after cycling. As with other discomforts, knee problems are better prevented than cured. In cycling this means proper bike fit, gradual conditioning, and good flexibility.

Bike fit. Correct saddle height and fore/aft positioning of the saddle are critical for efficient operation of the knees. (See chapter 5, "So You Want to Buy a Bike?") Positioning the shoe on the pedal properly should pose little problem because of the float built into most clipless pedal/shoe systems, but if you've chosen a fixed cleat, see the shoe section of chapter 8, "Clothes with Wheel Appeal."

Conditioning. John L. Beck, M.D., and Byron P. Wildermuth, P.T., in a symposium on "The Female Athlete's Knee" observed that injury rates are lower among well-conditioned women athletes than among less-trained females. Beck and Wildermuth also cited studies of highly trained athletes that confirmed that women can attain the same leg strength as their male counterparts when measurements are corrected for lean body mass. Don't let anyone tell you, Beck and Wildermuth said, that females are inherently weaker.

That's good news. We can get in condition more easily than we can change our anatomy! So let your legs catch up with your enthusiasm. That's why coaches encourage a gradual program of conditioning—high cadence and low gears—before tackling speedwork, big hills, and high gears.

This warning isn't just for racers. A few years ago I joined a group bike tour in Brittany on the northwest coast of France. One of our party was a friendly but hard-driving Wall Street lawyer, with plenty of gusto but little cycling experience. Unfortunately, she took the advice of a man in the group to pedal constantly in high gear. After two days her knees gave out, and she traveled the rest of the route in the sag wagon. A month of training before the tour and use of moderate gears would have made all the difference.

If you expect a lot from yourself as a cyclist, train year-round, indoors if necessary. Or in the winter substitute another activity that exercises cycling muscles, like cross-country skiing. Circuit weight training, aerobics, and vigorous ice skating can also supplement lower cycling mileage. Andy Pruitt, a former racer and certified athletic trainer who's worked with elite and recreational American women cyclists, warns that knee problems tend to bloom in the springtime, after the first races. Women must learn that cycling strength is something they build over many years, he adds.

Flexibility. Cold, tight muscles are much more liable to injury than supple, warm ones. In cool weather (below 65°) wear tights, knickers, or leg warmers to protect those "hinges." And make the first fifteen minutes of any ride a warm-up: Spin easy gears and get your blood racing. Likewise, the last ten or fifteen minutes of training should be at an easier, cool-down pace in low gear.

In addition, some top racers and sports medicine professionals emphasize the value of stretching to improve flexibility and relax muscles that might otherwise tighten with exercise. I usually stretch my legs after a ride. It takes only a few minutes. Sometimes if I forget, I'm noticeably stiff later on.

As Andy Pruitt points out, any sport requires a certain range of motion. For example, cycling demands flexible ankles and hamstrings, as well as good straight-leg hip flexion. Besides, if one muscle group is tight, other muscles have to work overtime to compensate. As you gradually become more supple, you'll probably find that you can comfortably achieve a more aerodynamic position.

In this chapter you'll find some stretches to help you improve flexibility for cycling.

LOOSENING UP YOUR BACK

Cycling is easier on the back than some other pursuits, so athletes sometimes turn to cycling when back problems force them out of more punishing sports. At the same time, biking can cause back muscles to tighten. I've experienced this myself when increasing my mileage too suddenly. The back stretches that follow helped me improve my flexibility.

Since cycling exercises the back muscles but does not work the abdominals, back muscles may tighten too much because the abdominal muscles aren't strong enough to counter them. "Crunches" strengthen the abs better than old-fashioned sit-ups, and they're easier to do.

In fact crunches are so simple you might wonder if that's all there is to it: To position yourself for a crunch, lie on your back on the floor with knees bent and feet flat on the floor; lace your fingers underneath your head with your arms flat out on the floor. Now you're ready. Lift your upper back no more than thirty degrees from the floor, keeping your spine straight and your head in line with your spine; at the same time breathe out and contract your abdominal muscles. Maintain this straight body alignment as you lower your back to the floor; inhale with the diaphragm while doing so.

Do fifteen to twenty-five of these three times a week (perhaps right after your ride). You'll derive back benefits and firm your abdomen.

STRETCHES FOR CYCLISTS

Work these stretches into your day whenever you choose—even while watching television—although just before or after a ride is best. Ten minutes a day spent on these stretches will let muscles work together efficiently without overworking any one muscle group.

Stretching motions should be smooth and sustained, not bouncy or jerky. It's fine to stretch until you feel it, but don't overdo it to the point of pain. Expect your flexibility to improve gradually over a few weeks, and recognize that there are individual differences in potential.

Fig. 19:
•For hamstrings, lie flat on your back. Keep your right leg on the floor and raise your left leg, clasping the back of that leg with your hands. With your knee straight, press your leg against your hands for a few seconds. Then relax the knee and pull the leg toward your chest. You should feel a stretch in the hamstring in the back of that leg. Hold for ten seconds. Then repeat the entire procedure; see if you aren't a little more flexible during this repetition. Now start over in reverse position to stretch your other leg.

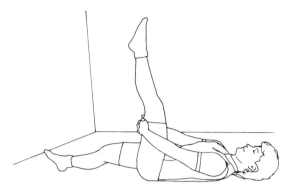

Fig. 20:
•To stretch the calf and the Achilles tendon (to improve ankle flexibility), lean against a wall, stepping forward with the left foot and bending the right knee. Keep that right heel flat against the floor and feel the stretch in the right calf and the ankle. Hold for thirty seconds, then reverse position with the right leg forward to stretch the left calf and ankle.

Fig. 21:
•For the top of the foot and ankle area, sit down (remove shoes if wearing them). With legs extended, point toes of both feet and hold the stretch for ten seconds.

•In this position you can do another stretch to improve ankle flexibility if you like: Flatten your feet so soles are perpendicular to the floor. Reach out and grab the toes with your hands and gently pull toes toward you. It's OK to bend your knees if you need to.

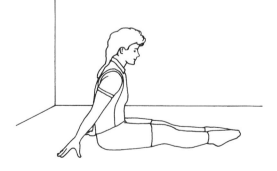

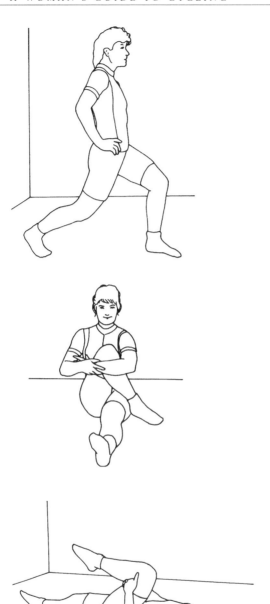

Fig. 22:

•For hip flexors and fronts of thighs, stand with feet shoulder-width apart and take a long stride forward with the left foot. Both feet should point straight ahead. Bend knees slightly, tucking hips under and keeping heels as close to the floor as you can. Do you feel the stretch in the front of your right thigh and through the hip? Hold for thirty seconds, then reverse for opposite leg.

Fig. 23:

•For the iliotibial band (the ITB, which runs along the side of the thigh and tends to tighten while cycling), do the "human pretzel." Sit with your back straight and left leg extended. Cross your right foot over your left knee and set it on the floor. Now, keeping your back at a ninety-degree angle to the floor, pull your right knee toward the left side of your chest. Feel the stretch near the right hip where the ITB inserts. Reverse position and stretch the other side.

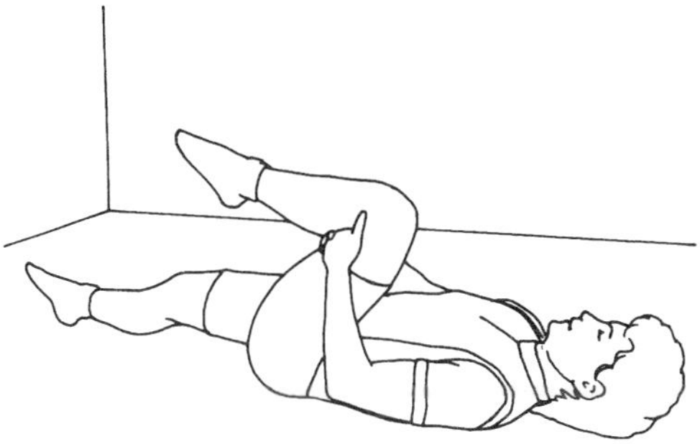

Fig. 24:

•Here's one for your lower back: Lie on your back with legs out flat and relaxed. Bend your right knee, bring it up and clasp your hands around the back of your thigh. Pull knee to chest, at the same time pulling abdominal muscles in. Reverse position and stretch again.

Fig. 25:

•To improve lateral flexibility in lower back: Sit up straight with legs extended in front of you. Cross your right foot over the left leg and rest it on the floor. Reach your right hand behind you and brace your left elbow against the outside of your right knee while keeping spine erect.

Fig. 26:

•For upper back: Stand with feet shoulder-width apart, knees slightly bent, and hips pulled under. Pull your belly-button toward your spine and, with hands resting on thighs, gently separate your shoulder blades.

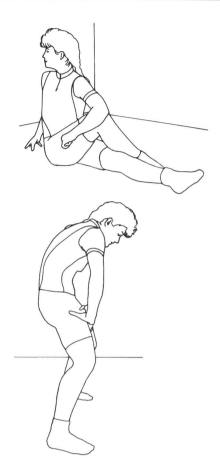

FOOT COMFORT

Clipless pedals have solved many "agonies of de feet" for cyclists who used to feel as if their feet were on fire because of too-tight toe straps. Just as feet swell in the heat or simply because of a long day of cycling, lacing your shoes too tight can have the same effect. Loosen them at the first hint of discomfort.

Not ready to go clipless? Riders using clips and straps for long rides might try leaving the straps a tad loose until you need to pull them tight for a big climb. Another trick is using two straps on each pedal. One goes in the usual spot; thread the other through the forward part of the pedal cage and over the toeclip. With double straps, neither has to be quite so tight; snug them up when you need to.

And if you're still trying to make do with running shoes or—worse—sneakers, treat yourself to some cycling shoes.

Tuning Up Your Technique

In bike racing and recreational cycling, the best riders demonstrate technique as well as strength and endurance. It's the old story of using grace, form, and brains to supplement brawn. Women cyclists not only need to do this, but possess a special affinity for it. Don't we often think our way around a problem instead of simply muscling through? Here we'll talk about improving efficiency in dealing with wind resistance, improving climbing skills, making the most of our gearing, and more.

CHEATING THE WIND

Even when the air seems still, a lone cyclist expends about 30 percent of her energy merely overcoming wind resistance. So it is that Silvia Sivret of Claremont, New Hampshire, noticed a dramatic difference in her first experience with drafting:

Once my husband realized my commitment to the sport, he made an effort to teach me more technique. On a training ride we did some paceline *work (he pulled the whole way), and it demanded my greatest concentration to stay as near his wheel as I dared and shift into the gear ratios he asked for. Aside from the concentration involved, our speed thrilled me. No wonder he and his cycling buddies have such fun! After the one-hour, eleven-minute ride, I felt less tired than I do following a ride with my friends at a touring pace and doing our own pulling.*

Drafting (riding closely behind) another rider enables you to go 2 to 3 mph faster than if you were alone. The closer you can stay to that wheel in front of you, the more energy you save. And the larger the paceline, if working efficiently, the faster you can go. Like Silvia says, paceline riding takes concentration, as you must respond to the cues of the rider in front. But you'll experience a new exhilaration, speeding along in the slipstream, part of a well-tuned group of cyclists, or a *chaingang,* as the Brits call it.

Even several bike lengths in back of another rider you can benefit from the slipstream, if you find the wake, or "bubble." When you're out there alone and another cyclist passes you, move into her wake, and you'll get a boost in speed. Turn on a burst of effort and you may be able to catch up and draft her.

Any cyclist can use paceline skills. If a group of tourists faces long mileage or a stiff headwind, a paceline could be the answer. For recreational riders who regularly train on the same route, working as teammates keeps it interesting.

Paceline Pussycat

My funniest, sickest, and grossest riding experience occurred on a cycling vacation in the Florida Keys, where my husband Tom and I failed to imagine the consequences of the many cats Ernest Hemingway had introduced to the area.

    We began a beautiful ride with Tom in the lead while I practiced drafting close to his wheel. Because of crosswinds and tractor trailers on the road we weren't talking much. And to stretch out after driving for two days, we were moving pretty fast. Suddenly without warning, Tom veered off the shoulder of the road. And what did he leave me to face? There on its back with all four feet sticking straight up in the air was the largest, deadest, stiffest cat I ever hope to see. It was big enough to do some very big wheel damage, I'm sure. I missed it, but I'm still not letting Tom forget that one.

–Pamela Gill, Cheverly, Maryland

Soon you'll be ready to draft on fun club rides and anticipate a faster century. Of course, in competition, much strategy involves use of the slipstream.

You could begin learning, as Silvia did, by drafting one experienced rider who's willing to *pull* (ride at the front) and who can maintain a steady pace. The cyclist pulling must remember never to stop suddenly and to give warning if a pothole or other road hazard needs dodging—since you may not see it. (Usually the lead rider points a finger at the offending pile of glass or whatever, and swerves. You follow suit.) Go over matters of communication with your partner before you start.

My patient friend, Ellen Dorsey (a top Veteran racer at the time) taught me that way. A smooth, strong rider, she could be trusted not to make a dangerous move. So I quickly got the hang of it. We didn't bother calling out gear ratios, but you could. Here's the technique:

- Try to follow about three feet behind the wheel in front of you.
- Ride an inch or so to one side of the wheel in front, so you have space to maneuver if there's a sudden slowdown. This gives you a better view of the road ahead, too.
- Don't overlap wheels. A swerve by the rider in front of you could take you down.
- Don't stare at the wheel ahead of you. Use peripheral vision to monitor the distance between your bike and the wheel preceding you, while you look at the road ahead.
- Don't brake if you can help it. That destroys the smoothness of the paceline and requires extra work to accelerate again. Instead, if you're gaining on your partner, briefly ease off, or *soft-pedal*. As the gap widens to the correct distance, smoothly resume normal pedaling. If you must go for the brakes, don't grab them hard but *feather* them (lightly squeeze and release).

•Fairly flat terrain works best for practice. If you do have downhills, for safety on the descent let a gap open up between you; regroup after the road levels.

Those are the basics. Usually cyclists share the work by taking turns pulling. To change the lead, the front rider looks back to make sure no cars are coming; this also signals you. Then she speeds up a little and moves over a few feet (to the left in North America, to the right in the United Kingdom). She eases her pedaling while you maintain a steady pace—check your speedometer if you have one. Don't accelerate; if you had other cyclists behind you, it would open up gaps in the line. When she is alongside you (or alongside the last rider if there are more), she accelerates a little and moves over to catch the draft. Now she can rest.

To reiterate, smooth moves are the key. At the front when you scan for overtaking traffic, glance over your shoulder while relaxing your other arm to prevent steering in the direction you're looking. On the drops, try looking back under your elbow.

How long does the leader stay at the front? That depends. At race pace the front rider really hammers, so racers may spell each other every ten pedal strokes or sooner. During your workout a stronger cyclist may pull longer than a weaker one; thus riders of varying abilities can train together and each get an appropriate workout. Or you can agree that each pull for a certain distance or, say, a minute apiece.

Fig. 27:
Single paceline

In a larger paceline of six or a dozen, the same principles apply.

With rapid turnover at the front, you'll see a circular flow of riders, with one line moving forward, the other back. Lines should stay close together to take best advantage of the slipstream and not use too much of the road.

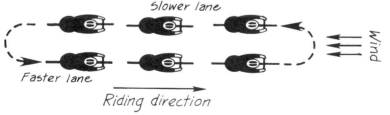

Fig. 28:
Circular paceline

In light traffic a large group can make a *double paceline*. This works like two pacelines riding side by side. To change the lead, front riders swing out to either side. They drift back and pair up again at the rear.

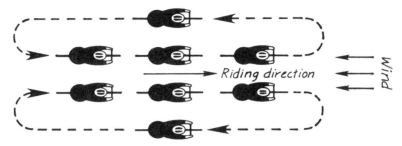

In a crosswind, a standard paceline proves less effective than the *echelon*, a diagonal formation across the road, because the pockets of still air are diagonally to the rear of each rider. With a partner, you can use echelon technique on a wide road, but larger groups should not unless the road is closed to traffic, as in a race.

Note: In this instance the wind blows from the left. If it is coming from the right, the lead rider should swing off to the right to avoid taking down a rider whose wheel is overlapped. In other words, pull off into the wind.

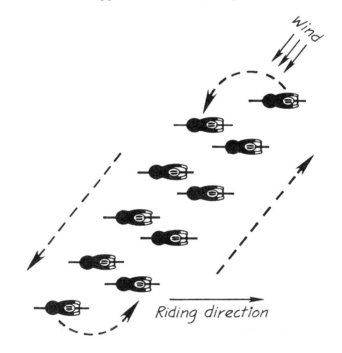

CLIMBING TO THE TOP

One of my friends calls hill climbing "the moment of truth" for cyclists. Some find it our true call to glory. "Steep and long, bring 'em on!" say the natural climbers—typically slender, muscular, and aerobically fit types. Others of us see hills as penance we do for the other pleasures in riding—like the view from the summit and the ice cream stand on the other side.

If that's how you feel, hang in there. As you continue to improve your fitness, climbing will get easier. Surprisingly soon some of your best memories will center on how you made it to the top. But don't wait for it to happen; good technique, practice, and determination will speed your progress.

For example, in June some years ago I joined a popular one-day ride from London (England) to the seashore resort of Brighton, a fifty-six-mile bit of mass hysteria shared by about 30,000 cyclists. Anyone who's taken part knows that plenty of hills stud the route, looming higher and steeper as you progress toward the coast. About six miles from the finish, when your legs have just about turned to cottage cheese, there's a real stinker called Ditchling Beacon. I confess I walked it.

I could see why, to the stalwart regulars, Ditchling Beacon becomes a point of pride. After the event, Helen White from South Hatfield, Hertfordshire told me she'd cycled all the way up two years running. She was so intent on pedaling up it the first time that she "even rode over a £10 note someone had dropped! There's determination."

So you supply the determination; here are some tips:

- Your bike must be geared low enough. I'm prejudiced toward triple chainrings on hilly roads, but if you have a double with wide-range gearing it might be fine for you. However, if your lowest low isn't down around 35 to 40 inches, look into modifying or replacing your bicycle—or all the determination in the world won't take you up much more than a pimple. Of course, the lighter the bicycle, the easier climbing becomes. Good road bikes weigh only about 22 or 23 pounds. A behemoth that tips the scales at 30 pounds or more will handicap you.
- Exploit downhill momentum. I love rolling hills because they vary the ride and let you take advantage of gearing. After you've crested a rise, you shift into high gear and pedal down. You may have to level out some before your pedaling actually makes a difference, but as it does, pedal rapidly to maintain speed as long as possible.

  On gentle rollers, you may ascend the next with a snappy cadence and surprisingly little effort. If not, shift down and keep pedaling. If you've just a short distance to the top, you could stand on the pedals for greater leverage. Once over the top, shift again into high for the next downhill. Such terrain is a joy to ride and an excellent opportunity to work on technique.

Fig. 31: This technique is especially good for 'honking' up a short hill: with hands on the brake hoods, get up off the saddle; rock the bike from side to side in opposition to each pedal stroke.

Likewise, beginning a long descent, shift into high as you start down so that when you resume pedaling, you'll be in the correct gear.

• Use cadence as a guide while you experiment to see which climbing style suits you best. Some cyclists climb out of the saddle; others sit and spin.

Let's say you usually ride at a cadence of 85 rpm. On a short climb, remain seated as you try to keep your cadence up. With hands on the tops of the bars or on the brake hoods (or bar ends if you have them), pull a little on the bars as you pedal, but otherwise keep your upper body relaxed. Pull up on the pedals as well as pushing down. (Toe clips or clipless pedals are essential.) Breathe deeply with your diaphragm.

As your cadence drops below 80 rpm, grip the brake hoods and get up off the saddle to pedal. Lean forward, centering yourself over the pedals. This makes use of your full body weight to turn them. Put muscle into it. With each pedal stroke, pull with the alternate hand. You'll feel the bike sway a little from side to side, which is expected. But keep the bike moving straight ahead; don't weave.

You may find yourself gasping for breath because the effort becomes *anaerobic* (requires more fuel than the oxygen you breathe in can provide). Slow your pedaling if necessary but keep going to the top; you'll catch your breath on the descent.

Beginning climbers, if you must stop on the ascent to rest, then next time you do a hill like this, forget cadence. Simply try to make it up without stopping. Do it by gearing down and pedaling slowly. In fact, the first time, go as slow as possible without wobbling the bike, even if you think you could go faster. It will probably feel easier to climb seated, but stand up if need be. Don't worry if other riders pass you. At the top, if you're not breathless, you'll know you can go faster the next time. Practice on hills like this once a week. You'll develop a sense of pacing and how much you can push yourself. As you improve, you can concern yourself more with cadence.

• Pace yourself on long climbs. Begin conservatively if you're not sure what you can do. If you start in an easy gear and halfway up you feel capable of more, you can shift higher. Try to keep your cadence up. Ride seated until you tire, then stand to use different muscles. Alternate the two positions.

If you must slow your cadence, it's no great sin. Remember to use deep, rhythmic breathing. Be patient with yourself and keep going. If you can take in the scenery while keeping an eye on the road, it's heartening. Just today I enjoyed a view of barns and fields in a patchwork valley and gauged my progress past rows of cornstalks as I pedaled up a long hill. Simply watching the road, you think you're going much slower than you actually are.

•A full stomach hampers you on a long, strenuous climb.

•When the going gets too tough, sometimes the smart stop going. It depends. If you have a competitive streak, you may battle your way to the top regardless. On the other hand, tourists have the perfect excuse for stopping during a climb: to better admire the view. You'll find a one- to three-minute rest long enough to catch your breath, maybe even snap a picture. Then climb back on and pedal. Try it. If it's too much, you can always get off again and walk.

You will improve.

DOWN THE OTHER SIDE

Some riders don't mind climbing hills but tremble at descents. I consider downhills one of cycling's great bonuses. With correct technique they can be a very safe thrill.

Whether you descend fast or slow, here's what not to do: Don't simply apply the brakes and keep them on until you reach the bottom of the hill. Why not? The sustained friction of rubber brake pads against your rims can melt the pads so they glaze over and aren't effective for stopping. Tires are also vulnerable to heat buildup in the rims; air inside tubes or tubulars can expand, causing a blowout.

Instead, feather your brakes. As your speed builds, apply the brakes briefly and just enough to dampen your speed, then release them. Coast until you want to slow again. Brake again briefly and so on.

Body position also affects your speed. To slow your descent, sit up to increase wind resistance, keeping your hands ready for braking. On a road bike this often means hands on the brake hoods. If you have difficulty braking from this position, check with your bike shop to see whether your levers are mounted in the proper spot. Or maybe you need smaller levers, which are now available.

The hands-on-hoods body position has other advantages, too. Compared to riding the drops, you see the road better and breathe more freely—helpful when you're recovering from the effort of ascent. On a winding, bumpy road, though, riding the curved part of the drops gives you the most secure grip and the levers are right there for you.

If you have an old bottom-of-the-line ten-speed with auxiliary brake levers, don't depend on them for descending; they could fail, as they come out of adjustment easily. And that hand position is not secure: If you bounce on an imperfection in the road, you could go over the handlebars.

Give yourself room on the road. Don't hug the edge on a descent. Having checked for traffic, I move out into the lane far enough to avoid sand or gravel that accumulates near the edge, and so that I can move either way to avoid rough spots. On a long, fairly straight downhill where I can be seen from a distance, I take the center of the lane. Should a driver approach from the rear, I may hold the center if I'm traveling about the speed limit, or I can move over to let him pass.

On a long downhill, pedaling in high gear, even if you are spun out, keeps legs from chilling and stiffening.

Cornering on a descent is the challenge, particularly at high speed. But as you develop competence, you'll love that feeling of mastery. Here are the basics:

- Brake before, not during, a turn. At the apex of the turn, where you'll be leaning most, be especially careful not to brake, or you could cause your tires to slide.
- In a turn, keep your inside pedal up to avoid scraping; on a right turn, that's right leg up. At the same time, put pressure on the left (outside) pedal and lean hard to the inside of the turn. The bike goes in the direction it's being leaned. (If you're a downhill skier, it's the same technique.) Weight the outside arm and grip the handlebar a little tighter with that hand. With knobby tires the same principles apply, but moderate the lean.
- As in normal cornering, pick in advance the line you'll take through the turn. The idea is to "straighten out" the curve as much as possible. Before you reach the corner, you must "set up" for the turn by controlling your speed and establishing your line. Traffic permitting, this typically means moving

Fig. 32: For faster downhill cornering, the idea is to "straighten out" the curve as much as possible. The dotted line shows the path a cyclist would take, traffic permitting, on North American (or other) roads, where traffic keeps to the right.

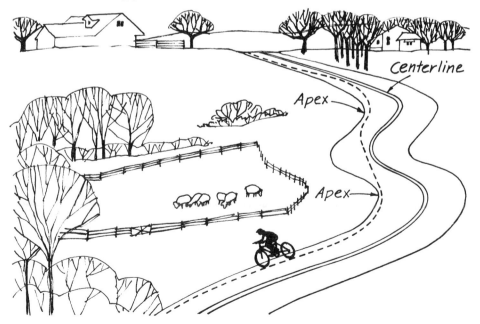

out into the road in advance of the turn. You then dive into the corner close to the apex, then swing out into the road again (see figure 32). Unless the road is closed to traffic, the centerline is as far out as you should go.

Developing this skill takes practice. If, to stay on the pavement, you find yourself having to brake hard as you come out of a corner, either your line was wrong or you were going too fast. Often one corner quickly follows another. In that case, you need to think ahead. Coming out of the first corner, take a line that allows you enough room to set up for the second corner.

Bear in mind, racers take downhill corners and descents generally faster than you or I might. Sometimes that's because they've familiarized themselves with the race route. I used to cover a now-defunct stage race in Colorado called the Coors Classic. I remember American Rebecca Twigg winning the women's division in 1983. On a mountainous stage, the road wound through sheer dropoffs of 1,000 feet overlooking rocks below. Rebecca had been outclimbed by her toughest competitor, Maria Canins of Italy, who was already descending toward the finish with another rider. But cornering more efficiently, Rebecca caught them on the downhill and then broke away just before a sharp curve leading to two back-to-back tunnels. It was dark in the tunnels, but she had scouted and rehearsed the descent. In a daring move, she maintained her speed in the tunnels and finished a minute and a half ahead of her rivals.

That kind of riding demands proficiency. After mastering the basic skills, one way to improve downhill technique is to follow a good bike handler who's willing to help you practice descents. Trace his or her path from a dozen yards behind.

In her first year of bike racing, Connie Carpenter Phinney recalls having trouble in practice with downhills on the world championship road course in Italy. Now a well-known coach and former Olympic champion, Connie says her coaches repeatedly drove her back up the road and had her follow a more experienced teammate through the sharp, difficult turns. The technique drill paid off: Connie was one of the first to complete the descent on race day.

If you have any doubt about your bike's frame and wheel alignment, she adds, have it checked out. It can make a difference.

A hill requires all your concentration, as Joy Crays from Banks, Oregon, learned the hard way. "Let me tell you about the time I got my fancy new bike computer!" she laughs. "It was so fascinating I couldn't keep my hands and eyes off it, which was a mistake. On my first fast descent I was checking my computer for speed while I should've been checking the road for turns. When I did see the turn, it was too late. I hit a blackberry patch and ruined a perfectly great jersey." Take a quick peek at your computer if you like, but do it on the straightaway.

GETTING THE MOST FROM YOUR GEARING

Though we worked on gearing in chapter 6, we didn't go into fully sorting out the shift pattern on your bike. Some cyclists expect to find all the lowest gears on the small chainring, the middle gears on the medium ring, and the high ones on the big chainring, all in orderly sequence.

That's not the case, as you've probably intuited by now. But if sometimes you're still fumbling a bit trying to find just the right gear, here's an easy way to demystify the situation: Chart your gears. Begin by counting the teeth on your chainrings and rear sprockets. (If the tooth numbers are engraved on your chainrings, you don't have to count.) Remove the rear wheel for counting sprocket teeth more easily.

Set up your chart with the teeth on the sprockets, from smallest to largest, running down on the left. Write the chainring-tooth numbers across the top. For example, my road bike has chainrings of 40 and 48 teeth. Its freewheel sprockets have 13, 15, 17, 20, 24, and 28 teeth. Here's my chart:

40T	48T	
13T	(83) inches	99½ inches
15T	72 inches	86½ inches
17T	63½ inches	76 inches
20T	54 inches	64½ inches
24T	45 inches	54 inches
28T	38½ inches	(46) inches

To figure the gear inches for each combination, I referred to the gear number chart at the back of the book. As you can see, the 28 x 40 combination gives me a lowest gear of 38½ inches.

Now let's look at my shifting pattern. I put parentheses around the 83-inch (13 x 40) and the 46-inch (28 x 48) gears because they are unusable. These are the small/small and big/big combinations, or "cross-chain" gears, which we avoid because they put the chain at an exaggerated angle that wears on the gear teeth. If I shift into one of these combinations accidentally, I'll hear an annoying rubbing sound as a warning.

It turns out I have a very simple shift pattern known as *crossover gearing*. Here's how I use it to shift up through the gears:

If I start in the lowest (38½ inches) I can stay on the small chainring as I shift up through 45, then 54, then 63½, then 72 inches. That is, I shift only my right lever.

To go still higher, I shift to the big chainring, or *cross over*. This gives me access to three more gears: 76, 86½, and 99½ inches.

In running through this progression, I've had to *double-shift* (shift both levers) only once—when I crossed over from the 72-inch to the 76-inch gear.

That was easy, and so is down-shifting from the highest gear. With the chain on the big chainring, I shift from 99½, to 86, to 76. I can cross over to 72 (double-shift) and continue to shift lower on the small chainring. Or I can continue down on the big chainring to 64½, then 54, and then cross over.

You've figured out by now that creating crossover gearing necessitated a couple of duplications. In effect this bicycle has only eight different, usable gears. But that's plenty if they're well-chosen. In fact, road racers use crossover gearing because a missed shift can be a costly error. Crossover gearing, which can be created using many different combinations of chainrings and rear sprockets, is useful for other cyclists, too. Its main drawback is that it doesn't work well for truly wide-range gearing for loaded touring and gigantic hills.

You can figure your own gears and shifting pattern similarly. If some of your chainring/sprocket combinations aren't on the chart, here, for your convenience, is the formula we used:

$$\text{Gear inches} = \frac{a}{b} \times c$$

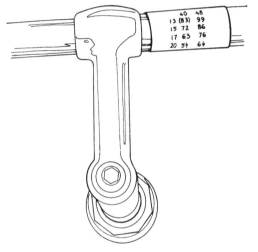

Fig. 33: Tape a gear chart to your handlebars to help you shift systematically.

where   a = number of front
              chainring teeth
          b = number of rear
              sprocket teeth
          c = rear wheel diameter

You may have a more complicated shifting pattern. To use it efficiently, tape your chart to your handlebars and practice with it. Shift in sequence from low to high, for example. If you need to double-shift, do it sequentially, not simultaneously. Also, using your chart, practice making the most efficient shifts to keep up a constant cadence over varying terrain. And don't be embarrassed about having your chart on the bars. A little kidding is a small price to pay for your new skill.

WORTHY WHEELS

As you hone your technique, you deserve a bike worthy of the effort. Assuming yours fits you well, if there's anything likely to be holding you back, it's heavy wheels.

Sherry Biddison of Bainbridge Island, Washington, discovered this by accident—literally. As she tells it, she followed her husband for four years while he rode a spiffy touring bike with lots of gears, and she chugged along on an old ten-speed "with heavy steel rims and all. Then my front rim got bent and was replaced with an aluminum one. If I had known it made that much difference, I would have done it years ago! I always felt like a wimp. I didn't know I was lugging around a handicap . . ."

Sherry proved the old maxim: "A pound off the wheels is worth two pounds off the frame." If you have an inexpensive bicycle with steel rims, the least costly way of perking up its performance is a switch to aluminum alloy rims and better tires. You'd reduce the bike's weight by about 2½ pounds. Furthermore, lighter wheels respond more quickly when you accelerate and when you brake. Aluminum alloy rims also reward you with much surer braking in rainy conditions when rims are wet.

New rims will require new tires. For a skinny tire bike, get high-pressure clinchers (at least 90 to 100 psi). The 27 x 1-inch or 700 x 25C tires are lighter and have less rolling resistance than the wider 1⅛-inch or 28C tire, so they'll be more responsive. They're ideal for training rides, day tours, or even "credit-card touring." At the same time, they should be sure-footed enough for you—just don't go with a treadless tire.

If you envision putting loaded panniers on the bike for touring, then a wider 1⅛-inch (28C) or 1¼-inch (32C) tire would be better. The mechanic at your bike shop can advise you on rim and tire selection if you describe your intentions.

As noted earlier, if you're pounding pavement with knobby tires on a mountain bike, a change to road treads would lessen rolling resistance and boost your speed.

Sharing the Road

The image we, as cyclists, present is extremely important!
–Patti Brehler, Clinton Township, Michigan

Cyclists who don't follow the rules of the road are one of Patti Brehler's pet peeves. Perhaps you agree. Among North American women participating in my survey, more are troubled by careless cyclists than by hills, bad weather, lack of equal opportunity, or even harassment from men. Seeing an irresponsible rider give the rest of us a bad name disturbs us.

Equally worrisome, cycling scofflaws endanger us. That wrong-way biker coming head-on in our road space is a potential accident. Of course, this is not the only cause when two riders collide. Among skilled cyclists, collisions with other bicycles happen just as frequently as collisions with automobiles. Surprised? The tendency among cyclists everywhere is to overestimate the danger from automobiles and underestimate the frequency of other kinds of accidents when cycling. According to a nationwide survey conducted by the Consumer Product Safety Commission in 1991, only 10 percent of the bike accidents resulting in non-fatal injuries involved collisions or near-collisions with moving motor vehicles.

At the same time, maybe we could sharpen up on a point or two to improve our relationships with drivers. Or perhaps we need to master some in-traffic techniques to build confidence and make the going easier. Developing road-use skills cuts cycling accidents by about 80 percent among adult cyclists, various studies have demonstrated. Once we have these skills, the evidence shows, cycling is a reasonably safe activity (contrary to loudly proclaimed opinions of the non-cycling establishment, which often attempts to deny us access to the road).

Additionally, we may have concerns about how to prevent or deal with harassment on the road. This chapter will help you be a more competent, assertive, and—possibly—more considerate cyclist in traffic.

THE GRACIOUS CYCLIST

"I train year-round in the Detroit area, which is motor city," says Patti Brehler, half of the marathon tandem team, the Pink Leopards (see chapter 9). "When I started wearing a helmet, I noticed I was getting more courtesy from drivers. I decided that the image I projected made a difference in the way they treated me."

She became conscious of cycling habits—her own and others'. "I'm bothered by some cycling clubs I observe around here on rides. They run red lights and disregard other traffic laws, ruining it for everyone," she adds. Even when Patti's riding after dark, she stops for red lights. "I think, 'What if someone would see me?'"

The ripple effect works both ways. Efficient, courteous riding helps show drivers that bicycles can be part of an orderly traffic flow. Bearing in mind the power inherent in the word, I suggest that we be *gracious* cyclists; that is, let's remember we have a right to share the road but be thoughtful doing so. We covered a few basics in chapter 6, including signaling your turns and riding with the flow of traffic like a vehicle. In addition, put yourself in the drivers' shoes to see why you would appreciate the following:

- Keep right (in the United States and Canada; left, in the United Kingdom). As a motorist, you'd be irritated to see bicyclists in the middle of the road for no obvious reason. If the shoulder of the road is clean and unobstructed by vehicles, potholes, sewer grates, or other hazards, it makes sense to use it. However, you need only ride as far right (or left) as is practicable. It's better not to ride at the far edge of the shoulder, but about three or four feet away from traffic, where you can still be seen by vehicles entering from a side road. Is the shoulder littered with bits of gravel and broken glass? Save your tires by riding just to the inside of the road edge, since car tires will have swept that area free of debris.
- When you stop to read a map or wait for a companion, pull well off the road. You'll avoid riling drivers and save your own skin in the bargain. Be especially careful in taking a breather at the top of a hill, where a motorist may have a tough time seeing you.
- On a busy road, leave the gabbing for later; don't ride two abreast, causing traffic to back up or cars to veer dangerously wide around you. If a string of cars slows behind you, even though you're in single file, pull off the road briefly to let them pass. In this situation a group of cyclists should break into subgroups of three or four, leaving a few car-lengths of space in between to facilitate passing.
- Remember intersection etiquette. The law requires you to stop for traffic lights. When you do, putting your foot down does much more for public relations than if you ride in circles in front of a motorist waiting for a red light. Save the track stand for the track. And in consideration of the other guy's wax job, don't lean on his or her car.
- Keep a turning lane open. If the law permits a turn on a red light but you're going straight, stop just on the inside of the straight-ahead lane so cars can go by.
- Don't cause drivers to repass you unnecessarily. Let's say you've been cycling a busy, narrow road on which cars have had trouble getting by you. At the next red light sit several drivers who have already patiently overtaken you. Should you whiz past them on the right to enter the intersection ahead of them when the light turns green? If you do and they get caught behind you again, could you blame them for feeling annoyed? A more gracious approach: Move up in line only far enough to just make the light.

DEFENSIVE TACTICS

Most of my cycling is in London, and actually I quite enjoy battling with the traffic. It's exhilarating. You've got to keep awake and concentrate to foresee things that are likely to happen, like cars pulling out of junctions, or turning across you . . . It's good for your reaction. –Julia King, London, England

As experienced motorists, we know the necessity for "defensive driving"—staying alert to traffic patterns around us and anticipating errors other drivers might make. We're not afraid, but ready to give a warning toot at another driver about to pull out without looking.

A cyclist must be similarly wary. These days, more than ever, drivers are distracted by their car phones or who knows what else. They can fail to see you or even a traffic light or stop sign. When you get the green, don't just go without looking for a driver who might be running the light.

Even when you have the right-of-way and are moving, scan driveways and side streets to see who's coming from where. Get in the habit of noting if a motorist is looking in your direction, and try to make eye contact. If you can't, a good, loud "Hey!" gains the driver's attention and is better than a bicycle bell (not loud enough in traffic) or a whistle (requires you to take one hand off the handlebar or ride with the whistle always in your mouth). You can also call to a pedestrian about to step into your path: "Heads up!" or "Watch out!" Maintain your pace but be ready to make an emergency turn to avoid collision, if a driver or pedestrian in a total fog fails to yield. (A quick turn maneuver takes practice; it's covered in the next section.)

Whenever possible, look for feedback that tells you vehicle operators have seen you and intend to cooperate with you. Eye contact helps in many situations. I also look for a car's turn signal or note which way the wheels are turned if, for example, I'm stopped at an intersection and want to proceed straight while making sure a driver doesn't turn into me. If I do make eye contact, the motorist may motion me to proceed. I check that no other traffic is coming (never assume the driver has done this for you) then nod my thanks and go on.

By the way, you can take a motorist's turn signal as a warning (as above), but don't count on a turn signal as a guarantee of anything. Don't pull out into his path. Maybe he's signaling a turn farther up the road or he's forgotten the blinker is on. This can really get you into trouble.

Use your ears, too, as sounds around you provide important cues. Don't wear your personal stereo when riding outdoors. As one San Francisco bike commuter, Greta S., puts it: "When I see cyclists using a Walkman, I wonder what they're listening to. Prayers? 'Lord, please get me home safely because I'm partially disabled in traffic?'"

Keep an eye peeled for hazards in your path before you get to them, so you have time to decide your course of action. And perfect your dodge (chapter 6).

Many accidents among experienced cyclists are falls in which no car, dog, or other bike is involved. Watch out for these dangers:

- Don't ride over gratings with wheel-grabbing slots parallel to the road edge. Gratings are often near the curb—another reason not to ride too close to it.
- Beware of an uneven surface where road and shoulder meet; often there's a slight drop to the shoulder. If you happen to drift off the road, you can't simply drift back. Your wheel could catch, knocking the bike out from under you. To cross back over the lip of the road, approach it at a fairly wide angle. (Watch out for traffic.) Or stop and place your bicycle back on the road.
- If bridge expansion joints are wide enough to be wheel swallowers, walk your bike.
- Water-filled potholes can be treacherous; water may camouflage a deeper hole than you think.
- Slow down for protruding railroad tracks and cattle grids. Hitting them too hard can dent a rim, especially on a skinny-tired road bike. To protect your wheels in this situation, get up off the saddle and crouch with knees and elbows flexed, centering your body weight evenly between the two wheels.
- Tracks that angle across the road necessitate extra caution or they will throw you. Experienced cyclists change course to encounter the tracks at a right angle. Just be wary not to weave into traffic.

Watch out for the inexperienced cyclist on the road. Merely passing such people can be risky, since many a careless bicyclist doesn't ride in a straight line on the road or could veer into you with a sudden turn from the curb. Making your presence known doesn't guarantee a correct response from such a rider. The smart thing is to treat this cyclist as you would a larger, slow-moving vehicle in your lane; that is, you change lanes to pass, after using the backward scan. If necessary, slow down behind this cyclist until it is safe to make the lane change.

To alert a trained cyclist before passing, say, "On your left," and ride by (on the left), allowing a safe margin of space between you. (In the U.K. say, "On your right," and pass right.)

Note that often the least safe place to ride is a cycle path, partly because of the mix of users, who may include inexperienced cyclists, walkers, joggers, skateboarders, in-line skaters, and more! Of course, the mass bike ride, another situation that brings folks of all ages and experience levels together, offers lots of opportunities for crashes with other cyclists. The safest place is the front of the pack or some other spot that gives you some breathing room.

EMERGENCY MANEUVERS

Like any other crisis, we respond best to traffic emergencies with advance preparation. You may not need these moves often, but even a single use in your cycling lifetime merits the practice.

The panic stop. To stop very quickly, you must strongly apply the front brake, which has double the stopping power of the rear. Here's how to do that without pitching over the handlebars.

As you're squeezing the front brake lever hard, apply the rear brake lightly and at the same time, move back on the saddle to place more weight over the back wheel. As the rear wheel starts to skid—your clue that it's about to lift off the ground—ease your pressure on the front brake.

Try this maneuver at slow speed in a traffic-free area, like an empty parking lot. Remember to use light pressure on the rear brake, or else you'll make the back wheel skid too soon. In your repeated practice stops, try increasing your force on the front brake a little bit each time, until the back wheel actually does begin to lift off. Immediately release the front brake lever.

The quick turn. What can you do when a thoughtless motorist makes a turn so close in front of you that you have no time to brake? To avoid plowing into the car, make a "quick turn" in the same direction as the car.

Since this requires a sharper turn than in normal cornering, you must modify your technique. If you need to make a quick turn to the right, you begin with a momentary turn of the handlebars to the left (away from where you want to go). This causes your bicycle to lean right; then you can steer right. In other words, it begins like the dodge (chapter 6). If you do no correcting, you'll find yourself leaning into a sharp turn in the opposite direction.

Practice this in an empty parking lot. Do the turn slowly at first, while you develop a feel for it. Gradually increase your speed with repeated practice. As you do, you'll see you don't have to steer so sharply to make the turn. Work on it during a few sessions to master it; then practice it from time to time. Do it now so you'll be ready if you ever need it.

CITY STREET-SMART

It's quite a jungle out there. Motorists are a mixed bunch. Some are tolerant and will sit behind you until there really is enough room to go past. But more often if they think they can get through a gap, well, they'll try it and see. And sometimes they can't. I'm not a cyclist to take risks. I won't go into a gap that I see is going to close up. I'll always cycle within my own limits and the limits of my machine, and I know what they are. Having said that, I suppose I'm quite pushy.

You've got to have the courage of your convictions. There's no use going out there thinking, "I'm going to be scared by this traffic." Because you'll wobble and you will get knocked off your bike. Or you'll try and ride too close to the side of the road and somebody will open a car door on you.
–Julia King, London, England

An overly-cautious crawl through traffic is not only maddeningly slow, it's also risky. Maintaining a brisk pace and riding the proper portion of the roadway makes it easier for drivers to see you and helps ensure that they'll yield right-of-way when traffic law requires. Be defensively aware, but don't hang back in fear.

While you should keep as far right (or left) as is practicable, you have the right to use as much of the road width as your safety prescribes. We've observed that weaving in and out among parked cars renders you less visible to drivers and that you must give yourself room in case a car door is flung open in your path. (Would you believe you might even be held liable for damage to the car?) Hugging a curb too closely also makes it easier for a driver to pass you and then cut you off by turning in front of you. Curb-huggers appear to be, and usually are, riding slowly; motorists are more likely to disregard them.

When a one-way street has two lanes, the best way to avoid being squeezed between parked cars and moving traffic is to position yourself far enough into a lane so that drivers are required to pass you in the other one. Check for traffic behind you before moving over. Then once you do, proceed in a straight line on the road. As a general rule, the proper place for you is the right lane (in North America), since the vehicle code decrees that slower traffic keep right. In the United Kingdom the opposite pertains, since slower traffic stays to the left.

Any time you change lanes, like a car, you must yield to traffic already occupying the lane you want to enter—thus the novice cyclist's biggest bugaboo in North America, the left-hand turn. (In the United Kingdom read "right-hand turn.") Mastering the left-hand turn will make riding in traffic less worrisome. The key is communication. Most drivers will cooperate if you make your intentions clear.

Let's say you'll have to cross two traffic lanes to make your turn. Begin some distance back from the anticipated turn.

- First, to gain the cooperation of a driver behind you to cross your own lane, give a clear hand signal and scan quickly over your shoulder. Repeated glances may be required until there's a break in traffic or the driver behind motions you over; then cross your own lane.
- Next signal and scan again for an assist from a driver in the next lane so you can cross it. When you can, move to the far side of the lane; or, if the lane is a turning lane, simply merge with it.
- Continue to signal the turn as you wait for your light; turn when it is safe to do so.

If overtaking traffic is coming on too fast for you to turn like a vehicle, you can always dismount and walk your bike across at a light like a pedestrian. Switching to the pedestrian mode may also let you turn left where a turn is prohibited to vehicles.

Your choice of roads makes a difference in the traffic conditions you'll encounter. Sometimes the decision is made for you by restrictions that prohibit bicycles from certain roads. Otherwise, it's your judgment call.

Give careful thought when picking a training or commuting route you expect to ride frequently. "I'm constantly fine-tuning for the shortest, flattest, most expedient way with the fewest stop signs where I have to wait for cross-traffic," reports Greta of her urban commute.

"I'll often choose a street with fewer cars—not so much for safety because it can be safe with a lot of cars—but because I'd rather not ride with my face in the exhaust pipe."

As a rule, if you wish to move quickly through a city or other built-up area, main streets will have fewer stop signs than will intersecting side streets. Traffic lights will be timed in your favor. Although traffic volume is likely to be heavier, the compensation is wider lanes with longer sight lines, where you'll be more visible. And you can expect fewer encounters with incompetent cyclists on these streets. Bear in mind, the fewer the intersections, the faster and safer the going. If you choose main streets and highways, it's best to ride at a snappy pace but leave yourself some reserve to accelerate if you need to.

If you prefer a more scenic route and slower going, back streets may be the better choice. "And I go out of my way for road quality," adds Greta. "Fresh pavement is such a thrill, especially with slick tires and a little downhill. There are many exciting ways to get from point A to point B, and the more options you give yourself, the better ride you'll have."

GETTING THROUGH GRIDLOCK

One of the many advantages of the bicycle is that it lets you keep moving when motor vehicle traffic is gridlocked. But proceed with caution and continue to obey traffic lights and other signals. Ride slowly enough to stop if an unwitting driver should open a door in front of you. Beware of other cyclists, hidden by vehicles ahead, who could pull into your path.

If a single car or truck stops in your lane in front of you for no obvious reason, take extra care, because the driver's course of action is unpredictable. Wait for the vehicle to move on, or pass it on the left (in North America; right in the United Kingdom), allowing plenty of room to spare.

Every stopped vehicle has a blind spot and a safety zone. For example, you have no worry next to the rear wheels, since they can't move sideways—only forward or back. You are also positioned where the next driver back can see you.

As you near the front of the car, you pass through a blind spot. Check the front wheels; if they are turned to pull out or if you hear the engine rev up, wait by the back wheels until the driver makes his move.

Be especially cautious when you see driveways or parking spaces along the road that the stopped motorist might pull into. In this situation, some cyclists rap on the back window to catch the motorist's attention before trying to pass. Then slowly move laterally away from the vehicle into the open space; look back to see if the driver has noticed you before you come in range of the front wheels.

Should you need to cut across a lane of traffic in front of a stopped vehicle, signal and catch the driver's eye first for assistance. Then check to make sure the car in front is not likely to roll back into you (as sometimes happens on an incline at a traffic light, or if a driver who's protruding too far into an intersection decides to back up without looking). When it's safe to cut across, before entering the next lane, scan back for another cyclist who might be approaching.

If your lane is clear of cars behind you but traffic is stopped in the next lane (a turning lane perhaps), move over in your lane for extra "breathing space." Watch for any turned wheels that suggest a driver might pull out into your lane. Give a yell if you need to warn that driver of your presence.

When a bus or truck is stopped in the curb lane, don't try to pass it on the right (in North America; left in the United Kingdom). You risk hitting passengers or drivers who may step into your path. Allow yourself plenty of room and pass on the left (North America), moving warily in case you encounter a passenger coming around the bus.

With these cautions in mind, you can move safely in stalled traffic while all those drivers sit fuming at the wheel. If traffic isn't fully stopped but merely crawling at a few miles per hour, you can still navigate through it. But be even more careful. Pass only when cars have nowhere to go but straight ahead. Stop and wait at a vehicle's rear wheels if its front wheels are turned, indicating the driver may pull out into you. Watch for long vehicles that might be turning; don't let yourself get caught between a bus or a truck and the curb.

ASSERTING YOURSELF ON NARROW ROADS

Lightly traveled country roads make lovely cycling, but we must be alert nonetheless. Especially on narrow roads, take care to avoid the inevitable squeeze play that occurs if one car passes another near you. You could be hit if, to avoid a head-on collision with the other car, a driver pulls back over too soon after passing you.

To prevent an unsafe situation, you must take the initiative while a motorist still has enough time and distance to respond to your action. For example, as soon as you sense traffic approaching in front of you, scan back for any coming from behind. Let's say a car is coming; to prevent a squeeze play, move out closer to the center of your lane. Monitor the driver's approach with a quick backward glance to signal your awareness of him. As the car nears, use a hand signal that says "hold back" to the motorist behind you. After the oncoming car has passed and you see the road is clear, return to your usual position near the road edge and let the waiting vehicle pass.

Likewise, when curves limit visibility, it's in your best interest to deter a driver behind you from trying to pass you unsafely. Why? Around the bend, if that driver comes face to face with an oncoming car, she'll pull back over, and you could get crunched.

How likely is it that the person behind the wheel will go ballistic at being slowed down? Not very, says Myrna Meyers, a triathlete and a retired Effective Cycling instructor from White Plains, New York. Remember, she says, you're simply requiring the motorist to do what the law requires, to reduce speed when passing is risky. Nine out of ten drivers will perceive you as helpful. But for safety's sake, Myrna observes the motorist's reaction in her cycling mirror. There are those odd drivers, she notes, who "will ignore my signal and pull madly around me." If Myrna sees she has a hothead back there who may not slow down, she's prepared to leave the road in a hurry. In this situation a mirror could be a lifesaver, and the fat tire bikes many of us ride can handle a quick exit off the pavement, especially if you practice doing it every now and again.

Keep a watchful eye for all oncoming traffic on narrow roads, especially if curves entice drivers to take their half out of the middle of the road. With a line of oncoming cars, beware of motorists who pull out to pass. Sometimes they don't see you or they underestimate the distance needed to pass without endangering you. If necessary, ride off the road.

As noted, simply being seen is a concern for cyclists. On rolling or hilly roads remember that—bright clothing or no—after you've crested a hill, you disappear for the driver approaching from the rear. Maybe you're out of breath, but don't dawdle at the top. In fact, your safest action is to speed up and quickly start on your descent. Your out-of-the-saddle, side-to-side movement and the bobbing of your brightly helmeted head as you crest the hill should catch the driver's attention before you drop out of sight. A speedy descent will help put some distance between you.

HANDLING HARASSMENT

I was riding on an isolated road in Tampa when a vehicle with three teenage boys passed very close. One boy slapped me hard on the back side. I noted the license plate number as they sped away, and being a private investigator, I was able to obtain the driver's name and address. I called the police, who found the culprits at their parents' home in my neighborhood. The boys' father apologized to me, then made his sons do the same. They will think twice before slapping another female again!

–Alison Boh, Temple Terrace, Florida

I find it extremely frustrating that, because of harassment, I talk myself out of taking overnight trips or short tours alone. It stops me from doing what I really want to do.

–Randy Lee Jablin, Brooklyn, New York

A rude slap or loud horn blast right in your ear is not only disconcerting, it's dangerous, possibly causing you to lose control and crash. Even worse are the offenders who throw bottles, shove you off the bike, or try to run you off the road. It probably doesn't help much for us to be told that male cyclists also worry about harassment; we feel vulnerable once it's happened to us.

The first time I ever had my rump thumped, I was too outraged and surprised to do anything but shout in anger. The next time I wrote down the license number. When I called the police, they refused to reprimand the driver unless I was willing to press charges. I didn't want to retaliate, I just wanted to make them think. So I dropped the matter. But I congratulate Alison for getting her point across.

How do we put a stop to this sort of thing and keep it from intimidating us? Patti Brehler has developed a great arsenal of responses. As she points out, the harasser wants a reaction. "So when it used to happen I'd call 'I love you!' instead of flipping them off. Laugh it off," she advises. "You don't solve anything by getting upset; you just stress yourself."

She believes that improving her own cycling skills has made her a less vulnerable-looking target. If you feel confident and project that, it makes a difference. Likewise, knowing how to make an emergency repair matters. "I do all the maintenance on our bikes. If women can take care of themselves, it shows," says Patti.

Good cycling skills offer another benefit. When you cycle like a vehicle driver, motorists don't have to deviate from obeying traffic law to accommodate you. So when somebody in a car is doing something unusual, it's easier for you to spot. Then you can take action sooner.

Patti finds that wearing a helmet mirror helps. "There've been times I've gotten off the road because I thought I'd better. Either the car looked like it was trying to get too close, or I saw that arm out the window." And the helmet itself helps disguise gender.

Sometimes dress can be a factor. Patti generally avoids halter tops or short crop tops, or anything else cut too low for leaning over the handlebars. "I wear outrageous things—bright pink leopard skin tights and neon green jackets—but that's to be visible to drivers," Patti says.

By contrast, Myrna Meyer is somewhat less optimistic. Even gray hair doesn't spare her. She's had kids riding straight at her on bikes, trying to play "chicken," and she's endured lots of verbal harassment. What she wears seems to make little difference.

Occasionally she's caught up with the troublemakers. Myrna, who doesn't scare easily, tells how a kid screamed at her from a summer camp bus, which she overtook at a light. "I got in front of the bus and went through obvious motions of writing the license number down. I told the bus driver he was responsible for his passengers' actions and that if it happened again I'd get the lawyers in our bike club to go after the camp. I made an impression and he apologized."

Myrna suggests that riding with a partner might cut down on the problem, but that usually she prefers to ride alone and continues to do so.

How much should you worry about harassment? I've talked with many cyclists who experience little trouble. The problem varies widely from one area to another. Says Myrna, "It has its ups and downs. Thirty years ago the attitude was 'You don't belong on the road.' Then as more people began cycling, the heckling and so on subsided. Today cycling is a yuppie thing and there's a backlash. Out of resentment, I think, harassment is on the rise again."

In her locale, Patti thinks harassment on the decline: More drivers themselves cycle now or have friends who ride. But we can't afford to act complacent. "There are pockets of harassment in some parts of Detroit. And suburban sprawl and deteriorating roads create places where cyclists and motorists compete for space on too-narrow roads, so drivers can get irritable." It pays to keep your cycling skills sharp and your wits about you.

For further instruction in safe riding techniques, I recommend taking an Effective Cycling course, offered in many communities around the United States; ask at your local bike shop or contact the League of American Bicyclists (see appendix) to locate an instructor.

True Grit

Both triathletes, my husband and I live in a small town in Wyoming. We are definitely freaks around here and take a lot of abuse from the local ranchers. We do much of our riding on a narrow two-lane highway leading to the Uinta Mountains. Ranchers who live along the route always haul long horse trailers or large semis full of cattle and just about push us off the road most of the time. We fought over space all last summer. However, by fall their attitude began to change. They realized I wasn't just a city slicker with a fancy bicycle and strange clothes when I was still out there in November in 25-degree weather, riding along enjoying the Wyoming countryside. A few of the ranchers even waved! –Linda Prater, Evanston, Wyoming

Fat Tire Freedom

Where the road ends, mountain bike freedom begins. I first tasted it on the back of a mountain bike tandem, hanging on behind a wild man I call Jarrin' John. Together we plunged—forever, it seemed—down a power-line cut in a Pennsylvania state forest about a half-hour's drive from home. On that fat-tired bicycle-built-for-two, we ricocheted from rock to rock, trees blurring to a smear of green on either side, my butt bouncing on the saddle.

I was a real beginner who didn't know how to use my legs for suspension. Once my right foot flew out of the toeclip and I yelped, fearing I would follow it. John slowed so I could settle in again. "You have to really shove 'em in there," he shouted. All I could do was hold on and go with it, telling myself that he knew what he was doing. I relaxed a little and thought how the ride reminded me of downhill skiing—the controlled speed, the nip of the wind, the challenge of working the terrain. You focus on exactly what you're doing, wiping out all other concerns.

We reached the bottom without mishap. In full adrenaline rush, I looked back up that mountain, awed at what a skilled rider on knobbies could do. I'd really been missing out by just cruising my bike on pavement.

But you don't have to be fearless to get into it. As in any other skill sport, if you ride within your ability, you minimize the risk. Since that day, I've found fat tire freedom on my own mountain bike and at my own pace.

With patient friends giving pointers, I mastered trails in the wooded parkway about a mile from my door: gravelly fire roads; steep singletrack through a grassy meadow; root-laced, rock-studded downhills; climbs that get the old ticker going; flat cinder paths for recovery and socializing. This varied terrain makes a fun practice loop, where I can still enjoy watching sunlight glitter on the Little Lehigh Creek and hearing the chatter of a kingfisher as it darts above the water.

Too much work? On lazier outings I've spent whole summer days rolling along a canal towpath, cool in the shade of trees overhead, without a worry about traffic. I was free to investigate the remains of forgotten canal towns and lockkeepers' houses from a vantage point the road didn't offer.

If you lack canal towpaths, you may instead find fire roads, gentle footpaths, or old railway beds converted to bike trails. On these, you need few special skills. Ask at the shop where you bought your mountain bike for good places to ride it. Or for converted rail-trails in your area, visit the web site of the Rails-to-Trails Conservancy (see appendix). And, no matter how easy the path looks, wear your helmet.

You may be surprised at what's waiting off-road, perhaps just outside your door. To Suzanne Vannell, home is "a huge apartment complex about thirty miles north of Detroit—an area no one would mistake for off-road heaven," where a golf course and cemetery provide the closest things to wilderness. Once, Suzanne remembers, she skirted a stand of trees bordering the cemetery and turned onto a short trail that passes a pond surrounded by cattails:

There I saw a deer, head down, drinking. Slowly I got off the bike and stood still. The deer drank on, then a second stepped from the bushes. It caught my scent, ears going up like flags, alerting the first deer, too. For a few sweet, electrifying seconds we stared at each other. Then in a flash of white tails they were gone. I rode to where they had been and looked at their tracks in the damp sand . . .

BACK TO NATURE

What's not to like about such serene, scenic rides? Find out what you can discover when you take your bike off the asphalt. These tips should ease the transition.

- Check your position. For both on- and off-road riding, your saddle height should allow a slight bend in the knee with your leg fully extended at the bottom of the pedal stroke. Keep your elbows bent and your shoulders relaxed to help soak up vibrations.
- Use toeclips and straps. Without them, even on flat trails, a slight bump could make your foot slip off the pedal. If you get caught by that whirling pedal in the back of the heel, it really smarts. Toeclips also help you climb more efficiently. Keep the straps a little loose so you can quickly slip your foot out when you need to. As noted in chapter 10, "Building Fitness," I recommend toeclips to new off-road riders, except for roadies already so comfortable with clipless pedals that you can release them in a nanosecond. (But beware in sloppy conditions, as clipless pedals can fail to let go of a muddy shoe.)
- Know your shifters. If you need to, play with them on flat, easy trails. Get used to shifting smoothly between the three chainrings without looking down, so you can focus your attention where it belongs—on the trail. (See chapter 6, "On Your Bike!," for gearing basics.) Then practice gearing to suit changes in terrain. You want a reasonably "spinny" cadence, between 60 and 80 rpm. As on the road, shift down before you begin a climb to avoid wear on the drivetrain or a missed shift. Aim to develop a sense of what gear you're in without looking at the drivetrain. Then on any terrain you'll be ready with a quick shift.
- Adjust tire pressure. On smooth, firm-surfaced trails that don't feel much different from pavement, try your tires almost fully inflated. But in other

situations, a little give in those knobbies (about 35 to 45 psi) takes out some of the bounce. You'll have better traction on climbs, too, because the tire will have a broader footprint. So put the squeeze on: If you can't press in the sidewall slightly with your thumb and forefinger, let out some air and try it again.

Experiment to see what works best. If you start getting pinch flats or bottom out and flatten a rim, you let out too much air. Generally, tires should be softer when you're riding on soft stuff, like sand with no rocks. For firmer, stonier ground, pump 'em up harder. Carry a frame pump in case of a flat and to pump up before emerging to ride on pavement later.

• Read the trail. Just as you need to scan a paved road for hazards, look ahead on even the smoothest of trails or four-wheel-drive roads for a possible washout, rut, erosion-control installation, broken glass, or whatever. To give yourself plenty of response time, bounce your gaze from directly in front of your wheel to about twenty feet up ahead. Scan back toward your wheel and then look farther ahead again. When you locate a hazard, like a rock in the center of the path, train your peepers on where you want to go—the cleanest route past it. If you stare at that rock too long, you'll plow right into it. We tend to steer where we look.

Should you have to get off and walk over or around some obstacle, that's OK. Just call it cross training.

• Use the ready position. If a section of trail is bumpy, level the pedals and stand on them with knees bent, so that they, not your butt, absorb the jarring as the bike bounces around under you. Shift your weight back with your thighs lightly gripping the wide sides of the saddle at the rear (the *flanges*. We call this the *ready position* because in it you're ready for almost anything. It's good for coasting (over rocks, for example) where you might hit a pedal if you had one down. Use it for descending, too, since on the downhills you need to move your center of gravity back some to keep weight over the rear wheel.

• Strategy for sand. A flat sandy road looks like easy going, but a deep drift of this dry, gritty stuff can make the bike wallow. To cope, slide back into the ready position to unweight the front wheel. Spin low gears and let the front wheel wander rather than fighting to keep it going straight. Stay loose and go with the flow, or as they told me in the Southwest, "keep smiling and say 'I love sand.'"

• Go easy on the brakes. Don't jam 'em on. If you need to come to a halt, squeeze both brakes and try to roll gently to a standstill. Whenever you do use the stoppers, shift your weight back to the rear of the saddle, as we do on the road. Should you forget, a quick stop could send you head-first over the bar—an *endo* in cycle speak.

• Review cornering basics. (See chapter 6, "On Your Bike.")

There you have the fundamentals, which will quickly become second nature to you. Like Suzanne, liberate the kid inside:

Mountain biking makes me feel like a kid again, flying down gravel roads, discovering the world all brand new, over and over again from my bike. I've found magic, riding in that free, unworried, ready-for-anything kind of way kids have and too many grown-ups have long forgotten. Sitting upright, I can actually see the scenery. And my fat, knobby tires hug the terrain, making for a stable, secure ride.

GETTING DIRTWISE

Now how about some vavoom along with the view? Develop a little more finesse, and you and your MTB can tackle paths with technical challenges—steeper ups and downs, bumps and rocks, ruts and roots. Soon you'll be sold on the thrill of the narrow trails we call *singletrack*.

To build skills and confidence, begin on easier terrain with few obstructions in the path. Progress gradually to more challenging geography and greater speed. If a portion of a trail seems beyond your current skills, don't be embarrassed to walk—especially the first time on a new trail. With practice the same technical sections get easier as you learn to anticipate the next move. My biking buddies and I proved that recently by riding a familiar but tricky loop in the opposite direction, something we hadn't tried before. Afterwards we all agreed it was as if we were experiencing the trail for the first time.

Always pedal with a partner on isolated trails, in case of a mishap. Besides, a quick way to improve is to learn from more accomplished friends. Just pick your companions carefully and ask them to take you for a nice, easy ride. Once you're rolling along, if they seem to forget how it felt to be a beginner, speak up. "Hey, hammerheads! I think we're going too fast. Do you mind if we slow down?" Take an active part in setting guidelines for the ride.

A true fat tire friend will stay with you to offer suggestions and an encouraging word, or at least wait for you at the top of a climb. I've known guys and gals both who've been great at this, so it's not necessarily a gender thing. Last year a couple of good friends, Carol Stickles and her husband Gene Krisukas, introduced my husband and me to some new trails in a park a half-hour's drive from home. The challenge level was about three notches above the local stuff in the parkway. On that first ride Gene led the way, stopping frequently to suggest we look over the hairier descents. "It gets kinda tricky here," he'd say with a laugh. "Don't be afraid to walk!" His no-pressure mentoring worked for us. We were hooked, and once or twice a week we met for rides all season long. Trust me, if you have a crummy time, you probably just chose the wrong partner. Try again.

Along with tips already discussed in the "Back to Nature" section, here's what you need to know.

• Learn to mount up. "Who needs to be told how to get on this rig?" you say. But mounting correctly on level ground will prepare you for those harder restarts in the middle of a climb. To mount on a hill, simultaneously squeeze the brake levers so that the bike can't roll and hold it upright, not tilted to one side. Straddle the top tube with one foot on the pedal in the power position (pedal up between top center and horizontal) while standing tiptoe on the other foot. Perch your butt on the saddle nose for stability. (Or if you can't, then let it poke you in the fanny so you can feel where it is.) Got all that? Now push down on the raised pedal as you release your brakes and lift that other foot onto your free pedal, meanwhile slide back on the seat. Practice moving smoothly to keep your balance. Don't try to clip in or slide into the toeclip until you have some forward momentum.

• Keep your eyes on the trail. The terrain changes quickly under your spinning wheels, so be attentive. If your bike—or your partner—makes a funny noise, it's best to stop safely, then turn your attention to bike diagnostics or your friend's booboo. If you must check out your machine while on the move, then scan the trail for clear going ahead before sneaking a quick peek at the problem.

• Allow room for error. When following, let several bike-lengths open up between yourself and your buddy ahead of you. That way, if she stops suddenly, you won't plow into her. If someone behind you is tailgating, don't hesitate to suggest that you need more space. Especially on technical sections, in our foursome we give each other a big gap to move and groove. After all, if you're going great through some gnarly part, you don't want to have to disrupt the flow because your partner has halted abruptly in the middle of the path just ahead.

• Pick a line. Leaving this gap also lets you read the section of trail in front of you and *pick your line* around a stump, tree root, or other obstacle on the path. As noted above, read the trail with a roving eye to take in the trail far enough ahead to respond. If you spy a tricky section coming up, plan "backwards" to choose a line of travel that will take you most efficiently through the tough part. As in a game of checkers or chess, plan several moves in advance.

   Sometimes that means riding over one rock in order to route yourself among a bunch of them just beyond. The bike wheel wants to go fairly straight instead of turning around every obstacle. With any kind of forward momentum, expect to make minor corrections rather than wiggling all over the path.

• Look where you want to go. Make a mental note of what you want to miss—that stump, for example—then focus your gaze on the line you've chosen.

   If you need to pick your way between two obstacles, center your gaze. Let's say some saplings close in on either side of the trail, or you want to

IMBA's Rules of the Trail

Trail access is a huge issue for our sport. Thousands of miles of dirt trails have been closed to mountain bikers. The irresponsible riding habits of a few cyclists have been a factor. Following the International Mountain Bicycling Association's six simple guidelines will contribute to your own safety and to good PR for mountain bikers in your area.

1. *Ride on open trails only.* My favorite park, for example, opens some multiuse trails for mountain biking while restricting others; to cycle on the prohibited trails would risk closure of the entire park to bicycles. Take care not to trespass on private land and be aware that federal and state wilderness areas are closed to cycling.

2. *Leave no trace.* Practice low-impact cycling, says IMBA. Stay on existing trails and dont create new ones. In some areas cycling even the legal trails in certain conditions, such as after a rain, can cause damage. Be sensitive to the dirt beneath you. And pack out your trash.

3. *Control your bicycle.* Inattention for even a second can cause problems, IMBA reminds us. Obey all bicycle speed regulations.

4. *Always yield trail.* Slow way down to pass hikers, or pull off the trail to let them by. When approaching from behind, use a bell or make your presence known with a polite "excuse me" or friendly "hello." This gives the person time to pick which side of the path to move to and time to move. Sometimes a bike is so quiet that a hiker or another cyclist doesn't know you're there. Anticipate other trail users around corners or in blind spots.

When you stop on the trail—e.g., you bailed out in the middle of a technical section—pull your bike over to the side so you don't impede another rider's progress.

5. *Don't scare animals.* All animals are startled by an unannounced approach, a sudden movement, or a loud noise. Slow your rig to a walk to pass horseback riders, or ask if it's OK to ride slowly past. If someone indicates a horse spooks easily, don't even speak as they go by. To have a horse with rider rear up on the path beside you is a terrifying and dangerous experience, as I learned by opening my mouth at the wrong moment. Giving these animals a wide berth is good horse sense.

IMBA adds: Running cattle or disturbing wildlife is a serious offense. Leave gates as you found them or as marked.

6. *Plan ahead.* Be self-sufficient, keep your equipment in good repair, and carry necessary clothing or supplies for changes in weather or other conditions, says IMBA. Always wear a helmet.

IMBA seeks to promote responsible off-road cycling. The organization works with other trail-user groups and aims to keep trails open and to gain access to new trails for mountain bikers. The $20 annual membership fee covers a newsletter and other materials. (See appendix.)

steer between two posts that close off the path to motor vehicles. The natural thought is "Aaack, I don't want to bump those with my handlebars!" Take note of them but direct your gaze midway between the obstacles, and you'll sail right through. The same is true for a narrow bridge—focus on the center of the far end of the bridge; don't stare straight down.

•Jump that log. Well, not any log. Start with a stick and gradually work up to logs several inches in diameter. I get a charge out of log jumping, and it's easier than I thought.

First practice lifting the front wheel, without a log, on an unobstructed trail. At cruising speed, stand crouched on level pedals over the handlebar, with elbows really bent. Push down with your arms to compress the tire (and suspension fork), then pull up while moving back on the saddle. The front wheel should lift. This method works for me on my bike with rigid forks, and with front suspension, it gives a good hop.

Practice doing this over sticks and then over small logs. Remember, pedals level. Timing is the key, as you'll quickly discover. Lift too soon and you're back on the ground and riding smack into the log. (If you do that to a big log, you would sail right over without your bike. That's why we're practicing with small ones.) If you lift too late, your bike will bump over the log anyway, assuming your weight is back.

As the front wheel rolls over the log, shift your weight forward just enough to unweight the rear wheel so it follows easily. You'll get it; it's almost intuitive.

DOWNHILL TECHNIQUE

I love the thrill of descending and letting gravity do most of the work! Here's how to develop downhill technique:

•Shift your weight and your chain. At the start of a descent, assume the ready position (standing on the pedals, butt back, thighs holding the saddle flanges), and keep elbows and knees relaxed, not locked. The steeper the downhill, the farther off the back of the saddle you should hang your buns to counterbalance.

Also, before a downhill run, shift your chain onto the large chainring and the next-to-largest rear cog. This takes up any slack in the chain so it doesn't come off if you hit a bump. Who wants to hear the slap-slap-slap of the chain, chipping the paint off your chainstay? Hold the handlebar firmly but don't white-knuckle it. Keep one or two fingers on the brake levers. Practice these things on gradual descents, then progress to gnarlier ones.

•Develop off-road braking habits. Brake to slow your speed before you initiate the descent. Usually you want to *feather your brakes*, lightly squeezing and releasing them repeatedly rather than just jamming them on. Use your brakes as a pair. Try squeezing them about equally as you practice braking on easy descents to learn what your brakes can do. This is the time to imprint on your brain which lever controls which brake: left hand—front brake, right hand—rear brake! Remember that the front brake is a powerful stopper, and use it lightly. The rear brake works well to slow the bike. If you want to use a little more back brake than front, go ahead, but don't apply it too long or too hard unless you want to lock up the rear wheel and make the tire skid.

Whenever you brake, remember to have your weight back. Should you forget, a quick stop could send you over the bars. I normally ride with two fingers on the brake lever (index and middle finger) and the other fingers on the bar for a secure grip. But if you find you're pulling the front brake too hard, try just your left index finger on that lever.

•Scout any unfamiliar dropoffs. As if I need to tell you, plunging blind into a descent could lead to bloodshed. Once you've checked out the downhill, if you decide it's ridable, turn around and go twenty yards back up the trail so you can pedal to the start of the descent in the ready position. Trying to mount up at the lip of the downslope could lead to disaster.

•Learn to roll over obstacles. When there are roots, small rocks, logs a few inches in diameter, or other minor obstacles in your way, don't panic. If you need to brake, do so as you approach, then release the levers before making contact. Meanwhile, shift your weight back farther and let yourself cruise over. When your front wheel has cleared, shift forward into the ready position. Now you can brake again if you need to. It's easy.

•Sometimes a little speed makes descending easier. You want to be under control, but don't ride the brakes. Squeeze and release. Let momentum carry you over small bumps; they feel larger if you take them slower. Should you momentarily go airborne, keep your weight back so that the rear wheel touches down a nanosecond before the front wheel. That's the safe way to land.

•The steeper the descent, the further back your weight needs to be. Practice this more advanced technique: Lift your butt up and over the back of your saddle so it's suspended over the rear wheel. As one friend puts it, "If you burn your bum on the knobs, you're doing it right!" You'll be surprised what you can ride down this way. Just watch you don't catch the crotch of your shorts on the back of the saddle as you "reseat."

CONQUERING CLIMBS

If you can ride down it, it's great to be able to pedal up it. But that's easier to say than do, especially as a beginner. Early on I carried a pair of clippers one day to cut back the blackberry brambles growing over the smooth part at the base of my favorite uphill practice trail. With those prickers trimmed back, I could get a good start, and my momentum and some heavy breathing took me up the rest of the way.

Try these techniques to help you fight the forces of gravity on those uphills:

- Approaching a hill, try to read it and pick the best gear and the best line of travel to avoid such stoppers as slippery rocks or roots.
- Pace yourself to conserve energy. Many climbs do not ascend at an even grade all the way up. Steeper sections intersperse with gentler rises where you can ease up (to a virtual crawl, if need be) and recover in preparation for mustering momentum to make it up the next steep bit. Using smart pacing, a less-fit rider can sometimes outperform a strong rider on this sort of climb.
- The basic climber's position puts your weight over both wheels and lowers your center of gravity. You sit with your butt a bit back on the saddle, elbows flexed, back straight, as you bend forward at the hips and lean toward the handlebar. Your nose should be about fifteen inches away from where the stem meets the handlebar. As long as the grade lets you maintain this position, it is the most energy-saving.
- As the climb steepens, one of your wheels may lose traction. Usually what you need to do is adopt a more aggressive lean, nose closer to the bar. Meanwhile, slide your buns back to keep weight over the rear tire. Experiment with slight variations. Try more lean if the front wheel isn't digging in or if it's weaving from side to side. If the back is spinning out, try less lean; also it may help to ease up on the pedals and shift to a smaller rear cog.
- When the going gets really steep—and you wish you were Spiderwoman—slide forward onto the tip of the saddle and lean far forward, with your nose in front of the bar and as close as four inches above the stem. Pull down on the handlebars toward your waist to help the back wheel bite into the trail. Don't pull up on the bars, or you could do an unintentional wheelie. This position and the grade burn energy fast. As soon as the hill permits, slide back on the saddle and relax your upper body.

   Experimenting and experience, plus increasing fitness, will help you conquer those singletrack slopes. So will your improving ability to balance. With mountain bikes geared as low as they are, you can ascend very slowly, but the slower you go, the more you teeter. (Work on your track stand at home in the backyard! Those skills will help you.)

   By the way, take note of your handlebars. If yours are higher than your friends' bars—some suspension forks, for example, raise the bars higher than on a rigid bike—you may have to exaggerate the lean to compensate.

- Want to experiment with standing while climbing? As Susan DeMattei points out, this is best saved for not-too-steep middle-chainring gradients (on an overly steep grade you'll immediately lose traction on your rear wheel). First, shift to a higher (harder) gear to keep the rear wheel from spinning out. As you get off the saddle, keep your weight back and your lower back straight. Your chest should be over the handlebar and your torso more upright than when you are seated on the same incline. Grip the bar ends if you have them and slightly sway the bike from side to side in rhythm with your pedaling, but never in an arc wider than your shoulders. Your downstroke will be more powerful, but try to push and pull through a full circle.

Wait for a level or near-level spot to sit back down. As you do, shift back to an easy gear. If you have a suspension fork, you'll probably want to stay seated most of the time. When standing, your power stroke makes the fork bob, diverting energy.

• Conditioning counts. It's no fun sucking air on the uphills like a trout out of water. If you need to get in shape aerobically, you may also need more base miles before challenging your knees on too many uphills. Work on technique but also give yourself time to improve fitness. You have the rest of your life to enjoy this great sport.

• While you're scrambling and skill building on the local trails, have fun. Go your own pace. Laugh a lot. Glory in the surroundings. You'll soon get the hang of off-road. As you do, look for new adventures—day trips and beyond. And pass along what you've learned to riders who are even greener than you. They may turn out to be great riding buddies.

Desperately Seeking Dirt Pals

You might connect with riding partners through your local bike shop (some shops lead rides) or the cycling club in your area. Or go to the trail and introduce yourself to other cyclists in the parking lot.

Among women's mountain bike clubs, the longest standing is the WOMBATS (Women's Mountain Bike and Tea Society). It's a networking organization that aims to make off-roading fun and accessible for women, founded by American mountain bike racer Jacquie Phelan. As you surmise, Jacquie's got a sense of humor. WOMBATS has a newsletter and events, with chapters in a number of states around the United States. Or you could start your own chapter and affiliate. Write and inquire. (See appendix.)

BE PREPARED

Prevention is the best doctoring, so I'm big on bug repellent and baby wipes.

Ticks, most likely to be found in woods or rural areas, don't fly or hop on you. They lurk in vegetation, waiting for you to brush by. Especially in areas where Lyme disease poses a threat (as in the northeastern United States), use a repellent with DEET and check for those tiny deer ticks when you leave the trail and more carefully again as you shower. According to Arnie Baker, M.D., "Ticks usually wait until you're at rest before biting, often at the top of socks or at the neckline." Quick removal of a tick cuts the chance of infection way down. That's the good news. The not-so-good news: Some experts now suspect that other insects, such as fleas and blood-sucking flies, may also carry Lyme disease, even more reason to use repellent. If you do have symptoms—a rash (especially the classic bull's-eye), muscle aches and pains, fatigue—see your doctor. Complications from Lyme disease are serious.

As for the baby wipes, I keep a container of them in the car, to clean off legs in case we've stepped into poison ivy or just to spiff up if we're stopping for dinner on the way home. During the ride, if you see you're standing in the midst of that toxic vine and you have a moist towelette in your bike bag, use it; you have about thirty minutes before that bad stuff starts to work on your skin.

In fact, it's smart to carry a few emergency items with you in your bag. You can put together your own kit or buy a nifty, compact Road Rash first-aid pouch with the essentials in small foil packets. I've already dispensed ibuprofen and antibiotic ointment from mine. For $6 it saves a lot of hunting and assembling: You get various adhesive bandages, a knuckle bandage, a gauze pad, three antiseptic towelettes, antibiotic ointment, two ibuprofen tablets, two electrolyte tablets, a sterile lancet splinter remover, and a towelette for insect bite/sting relief. It has a card for noting your vital statistics and a little extra room for you to add a few small items to customize the kit—such as antihistamine tablets. (See appendix.)

Speaking of prevention, beware during hunting season. Inquire at your local wildlife office to learn when and where hunting is permitted. Rounding a bend and encountering a bow hunter in a tree, looking deadly serious with arrow poised, convinced me quickly last fall that I don't care to risk becoming a Bambi. But if you choose to venture onto game lands during hunting season, put jingle bells on your handlebars and wear bright colors like the classic blaze orange. Avoid camouflage and don't wear white unless you want to look like a deer's hind end.

Best of Both Worlds

I got into mountain biking as soon as the first stock bikes were available in a frame size to (almost) fit me. I felt like a kid in a candy store! I wanted to pinch myself and ask, "Is this true? Can I really combine the two things I love to do most—backcountry hiking and bicycling?" The answer is still "Yeah! And it's great!" Just a week ago three of us rode along a ridgeline on singletrack through a field of wildflowers, a view of the Pacific Ocean on our right. There's nothing quite like it!

–Naomi Bloom, Cupertino, California

Cycling with the Family

Because we enjoy cycling, we want to share it with those close to us. Usually that's the family: husband (and by extension, boyfriend or lover), children if we have them, or sometimes grown sisters, brothers, even parents. Besides, we're often in a bind, wanting more time to spend with the family, yet wishing we could fit in more riding. So combine the two!

"Cycling was the only exercise I could do with a three-year-old who would no longer stay in the stroller," says Suzanne Bailey of Harrisville, Rhode Island. Able to manage, at most, an hour's ride before her son got squirmy, Suzanne extended the distance with a 23-mile loop. "At the halfway point is a state forest with a park, where we would stop, eat, swim, play, and then head home."

At its best, cycling draws a family closer together not only while caught up in it, but later in remembering. Laura Castle of Selma, Indiana, was eleven when she wrote to me:

> Last summer I had many interesting experiences bicycle vacationing with my parents. One night when we were sleeping in our tent, my mother was awakened by the beeping of the computer on her bicycle. When she went out to see what it was, there was a raccoon sitting on her bike bag, happily punching the buttons. He must have been fascinated by the sound. Anyway, he and his buddy ate a lot of our food and carried utensils and other things all over the campground. My father got the idea to scare them away with my camera flash, so in the process I got two super pictures of raccoons.

As we start our children on a sport for life, they'll derive fitness and psychological benefits, just as we do. Equally important is the chance to teach them bicycle safety by example. I don't have kids, but I cringe at seeing somebody else's riding after dark without lights or on the handlebars of another kid's bike. No wonder children in the five- to fourteen-year-old age group are five times as likely to have an accident, compared to older cyclists! If we ride with our children, we see which lessons are really being learned.

But there's more to family cycling than meeting the needs of our youngsters. Bicycling is a pleasure we can share with any family member willing to be included. Sometimes we have to wait until they ask or we sense the time is right, as Linda Cave of Sunnyvale, California, relates:

One day my father asked to come riding with me, and I told him yes. At the time he was overweight and smoked—unfiltered Camels, no less. He had done nothing vaguely athletic in thirty years and spent most of his time reading at home. His biggest outing was to drive down to the local Sears and Roebuck.

After several rides with me on my favorite routes, he quit smoking.

Two years later we were on our second bike tour, this time down the coast of New Jersey on our way to Assateague Island, which is home to wild ponies and many shore birds. Our journey included a ferry ride from Cape May, New Jersey, to Lewes, Delaware. We awoke that morning to a clear day and rode fast to catch the first ferry. Once underway, my father and I stood at the bow watching our escort of dolphins play in the boat's wake. After several quiet moments he turned to me and thanked me for showing him what he'd been missing all these years.

PEDALING WITH YOUR PARTNER

One Sunday afternoon my husband, a friend, and I took a long ride to a lake. On the way back I had a tough time staying with the guys. The sun was scorching, the headwind was fierce, my calories were all depleted, and my husband was irritated. Our friend needed to get home, so he decided to let my husband and me fend for ourselves. This made my husband more irritated with me (if that's possible). Eventually he, too, left me miles behind.

Since the community where I teach wasn't too far off, I headed there rather than home. I figured I could get help if I felt any weaker. Finally I made it to the little corner store across from the high school. But I could barely muster the courage to go inside. I was wearing my triathlon suit, which is very revealing, and I was afraid I'd run into a student or, worse yet, a school-board member. —Gailyn Sutton, Longview, Texas

Sharing the sport with a spouse, boyfriend, or other adult partner is often the first challenge in family cycling. You want to have a good time, not fight the battle of the sexes over it. What if you're the slower or less-experienced cyclist?

Meet the Kornbluhs of Pittsgrove, New Jersey. When they were dating twenty-seven years ago, Barbara was a concert pianist whose athleticism was mostly in her arms, hands, and fingers; Mel was an avid cyclist. So she gamely bought her first adult bike, but whenever they tried to ride together, she says, the last she'd see of Mel was him pedaling down the driveway. Because they were determined to share their loves, because she spoke up about how she felt, and because he was patient enough to put himself in her cycling shoes, so to speak, they made it work. You'll see how, in some of the following tips and throughout this chapter.

•Be generous with yourself. Sometimes a woman skimps on a bicycle for herself because she's unsure just how involved she wants to get in the sport. But in buying a cheap, heavy bike she guarantees herself less enjoyment.

   "She needs comparable or better equipment than her partner," says Mel Kornbluh. "When some of my friends say their wives don't enjoy cycling, I look at their bikes, and I can see why. My wife Barbara has a nice, light-weight bike, and one time I encouraged a fellow's wife to try it. Normally she rides a heavy mixte, but she tried this bike and she couldn't stop grinning. She loved it."

•If you train together, suggest that you lead and set the pace. Always struggling to keep up is demoralizing.

•Or practice paceline riding (see chapter 13, "Tuning Up Your Technique"). If you're continually losing ground, draft. In front, your partner gets a more intense workout while you whizz along faster than normal, sheltered from the wind.

•Train on your own or with others of a similar fitness level. Join a club or organize a few friends. Riding separately may ease the tension between you and your partner, providing you each have your own companions. But don't pass up all chances to go out with more accomplished cyclists. You can learn from them.

•A tandem is a great equalizer, as the Kornbluhs discovered. Providing you work well as a team, you can combine your strengths. And you'll like no longer having to shout conversation into the wind. Tandeming does take trust, patience, and communication. Says Barbara, "Mel had to learn to keep me informed because I couldn't see over his shoulder. Otherwise I'd look up, see a car coming, and jump." The tandem isn't for everyone (see chapter 5, "So You Want to Buy a Bike?"), but for many couples it has been the answer. Do train on your single bike when you don't pair up on the tandem.

•Prepare in case you might be left behind by your partner or become a straggler on a club ride. If you're ready to be self-sufficient, you can handle it. Carry snacks with you for an emergency energy boost, and carry your own copy of the route map. Equip yourself with a pump and repair kit and know how to fix a puncture. Keep phone change in your bike bag so, if necessary, you can call a cab. Then if you find yourself on your own, it's just another of cycling's challenges.

   Don't get me wrong. I'm not saying it's OK for one cyclist to abandon another, especially a new rider, in strange surroundings. This sport can test a relationship. Assert yourself if your needs aren't being met. A partner who really wants you to be a cycling companion should consider your feelings.

•Are household, work, and family responsibilities divided fairly so you, too, have enough time to train? If not, negotiate. As Kate Bauer of Ewa Beach, Hawaii, puts it, "Let's see the guys support us for a while. Give us encouragement and

The Rewards

After cycling since only last spring, in August my husband and I signed up for a sixty-two-mile ride. And as we thought it ridiculous to pedal sixty-two miles and then drive home from the finish, it would be a seventy-miler, nearly double our previous longest distance of forty miles. The night before, I was actually scared. What if we really couldn't make it?

Leaving the start, I couldn't believe how hard it was to pedal—panic set in. When logic returned, I realized I had a flat tire! My husband was so charged up, he didn't hear me call him and left with the pack. A friend stopped to help and became my cycling partner until my husband finally missed me, fifteen miles down the road.

Even though it rained and we were sopping wet most of the trip, it was really fun. Though too inexperienced to realize it, we "hit the wall," seven miles from the official finish. We stopped in the shelter of a drive-in and took out little chocolate bars and started giving each other shoulder rubs. The oohs and aahs plus the sugar shot sent us into fits of laughter until tears poured down our faces. A sag-wagon driver spotted us and called, "Only seven more miles, you can do it!" and we knew we could but were laughing too hard to answer.

The finish line itself was anticlimactic: A few people standing in the rain, waiting for the stragglers. We chatted with them, then hopped on our bikes for the eight miles home, an awful ride through heavy, downtown traffic.

Near home it rained again, and even now I wonder what the neighbors thought, seeing us ride up and down the block in the rain as if unable to find our driveway. But no way was I getting off the bike until my odometer hit exactly 70.0 miles, not 68.9 or 69.5, but 70.0.

After stumbling into the house and out of our wet clothes, we fell into a steaming shower and laughed again, enjoying our tremendous sense of accomplishment and the bonding of our love and friendship.   –Stephanie A. Johanns, Lincoln, Nebraska

time to ride. I think that's one of our biggest problems. Let's get men to take us seriously and give us some of the support and time back that we've given them."

•Stick with it. Building fitness takes time, as Anne Smith of Colorado Springs testifies:

My husband and I began cycling in our early forties. He was fairly athletic, but I wasn't. I spent the first year trying to keep up with the group—any group. He spent it trying to keep up with me—waiting or going back to find me!

About the time I finally got stronger, we moved from Texas to Colorado, and the altitude and hills put me back to square one. Three years later, with much determination and hard work, I could ride in a group without my husband and not worry about being left behind or that some friend must look out for me. It's a great feeling and worth all my training.

If you're the cycling enthusiast and your partner is new to the sport, it will be up to you to make bicycling appealing. Without smothering the other party, try to anticipate the typical newbie mistakes and head them off.

I introduced my husband (then boyfriend) Joe to cycling in much the same way I've encouraged readers of this book to begin. I lent him a bike that fit and was geared for the hills in our area and made sure he had a helmet and comfortable shorts. Derailleur shifting was new to him, but I explained the basics and he quickly got the hang of it. He also discovered the bike seat was too hard, and we substituted an anatomic saddle (yes, many men find them comfortable, too).

We were lucky. From his door we could take off on a variety of scenic, rural roads with little traffic. Some climbs sent us into oxygen debt (me worse than Joe), but the patchwork view of fields and farm buildings repaid the effort, and we enjoyed our Sunday and after-work rides there from the start. I prefer the carrot to the stick, so we planned a fall bike tour in Italy with an exciting ultimate destination: Venice. Anticipating it gave us incentive, and the tour was *magnifico!*

More recently we've discovered biking off-road, and we love the sport even more.

KID STUFF

If you've decided to make cycling kid stuff, you can put a child on wheels at virtually any age. To ensure that it's fun for everyone, you have to think like your youngster. Here's what two child development experts, interviewed by phone, recommended that we keep in mind.

As you know, kids aren't the patient plodders adults tend to be. Before about age 6½, long-term goals mean nothing to them. Their concerns are immediate and can change within minutes, especially if the activity becomes boring or uncomfortable. "They stop doing whatever's displeasing or discomforting. They become belligerent about not continuing," noted Vern Seefeldt, Ph.D., director of the Youth Sports Institute at Michigan State University.

Kids typically pace themselves with bursts of energy. They go pell-mell, then tire and poke for a while. They recover and want to go top speed again.

Between 6½ and 7½, a child's motor skills and the ability to concentrate improve tremendously, said Dr. Seefeldt. A natural competitiveness usually emerges about this point, and kids push themselves more. It's important to encourage gradual conditioning, since older children, adolescents, and teens (like adults) can suffer overuse injuries if they do too much too soon.

"They can get all the various 'itises,'" observed orthopedic surgeon Lyle J. Micheli, M.D. These include bursitis, tendonitis, stress fractures, and *chondromalacia* (cartilage degeneration on the underside of the kneecap). Head these problems off with slow, progressive increases in training. Increments of no more than 10 percent a week work well for youngsters.

If injury should occur to your child's growing bones, cartilage, or joints, don't ignore it, warned Dr. Micheli, director of sports medicine at Boston's Children's Hospital and assistant clinical professor at Harvard Medical School. Discomfort and swelling after a long day's pedaling should be checked by a doctor. Kids differ from adults in that children rarely experience "muscle injury or muscle strain. If you think your child has a muscle injury, it usually means something else is wrong."

Youngsters need to stretch, as not all kids are naturally flexible, Dr. Micheli added. "Some kids, particularly more athletic kids, are relatively tight compared to adults."

Prevent head injury by providing approved helmets that fit properly (see chapter 7, "Accessories"). Insist that your children wear their helmets every time they ride. With the cool graphics on kids' brain buckets these days, letting your junior cyclists pick out their own should encourage cooperation. Helmets come in small sizes, so even a baby should wear one as soon as she can hold her head up. In a study of injuries to passengers in child seats, head trauma was the most commonly occurring injury in the case of a crash or a bicycle toppling over with a little one on board.

Remind children to drink water often. (If concerned that yours aren't getting enough fluids, weigh them on an accurate scale before and after a ride. If there's a noticeable weight loss, have them drink more on the next ride.) Carry sterile water in a bottle for your infant to supplement feedings in hot weather. Remember sunglasses for baby and older children, plus sunscreen.

Finally, be generous with praise. Each little success along the way builds your youngster's confidence and encourages him to keep trying.

Now let's see how parents combine cycling savvy with knowledge of their kids' abilities to nurture their growing bicyclists.

BIKING WITH BABY

I've known parents who've cycled clear across the United States with their two-year-old in a bicycle trailer, happily clutching his hobbyhorse as a companion. More likely, your first thoughts are of riding close to home. Regardless, you share a concern for your child's safety.

For starters, select the right hardware. Buy at a good bike shop, or keep your eyes open for outgrown gear from other cycling families in your club. And check the classifieds in *Tandem and Family Cycling* magazine (see appendix). In the Northeast another network for equipping children of all ages is the Family Cycling Club.

Here are your options:

Trailers. Although often expensive, a trailer is the safest way to cycle with one or two young children up to several years of age. By securely mounting an infant seat inside, you can provide good head and neck support for even a small baby.

A car seat would also work. For toddlers and other tykes, a seat insert with a restraining harness or the like is essential for comfort and safety.

The trailer can hold not only your small passenger(s), but also some gear if you choose to go touring. It's versatile; once your child outgrows the trailer, you can use it to haul luggage. Typically the advertised load limit is 100 pounds. Admittedly, trailers themselves aren't light (about twenty-some pounds, empty), so remember the combined weights as you consider where and how you will use this setup.

Safety features to look for are lap and chest harnesses, and a coupling designed to keep the trailer upright even if your bike should fall. A bright color like red or orange increases visibility, especially in fair weather, while yellow is particularly good for overcast days. Many trailers come with a safety flag (for even better conspicuity), as well as a rain cover and a screen to protect against insects or a chasing dog. If your trailer lacks a screen, check to see that your tot's fingers can't reach into the spokes; some parents rig plywood fenders to be sure. A good bike shop can help you choose and should let you test-ride a trailer you're considering.

Preferences vary as to whether the trailer should face a child in the direction of travel (less likelihood of dogs jumping or nipping) or facing back (to see and talk to a parent riding a second bicycle behind). For convenient storage and transporting, many models fold; some convert into strollers.

Trailers are wider than a bicycle, so avoid congested streets with yours. Their low center of gravity makes them quite stable, but any trailer could tip if you ride over a curb or into a pothole with one wheel. Constantly be aware of the trailer's path to avoid hazards. For greatest stability your child's weight should be carried lower than the trailer wheel hubs.

Baby packs. In the early months some parents choose the sort of carrier that the baby wears like a sunsuit. A panel of fabric gives head support, and Mom or Dad wears the carrier on chest or back. It gives no protection in case of an accident, however.

Child seats. At about one year, when he can sit and hold his head up well, a child is usually old enough for a child seat and too big for the above carrier. A rear-mounting child-seat is preferable, as it interferes less with bike handling than a front-mounted one, and your view will be unobstructed.

Select a child seat with a waist belt and a chest harness or slots for adding one. The seat back should be high enough to support the neck and shoulders, but not so high that the helmet makes your little one lean forward uncomfortably. Look for a child seat with integral foot buckets; dangling legs not only tire, but also there's the danger of frisky feet kicking you black and blue or getting caught in the spokes. To prevent the latter, spoke protectors that mount on your wheel often come with a child seat and should be used. Cloth-covered cushions are better than plastic ones, because they don't heat up in the sun.

Take your bike with you so a salesperson can help you make sure the seat will fit it properly. For greatest stability, have the seat mounted so that it places your tot's center of gravity ahead of your rear axle. You don't want to pop a wheelie with baby on board! Also make sure the child seat won't rub on tires or brakes. If uncertain you can mount the seat correctly, have it installed at the shop.

Speaking of your bike, a true racing bike with a short wheelbase and quick handling is not so great for mounting a child seat. Just about any other bike would be more stable. If you're likely to be splashing through wet streets after a rain storm, add fenders to your bike, or you'll dampen more than your child's enthusiasm.

Whatever equipment you choose, be sure your cycling skills are top-notch. Before putting baby in the trailer or child seat, practice first with something you love less dearly but that weighs the same, like a bag of potatoes. Strap it in and ride so that you accustom yourself to cornering with the trailer and are mindful of its width. Get used to the effect of extra weight in the child seat. Because of the load, allow more time to brake when toting a passenger in the child seat or towing a trailer.

Never go off and leave baby in the child seat unless someone else is standing there, holding your bicycle for you. A parked bike can topple over.

PUTTING GROWING KIDS ON WHEELS

Eventually a child grows too heavy for a child seat. Consider thirty-five to forty pounds a maximum weight, but you may find your bike handling compromised earlier. A trailer remains safe for a longer period of time, but sooner or later your passenger will decide she'd rather pedal than just sit.

In cycling this is an awkward age. The child is too small for the smallest (20-inch wheel) bikes with multiple gears, which are necessary for cycling anything but flat terrain. She may have a single-gear bike, but she poops out before pedaling it very far.

The solution? Put your child on the back of a tandem or on a trailer bike, which resembles a bicycle missing a front wheel and turns your single bike into a tandem. Though you must start with short rides and gradually build up, a youngster can go longer distances on a tandem more quickly. With a parent in front as captain, the child can ride through traffic and road conditions that would otherwise be risky. She shares the fun of cycling, becomes traffic-wise, and develops some of the balance needed to solo on a bicycle before even trying it.

Fairly new, the trailer bike offers a relatively inexpensive option for parents who already own single bikes and don't wish to invest in a tandem or to deal with the complications of transporting one. You can also use one to turn a tandem into a triplet. Several companies make these attachments, but Burley's Piccolo (see appendix) is ahead of the pack because of its safety features and smooth ride. The key is a hitch system which mounts on a superstrong rack (included) on the parent's bike; ball bearings in the hitch eliminate any slop that otherwise could cause shimmying or poor tracking. Six-speed gearing (which can be locked out if the parent chooses), adjustable handles and seat, and chromoly tubing complete the Piccolo, intended for children ages four to ten.

Before trailer bikes, tandems were the answer. Some families continue to choose them, and—again—there are more options than before. A lucky contact with other cycling parents might get you a custom-built tandem with the correct frame geometry to fit your pint-sized pedaler. Or, if you have some extra do-re-mi, you could have a builder make you a tandem with a rear-seat tube as short as 12 inches.

Alternatively, some families are spending less (still a couple thousand) and buying a Tandem Two'sDay from Green Gear Cycling, with very quick delivery. This is a folding tandem (yes, it fits into two suitcases for travel), made with 20-inch wheels to your custom specifications. It can accommodate a captain as tall as six-foot-six and yet be small enough in the rear for a kid stoker. Occasionally Green Gear sells used Two'sDays, for a smaller bite on the wallet.

Yet another choice, parents can modify an adult-sized tandem they already have, or buy one and convert it with a Junior Pedaling Attachment, or "kiddy crank." The unit comes assembled, ready to attach to the rear seat tube. It's complete with short cranks, chainring, fixed sprocket, boss, and allen keys. The *fixed sprocket* means that, as on a standard tandem, when the parent pedals, the child pedals; when Mom or Dad coasts, the child coasts, too.

Adding a kiddy crank is not a do-it-yourself project or something even every bike shop mechanic can do. Contact one of the listed tandem sources (see appendix) or the Family Cycling Club if you can't find someone to make this change.

When a youngster outgrows the kidback conversion, adjustable crank shorteners are available so that kids eight to eleven years old can still ride the tandem.

Just as there are child back tandems, there are triplets for a parent who wants to cycle with two children, or for a couple who relish togetherness and wish to add on for a child. Talk about special equipment! Some custom builders, like Santana of Claremont, California, make them, or contact another of the listed tandem sources. Triplets of good quality will be pricey.

So, take your choice. You can put your kids on wheels, but it will require at least a modest investment. If you connect with other families to recycle equipment, however, you can save money up front and recoup some of your investment on resale.

MAKING IT FUN

If it's important to make cycling pleasurable for yourself and your partner, it's doubly desirable to make it fun for the kids. Or, as the Kornbluhs put it, "You have to sort of nurture the whole thing."

Remember your child's attention span in planning rides. If you don't, she may quickly remind you. At age two, the Kornbluhs' daughter Natalie was good in the baby seat for about twenty miles. "But when she didn't want to ride any more," laughs Mel, "she'd throw her pacifier overboard or kick Barbara in the butt."

"Infants are easy because they'll sleep," adds Barbara, "but the toddler stage is awkward, as they don't want to be held down and, since they can't verbalize, they scream."

For a youngster in a baby seat, tie a toy within reach. Give an older child in a trailer a bag of toys or a personal stereo to listen to. Take more breaks while riding than you normally do. On a warm day a child in a trailer, for example, heats up faster than you because you have a cooling breeze. Even if you provide your passenger with a water bottle, help your child drink when you stop. On a cool day, because she's not exercising, a child will feel cold sooner and should be dressed more warmly. To boost circulation and burn some energy, let your youngster run around a little when you take a rest stop. Besides, when it's time to move on, kids are easier to coax back into the child seat or trailer if you say you'll stop again soon, where they can play some more.

All kids welcome a change in activity. They "recuperate" miraculously from tiredness at a rest stop if you pull out a Frisbee or a ball to play catch. One mother says she never passes up intriguing looking playground equipment when she and the kids are biking by.

Plan an activity for every ride. Pedal to the park or zoo, to a museum or Grandma's, to a lake or your favorite ice cream stand—some place fun for your youngster. This is especially helpful at the stage when the kids are getting heavy back there on the tandem but aren't contributing much to the effort. "You're doing a lot of work and they're doing a lot of complaining," says Mel. "This isn't the time when it's most fun to ride with them. Having a destination helps cut down on complaints."

Tell children in advance how long the ride will be. Mel and Barbara didn't speak in terms of miles, which can sound too long. More likely they'd say, "Well, our first rest stop will come after about as long as it takes you to watch *He-Man* (a favorite cartoon show)."

Riding with other folks who have kids is the most surefire way to keep yours interested. "If they see John or Jennie doing it, they say, 'Hey, this is normal for me,'" says Mel. If they never get to ride with other families, they feel as if they're freaks in a way, he adds.

Look for cycling families through your local YMCA or cycling club. Sixteen years ago the Kornbluhs and some other tandeming families formed the nucleus of a regional Family Cycling Club, still in existence with some thirty member families from several states. With a little organization, you could do the same in your area.

On a typical Family Cycling Club weekend tour, the small fry outnumber the adults. A reasonable mileage limit is set for the day, about thirty-five to forty miles. A sag wagon carries luggage, and pooped-out kids when necessary, although the club's agreed on a five-mile limit for van rides. That seems to be ample time for children to rekindle their energy and realize they're missing out on some fun.

Sometimes youngsters play "musical parents," pairing up with an adult other than Mom or Pop. They seem to try harder and bike without griping for somebody else.

GRADUATING TO THEIR OWN BIKES

Sooner or later youngsters want to ride small bikes of their own. To ease the transition, let them continue on the tandem or in the trailer for longer excursions, while building stamina on their own bikes with shorter rides. On tour the Family Cycling Club handles it this way: First thing in the morning there's a pre-ride spin of a few miles for tykes on their single bikes; then for the rest of the day they're back on the tandem or in a trailer.

At this stage you may find it wise to start with one bike for learning and wait to buy a second, lighter bicycle at a later time.

To save your back while teaching a child to balance on a bike, Mel Kornbluh recommends that, rather than holding on to the seat with your hand when running behind a child and trying to steer the handlebars, you should fasten a piece of rope or a leather belt to the center of the back of the saddle. That's a more natural position to run in, and you'll be able to stay with your child longer.

As soon as children can ride independently, parents should work with them to reinforce the rules of the road. Head off these typical kids' errors to dramatically reduce your youngster's chance of being hit by a car:

- Failing to look for traffic before entering the street from driveway or sidewalk
- Not stopping for stop signs or traffic lights at an intersection
- Not looking for oncoming vehicles before moving sideways or otherwise swerving into traffic

All along children need lots of positive reinforcement for their efforts, and this continues to be the case as they progress to riding their own single bikes. Within their level of ability, your children try hard to please you and are waiting to hear they're doing just that.

When your growing rider is ready for a multispeed bike with 20- or 24-inch wheels, the mountain bike style is a good choice. The upright position will help a child see and balance more easily. Kids will need some practice at first (in a big, empty parking lot) to coordinate pedaling and braking. Shifting can be a puzzle, too. When riding together, you can help by looking at the terrain from time to time, then looking at your child. Is he or she pedaling too slowly? Spinning wildly? Explain how to shift up or down as needed to find a comfortable cadence.

At the transition to single bikes, certain commands from a parent need to be followed unquestioningly. When Mel and Barbara's children made the switch, the Kornbluhs felt they couldn't allow as much talking back and forth as before. The kids needed to be able to hear important instructions.

"On many occasions we'd say, 'This is not a time to talk' because we're in a busy area where you need to be aware of everything around you, and talking would distract," recalls Mel.

"But then," adds Barbara, "we'd go in other areas where there's not much traffic and we could sing songs and tell jokes and ride two abreast."

Sometimes you can discuss traffic situations as they arise. Ask your children's opinion and offer your own. Praise their good judgment and improving bike handling. Encourage your youngsters to be proud of cycling well.

Who can predict what will happen? Several years ago I chatted with the Kornbluhs, and I asked the kids what cycling has meant to them. Natalie, 15, mentioned that she'd developed confidence meeting other kids at the rallies, which made a recent move to a new school easier.

Jed, 12, also had a sense of accomplishment. "On the last family tour," he recalled, "the lead group was me and my friend. We reached the lunch stop before the sag wagon. And last summer I entered two races. I finished first in my age category in one and second in the other."

Later Barbara tried to sum it up:

> There's a Yiddish word, naches. It means "a warming in your heart." In this case it comes from your kids doing what you want them to do, without asking them. This is more than we ever expected out of cycling.

Just last fall I called to catch up with the family. I reached Mel in the garage, headquarters of Tandems East, a part-time dealership he and Barbara opened several years ago. Enthusiastic as ever about family cycling, he told me about a customer who pedals her two kids to school year-round on a tandem with a Piccolo trailer bike attached to the rear.

As for the Kornbluhs, Natalie, embarking on a career as a graphic designer, has cycled only casually lately, Mel reported. Jed now goes to college in Philadelphia and works as a bike messenger on the side. "He loves it," said Mel. "He's got a few earrings and a patch of purple hair here and there, but what can you do?" Apparently the kids haven't strayed too far: Next week the four Kornbluhs are off for a bike tour of Spain over semester break.

Fitter and Faster

Last month I rode a ten-mile criterium and captured third. I've never felt more proud and exhilarated. I remember hoping that, since I was ten years older than the rest of the field, strategy—not strength or youth—would win the race. Then I noticed a two-member team signaling each other. They worked their way to the front, and one of them took a flyer. Everyone else meekly let the teammate hold them back, but I went for it. I tried to catch the breakaway rider but failed. The pack swallowed me up, and I decided to settle for placing. Heck, she could always crash.

I planned my strategy for the final lap. I'd come around the last corner in somebody's slipstream. When I was close enough to sprint, I'd take her! Amazingly, everything went as planned. I set myself up perfectly. I began my sprint. My thighs had never burned like this before. My throat was parched, my breathing labored. I was gonna throw up! I'd never pushed myself this hard.

The finish line was just meters away . . . when reality struck. The teammate had used my strategy—on me! How dare she! She squeaked past me and claimed second by half a wheel.

But I was still ecstatic. I'd almost thrown up! I'd kicked butt that day!
–Barb Tanner-Hury, Altamonte Springs, Florida

There are many measures of satisfaction in cycling, and sometimes they center around making a greater effort, finishing a certain distance, achieving a particular speed, entering a first race, or winning in competition. In some way you see proof of your progress toward being a fitter and faster cyclist.

Fast is not always best or even everyone's ultimate goal. But all of us can use some speed in our legs—if only to cross a busy intersection more quickly and safely. Or on an organized ride when an efficient paceline speeds by, maybe we'd like to jump into overdrive and catch it. We'll talk in this chapter about ways to improve speed that even weekend warriors and beginners will find fun. We'll also cover more structured kinds of training, along with some race strategy pointers.

STARTING SPEEDWORK

I'm assuming that you've built a good foundation of conditioning with a couple months of spinning in easy gears (see chapter 10, "Building Fitness"). Now, to improve your speed there are various approaches you might take, but all are based on the following principles:

- Developing leg speed. It's this simple: If you can turn the pedals faster in the same gears you're using now, you will go faster.
- A gradual increase in workload. Training involves stressing the body and giving it time to recover. This allows the body to adapt by becoming stronger. To continue to improve, you must continue to push past your current limitations by small increments. If you haven't been doing any speed-work, start with one session a week. After some weeks, you could increase to two sessions. But remember, the more you push yourself, the more essential rest becomes.
- The importance of *active rest*. The day after a long ride or a hard training session, for example, it's better to go out for an easy cruise, using low gears, than to sit at home with your feet up. The spinning and increased circulation help keep your muscles supple.
- Begin each speedwork session with a warm-up; end with a cool-down.
- Roadwork for everyone. Dirt riders, if you want to sizzle on the singletrack, you could do some *fartlek* ("speedplay") training on easy trails, but generally the road is more conducive for concentrating on speed. According to Skip Hamilton, who's coached U.S. Olympic mountain bikers, elite off-road racers do at least 60 percent of their training on a road bike on the road, without the mental demands of technical riding to distract them or sloppy trail conditions slowing them down. Likewise, track racers devote much of their training time to the road. "You'd go nuts, riding around and around in circles on the track all the time," says Pat McDonough, a former Olympic track medalist and now director of the Lehigh County (Pennsylvania) Velodrome.

GROUP PSYCH

A fun fitness builder for any rider, a group paceline workout on the road lets you build team riding skills, crank up your cadence, and make the most of precious training time. The pace set will depend on the particular group you organize or choose to join—and its goals. As I know from my own group training rides, it's exhilarating. You're motivated to put forth something extra, and you get results. If unaccustomed to riding this hard, limit it to once a week with an easy *recovery ride* scheduled for the next day.

Serious about building speed? One of the best things you can do is train with stronger cyclists, which could mean riding with men. This is one of the secrets of Seana Hogan's success. A four-time winner of the Race Across AMerica women's division, Seana tells us:

I trained with a group of guys—racers—at work. This made me go harder because men push themselves more. Women could be a lot faster than they are if they just set their standards higher. But they're expected to go slower, so they do. When I ride with friends—guys—we don't talk much. We're mostly pushing each other. I think the importance of riding with somebody is so you don't daydream.

If you're game but not quite competitive with the local men, you could still join them on training sessions, riding at the back of the paceline, as female racers often do when there's a shortage of competitive women to train with. It's almost like motor pacing: In the shelter of the paceline you try to keep a high cadence, 110 rpm or so. Aim to use the same gears you're using now but spin faster, increasing cardiovascular demand.

You don't have to be a racer to benefit from group rides, and the group could be any bunch that's willing to cooperate. If you can't take a pull, let the rider who's dropping back (after his pull) slip in front of you. Just tell the others to pretend you're not there. To find the right spot for the best draft, you do need to be comfortable with bike handling and drafting (see chapter 13, "Tuning Up Your Technique").

Nancy Neely of Wescosville, Pennsylvania, knows firsthand about keeping fast company. A former national-class track racer and, until last year, technical director at the Lehigh County Velodrome, Nancy and another woman regularly joined weekly rides with a group of elite male track riders who were drawn to the area by the 'drome.

They'd roll out at a moderate pace, and Nancy would take her turn at the front or, she says, "some guys will tease you if you don't." Usually the other woman was in line behind her, so each took a short pull. After a while they simply *sat in* (rode at the back) and stayed with the men as long as possible. Eventually the group would break up as the pace increased.

This is the moment many women fear—and the reason why it helps to have another person of your ability level on the ride. "I've been dropped so many times out in the middle of nowhere," says Nancy. "As one of the guys jokes, 'Bring along some money and a map, and you'll be fine.'"

Typically riders regroup at an established halfway point, and everyone has another chance to try to hang on.

FARTLEK

For another approach, incorporate *fartlek*, or "speedplay," into your training. On some group rides, there's an unspoken pact that everyone goes nuts, sprinting for the "town limits" signs. To do fartlek when training alone, pick up your speed now and again; sprint the distance between two telephone poles, suggests Rebecca Twigg, five-time world champion in the pursuit.

What distinguishes fartlek from other speedwork is its spontaneity. "There are so many games you can play," says Nancy Neely, crediting her coach, Pat McDonough, with making it fun. At the time, Pat was working with riders at the

Lehigh County Velodrome and would later coach U.S. junior and senior teams at three world track championships.

Pat had taken it upon himself to study the training methods of elite athletes around the world—not just in cycling, but in swimming and track and field, as well. Cyclists, he became convinced, must allot more time for speedwork. He's taken this tack with his riders, including Janie Eickhoff Quigley, a six-time world championship medalist, and Marty Nothstein, who would go on to win three world championships and the match sprints silver in the '96 Olympics.

Group fartlek sessions, Pat explains, simulate many different situations that might occur during a race. These games build confidence for the real thing, and they spice up a group ride.

He calls a favorite simulation "Cowboys and Indians." "I'll pick a couple or more Indians," he says. "They'll take off from the pack, which is moving fairly slow. Depending on who they are, we'll let them get fairly far away, and then the pack will try to catch them."

Both the Indians and the chasing cowboys practice working together in their respective groups—just like in a race, where riders in a breakaway or a chase group join efforts regardless of team affiliation.

"I demand that the groups work in paceline or echelon formation," Pat says. "So you're practicing many things besides just speed training. The Indians are thinking, 'I'm going to go out there and make an attack and try to make it stick.'" The chasers try just as hard to reel them in. Such speed games give riders who're thinking about racing a taste of it. "It's unstructured, but it's fun and," he adds laughing, "it can hurt like hell."

As Nancy attests, in the heat of the chase, you don't mind so much. Even a pair of riders can chase for some speedplay. If one is stronger, let the weaker one take off first.

INTERVAL TRAINING

By contrast, interval training is best done alone, since it's unlikely that two riders will be at precisely the same fitness level. "If you start doing intervals with your friend, one of you will get more out of it than the other," says Pat McDonough. Instead, he encourages monitoring the intervals in some way, using a training diary to keep track of speeds attained or an improvement in the length of the work period or cadence.

"Do that," he adds, "and I can guarantee the intervals will help you because many times, as my riders can confirm, you'll get to a race and it will seem easy compared to training. If you do intervals right, they hurt."

To set up a program, decide first what your goals are—because there are many different types of intervals you could do. Pat categorizes them according to which of the various energy systems is being trained.

The aerobic system. A rider wanting to improve her speed at a steady pace—a time trialist or triathlete, for example—would be training her use of that energy system that draws on both glycogen and, to a lesser degree, free fatty acids (see chapter 11, "Fueling the Engine"). These intervals are done with a relatively moderate output of energy but with short rest periods. Work periods might be five minutes or longer; the rest is five minutes or usually shorter, maybe half that.

"I call them *pace* intervals," says McDonough. "I say to myself, 'What sort of pace would I be doing in a road race?'" He assumes it would be an aerobic pace but faster than his solo training pace, when he has no competition to keep him going. With these intervals he gets an aerobic workout if he keeps it up long enough. Generally he recommends a 1½-hour session to his riders—and that takes discipline.

The lactate system. This anaerobic system fuels efforts that use more energy than oxygen can sustain. Within your body, this system involves the conversion of glucose into the fuel known as *ATP* (adenosine triphosphate). In the process *lactic acid,* or *lactate,* is created; as it builds up in the muscles, it causes a temporary but painful fatigue. Eventually your blood carries the lactate away to the liver. There, when oxygen is available, the lactic acid is converted into glucose.

This amazing cycle can provide energy for more intense efforts that might last from thirty seconds up to about three minutes. In track, road, criterium, and mountain bike racing, all of which involve bursts of speed—and often repeated bursts of speed—this system is key. McDonough's racers do a variety of intervals to train it.

A criterium racer, for example, might use a heart monitor and do her speed-work at about 80 percent of MHR, or right around her *anaerobic threshold,* the point at which muscles must start depending on the lactic acid system for energy.

"You're trying to train your body to operate with a certain amount of lactate, and also to ultimately put off producing lactate until you're at a higher speed. In other words," McDonough explains, "you're trying to push back your anaerobic threshold."

To do this, the cyclist rides at about 80 percent of MHR for about five to ten minutes, so long as the heart rate is being maintained and speed (mph) decreases no more than about 3 percent. When the speed drops, the work period ends. Five minutes of rolling rest follow immediately, in which the rider spins low gears but keeps the heart rate up to 100 or 110 beats per minute (bpm). This active rest, Pat explains, keeps circulation up and speeds removal of lactic acid from the muscles via the bloodstream. If you stopped completely, you would load up even more with lactate.

In this manner, work sessions alternate with rolling rest. A cyclist would start with two five- to seven-minute work periods with ten minutes of active rest in between. Gradually she might increase to four work periods of ten minutes each, with seven minutes of active rest in between. It takes time and conditioning to build up to this level, as the difficulty of each succeeding work interval increases with the accumulation of lactic acid.

The ATP-PC system. This system kicks in for those photo-finish victories. In the muscles, we have limited amounts of a substance called *PC* (phosphocreatine), which can be transformed instantly into ATP for very short bursts of intense speed, usually less than thirty seconds. Maximum-speed workouts are important for track sprinters and for other competitive cyclists who want to improve their finishing sprint.

The work interval lasts at most fifteen or twenty seconds, an all-out sprint, with at least six minutes of rolling rest in between, probably more like twelve minutes, Pat suggests. He recommends doing this sort of workout about once every two weeks, with a minimum of four work intervals and no more than eight.

To sum up, a racer who prefers to be well-rounded, rather than specialize in a certain event, must train all systems. Too many cyclists think of their conditioning only in terms of quantity. "If you spend 80 or 90 percent of your time riding slow and steady, that's how you're going to ride in the race," says McDonough. "And with the exception of the Race Across AMerica, there aren't too many races that are slow and steady!"

HILLWORK

Just as you can improve your speed, you can better your climbing by devoting one day a week to repeat efforts on a hill. For example, pick one that's challenging enough but that you know you can climb sitting down. Devise a short circuit route that lets you do the ascent a half-dozen or so times. Put your bike in a gear low enough to use all the way to the top and try to maintain a high cadence.

In the succeeding weeks, when that hill starts to feel easy, practice attacking near the top. And look for another hill more worthy of your efforts.

Why We Do It

There was a man picking up his entry packet at a local mini-triathlon at the same time I was. He was obviously amused at the gray-haired woman entering a triathlon, and he didn't try to conceal his contempt. I had the pleasure of passing him as he struggled up a steep hill near the end of the bike portion of the triathlon.

"You're looking good, son," I said "encouragingly" as I spun by.

—Myrna Meyer, White Plains, New York

GOING THE DISTANCE: CENTURY TRAINING

For me, completing my first century ride was a real adventure. I'd been riding year-round for four years and had had a century as my goal for about a year. This spring I began a ten-week training program which would culminate in a century ride of my own—not a group or club event—just my own personal goal.

The whole training time was exciting. My first forty-mile, then fifty-mile, then seventy-mile rides were real peaks (and valleys)! The adrenaline rush amazed me. How good I felt after a long ride surprised me, too—though I did move slower for a day or two. The most depressing thing was bad weather—cold and rain—for the forty- and fifty-mile rides.

The century itself was truly a climax, a perfect day except for a brutal south wind that blew me home since the last part of the ride went north. I feel really good that I could do it and more confident than ever about riding anywhere I want to go. –Susan Ripple, Rapid City, South Dakota

Centuries, organized 100-mile events, give cyclists a goal to shoot for during the season. Some clubs sponsor less daunting *metric centuries* (100 kilometers, or sixty-two miles). In either case, finishers often earn decorative patches and keep a record of their times (subtracting time spent at lunch and rest stops). If a century is a race at all, it's a race against yourself.

To prep for any long event, gradually build endurance through regular mileage increases, including one long ride each week. Here we'll talk about training for a century, but you can apply the principles to create your own program for goals of other lengths.

Some experienced cyclists, already fairly disciplined in their training, may not need a highly structured schedule to prepare for 100 miles. My friend Ellen Dorsey says that in her racing years, she typically rode twenty to twenty-five miles a day on weekdays, and in the last couple of months before a century, she'd try to do some fifty-mile rides on weekends and work in a sixty-five-miler a couple weeks before the event. You don't need to do the entire 100 miles in training to complete it on century day. Save the thrill of accomplishment for the actual event.

Many riders do benefit from a schedule. The two offered here cover the preceding ten weeks. You can truly improve performance over this period of time, yet it's a short enough span that you don't feel you're giving a lifetime over to training. (And you may love it and find yourself elevated to a new standard in your cycling.)

Program 1 is for first-timers and those who've been cycling about forty-five to fifty miles per week. If you've been doing a little more, you could increase distances slightly.

Program 2, for cyclists already training over seventy-five miles a week, should ensure a comfortable finish or a new best time.

In both, "easy" refers to a leisurely ride; "pace" suggests riding at the pace you expect to keep during the actual event; and "brisk" means that you'll exceed your century pace. On one of your "pace" days you might want to do the aerobic pace intervals described earlier. If so, ride the work period about 1 mph faster than your intended century pace, and do the active rest period at about 1 mph slower than your expected pace.

Note that the long ride of the week (crucial for building endurance) is planned for Saturday—a good idea, so if that day should be rained out or otherwise impossible for riding, then you have another chance on Sunday. These schedules assume century day is a Sunday. If yours is on Saturday, shift that entire week's program accordingly so that the day off, for example, falls on Wednesday.

Program 1: To Survive

Week	Mon. (easy)	Tues. (pace)	Wed. (brisk)	Thurs.	Fri. (pace)	Sat. (pace)	Sun. (pace)	Weekly Mileage
1.	6	10	12	Off	10	30	9	77
2.	7	11	13	Off	11	34	10	86
3.	8	13	15	Off	13	38	11	98
4.	8	14	17	Off	14	42	13	108
5.	9	15	19	Off	15	47	14	119
6.	11	15	21	Off	15	53	16	131
7.	12	15	24	Off	15	59	18	143
8.	15	15	25	Off	15	65	20	153
9.	15	15	25	Off	15	65	20	155
10.	15	15	25	Off	10	5 (easy)	Century	170

Program 2: To Thrive

Week	Mon. (easy)	Tues. (pace)	Wed. (brisk)	Thurs.	Fri. (pace)	Sat. (pace)	Sun. (pace)	Weekly Mileage
1.	10	12	14	Off	12	40	15	103
2.	10	13	15	Off	13	44	17	112
3.	10	15	17	Off	15	48	18	123
4.	11	16	19	Off	16	53	20	135
5.	12	18	20	Off	18	59	22	149
6.	13	19	23	Off	19	64	24	162
7.	14	20	25	Off	20	71	27	177
8.	16	20	27	Off	20	75	29	187
9.	17	20	30	Off	20	75	32	194
10.	19	20	30	Off	10	5 (easy)	Century	184

Source: *Bicycling* magazine.

Schedules look dreadfully uncompromising, but use your good sense. Suppose heavy pressure at work, for example, creates such stress that trying to complete every ride one week according to plan feels like too much. In that case, ease off a little on training to avoid burnout.

To some extent, you can also shift things within the schedule. On a particular day, even after your warm-up, you may feel tired and sluggish. But a "brisk" ride is scheduled. You'd probably be better off to make this a "pace" or "easy" ride.

On the other hand, don't skip a day merely because you don't feel up to it. At least go out and warm up. Sometimes you'll be surprised how good you feel once you're on the bike. We have more toughness and resiliency than we sometimes give ourselves credit for. Finding that out is one of the great rewards of mastering the century.

While training, at least during the long ride, eat and drink regularly so that you get comfortable with the habit and know what digests well for you.

For the big day, keep in mind these tips from the pros:

- Pick your century wisely. Choose a flat, well-supported event and avoid ones with words like "Hotter than Hell" or "Killer Hills" in the title, advises Rose Costin, who in 1994 rode 111 centuries and broke both the women's record for centuries in one year (77) and the men's (110).
- Divide and conquer. "I remember my first century back in 1989," says Seana Hogan. "My thought was to get to the first stop. If a century has rest stops every twenty-five miles, think about riding that distance four times." Seana notes that she applies the same strategy to the 2,911-mile RAAM (Race Across AMerica), dividing it by the sixty-four time stations. "It's less intimidating."
- Expect highs and lows. In a century, as Seana points out, pain has time to move around, making it a little easier to handle. Your feet might hurt for awhile, then your butt, then your hands. Stretch and try to relax, and don't get discouraged thinking that once you get an ache you can't ride through it.
- Don't experiment with anything the day of the event, says Susan I. Barr, Ph.D., a nutritionist and marathon rider. Want to wear a stylin' new outfit on century day? Try it out in training, ditto for shoes, gloves, a new energy drink, etc., or you might be in for an unpleasant surprise.
- At the top of a long climb, take a minute to pull off the road and look back, Rose urges. "The spectacular view is your reward for all that hard work."

Regarding carbo loading and other nutrition tips, see chapter 11, "Fueling the Engine." For on-bike comfort review chapter 12, "Ouch-less Riding." On century day, limit rest stops to ten minutes each so you'll be less likely to stiffen up; make each stop an opportunity to stretch, as well as eat and drink. Even if rest stops will provide food, carry a few snacks of your own in case you need an energy boost toward the end. Go for it! If you discover you're really strong at riding long, check out the Ultra-Marathon Cycling Association (see appendix).

VOICE OF EXPERIENCE

At the opening of this chapter, Barb Tanner-Hury hoped that strategy rather than mere fitness would win the criterium. As it turned out, "race brains" did affect the outcome, as they often will in competition. So if you're interested in racing, you'll want to learn as much as you can about race tactics from fellow club members, clinics (see appendix), and further reading. British Olympian Maria Blower reports that her knowledge of teamwork and racing strategy came from her pro-racer father. "I'm so familiar with it, I'm amazed when other girls don't know these things," she says. Here she and two Olympic teammates—Lisa Brambani and Sally Hodge—share insights garnered in years of international road racing.

Conditioning. *Sally Hodge:* Include speedwork in your training. When I started, distance was all-important to me. Now I do more quality work and less distance than ever.

Lisa Brambani: A lot of people fall into the trap of pushing big gears. You'll get the blood to your muscles quicker if you twiddle (spin) lower gears. In a race you can attack better if you twiddle, and you'll remain more supple, too.

And increase your strength. Valerie Rushworth, my coach (a former national champion), is always going on about this. Your arms play a big part in climbing, and sometimes they do ache on a hill. I'm very weak in the upper body. I have weights at home, but I have to get psyched up to do it. So when I'm lifting this winter, I'll think about some miserable hill to get motivated.

Sally: Do circuit [weight] training in the winter, two to three times a week. I do this more perhaps than the other girls because I have a track-racing background. Circuit training is a good change of pace in the winter, and a change is as good as a rest.

Rest is important. I don't have a set rest day, but I use Monday as an easy day, with fewer hills, if it's been a hard weekend. I ride low gears and just enjoy looking around on the country lanes. If I took a set day off completely, then I might really need a rest day later on in the week and I'd miss two days. So I train seven days a week and make sure to take one rest day every two weeks.

On equipment. *Lisa:* The average person doesn't need to worry about internal cable routing and aerodynamic rims. That sort of equipment only matters at the highest levels. I started from humble beginnings. "I'll show them I can beat them on my cheaper bike"—that was my attitude.

Learning to ride in close quarters. *Lisa:* Don't stick at the back of the pack all the time. If you're back there and there's a crash in the middle of the bunch, it's hard to avoid it. After awhile you know the people who are good bike handlers. Try to stay with them.

If somebody's leaning on you, learn to lean back. If you lean the other way, you're bound to fall. Sometimes my coach will go out on her bike with me and rough me up a bit. She'll ride me into the gutter and elbow me, to accustom me to riding in a pack. But you're bound to crash at times. Try to think of it as just part of the glory.

Before the race. *Maria Blower:* When you get a race program (or profile) write the information on your handlebars. Note, for example, that where there's a hill, the top is a likely spot for a sprint, so you'd want to move up within the pack to be ready for it. Use your watch or cycle computer to keep track of the mileage to these various points.

It's important to know the course—where the hills are, for instance. So if you're a weak hill climber, you try to dominate the pace and then on a hill, as you drift back through the bunch, there are some wheels left at the top you can sit behind and draft. If it's a long climb, get behind a steady climber. Otherwise, it's easy to get carried away and blow up.

Always check your gears before the race starts. If you discover a problem, hopefully you can have it fixed. It's demoralizing to try to shift on a hill and have it not work.

If you have a jersey with pockets, don't pin the pockets shut when you put your race number on. It's hard to get the food in that way! If somebody else pins your number on, check to make sure they don't make that mistake.

Sally: A good warm-up is important. Races go from the gun—partly because they are shorter in distance than they need to be, and partly because better riders want to get out ahead of less-experienced ones, to avoid crashes. If the road or track isn't clear for a warm-up, perhaps because of another race, warm up on rollers. Also we might use them afterwards for a cool-down.

During the race. *Maria:* New racers, don't be afraid to attack. You might feel overawed, but the way to improve is to attack. The way to race is to race.

Don't stop immediately if you puncture. Sit on the back of the pack until the support vehicle (if any) is near. Put your right hand up to signal you need a back wheel, your left for a front wheel.

If you crash, look around you to see who's getting it back together to chase. Try to ride back up to the pack as a group. Don't go racing off alone if you can help it.

When you sprint, always position yourself so your opponent has to sprint into the wind. Say the wind's coming from the left. Sprint in the right-hand gutter, so if anyone comes by you, she blocks the wind. That's why it's really important to check out the finish before a race. Get out of the car and check to see which way the wind is blowing.

Energy needs. *Maria:* In a stage race eat right after the stage so you can get your glycogen replenished. If a race is short, you don't have to eat during the race; an energy drink will do. In a race you can get so nervous your stomach is unsettled—I hate eating during a race for that reason.

On drugs to enhance performance. *Maria:* I've never been offered drugs. But I wouldn't do it if I were. I want to win on my own. And I don't want to change my body. I want to have children some day. Besides, what would it do to my family, my grandparents, my friends? What a stigma! If you're caught cheating once, people think you do it all the time.

Want to get in on the excitement of road or track racing? For a license, contact the United States Cycling Federation (USCF), the Canadian Cycling Association (CCA) (see appendix), or other federation, as appropriate.

FUN IN THE DIRT

Whether you race off-road or simply ride trails for a change of pace, "it's a great training tool for bike handling," says a top-ranked American roadie, Jeanne Golay. "Ride on rocks and dirt and get used to your tires skidding in corners," adds the '96 Olympian. She recalls that she raced off-road early one season—and then later in a criterium, a racer crashed directly in front of her. Instinctively Jeanne bunny-hopped the downed rider's front wheel and stayed upright, like hopping a log out on the trail. "Mountain biking reinforced those instincts. It's good strength training, too."

If you're curious to try racing, your local bike shop is the place to start inquiring about races in the area or (although not all races require it) to ask about an application for membership in NORBA, the National Off-Road Bicycle Association (see appendix). You can join NORBA with a full membership, or take out a one-day license. Most events fall into one of three categories: cross-country, downhill, and dual slalom, with the majority of newbies gravitating to cross-country. In this event, stamina, moderate trail-riding skills, and some good sense will get you to the finish in one piece and let you have fun doing it—reasonable goals for an initial foray onto the fast track. Here, a few tips for your initiation:

- If possible, preride the course a day or so before the race. Practice on technical sections and plan your pacing. Can't do that? Then walk it on race day.
- Carry sufficient water and use a hydration system so you can keep your hands on the bars.
- Be prepared for an emergency repair on the trail; rules prohibit receiving hands-on help or borrowing tools from another racer. (You'll be set if you have a hand pump or two CO_2 cartridges and an adapter, a tube, and a multitool that includes a chain tool and 4, 5, and 6 mm Allen keys in your seat pack—and know how to use them.)
- Warm up before the start. Ride for about twenty to thirty minutes, with four to eight sprints and a few minutes of "race-pace" speed.
- At the gun, don't go out too fast. As Olympic bronze medalist Susan DeMattei points out, staying out of oxygen debt in the first half of the race

gives you a better chance of being where you want to be in the second half. She proved that in Atlanta in 1996: Everybody charged at the gun, but Susan had trouble getting her foot on the pedal. Suddenly left at the back of the pack, she was tempted to blast to the front. "But I told myself, 'Hey, you have two hours to go—don't be stupid.' I just tried to save myself and pass people at opportune moments." Gradually she worked her way up to the contenders, pacing herself to endure until the end, and earned a spot on the podium.

•If you don't know the course, ride with a controlled speed so you can handle whatever's around the corner.

•Don't be embarrassed to jump off your bike and run with it if you need to. You may be surrounded by lemmings who are so excited they plunge into a too-difficult downhill and then crash. Ride consistently at your ability level, and you'll have more fun.

•If you miss a shift or feel you're riding poorly, don't telegraph your dismay. "When I hear someone say, 'Oh, shit!' that's my signal to attack," says Jacquie Phelan, MTB racing pioneer and founder of the WOMBATS. "Just bite your tongue. Otherwise, racers will see your distress and use it as an opportunity to get ahead."

If you temper your gutsiness with a bit of caution at first, you'll stay in the race game and grow with it. After all, every Expert and Pro started out once in the Beginner class. And what seems extreme to you now, you may find yourself doing some time in the future.

During some recent projects with *Bicycling* magazine, I've come to know staffer Carlotta Cuerdon—a super-strong racer who's discovered a taste for relay events. Down in West Virginia at the 24 Hours of Canaan (rhymes with "insane"), she and her three teammates have won the women's Expert-pro class event three times. This mountain marathon calls on the whole woman—her strength, stamina, and bike-handling skills, plus quick thinking and courage. The course features a long dirt-road climb, a steep-loamy-rooty (nasty!) descent, bumpy meadows, and hairpin turns. Here Carlotta describes her first nighttime lap of 11.5 miles in the '94 race:

It was the middle of a loop, the middle of the night, and my vision was failing. I wiped my clear-lensed glasses, thinking they were fogging up, but it wasn't my glasses. My lights were dying and soon dead.

In order to see anything and keep my team's chances alive, I would have to hang on the wheel of an unsuspecting rider who had lights, using him as my beacon through the hairy singletrack. The first rider by was too fast, but I hopped on the wheel of the next one. Adrenaline coursed through my body as we bumped and wound our way over rocks, down dips, and through puddles.

He was going faster than I would have, even in the daylight. And in the dark, the speed was frightening. I had tunnel vision, concentrating all my efforts on his rear wheel. I knew nothing of the trail that flew by.

At one point I went astray in a puddle, mired in deep mud, and desperately wrenched my bike out of the muck. I had to run through water and thick darkness to catch him again. When I hit an unexpected bump, all seemed lost. My right hand flew off the bar and I started to fall forward. Somehow I managed to regain control, but again I had lost my eyes. I had to sprint through a black hole to catch him. I prayed he knew what he was doing. It was like a wild carnival ride with no lights, my body being whipped through the air and all I could do was hang on and wait for it to end. At the tag zone, my beacon disappeared into the darkness. I owe that guy—not just for our victory that year, but for the ride of my life.

Nothing Flat—
And More Repairs You
Can Do Yourself

Bikes, unlike cars, are easy to maintain and the cost for parts is much cheaper. —Elaine Fisher, Stockport, Cheshire, England

I want to learn more about repairing and upgrading my bike. Like most women, I grew up convinced that only the Y chromosome has the gene for mechanical ability. I've worked hard to overcome this internalized assumption that because I'm female I can't fix things.
—Amy Hubbard, Syracuse, New York

Learn at least basic repairs such as punctures, and always carry tire levers and a puncture kit/spare tube, so that you're not forced to ask strangers for help. —Susan Richardson, Liverpool, England

Soon I'm off to Oregon to take a two-week bike mechanics course so that I can go anywhere in the world and feel confident in maintaining and fixing my bike by myself. Bicycles are the first mechanical things I have ever dealt with, and both riding them and conquering their complexities give me great pleasure. —Gillian Lancaster, San Diego, California

I have a few friends who do my repairs. I haven't a clue myself. My boyfriend does most of it. He tries to show me how to do things, but I think I'm a little too lazy to learn, as he will do it for me. Naughty, eh!
—L. J. Widger, St. Blazey Gate, Cornwall, England

When it comes to bike repair, many women like to take matters into their own hands—literally. But not everyone. If you're in the latter group, what do you do? The guise of feminine helplessness may work if you have indulgent friends or a handy spouse, and there's always the bike shop.

Sooner or later, though, you'll want to learn at least the basics of repair to give you greater freedom in your cycling. Otherwise, some day you might find yourself inconvenienced—maybe stranded—because of your ignorance. Besides, to remain totally at a standoff with wrenches, chain tools, tire levers, and patch kits is to miss one of cycling's great benefits—the discovery of our mechanical aptitude. While some of us grew up learning to use tools, many of us didn't. Fixing things often seems a male domain we don't dare enter. But we can!

In the first place, not too much goes wrong with a bike if you take care of it. Second, many of the working parts carry on their duties in full view, which makes things easy. Take time to observe how they work, and you'll discover it's not so mysterious after all.

In this chapter we'll cover the most common repair situations: fixing a flat, putting your chain back on, and remedying wheel wobbles. We'll also talk about good workshop habits and a schedule for maintenance. But we're going to begin with a bicycle safety checkup you should do right now if your bike hasn't been given a "physical" lately.

SAFETY CHECKUP

Anyone can do this beginning-of-the-season checkup—needed for any bike that hasn't been ridden for awhile. Then, should you need to head for the local bike shop, you'll be prepared to talk about repairs. Also, use this check to evaluate any used bike you consider purchasing.

YOU'LL NEED:

- Clean rags
- Bike lubricant (see chapter 7, "Accessories")
- Degreaser
- WD-40 or bike frame cleaner/wax
- Six-inch adjustable wrench
- Set of Allen keys (These come on a handy ring to keep them together; other sets fold out like blades of a pen knife.)
- Small screwdriver
- Floor pump (see chapter 7, "Accessories")
- Chain cleaner kit (optional)

1. *Clean and lube.* The bike's bound to be dusty, so wipe it down with a clean rag, all except for the chain and cogs. Remove any grease spots with a little degreaser on your rag. As you clean the frame, keep an eye open for dents, severe rust, loose welds, or other damage. (If you discover damage to the frame, have it checked at a bike shop before riding.) Did you find scratches in the paint? Spray a little bike frame cleaner/wax or WD-40 on a rag and wipe the scratched area. Do this after every ride to prevent rust.

A rusty chain should be discarded and replaced. If yours is OK, squirt some bike lubricant on a section of it. Wipe off grit and excess lubricant by grasping the chain with another clean rag while rotating the crank backwards to move the chain through the rag. Clean the entire chain this way. A little lubricant will remain on it to prevent wear and make for easier shifting.

If you want to clean the chain before lubing, you might appreciate an ingenious cleaning device which is available from a couple of different manufacturers. I use one made by Finish Line. It has a plastic housing that snaps over the chain and brushes that turn to clean it. You fill the reservoir with degreaser (use full-strength for this job) and turn the pedals. Lubricate the chain afterwards.

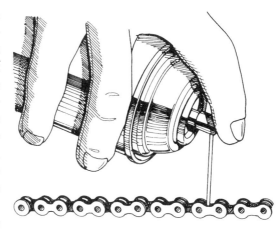

Fig. 34: Lubricating the chain: do this every week or so. And if you ride in the rain, lube your chain before taking the bike out next time.

If the chain has come off the chainring, see "Putting a Chain Back On," later in this chapter.

2. *Tires.* Examine them and remove any bits of embedded stone or glass. If tires have sizable cuts, dry rot, odd bulges, or badly worn tread, buy new ones. Pump up the tires to the correct pressure, marked on the sidewalls. The pressure will be given in *psi,* pounds per square inch. To inflate tubes with Presta valves, loosen the

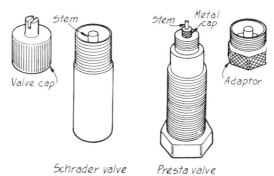

Schrader valve   Presta valve

Fig. 35: Know which kind of valve you have, so you can buy the proper tubes. If you have Presta valves, you may need an adapter for your pump.

knurled metal cap and press the stem until you hear a hiss. This tells you the valve is open; however, if air doesn't seem to be going in when you pump, loosen the cap a little more and try again.

3. *Wheels.* Loose spokes weaken a wheel. With your fingers squeeze together two adjacent spokes on the same side of a wheel. They should feel tight. Continue around that side of the wheel until you've tested the tension of all those spokes. All should have about the same tightness. If some are much looser than others, your wheel probably needs truing, usually a task for a professional.

Progress to the other side and then the other wheel. Note: On derailleur bicycles normally the right-side spokes of the back wheel are tighter than the left-side spokes.

Check rims for dents.

Are the wheels mounted securely? If attached with nuts, test them with your adjustable wrench to be sure the nuts are tight. If wheels have quick-release levers, test to be sure the levers are snug in the closed position. (Levers are meant to be flipped open and closed. They should be screwed only if they need adjustment so that the lever flips closed with some resistance. For further discussion, see "Fixing That Flat" later in this chapter.)

Check for loose bearings in each wheel hub: Grasp the wheel rim on opposite sides with your hands and wiggle it sideways. If there is more than a little play, have the bearings checked. (Loose bearings can cause excessive wear in the hubs or lead to an accident by making the bike shudder uncontrollably on a downhill.)

4. *Brakes.* If you have *hub brakes*—for example, coaster brakes—which work through pressure applied inside a wheel hub, ride the bike a short distance and brake by backpedaling. Pedals should rotate less than a quarter turn before braking action occurs. If not, have them checked at the shop.

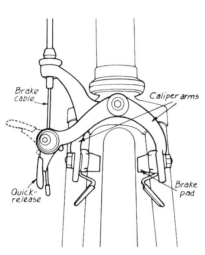

Fig. 36: This sidepull brake has a quick-release which flips up to open but is now closed. Note that the wheel is centered between brake pads with a little clearance on each side.

If, like most bikes, yours has *rim brakes*, which operate by applying pressure on both sides of the wheel rim, do you have plenty of rubber left on all four brake pads? If pads are worn past their grooves, replace them.

If your brakes have a quick-release system, check to be sure releases are in the closed position; brakes don't work normally with quick-releases open. On road bikes with standard caliper brakes, the quick-release is usually attached to one of the calipers (see figure 36), although some older bikes have them on the brake lever (see figure 37). On bikes with Campagnolo dual-control levers, look for a pin on the brake lever that you push in to let it open farther and spread the pads. With cantilever brakes on mountain bikes, usually one end of the straddle cable or link wire unhooks, which allows the brake arms to move away from the rim for wheel removal (see figure 38); brakes are inoperable in this position. On direct-pull brakes such as Shimano's V-brakes, the brake cable unhooks at the top of the brake caliper (see figure 39).

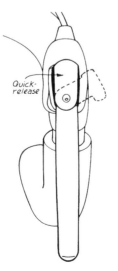

Fig. 37: A brake quick-release on the lever is shown in the closed position. It flips open to the side.

Then spin one of the wheels and squeeze the hand brake that controls it. Both brake pads should contact the rim squarely and "toed in," with the leading edge hitting just a little (1–2 mm) before the trailing

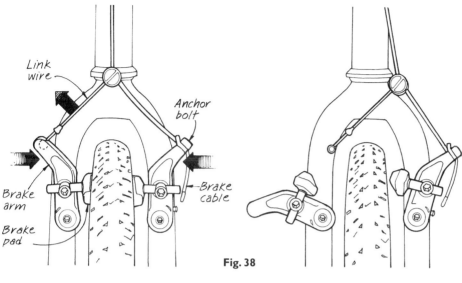

Link wire

Anchor bolt

Brake cable

Brake arm

Brake pad

Fig. 38

Fig. 38: (left) To increase clearance for wheel removal with this cantilever brake, squeeze the brake arms together with one hand and lift the end of the link wire out of its pocket in the brake arm. (right) Brake pads now allow clearance for wheel removal. Brakes are inoperable in this position.

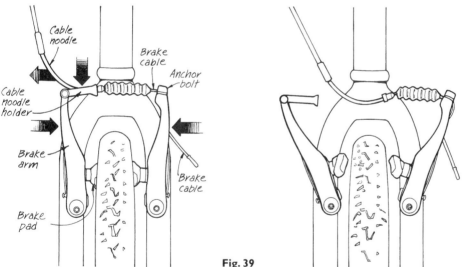

Cable noodle

Brake cable

Anchor bolt

Cable noodle holder

Brake arm

Brake cable

Brake pad

Fig. 39

Fig. 39: (left) To increase clearance on this direct-pull or V-brake, squeeze the brake arms together with one hand; meanwhile, with that pointer finger, push down on the cable noodle holder while pulling on the cable noodle with the other hand. (On a new bike, some cable stretch may be necessary before you can unhook the brake. If you have difficulty, ask the shop mechanic to assist you.) (right) The wheel can now be removed. The brakes are disabled in this position.

edge. Spin the wheel again. Is a brake pad rubbing when you aren't braking? If so, check to see whether the wheel is centered. (Need help? See "Fixing That Flat.")

If one side is rubbing despite centering the wheel, have it checked at the shop; you may need a new rim or to have the wheel trued.

Repeat these steps with the other brake and wheel.

Finally, look over each brake cable (where visible) for broken strands or frayed cable where it enters the hand lever and where it fastens to the brake. Squeeze each brake lever and look into the opening for any fraying in there next to the end button, the usual point of wear. If you find damage, cables need replacing. Spray a bit of lubricant into each end of the plastic casing.

5. *Handlebars and stem*. Face your bike, holding the front wheel firmly between your legs and gently try to twist the handlebars left and right. If they move, the stem, which attaches them, is loose and the bolt on top of the stem needs tightening.

Try to rotate the handlebars. If they move, the binder bolt on the stem part that holds the bars should be tightened.

Look the stem over. A hairline crack anywhere is a sign of metal fatigue and means the stem needs replacement. Don't ride your bike until you have it checked at a shop.

6. *Seatpost and saddle*. Examine the seatpost. Any hairline cracks signal a need for replacement.

Does the saddle need tightening? Try to twist it up and then down, left and then right. If it doesn't move, it's secure.

For a comfortable ride, check that the saddle is level. If not, adjust it using the bolt under the saddle.

Check saddle height. Find a wall or something else to support yourself while you sit on the saddle, or ask someone to hold the bike for you. Put your heels on the pedals. With your leg extended at the bottom of the pedal stroke, you should have a very slight bend in your knee. Adjust the saddle height if necessary. (If there's no quick-release, you'll find the seatpost binder bolt on the back of the seat lug.)

When raising the saddle, don't go past the minimum insertion line, which marks the safe limit for raising it. (If you need to raise the saddle higher than this, the bike is probably too small for you.) For more on saddle height, see chapter 5, "So You Want to Buy a Bike?"

7. *Gears*. Examine all visible gear cable for any broken strands or fraying, and check to see that the cable is attached firmly at a few points along the frame. Squirt some lubricant into each end of the casing, as you did with the brake cables. Check that shifters are securely attached to the bike.

OK so far? Then proceed by suspending the bike (or ask someone to hold it for you) so the rear wheel is off the ground and can turn freely. Rotate the pedals forward as you test the gears. Does the chain shift smoothly in each position? Also, as you turn the pedals, watch to see if the lever moves by itself from one setting to another. (It shouldn't.) If you have two derailleurs, test the gears with each one.

If the bicycle slips from one gear to another by itself, adjustment is necessary. *Internally geared* bicycles may have a problem within the hub that needs repair at the shop. On a road bike that has shifters on the down tube, you may be able to adjust *derailleur gears* yourself: Simply tighten the gear shift lever screw slightly with a screwdriver; some bikes have a D-ring you can turn by hand. Test again to see whether slippage is corrected. On most other bikes, locate the barrel adjuster and turn it.

During this test, if the chain should fall completely off the chainring, other minor adjustments may be needed and are probably best handled in a shop.

OK so far? Rotate the pedals again, looking for any stiffness where the chain curves around a sprocket at the rear hub. Let any stiff link travel around to where you can get at it with both hands, and flex it sideways with your thumbs, until it loosens up.

8. *Pedals and cranks.* Look for any tiny cracks here or in the components that make up the bottom bracket. (See any? Have the parts looked over by your shop mechanic before riding.)

Do you hear any peculiar noises as you turn the pedals? Hold one crank in your hand and feel whether the pedal is attached securely. The pedal should turn on the pedal spindle, but you don't want the spindle to wobble where it attaches to the crank.

For the cranks, grasp one in each hand and check for play by rocking them from side to side at several positions in the rotation of the crank. If there's any play, have the cranks checked at a bike shop.

9. *Headset.* To test the bearings in the *headset,* which holds the front fork onto the frame, lift the front end of the bike off the ground a few inches and drop it. If you hear a clank, the headset is loose and needs attention. Here's another check: With one hand grab the handlebars and stem at the centerpoint. With the other hand grasp a fork blade end. Push on the handlebars and pull on the fork blade simultaneously. Then reverse the motion; repeat several times. If you feel any play or hear a slight clicking sound, your headset bearings could be loose and should be checked at the shop.

10. *Details.* Is anything hanging loose? If there are fenders or bike bags, check to be sure they aren't rubbing against the tires. Is there anything sharp that could cut you if you fell or brushed against it? If the metal handlebar ends are exposed, for example, replace the grips or have new plugs inserted, as appropriate.

11. *Bike fit.* We talk about it in detail in chapter 5. Proper fit is important. Otherwise, you'll have unnecessary aches and pains—especially in shoulders, neck, or back if the reach is too long for you—and a bike that's too big or too small is more difficult to control. Whether it's your own old bike or someone else's, even if it's free, it's no bargain if it doesn't fit.

12. *Saddle.* Especially on older bikes, usually the saddle that came as original equipment was cheap and poorly designed for a woman's anatomy. (See chapter 12, "Ouch-less Riding," before buying a new one.) The wrong saddle can be torture and will limit your riding potential.

That's it. If your bike failed inspection on any of these points, take it to a shop for repair. Tell the mechanic what you found in your checkup, and ask for an estimate of costs before you leave the bike. This will help you make sure the bike is worth repairing.

Don't be reluctant to ask questions. Bike shops depend on return business from their customers—all of their customers, including you. As Caroline Della Porta, of London, England, puts it:

> Don't be afraid to ask about repairs or parts in bike shops. Before your bike is repaired, make note of the work to be done and check it when you pick the bike up. Have a quick cycle 'round the block and come back if anything feels wrong. If you use that shop again, they will remember you. Make use of your experience there to learn about your bike.

MS. WRENCH

Even if you don't have a lot of experience, you can tackle the easier maintenance and repair tasks with the help of a clearly written, well illustrated manual. Also, crack open the owner's manual that came with your bike and—if you have a suspension fork—the manual for that, too. These guides, written especially for your equipment, should cover maintenance needs which other repair books might overlook. Check out repair articles in the cycling magazines, too.

When possible, live instruction and hands-on experience are a great way to learn. Spend time with friends when they're working on their bikes. Watch and ask questions; help if you can. Take advantage of repair clinics offered in your area, or organize one through your club; allow time for hands-on practice. Ask whether your local shop offers a bike maintenance course.

Whatever repair jobs you decide to try, orderly work habits will get it done faster and save a lot of frustration.

- Work in a clean, uncluttered, well-lighted area. Tools are easier to keep track of and dropped parts are found more quickly. Remember the bike mechanic's law: The smaller the screw, the more likely you are to drop it. And the corollary: If you can't find it, the bike shop is sure to be closed. Be neat.
- Observe and analyze. Anything you take apart has to be put back together again. While disassembling, observe how the parts went together. This is learning opportunity number one. To reinforce it, as you remove parts, lay them out in a row (in the order of removal) on a clean piece of newspaper or in a small styrofoam tray. Don't take apart more than necessary.
- Most screws and bolts on a bike unscrew in a counterclockwise direction, as they do generally in the world of hardware. Remember: "Righty-tighty, lefty-loosey." (There are two exceptions, left pedals and some left-side bottom bracket parts. The left pedal is threaded differently from the right so that it doesn't accidentally become unscrewed as you pedal.)
- Not into the greasy-hands look? Keeping them clean is easier if you apply

hand cream before doing the dirty work. Another trick: Before handling the chain, pull on disposable latex gloves or slip a plastic bag over each hand. (Next time you get a pinhole in your rubber gloves so they won't do for washing dishes, demote them to the bike workshop for such jobs.)

- It's helpful to have a workstand that holds the bike up off the floor so that wheels can turn freely.
- If you do have to lay your rig on its side to work on it (and whenever you rest it on its side), don't lay it on the chain side. You'll avoid bending the derailleurs out of line. Always protect this side of the bike, and you'll save yourself some hassles.
- Prevent extra repair work by riding with one ear tuned to the sounds of your bike. If you hear a funny noise, stop and check it out.
- Be sensitive also to performance. For example, indexed shifting is great for easy, precise gear shifts, but it can come out of adjustment. If you notice you're no longer getting those crisp shifts, have it looked at or adjust it yourself. (Usually it's simply that the gear cable has stretched a little and needs tightening. A small adjustment can be made with the barrel adjuster—on bikes that have them.)

TOOLS TO CARRY ON EVERY RIDE

Inconvenient, but true: Most mechanical breakdowns occur, not in your home workshop or garage, but out on the road or trail. If you carry the following tools on all rides, you'll be prepared for the most common emergency repairs (covered in the sections which follow):

- 1 pair disposable latex gloves (tuck them in a small plastic bag for protection)
- 2 or 3 tire levers (I especially like the VAR lever for skinny road bike tires)
- spare tube (if you have two different wheel sizes, carry one for each wheel)
- patch kit
- frame pump (a full-size pump works more efficiently than a mini)
- set of Allen keys or a multi-tool
- chain tool
- moist towelette

PUTTING A CHAIN BACK ON

You're riding along, you shift gears, and suddenly, with a strange chunking sound, your bike stops. You look down and see the chain hanging slack, no longer wrapped neatly around one of your front chainrings.

Don't groan. Here's what to do. Check whether your chain has fallen off to the inside (near the frame) or the outside. Now while continuing to ride, move the front derailleur shift lever so the chain moves away from where it's fallen. If it fell to the inside, for example, shift it to the outside chainring. Like magic, the chain will often reseat itself.

If not, you can usually put that chain back on without getting your hands dirty. First, shift your chain onto the smallest rear cog; this gives you more chain to work with. Now, if the chain has become tangled or oddly kinked, you'll have to untangle it. To lift the chain, use a stick you find beside the road or a tool you're carrying. One woman I know uses the toe of her (black) cycling shoe. If the chain is really tangled, you may have to work the kinks out by hand, so think: Did you put those latex gloves in your bike bag? Are you carrying a snack in some plastic wrap or a bag you can slip your hand into?

Lay the chain in position on the top of the smallest of the rear cogs. Now pick up the chain near the top of the small front chainring and lay it in place around the chainring. With derailleur bikes, as you do this, push forward on the rear derailleur if you need more slack.

Rotate the pedals a full revolution forward to check that the chain is running smoothly. Don't turn them backward, or the chain can fall off. P.S., if you did get chain grease on your hands and you're wearing black cycling shorts, that's where you can wipe them if you don't have a rag.

CLICK SHIFTING THAT DOESN'T CLICK

If your indexed (click) shifting comes out of adjustment in the middle of a ride, on some older bikes you can switch to friction shifting so that you can still operate your gears to get home.

FIX THAT FLAT

When I first got my new bike, I went for a ride after fixing a front flat. I was-n't sure how the quick-release mechanism worked, but I thought I had it back on right. Well, after riding ten miles, I lifted the front of the bike up over a curb, and the wheel fell off! —Janet Fons, Denver, Colorado

That was a close one. I know people who've had some very bloody accidents when their front wheel came off, so let's cover changing a tire from start to finish.

1. Remove the wheel. The front one's pretty easy. If the brakes don't allow enough room for the wheel to pass between them, there is usually a quick-release mechanism that lets you spread them wider temporarily (discussed above in point four of "Safety Checkup").

Flip open (don't unscrew) the wheel hub quick-release (QR) lever. On some bikes you can now slide the wheel out of the dropout slots at the fork ends. But, for safety, many bikes have nubs on the dropouts that prevent the wheel from dislodging if the lever is incorrectly tightened. If you have this feature, grasp either side of the QR and unscrew the other side until the QR clears the nubs. Then take out the wheel. (If the wheel is nutted, loosen the nuts with your wrench.)

To take off the rear wheel: While hand pedaling, shift the chain onto the innermost chainring and the smallest rear cog to give you slack. Now lean the front end of your bike so that the front wheel won't pivot. Open the brake quick-release or unhook the brakes.

Flip open the wheel's QR lever (or loosen the axle nuts). Notice the open ends of the dropouts: You'll be sliding the wheel forward out of those slots. Standing behind the bike, grasp the left seatstay just below the brake and lift the rear of the bike. The wheel may fall right out. If not, with your right hand push the wheel down and slightly forward until the top of the tire clears the bike. Then maneuver the wheel a little left until the cogs clear the chain. If the chain gets caught up on the cogs, wiggle the wheel gently to free it. It's a bit of a juggling act, but you can get the wheel out without removing the chain from the front chainring.

Now to lay the bike down without damaging anything: Move the left pedal up into the twelve o' clock position. Lay the bicycle on its left side, propping it on the left pedal and the front tire and handlebar. Your frame, drivetrain, and saddle stay off the ground, clean and unscratched.

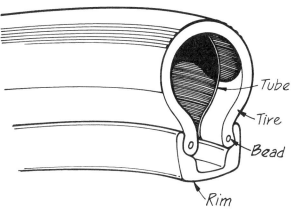

Fig. 40: A clincher tire and rim shown in cross section.

2. Remove the tire from the rim. The kind of tire most riders use, the "clincher" or "wired-on" tire, gets its name because the tire has two steel wires, or *beads,* on the side edges. A separate inner tube is inside the tire, and all of this fits under the edges of the rim.

To take off the tire, let out any air left in the tube. Depress a Schrader valve with a fingernail or a corner of a tire lever; unscrew and depress the stem of a Presta valve. Presta valves are easily damaged, so screw the valve shut before continuing. (If

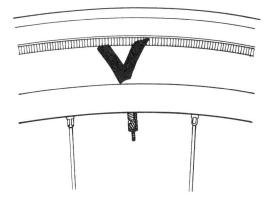

Fig. 41: Before removing a tire to repair it, mark the location of the valve on the tire with a pen or marker.

your tire isn't flat but you want to practice, deflate the tire.) Mark the location of the valve on the tire with a pen or marker.

Then remove the tire. Hold the wheel upright. On the side opposite the valve stem, slip the large, flat end of a tire lever under one side of the bead. Don't push the lever in any farther than necessary, or you'll pinch the tube. Pull the free end of the lever down toward the spokes to pry the bead up from inside the rim. Leave that tool in place, hooked around a spoke (if it has a hook). Do the same with the second lever, four to six inches away from the first. Remove the first lever and repeat, leapfrogging the levers. Eventually you'll be able to free the remaining portion of the bead by running one lever around between the bead and the rim.

Fig. 42: Remove one side of the tire with tire levers.

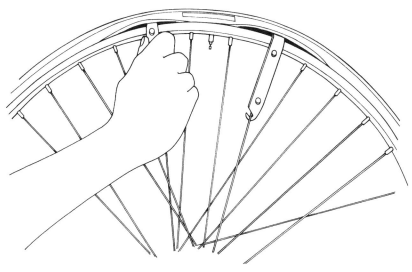

Now reach inside and pull out the tube, except where the valve stem goes through the rim.

To take the other side of the tire off the rim, start at the point farthest from the valve stem. You can probably pull the tire up and off the rim with your hands. If not, use the levers. Finish removing the tube; if you have Presta valves, there may be a nut or knurled ring next to the rim that needs to be unscrewed first. (If it has rusted, you will probably need a wrench or pliers to loosen it. For this reason, some mechanics say to discard this part. It's designed to keep the valve straight in the rim, but it's not essential.)

3. Locate the leak. Inflate the tube and listen for a tattletale hiss, or immerse the tube in water and watch for bubbles. You might find a pair of holes if you hit a bump hard and the rim pinched your tube.

Now look inside the tire in case the thorn, glass, etc. is still in there, waiting to do more damage. Use that mark you made on the tire as a point of reference to figure where the puncture is on the tire. If you don't see anything that might have made the puncture, feel the inside of the tire carefully with your fingers or slide a wadded rag around in both directions. There might be a piece of glass or a tack lodged in the tire. Remove it. Check also for a sharp spoke tail sticking through the rim, needing fixing.

Still looking for a clue to the trouble? Immerse the valve and check it for leaks.

4. Patch or change the tube. For a speedy repair on a ride, install a fresh spare and take the punctured one home to patch later; it then becomes the spare. (If the hole is small, like a pin prick, you can mend the tube following patch kit instructions. If the trouble is a leaky valve or a larger hole, discard the tube.)

5. Reinforce the tire if it's badly cut. For a cut more than ¼ inch long, *boot* the tire. That is, put something over the cut on the inside of the tire to keep the tube from blowing out through the cut. Carry a piece of old tire about 1½ inches long or a strip of handlebar tape in your repair kit for this purpose. In a pinch a folded dollar bill, a mylar energy bar wrapper, or a scrap of cloth will do.

6. Pump some air into the replacement tube, just enough to round it out. Put it into the tire. Lay the wheel on its side, with the tire-and-tube combo on top and the valve lined up with the valve hole.

7. Remount the tire. Stick the valve stem partway into the valve hole in the rim. Start to work the bead over the rim all the way around, using your thumbs, not the levers (so as not to pinch the tube). Work away from the valve in both directions simultaneously.

Then remount the second side of the tire, starting at the valve stem, and working the tire over the rim with both hands. To give yourself a little slack, pinch the two beads of the tire together in the deep center part of the rim; keep them there by maintaining tension on the tire as you go. That will make the last bit easier.

Try (if you can) to remount those last few inches without using the tire levers (since the levers could puncture the tube). Toward the end, fully deflating the tube can help. Then place the wheel on your knee, hold one end of the uninstalled section to keep it in place, then with the heel of your stronger hand roll the bead up and over the rim.

Some tire/wheel combinations are tougher than others to remount with just your hands; skinny road-bike tires can be especially persnickety. If you have a VAR tire lever (see chapter 7, "Accessories"), you can use it at the end without fear of pinching the tube.

After the tire's completely mounted, press the valve down into the tire and then pull it back out to make sure the tube isn't being pinched near the valve.

8. Pump up the tire. Put your frame pump on the valve and brace it by wrapping your thumb over the tire and one finger behind a spoke to prevent damaging the valve stem with the force of your strokes. Inflate to half the recommended pressure.

Fig. 43: To make the most of your muscle when using a frame pump—and to hold the wheel steady so as to avoid damaging the tire valve—lean the wheel against a tree, a wall (as shown), or whatever else is handy. Turn the wheel so the valve is at the right height for you to brace your elbow against your knee while you pump with the opposite hand. Here the cyclist holds the pump head firmly in place with her left hand and grips the tire with her thumb. This position lets her lean into the pumping motion with her upper body weight—helpful because pumping becomes more difficult as air pressure inside the tire increases.

When buying a frame pump, try it out in the shop first. And ask whether a high-volume pump would be beneficial for the type of bicycle you own.

Spin the wheel, eyeballing the tire to be sure it's mounted evenly—that nowhere is it too far up under the rim or too far out. If necessary, let a little air out and wiggle any uneven sections to reseat the tire. Fully inflate and recheck. Not getting this right can prevent the tire from rolling smoothly, or the tube might squeeze through and blow out.

9. **Replace the wheel.** For the front wheel, simply reverse the removal procedure: Make sure the QR lever is open (or axle nuts are loose). Center the wheel in the fork with the quick-release lever on the bike's left (non-chain) side and the wheel axle fully inserted in the dropout slots. If you had to unscrew the QR lever to get past the dropout nubs, hold it and turn one end clockwise to tighten. You want to adjust this so that when you flip the quick-release closed, you start feeling resistance with the lever at a ninety-degree angle to the fork blade. It should end up closed neatly beside the fork blade, and it should take enough force that an impression of the lever is left on your palm. Grasp the front fork while pushing, for some extra leverage. Close brake quick-releases or hook up the brakes if you opened them. Spin the wheel and make sure it's centered between the brakes and not rubbing either brake shoe. If necessary, loosen and center the wheel; then retighten.

For the rear wheel, again your bike should be in its highest gear in back (smallest cog). Check that the quick-release lever is open (or nuts are loose). Lift the bike from behind, holding the seatstay with your left hand. With your right, roll the wheel between the brake calipers—keeping it grounded stabilizes this operation. Hook the upper run of the chain over the smallest cog by manipulating both bike and wheel. If you need to, pull back on the rear derailleur to get it out of the way (or on an internally geared bicycle, pull on the chain itself to get enough slack). Center the wheel between the chainstays as you line up the dropouts over the axle, then drop the frame into place. Pull the wheel back and up to position the wheel securely in the dropouts. Check for centering between the chainstays, seatstays, and brake pads. Flip the wheel QR closed (or tighten the nuts), and hook up the brake again or close its quick-release.

REMEDYING WHEEL WOBBLE

If you ride through a pothole and bend a rim, what can you do for an on-the-road fix-up? If your wheel isn't bent too badly—that is, when you rotate the wheel if it hits the brakes but not the frame—you can make a stopgap repair. On a road bike, simply open the brake calipers a little with the brake quick-release. On an MTB if you're carrying your Allen keys (as you should), you can loosen the anchor bolt at the top of the brake arm (see figures 38 and 39) and pull on the cable to give a little slack (no more than ¼ inch) so the brakes open wider; tighten the bolt and check that you still have some stopping power.

You can continue on your way, but allow extra braking time because you won't be able to stop suddenly. After your ride take your wheel in for truing, or do it yourself if you're good with a spoke wrench.

REGULAR UPKEEP

"Not maintaining our equipment leads to problems down the road," says mountain bike racer Cindy Whitehead. Three times a national champion (including Veteran downhill champ in 1996), Cindy knows that routine upkeep extends bike life and helps avoid equipment failures. She learned that lesson in the Sierra 7500, a California race so named because it climbs 7,500 feet in the first half of its fifty miles. In 1986 Cindy rode forty-nine of them standing up without a saddle—an amazing feat of strength and determination—after breaking her seatpost binder bolt.

What happened that day was a triple-whammy of bad luck, manufacturer's error, and bicycle neglect. Cindy dismounted for the first water crossing. When she jumped back on, her weight on the saddle sheared off the lightweight aluminum alloy bolt—which, after a previous failure, a savvier mechanic would have replaced with a sturdier steel bolt. The saddle gone, she tried to remove the protruding seatpost, but it was rusted in place. "I'm lax about maintenance but a nut for a clean bike," she reflects. "I'd hosed it off without removing the seatpost afterwards and lubing it. Water had got in there and rusted it."

But that's not all, folks. Later in the race she crashed and knocked her handlebars askew. She tried to straighten them, but the stem, too, was rusted in. Now she was riding a little lopsided, but she hammered. And she won. Those who saw it won't ever forget it. But Cindy laughs modestly. "I do much better with mechanical things now. As a novice, I was really green and had to learn the hard way."

How quickly wear and tear take a toll on your machine depends partly on how much and what kind of riding you do. In most cases, if you follow these guidelines, your routine maintenance and repair of minor problems will prevent major ones.

Some tasks need to be done often, while others should be scheduled monthly or yearly. For these less-frequent jobs, keep a record (perhaps in your training diary) of the date and service performed. Later if you should wonder how long it's been since you installed those tires or had the wheels trued, you can look it up.

Before each ride. This quick check takes less than a minute. It covers those parts that can get out of whack from one ride to the next and cause a problem. If you want a refresher on how to check something, refer to the numbered section of the "Safety Checkup" provided in parentheses.

- Look at the chain, which should appear at least slightly wet with lubricant. Lube (1) if needed. Any time your chain gets a dousing on wet trails or streets, lubricate before your next ride.
- Check the brakes. Brake pads should contact the wheel rim only, not the tire, and brake levers should not touch the handlebars when squeezed (4).
- Check tire pressure with a pressure gauge before a road ride; for serious trail riding, you should be able to press in the tire sidewall slightly with your thumb and forefinger. Lift the front end of your bicycle and spin the front wheel as you watch for any wheel wobble or rubbing against the brakes, the front fork, or a mudguard stay (3). (Rubbing increases the work of pedaling and can put a hole in your tire.) If you have wheel wobble, look for a bend in the rim or loose bearings in the hub and have it repaired. Repeat these checks with the back wheel.
- Check for play in the headset (9).

Every week or two.
- Lube the chain, brake pivot points, and derailleurs. To avoid overdoing it, use a drip-bottle lubricant.
- Check the tightness of all nuts and bolts and tighten any that have started to come loose. Otherwise, the vibration from riding will gradually shake them looser. Test bolts that attach lights, reflectors, mudguards, racks, brakes, and brake shoes.

Every month.
- Check for frayed brake (4) and gear (7) cables. If even one of the several strands of wire that make up a cable is broken, the cable should be replaced immediately. If there is a kink in the cable housing (which wears the cable and makes braking less responsive) have it replaced. Put a drop of bicycle

oil on the bit of cable you see when you squeeze the brake lever and peer inside. Squirt some lubricant into each end of the gear cable casing.

- Examine brake pads. If they are worn down past the grooves, install new ones.
- Check tires for wear, bulges, and embedded stones or glass (2). If you have sew-ups, check that rim glue is holding.
- Check for chain stretch on a derailleur bike. (A stretched chain causes the rear cogs to wear faster.) Since a new chain's links are precisely 1 inch long, this test is easy: Place an accurate ruler alongside a 1-foot length of chain. Line up the end of the ruler with the center of a rivet; the 12-inch mark should come at the center of a rivet on a new, unstretched chain. If the rivet actually measures up at 12 ⅛ inches or longer, the chain is stretched and the cogs will have already worn. Cogs and chain should be replaced, as worn cogs can age a new chain quickly.

    If you watch for chain stretch regularly, you'll be clued in when the chain has just stretched ¹⁄₁₆ of an inch. Replace it then, and your cogs should be OK.

- Clean and lube the entire drivetrain—the cogs, chain, derailleurs, crankset, and pedals. (Do this more often if you see grunge building up on the chain, derailleur pulleys, or cogs.) For the most thorough chain cleaning, remove the chain from the bike with a chain tool. Soak the chain several hours or overnight in cleaning solvent, which is available from your bike shop. Then use an old toothbrush to scrub the chain, link by link. Afterwards, hang the chain to dry in a dry place or blow it dry with compressed air. (Don't try using a hair drier on it, as some solvents are combustible.)
- Check the bearings. Are wheel bearings too loose (3)? Are they too tight? Lift the front of the bike. Does the wheel turn on its own, swinging back and forth a few times before gradually coming to a stop? If it stops suddenly or jerkily, the bearings may be dirty, overtight, or need lubricating. (This test is possible because the part of the wheel with the tire valve is heavier. If the wheel doesn't turn when you pick up the bike, you may already have the heavy part at the bottom. Try again—give the wheel a partial turn, stop it, and then release.)

    On a derailleur bike you can test the rear wheel in a similar way, but first disconnect the chain by removing the wheel and taking the chain off the cogs; then replace the wheel, letting the chain dangle underneath.

    Before replacing the chain, test the crank bearings by spinning the cranks to see if they turn freely. To see if they're too loose, turn one crank so it's parallel with a rear chainstay, place your thumb between the crank and the chainstay, and try to move the crank sideways; any play indicates looseness. Now replace the rear wheel.

    Check pedal bearings by trying to spin a pedal with your finger: It should spin easily and smoothly unless bearings are too tight. Grasp the pedal in your hand and try to wiggle it; any play means the bearings are too loose. Test both pedals.

To test headset bearings, remove the front wheel. Hold your bicycle by the top tube with one hand and tilt the bike slightly to one side and then to the other. Handlebars should move freely left and right without sticking, or the headset is too tight.

With an internally geared or coaster brake bike, check the bearings by spinning the rear wheel forward. Tight bearings will grab the rear sprocket and cause the chain and cranks to move forward at full speed. (Don't worry if they move a little; that's normal.)

•Test spoke tension (3).

Annually. If you cycle over 2,000 miles a year, at least once a year your bicycle needs a full overhaul, with all moving parts disassembled, cleaned, inspected, replaced as needed, lubricated, put back together, and adjusted. Consider replacing brake cable and housing; some manufacturers of brake systems recommend doing this yearly as a precaution. Have the frame looked over for any damage or misalignment.

Think of the annual overhaul as an investment that will ultimately save you money because replacing a few worn parts will prevent damage to other, pricier components. Schedule this task for wintertime, when shop mechanics are not so busy. Ultimately, you may want to learn to do some of this yourself and will find the knowledge rewarding.

A Real Fix

As a rather inexperienced leader on a two-week bike trip for American Youth Hostels, I had one kid who thought he was from outer space (he would talk via invisible transmitter to someone on another planet). In the initial hour of day one, we had our first of many mishaps with him. I was the only leader, the other kids had gone ahead, and "John" was bringing up the rear when he ran straight into a parked car. It was eight A.M. on a Sunday in a small town with no bike shop. I threw the bags off his bike, told him to sit on the rear wheel of his upturned bike, and flagged down a stranger to hold the pedals. Meanwhile, I sat on the sidewalk, put my feet on the bottom bracket, and pulled as hard as I could on the fork. I guess my nervousness about the rest of the group, off without a leader, and my anger that all this had happened so early in the trip gave me strength. In seconds flat the fork was straightened, the brakes were readjusted, and the bags back on the bike. The kid was OK, I thanked the stranger, and we resumed riding. The bike was fine for the rest of the trip, though I kept a close eye on "John."

–Cynthia McArthur, St. Paul, Minnesota

Two-Wheel Travel— Cycle Touring and Other Adventures

Not to romanticize too much, but my first bicycle tour had an incredible impact on me. A month before my friend was to cycle across the United States from Maine to Oregon, he asked if I cared to join him. I laughed at the absurdity. Hours later I accepted on the allure. Why not, I thought. I was bored, cynical of my academic world, and in dire need of change. I was twenty-one. Little did I know, I was also out of shape and ignorant about the mechanics, not to mention the demands, of bicycling that distance. I was ripe for a full share of peaks and pitfalls, aches and ecstasies. What one peak experience do I recall now, nine years later?

Maybe it was the smell of homemade New Hampshire maple syrup pouring over hot pancakes after my first mountain pass the day before. Or perhaps the freshly grilled trout on the first sunny afternoon after two days spent dodging the splash of cars and eating cold peanut butter and honey sandwiches in a downpour. Might it have been the view from the top of Rocky Mountain National Park after two hours of climbing, or moonlit cycling in the high desert? Or was it the sight of the Pacific Ocean as we finished our tour?

Rather than a single event, an embracing sense of learning and accomplishment paints my outlook. I was sore at first—thirty miles my first day and I thought I would die. Thirty-five miles the second day felt even worse, as I was still sore from the first. I'd never ridden more than ten miles before. How would I ever get through this? To make matters worse, my running shorts chafed my inner thighs, the pedals soon destroyed the soles of my $5 sneakers, and the fingers of my right hand went numb without gloves or handlebar padding to cushion them. All the things I've since read not to do, I did. I cried and cursed my way through (or rather up) New England, but I never missed the chance to laugh or smell the morning air as a breeze whispered her hellos. Blue skies and no traffic were always warmly welcomed.

I felt my strength and determination grow steadily, my ability become evident. Even my father admitted I really could make it home to West Virginia as I rode up with 1000 miles on my odometer. He stopped offering me bus tickets. I stopped doubting myself and wondering whether I'd have to accept them. I was no longer out of shape, I was learning about bike mechanics, and I was meeting the demands of a long-distance tour. Luckily, I also discovered cycling shoes, gloves, and handlebar padding in West Virginia.

And when I saw the Colorado Rockies 3,000 miles later, I fell in love with cycling. We re-routed ourselves to stay there longer . . . and to cross the Continental Divide seven times, spending a glorious month while I enjoyed the climbing for its beauty, its challenge, and its rewards down the other side.

To be honest, my first sight of the Pacific Ocean wasn't the peak of this tour. It meant the end. Oregon was cold and wet, the beach clouded in. We felt tired. Six thousand miles had passed by. Beds, showers, and stoves with ovens began to look very appealing. We had $3 between the two of us. We unpacked our bikes and looked for jobs. –Beverly Rue, Berkeley, California

Many women have jumped into bicycle touring as Beverly did, inexperienced and ill-prepared, and come through their sudden immersion in the sport as born-again bicycle tourists. One woman describes a similarly challenging tour as "the most rewarding venture of my life." A much shorter 300 miles were still formidable to first-timer Nilce Moraes from Willow Grove, Pennsylvania, then an out-of-shape student who "had only ridden seventeen miles before the trip from New Jersey to New York's Adirondack Mountains." No one thought she could manage it, but she did. "I learned so much about myself," she says. "Soon to enter my senior year in college, I experienced more inner growth on that five-day trip than in three years of school."

Admittedly, the ride-yourself-into-fitness approach works best on a longer tour, especially if you keep mileage low at the start. The first days or weeks can be misery if you do too much. Some would-be adventurers—male and female—end up abandoning their trips, swearing never to see a bicycle again. And there are dangers, as inexperience and fatigue combine with the bike handling surprises of a loaded bicycle to increase the potential for accidents.

Strong knees, however, plus a modicum of luck and mounds of determination (not to mention the company of an experienced riding partner) have helped many a novice through. Out of an ambitious itinerary can emerge a well-conditioned and wiser bicycle tourist—a true picaresque heroine. Some before-you-go planning and training will enhance the likelihood of a fulfilling experience. (See chapter 22, "Planning Your Own Tour.")

Or you may prefer a gentler approach. An increasingly popular option for a first effort is to join a group on a commercial cycling tour, prefaced by appropriate training. Such an adventure can impart freshness and inspiration to your entire cycling year—motivating you as you increase your mileage in preparation and revisiting you in memories of the good times and accomplishments.

Years ago most partakers on organized bike tours were either impecunious students doing the youth hostel thing or avid adult members of cycle-touring clubs, whose legs were well-seasoned for eighty-mile days on the typical club trip. To the novice bicyclist or average sedentary traveler, the apparent discomforts of two-wheel travel seemed too daunting, its pleasures a well-kept secret.

But no more. With the fitness boom has come the development of the bike tour industry, which caters to a far more diverse crowd than hard-core cycle-tourists of the past decades. One nice feature of these trips is that they're enjoyable for novice and experienced cyclists alike. That's because participants aren't forced to ride as a group; individual maps and route instructions allow each cyclist to pedal his or her own pace, stopping to rest or explore some out-of-the-way village or ruin. First-time cycle-tourists often express surprise at how easy it is to ride thirty miles this way, and that they can accomplish much more than they thought possible.

Many participants don't think of themselves so much as cyclists, but rather people who enjoy "active travel" along with a certain amount of security and comfort. Often companies report that, by a small margin, women constitute the majority of their clientele.

ORGANIZED TOUR OPTIONS

Bicycle travel doesn't have to mean roughing it. Here's what you should be able to expect from a professional operator.

Pick a **luxury tour**, and accommodations and meals can be as elegant as any you might find on an upscale noncycling vacation. After a day of exploring á la bicycle, you trade stories with fellow guests over a glass of wine at that evening's country inn, Mediterranean villa, turreted chateau, or old-manor-house-turned-hotel. A meal fit for a duchess satisfies your well-earned appetite.

Plus you have the services of a van to carry luggage (and wilted cyclists if necessary), although finishing the day in the van doesn't happen too often; distances tend to be moderate enough for newbies. Typically outgoing and personable, guides are also knowledgeable cyclists who brief you on biking basics and provide mechanical assistance if you need help with a puncture or other repair. A route is suggested for each day, with maps and/or written directions provided to each guest. Typically you're encouraged to set your own pace, traveling alone or with others from the group, as you choose. You can have a fantastic holiday and learn more about cycling at the same time.

Select a **midprice tour**, and you can expect lodgings in less glamorous yet comfortable bed-and-breakfasts or hotels. You should still get impeccable service—hospitable leaders, support vehicle, route maps, and well-scouted itineraries. Some of these tours offer more challenging riding for serious cyclists eager to test themselves on the classic Tour de France climbs, for example, or the venues of the Giro d'Italia. Occasionally you'll find self-guided tours, which can save money for experienced cyclists who might still appreciate the convenience of a planned itinerary and lodging arrangements.

Prefer tenting or sleeping under the stars? Sign on for a **backcountry vacation,** and you can escape to the wilderness via mountain bike for several days, fully supported. You ride unencumbered, thanks to the four-wheel drive truck that carries camping gear, food for the trip, possibly even a solar shower. After some riding tips, you're off for the day's scenic discoveries, to be made at your own speed. At day's end your guides serve up hearty, delicious, from-scratch meals, fresh off the camp stove; you might be invited to chop a few veggies, but that's part of the fun. Haven't pitched a tent in a while? Your guide will show you. This is camping, but carefree camping, for sure.

For those who prefer not to be without a real bed and a private bath, some **inn-to-inn wilderness biking** trips are planned around hotel/motel lodgings, where a memorable evening meal tops off the day.

Other tours feature **road riding and camping,** again a fairly pampered approach—van-supported, of course. Guides walk you through tent setup, if needed, and prepare a gourmet feast from their kitchen-on-wheels.

Is your motto "So many sports, so little time"? **Multisport tours** combine cycling with other activities—whitewater rafting, sea kayaking, hiking, or sailing, for instance. This approach lets you sample a new sport and discover the region from a variety of perspectives.

DISCOVER YOUR OWN COUNTRY

Regardless of which type of tour you choose, a well-planned bicycle vacation adds unforgettable depth to domestic travel as the two-wheeled pace lets you know the landscape intimately. Recently I responded to the call of the back country, and joined Nichols Expeditions of Moab, Utah, for five days in Canyonlands National Park. As an Easterner used to suburban sprawl, I found all that open space completely liberating.

An even dozen (counting our guides), we pedaled the eighty-five–mile White Rim Trail, which parallels a deep gorge carved by the Green and Colorado Rivers. Aside from a four-wheel drive vehicle, the only way to explore this sculptured landscape of buttes and mesas, spires and sinuous canyons is by mountain bike. I found few signs of human interlopers, aside from the Jeep road built in the 1950s for uranium prospecting—no piped-in water, no guardrails, few signs even; it was just ourselves and the amazing panorama of rock formations in hues of crimson, pink, apricot, reddish-brown, and lavender.

A trip in the Canyonlands is a mix of luxuries and privations. For me it was the right mix. I hadn't tented in years, but I found it magical to sleep out under the stars and to get up and watch the sun rise—which in October came at the civilized hour of 7:15. The group quickly developed a sense of humor about the pit toilets and bathing with baby wipes after riding all day under the desert sun.

You might think rain would be a drag, but no. Under darkening skies, the last afternoon, we pitched our tents just in time. As the wind blew up and tarps flapped in their faces, our two guides strung up a dry haven for us to watch the rain.

"Can we do anything to help?" somebody asked.

"No, just get in your tents and hold 'em down!"

After a few tense moments our guides were cracking jokes again and organizing dinner. Before dark the storm abated and a double rainbow arched over the red butte that rose above our campsite. We were awed, ecstatic. Soon after, we sat down to barbecued chicken, garlic mashed potatoes, gourmet coleslaw, and brownies baked in a Dutch oven.

As luxuries, aside from the truck support and good cooking, I counted our trip guides, who could spin a yarn, play guitar for an evening sing-along, describe the canyons' geology, and point out ancient ruins of Anasazi granaries I'd never have noticed along the road. Our mentors offered plenty of cycling tips and cautioned us where the riding was tricky. And when I didn't take the hint and bent a crankarm in a crash, our guide's mechanical skills and a crank-swap with another bike got me riding again, restoring my sinking spirits and saving me from riding the last two days of the tour in the truck.

A PERFECT VEHICLE FOR FOREIGN TRAVEL

When it comes to discovering another culture, bicycle travel has time and again broken the ice for me, partly because a bike is not as invasive as a car. It's easy to stop for a conversation, to ride up a driveway, to stop on impulse for a photograph, to indulge a healthy curiosity.

One June I spent eight days cycle touring in the Cotswold Hills of England, a region near the Welsh border that preserves the quintessence of English country life in its estates and farms, fairy-tale towns, and medieval churches endowed by wealthy wool merchants of an earlier era.

The Cotswolds deserve to be experienced with all your senses, and cycling lets you do it. Here small villages of limestone cottages—centuries old, with roofs of thatch or stone—appear almost to have grown from among the green fields. Dry stone walls pattern the hillsides. In the drama of changing light, well appreciated from a bicycle, the Cotswold stone glows tawny-gold in the afternoon sun; pales to cream in the dusk; stands a stolid gray on a rainy day.

Without the roar of a car engine, I appreciated subtle sounds. A pheasant rustled in roadside weeds and took flight. Sheep at pasture amused me. As I cycled by, they bleated urgently to each other, lambs in soprano, ewes (I supposed) in alto, rams adding bass. A pair of lambs sang out from opposite ends of a field and bounded toward their mother to feed. Their straight little tails wagged as they nursed.

I breathed in the smells: new-cut hay, flowers in a cottage garden, earthy animal aromas, after-rain freshness. And when I wanted to, I stopped. I photographed wild poppies that turned an oat field to red and green damask. By chance my companions and I happened across a "benefit" tour, which opened private gardens to view in the village of Kencot. We bought tickets and wheeled our bikes from house to house—wonderful.

I found, as usual, that a bicycle is disarming. I talked to a gardener hoeing a strawberry patch, later to a woman walking four bouncing black Scotties. A church sexton opined about rising real estate prices and other local issues. Amazingly, a seller of antique cameos trusted me to mail her a traveler's cheque for a pin I wanted to buy.

There's the sense of accomplishment, too, conquering the hills and pedaling from Crudwell to Tetbury to Chippenham and so on, under my own power. I saw the points on my map, the route for the day, and my progress was clear. Life isn't always that way.

Women-Only Tours

"We like men, but who needs them to show how fast they can do it? From my experience, women working together are generous and supportive, and opportunities for sharing expertise and experience arise. The atmosphere is one where women from all walks of life feel free to learn new skills, test their abilities, and make new friendships that can last a lifetime." Thus Gloria Smith explains why, in 1994, she founded WomanTours, which focuses on road bike tours in regions as diverse as California wine country and the Canadian Rockies, New Zealand and the Natchez Trace.

By contrast, the adventure travel company Woodswomen has been offering women's bike tours since 1980. Other trips in their mix focus on activities such as cross-country skiing, rock climbing, backpacking, canoeing, and sea kayaking. Peggy Willens, administrative manager of Woodswomen, says of their bike tours' continuing appeal: "Many women join us because we travel to some pretty exciting destinations—Hawaii; Tuscany, Italy; Utah's Canyonlands—at times when they want to go and at a better price.

"Besides, many women say that in mixed groups they don't feel as safe as with an all-women's tour. We interpret safety fairly broadly, to include emotional security. Without men along," she notes, "women feel OK saying 'I need to take a break now' or 'I'm tired' or 'I'm thirsty.' When we remove the fear of keeping up, women are actually more safe, especially when learning a new activity."

What about you? Would you like a break from male competition and conversation? A chance to meet more women with interests similar to your own? While a considerable number of tour operators offer some trips limited to women (see appendix), the following specialize in all-female tours with women guides.

WomanTours
P.O. Box 931
Driggs, Idaho 83422
(800) 247-1444
(208) 354-8804

Woodswomen, Inc.
25 West Diamond Lake Rd.
Minneapolis, MN 55419
(800) 279-0555
(612) 822-3809 (phone)
(612) 822-3814 (fax)

Now, with plenty of B&B's, the Cotswolds is an excellent area for a budget tour. As it happened, though, I traveled with Butterfield & Robinson (B&R) and stayed in charmingly restored country manor hotels, all predating the twentieth century and as English as strawberries and clotted cream. My favorite: the aptly named Lords of the Manor Hotel in a quaint hamlet where a Burberry's fashion ad was being photographed at that quiet intersection as I pulled up on my bicycle. That's elegance. B&R, by the way, is a Canada-based company that pioneered adult luxury bicycle travel in Europe in 1981. Their first tour proved a hit—I could see why—and became the prototype for today's luxury package.

CHOOSING A TOUR

You've zeroed in on your destination, and you've had your appetite whetted as the tour brochures arrived in the mail. Now how do you make the best choice?

First read over the brochures with a critical eye and note what each tour offers. Below are some points to consider that may or may not be covered in the literature. Call each company with a list of questions and note their answers. Once you've narrowed your choices, ask for references you can contact for a recommendation—a few names of past guests who've taken the trip that interests you.

Companions. If you had your druthers, what sort of folks would you wish to travel with? In addition to mixed groups, some companies offer women-only tours. You'll also find trips limited to singles—adults traveling on their own or with a friend, but not as part of a couple. Family-oriented trips with more relaxed schedules and activities that children enjoy may be an option. So may be gay/lesbian groups.

Do you care about the ages of the other guests? If so, don't fall for the line, "We have clientele of all ages." Ask for some concrete averages.

Season. When's the best time to experience what interests you most about the destination? If you want to see the fall color in Vermont or the tulips in Holland, when do you go? And how early must you sign up for these popular departures?

Trip choice. Ask whether the company has previously taken the tour you're considering. The thought of joining the company's first trip to Uzbekistan may be tempting, but do you really want to be a guinea pig on an itinerary where roads might prove dangerous or the meals disappointing? Wait and take that tour next year.

Are there specialty tours offered for your destination? You're interested in gardens, wine-tastings, art? You'd like cooking classes or photography instruction? No guarantees here, but mention your special interests and ask whether any tours address them.

What's included? Are bike rentals and shuttles from the airport included for the price? Are any activities described as part of the itinerary, in fact, optional? If so, what's the extra cost?

Routes, mileage, and other cycling specifics. Are maps and/or route directions provided to each participant? Are there options each day for riders of varying fitness levels—longer routes for the ambitious, short alternatives or van shuttles for less-conditioned cyclists? How hilly is the terrain? For road tours, what types of roads are featured? How heavy is the traffic? For off-road tours, are trails singletrack? Doubletrack? How technically challenging are they, and over what sort of terrain?

Accommodations. Where will you be lodging? Ask for the names of the inns, something of their ambiance and history, and their location. Is it worth a walking tour once you arrive? Do you pedal to a different hotel each day, or spend a few nights at each? (Would you enjoy the variety or prefer instead not having to repack each morning before the day's ride?) If you want a room to yourself, what's the extra cost? Say you're willing to be assigned a roommate but none is available, must you pay the single supplement? What are the smoking policies at these lodgings? Are you assured a private bathroom?

Are boat lodgings a possibility? An interesting change from hotels, a bicycling/barging tour I took in the Netherlands required unpacking and repacking only once, a plus. For a trip with boat accommodations, ask about the size of your cabin and how much space is provided for luggage and hanging clothing.

On a camping tour, how scenic are the campsites? What sorts of toilet facilities can you expect? What about showers? Any other amenities? Do site restrictions permit campfires? What camping equipment is provided for the basic price? What additional items would you need to rent, and what is the cost?

Meals. Again, what's included? Full breakfast or continental? Are you on your own for lunches? All dinners included? What are the restrictions on choice? (Sometimes there's one set menu for the group, or a choice of two or three. I've heard of tours where you can order anything on the menu, but this costs the operator more.) Can you count on plenty of fresh vegetables and salads? What about any dietary restrictions you may have? Does the trip price cover wine or other alcoholic beverages?

Guides. How experienced are the tour leaders? Will they offer tips on riding skills? Do they know the culture, history, and ecology of the area you're touring? In a foreign country, do they speak the language? Some companies put a male and female guide with each tour; if this matters, ask.

Support vehicle. Where is the sag wagon during the day's ride; with more than one daily route option, for example, which one does the sag follow? Can it comfortably carry the group if severe weather curtails riding? (In my experience, riding in the rain is more fun than peering out the van window, unless it's a real deluge.)

Bicycles and other rental equipment. Are rental bikes and camping gear of high quality? Whether or not you plan to rent, the tour company's equipment should tell you something about its approach to cycling and commitment to good service.

Transfer requests and cancellations. Study the policy section of the brochures; some companies' policies are more liberal than others'. What happens to your deposit if an emergency should force you to change your plans? Can you transfer your reservation to another tour without penalty? Does the company reserve the right to cancel a trip because of low enrollment? Is trip cancellation insurance a good idea?

IF YOU GO

Ready to sign on? Consider these tips for a great trip:

Daily mileage. Pick an itinerary that challenges but doesn't exceed your cycling ability. Tour organizers say the biggest mistake first-timers make is overestimating how much mileage they can handle. Most people can cycle forty-five to fifty miles once, but day after day for a week is more demanding. I find twenty-five to thirty-five miles a day plenty because cycling is only part of the experience. I like to reserve time and energy for sight-seeing, taking photos, and striking up chance conversations en route.

One time on a bike tour in northern Italy, a friend and I were hailed by a local, all-men's bike club just back from their training ride, *"Bellissima, bellissima!"* One minute we were on our bikes, rounding the corner for a closer look, and the next we stood among them, a salami sandwich in one hand and a paper cup of wine in the other, their blue-and-white cycling caps perched rakishly on our heads. They made a great fuss over us, wanted to know where we were going, and insisted on a group photo. It was one of the highlights of that trip.

Bike fit. If you opt for a bike provided by the tour operator, call and discuss fit issues with the tour staff. Whether or not it's asked on the application form, provide your inseam measurement as well as your height. If, like me, you're shorter than five-foot-five, you'll probably get a better fit on a hybrid or mountain bike than on a drop handlebar road bike. If you're used to riding with toeclips, say so. Take along your own clipless pedals, if you use them, and your own saddle. A comfortable seat makes a big difference, even if the bike doesn't fit perfectly.

Rain gear. Be prepared with a rain jacket and pants or rain poncho, plus full-fingered water-resistant gloves if temperatures could be chilly. If it isn't absolutely pouring, I've even welcomed a bit of rain as a change of pace; the softer colors and quiet mood of the landscape can make a drizzly day quite beautiful.

Helmets. Take yours and use it. Some tour companies now require all participants to wear them.

Noncycling attire. Ask how guests usually dress in the evenings and for off-bike activities. On luxury tours, since the van will be carrying your luggage, you'll be able to pack some good casual clothes and/or dressy outfits as appropriate.

If carrying your own gear in panniers, you'll want something basic for non-cycling attire, like a pair of solid-color slacks you can dress up or down, which can be washed and hung up to dry overnight. Once I took a pair of plaid pants as my only off-bike attire on a three-week cycle tour and wanted to burn them well before the end.

Breakfast. The standard continental breakfast isn't substantial enough to see you through a morning of cycling. I stop soon after at a shop for some real food—fruit, a little sandwich, or some cheese and bread to tide me over until lunch. Fortunately, even in Europe a heartier breakfast will frequently be offered. Take advantage of it. And don't even think of picking your bike tour as a time to try to lose weight; you need that energy to ride.

Communication and culture. Read as much as you can about the territory you'll be cycling through; tour organizers often provide a bibliography. If it's another country, learn something about the language and culture. No time to take a language course? The knowledge of even a few words and the courage to use them can mean the difference between awkward, helpless silence and a smile that will light up your day.

Bicycling is one of the least-insulated forms of tourism, a reason for its growing appeal. On a bike you're not just exposed to terrain and weather, you're also a potential actor in the little dramas of daily life going on all about you. The man hoeing artichokes in a field, the old couple picking berries on a steep hillside above the sea, the kids walking home from school in a small town—all are at least as curious about you as you are about them. The more you're able to extend yourself, the richer your experience will be.

Training Tips for Any Tour

Along with following the basics for conditioning outlined in chapter 10, "Building Fitness," you'll be better able to enjoy riding day after day if you:

- Cycle the distance of the tour's longest day at least once or twice. Do it, say, three and two weeks before departure.
- Accustom yourself to riding several days in a row without a rest day. Don't feel you have to go the full distance; just get your muscles used to the idea.
- Resist any temptation to cram in extra training during your last week before the tour. It won't benefit you, and it could keep you from being fresh and rested. Do ride in the last few days before departure, but decrease distances if you'd normally be taking long rides.

CROSS-STATE RIDES

"I've ridden on tours with all the comforts, and they are not as memorable as RAGBRAI!" says one cyclist, speaking of the granddaddy and the biggest of the cross-state rides, the Register's Annual Great Bike Ride Across Iowa.

RAGBRAI participants don't come so much for the scenery, unless they happen to like cornfields mile after mile. They rally for a good time "with 10,000 of their closest friends" and to be welcomed into every small Iowa community with corn roasts and pork barbecue, lemonade stands and cake sales to benefit local Lions Clubs, ambulance auxiliaries, and every other civic group imaginable. Square dances and concerts (from barbershop quartets to banjos to kazoo bands) at day's end make for down-home fun and a feeling that Iowans must be the friendliest people in the world.

RAGBRAI, which dates to 1973, originated the cross-state ride, and the idea was contagious. Like to think big? Cross-state rides operate on the "more is more" principle. If you want to see more, do more, and be with more people—while paying less—you can traverse an entire state. How's that for bragging rights?

In 1997 nearly thirty states boasted a ride. Not all of them crossed the entire state. Some followed a border or created a loop, but all lasted three days or more. And while they give you a good cycling workout, most go easy on your budget. You'll find a current listing on the National Bicycle Tour Directors Association Web site: http://pages.prodigy.com/freewheel/nbtda.htm.

The flavor of these rides will vary, beginning with limitations on group size, ranging from less than 100 for some and up to 8,000 registered participants on RAGBRAI. Like RAGBRAI, some cross-state tours focus on the homey entertainments of small-town America, while others showcase the state's scenic parks or off-road rail trails. Typically these are long-distance camping parties on wheels with sag wagon support, transportation for gear, snacks at designated rest stops, camping arrangements, route directions, and the proof you did it—a souvenir T-shirt. Some rides include meals or provide indoor camping or offer a motel option.

Each state ride has its own stalwart supporters, some of whom return year after year to repeat the experience. Deborah Crane of Tulsa describes a cross-Oklahoma ride called FREEWHEEL:

> I just completed my third FREEWHEEL, and it will take a major disaster in my life for me to miss one—I love it! Everyone on a bike becomes your friend that week, and each year is like a reunion. There must have been twenty people who complimented me on my new bike this year because they actually remembered my other bike from the year before.

> I gain such a sense of accomplishment on this ride. There's so much energy and electricity in the air that you know you can climb that hill. The entire tour is friendly and therapeutic. I don't remember how many hugs I got last week, but I relished every one of them.

Emotions run high in camp the last night. People know it's almost over, and they don't want it to be. No wonder: People in the little towns have been wonderful, greeting us with banners across Main Street and fantastic hospitality. As we rode into our final town, the mayor sat in a yard under a tree, welcoming every rider over a loud speaker. I didn't want the ride to end. I felt so overwhelmed, tears rolled down my cheeks. To that town, all 2,000 riders in FREEWHEEL were celebrities. Besides riding 480 miles last week, I was a star. How can you beat that?!

To get in on the fun, since most rides limit the number of participants, inquire early and enclose a self-addressed stamped envelope.

BENEFIT RIDES

Back when I started cycling we had twenty-five-mile bike-athons to raise money for charities. I remember one where a guy showed up with a bed pillow strapped to his bike seat—obviously the first ride of the season. You wouldn't dare start out like that for one of today's megamile fund-raisers, but you could anticipate considerably more adventure as a reward for training and taking part. Some of these rides boast a long history and impressive organization, with well-mapped and clearly marked routes, luggage transport, and food worth pedaling up an appetite for.

Ah, yes, there is that matter of soliciting pledges. I suppose it's a rare individual who likes putting the bite on friends and family, but talk up the event and they'll probably feel proud and excited that you're fit enough to tackle it. And you have the satisfaction of knowing you're making a difference by working toward a good cause.

Whatever length ride appeals to you, in the appendix you'll find something that suits your style—from short day-rides to cross-America odysseys. This might be the way to do the ride of your dreams.

MOUNTAIN BIKE FESTIVALS

Here's another sort of biking bash to give you great stories to share around the office watercooler and with local riding buddies. Come to think of it, why not encourage some pals to pile in the car with you and head off together to the nearest fat tire fest? It's a great way to discover the most scenic singletrack without that am-I-gonna-get-lost feeling that comes with braving uncharted territory solo. Plus you'll meet a whole new crowd of like-minded off-roadies, while you take in the ancillary activities—spectate or join in the races, test out the latest front suspensions, laugh yourself looney over the Huffy toss or mud-bog drag racing or whatever, and improve your skills at a riding clinic. No doubt you'll also picnic on good, maybe gourmet, grub; listen to some bluegrass or rock; and gaze into the bonfire as you swap tales about the day's high points.

To locate the nearest festivals and get a run-down on the activities, ask at your local bike shops. You'll find a starter list in the appendix.

TAKE YOUR BIKE TO CAMP

"Skill-building and chick-bonding at its best"—that's how Penny Pisaneschi, 29, of Morgan Hill, California, describes her week at cycling camp in Sun Valley, Idaho. A beginning racer, she had gone to "learn better cornering and bike-handling skills and to climb a real mountain" with the help of some of cycling's top coaches, Connie Carpenter and Davis Phinney, at their PowerBar Women's Camp. She came away with a couple dozen new friends and the accomplishment of all her goals.

Cornering was the toughie. "I was hopeless at cornering," says Penny, "so I'd avoided the most common type of road race, the criterium, because I couldn't corner well enough to keep up." At camp, coaches described and demonstrated the techniques, cornering around traffic cones on the practice course. Penny tried but couldn't get it—more patient explanations, more frustration. Finally she rode directly behind her coach, mimicking his moves, starting a turn when he'd yell "Now!"

"After about ten minutes, it clicked. I felt it! A seamless flow around one cone and then another, left turn, right turn, left turn, right turn. I practiced until I was the only one left in the lot. Criteriums, here I come!"

Penny quickly points out, however, that a good number of her campmates were not racers and that cycling camp can be for anyone. An important aspect of the coaching, Connie Carpenter observes, is anticipating that women will have fears—concerns about getting hurt, dropping behind, or being excluded. Enabling them to get to know each other, to articulate goals and worries, breaks the ice and lets the coaches see "what's holding them back so we can help them move forward."

While the Carpenter-Phinney camp is for roadies, plenty of mountain biking skills clinics exist to teach what Jacquie Phelan calls "fat tire finesse." An off-road racing pioneer, Jacquie has introduced many women to trail riding through her WOMBATS (Women's Mountain Bike and Tea Society) rides, camps, and other events, which she paces to put beginners at ease and overcome the gnarly, dangerous image that a lot of the sport's advertising and media coverage have engendered.

As the sport has caught on, so has the idea of MTB clinics just for women, where asking "a dumb question" may be less intimidating, and participants can work on basic skills with less self-consciousness. Other women's camps teach more advanced racing and riding skills, with coaching by such pros as 1996 Olympic bronze medalist Susan DeMattei and Sara Ballantyne. For a list of weekend and longer clinics, see the appendix. Some clinics have mixed sessions, too.

Cycling for Two 20

You're pregnant. You also love bicycling. You want to know how you can keep riding yet protect the health of your unborn child, what limitations you should impose on yourself, and what level of fitness you can hope for. Or maybe, though inactive, you've simultaneously become pregnant and been bitten by the fitness bug. What to do? Today you can anticipate much more encouraging answers to those questions than our sisters received only a decade or so ago.

I believe it was athletes like American cyclist Mary Jane ("Miji") Reoch who turned the Western scientific community away from their conservative approach to exercise during pregnancy. Winner of nine national cycling championships in four different events and a silver medal in pursuit at the world championships in 1975, Miji was still cycling and coaching when she became pregnant with her first child at thirty-five. She pedaled from conception to delivery and even raced a criterium during her fifth month. "I got criticized a lot by people who thought I was hurting the baby," she says, "but my doctors were supportive. I felt I was so attuned to my body as an athlete, I'd know if I was overdoing it."

In fact, she felt so confident about it all that she cycled the ten-mile trip to the delivery room. On the way she spied a boy struggling in too high a gear; she picked up her pace to catch him and explained the advantages of gearing down. Then she excused herself and continued to the hospital, where twelve hours later she gave birth to a healthy, seven-pound, twelve-ounce baby girl.

That was 1981, when the medical establishment had just begun to rethink the previously standard advice to expecting moms to rest and avoid heavy exertion. In 1985 the American College of Obstetricians and Gynecololgists (ACOG) issued the first written guidelines for exercise during pregnancy. These guidelines gave the green light to women in healthy, normal pregnancies to continue exercising or even to initiate a fitness program. But for already fit females these were fairly conservative recommendations, as they advised women to keep their heart rate below 141 bpm. ACOG was concerned with oxygen flow to the fetus; sometimes a temporary decline in fetal heart rate (called *bradycardia*) occurs after heavy exertion by the mother.

A study reported in 1988 in the *Journal of the American Medical Association* suggested a more liberal limit: That pregnant women not push their heart rate beyond 150. In all but one case, the babies' heart rates declined only after exercise that considerably exceeded 150 bpm.

NEW ACOG RECOMMENDATIONS

After a review of current research, the ACOG changed their guidelines in 1994. The new advice takes individual differences into account, encouraging women to heed signs of overdoing it, such as overheating, pain, or fatigue. For women without additional risk factors, the following recommendations were made:

- Continue mild-to-moderate exercise routines, preferably on a regular basis (three times a week or more), rather than intermittently.
- Be attuned to your body. Stop when fatigued; don't exercise to exhaustion. "Non-weight bearing exercises such as cycling or swimming will minimize the risk of injury and facilitate the continuation of exercise during pregnancy," says the ACOG.
- After the first trimester, don't work out in the *supine* position (lying on the back), or you may compromise blood flow to the uterus. Also avoid prolonged periods of standing still, which can have the same effect.
- Don't risk raising body core temperature during the first trimester. Drink plenty of fluids before and during cycling to avoid dehydration. In hot weather ride during the cooler times of the day and dress to promote heat dissipation.
- Note body changes that may affect your sense of balance, especially in the third trimester. Avoid any exercise that might result in "even mild abdominal trauma" (which includes falling off your bike).
- Ensure adequate nutrition. The metabolic demands of being pregnant use up an extra 300 calories per day.
- Many of the body changes during pregnancy persist for four to six weeks after delivery. Ease back into your prepregnancy exercise routines according to your capabilities.
- The following factors would make exercise risky: pregnancy-induced high blood pressure, preterm rupture of membranes, premature labor in this or previous pregnancy, cervical abnormality, persistent bleeding in second or third trimester, slowed fetal growth, or multiple-birth pregnancy.
- Additionally, women with certain conditions, such as "chronic hypertension or active thyroid, cardiac, vascular, or pulmonary disease, should be evaluated carefully in order to determine whether an exercise program is appropriate."

APPLYING THE GUIDELINES TO YOU

Every pregnant woman should consult her health-care provider about plans to exercise, to be sure there are no problems that contraindicate it. If advised against exercising during these months, you have a right to a clear understanding why. Should you want a second opinion, don't hesitate to get it. Consult a medical practitioner who's athletic or accustomed to treating athletes. If necessary, ask for a referral from a women's coach or physician at your local high school or college.

Once you have the approval and guidance of your health practitioner, you can feel confident that by staying active you'll avoid some health problems like excessive weight gain, poor self-image, lower back pain, faulty posture, and fatigue. Ignore worrywarts who haven't informed themselves on the subject. You might share this chapter with the baby's father and whomever else you turn to for support.

Now, given the go-ahead, what can you expect when you're expecting?

- Cardiovascular changes with pregnancy will affect your perceived level of exertion. "Your blood volume, *cardiac output* (amount of blood your heart pumps with each beat), and resting pulse all increase to help support the growing needs of the fetus as well as your own increase in size," writes Joan Marie Butler, R.N.C., C.N.M., in her helpful book, *Fit & Pregnant: The Pregnant Woman's Guide to Exercise* (Waverly, NY: Acorn Publishing, 1996). "This is all happening while you are resting and not even exercising." You will notice it as you work out.

- As a rule, things seem to require more effort during the first trimester than in the second or third. If you start a ride and, even after a warm-up, you're not up to it, don't feel guilty if you make it an easy spin. In fact, early in your pregnancy you may not wish to ride at all. If so, take some time off but don't be discouraged. (Maybe a walk or a swim would feel better.) In a few weeks or months cycling will probably appeal to you again.

- You can expect some discomfort when you exercise—sore legs and knees, perhaps a sensation of needing to urinate, or contraction cramps. You'll probably experience shortness of breath as your growing uterus crowds your diaphragm upward, shrinking the space where your lungs normally expand. You may also find yourself hyperventilating—both when you're exercising and when at rest—because pregnancy hormones increase your sensitivity to carbon dioxide.

- Joints tend to be a little looser during pregnancy as a result of a hormonal secretion, *relaxin*, which relaxes the ligaments to prepare for expansion of the uterus and eventual delivery. Usually the effects are felt during the third trimester, although some women notice them in the second. According to Katherine Brubaker, M.D., an obstetrician/gynecologist and cyclist, joint laxity is usually not troublesome for cyclists but is more a problem for runners.

  Looseness can be felt in hips, knees, pelvic girdle, lower back, and shoulders. (The back exercises in chapter 12, "Ouch-less Riding" can help during this time when lower back discomfort seems inevitable.) You may notice that your hip "pops" or doesn't seem to support you. Dr. Brubaker says a woman may feel pain on her saddle, caused by the loosening of a ligament joining two bones in the pubic arch (which actually separate to enable delivery). Pelvic rock (pelvic tilt) exercises can help compensate, along with making sure to sit properly on the sit-bones when cycling. Take the usual precautions for not overtaxing knees. Wear padded bike gloves and change hand positions as often as possible while cycling to overcome any tendency toward carpal tunnel syndrome.

- Pay attention to subtle changes in your sense of balance. Fortunately, you have a chance to adjust daily, so you may not feel bothered. And the currently popular mountain bikes or other bike types with upright handlebars are a boon to comfort and balance in the later months. On road bikes, riding the brake hoods will be more comfortable than bending over on the drops; aero bars can lessen stability—consider removing them. Still, around the sixth or seventh month some moms-to-be may feel safer on a stationary bicycle or trainer than on road or trail.
- Even a minor fall can result in separation of the placenta, so if you do dump, especially in the final twenty weeks, see your health-care provider right away.

Clearly, during pregnancy is not the time to strive for high performance. Your "personal best" during this period is a healthy baby, not a faster time on the bike. A fit cyclist in a normal pregnancy, however, can usually adapt to the physical changes and maintain much, if not all, of her conditioning. To do so safely, you must recognize the distinction between overlooking minor discomfort and going into competitive overdrive or pushing yourself past the point of pain. As you and your health care provider plan your cycling program, consider these additional precautions:

- Set reasonable goals. If you're highly fit and used to training hard, don't be compulsive about it now. Avoid vigorous, intense efforts that get you "out of breath."
- During a normal, healthy pregnancy, the safe ceiling on exertion, some researchers say, is 70 percent of maximum heart rate. Other experts recommend staying within 60 to 75 percent of MHR. Prior to pregnancy, if you were using a heart monitor to exercise within a target heart rate zone, recalculate it to take into account your higher resting pulse. Furthermore, recognize that target heart rates are approximate. On a particular day, stress or tiredness may reduce aerobic capacity. "Listen to your body," as the saying goes.

  In fact, in *Fit & Pregnant*, Joan Butler, a Masters athlete who trained through her own pregnancy, observes that "it is unclear what maximal heart rate is for pregnancy." She suggests that perceived exertion might be "a better measure of exercise intensity." Highly trained athletes develop a sense of how hard they're working, and some don't feel a need for a heart monitor. Aware of athletes' ability to "guesstimate," a Swedish physiologist named Borg created a scale he called "Rating of Perceived Exertion" (RPE), which assigns numbers to perceived exercise intensities. It starts at six (for a very, very light workout) and goes to twenty (very, very hard). "During pregnancy," writes Butler, "you should stay around 12–14, (somewhat hard) when exercising. At this intensity of exercise, you should be able to pass the 'Talk Test' and easily carry on a conversation." Obviously that excludes sprints and intense speedwork.

- Thin air at high altitude can put extra stress on you and the baby you're carrying. Don't go above 10,000 feet and avoid exerting yourself at 8,000 feet or above. A few days to acclimate before exercising at altitude is a good idea.

- Don't risk raising core body temperature. One possible cause of birth defects, researchers believe, is *hyperthermia,* a condition in which body core temperature is elevated. Drink lots of water to stay hydrated. (Sport drinks, Butler points out, have not been studied for use during pregnancy.) Soaking in a hot tub or whirlpool or taking a sauna is unwise. So is a hard workout in hot, humid weather. And don't exercise if you are sick with a fever.

- Let appetite be your guide as you eat a balanced diet, including the supplements usually recommended in pregnancy, especially iron and calcium. Take in some extra protein—about 10 grams above your normal needs—an additional big glass of milk, 1½ ounces of meat or fish, or a cup of beans, for example.

    Appropriate weight gain indicates that you are meeting your caloric needs. If you're not gaining as you should, discuss the situation and your exercise program with your health-care provider.

- Should you have questions about your safety or experience anything unusual, like vaginal bleeding, raised blood pressure, dizzy spells, or pains in joints, cease riding and confer with your doctor before continuing. If cycling aggravates varicose veins, support hose may help, or you may have to shorten your rides or find an exercise alternative.

- During the last three months you may have *Braxton Hicks contractions,* rhythmic tightenings of the lower abdomen. If you feel these while cycling, slow down and concentrate on taking deep breaths, says Butler. Sit more upright, or take a break off your bike and drink some water.

- Pregnancy hormones can make you more vulnerable to yeast infections, so change out of cycling shorts right after cycling, and always wear a clean pair on each ride.

Supplement this advice with a good measure of common sense:

- Cycle with a partner, or at least let someone know when and where you are riding. Carry change for a phone call.
- Choose a route that you can shorten if you poop out sooner than you expected.
- Forego risks you might routinely take if you weren't pregnant—like mountain biking on challenging trails where there's a chance of crashing.

One of my survey respondents tells how, eight months pregnant, she rode home from the grocery store on her three-speed with a sack of groceries in hand and a three-year-old on the back in a baby seat. She was descending a hill when a motorist turned in front of her, causing them to fall. Luckily, they were unhurt.

Yes, a three-year-old is lighter than the recommended limit—about forty pounds—for these rear baby seats, but the extra weight creates instability. Carrying something in one hand hampers bike handling and braking. Now add in the compromised balance at eight months, and we have an accident waiting to happen. Although the motorist erred, an unencumbered cyclist might have avoided the crash. Take extra care to avoid riding in dangerous conditions.

If the unfortunate occurs and you're injured, experts advise not taking anti-inflammatory agents or other drugs that might affect development of the unborn child. If X rays are absolutely required, make sure a lead apron is used to shield the uterus.

But let's not allow this cautionary tale to distract us from the main point: Every active woman knows the sense of vitality that fitness brings. What could be more appropriate than maintaining that feeling of well-being as you bring a new life into the world? That's what Kristen Proffitt believes, as she demonstrates in her diary, "Nine Special Months of Cycling":

"Any questions?" the doctor asks. I have a flood of them. Can you ride centuries and time trials when you're pregnant? Do you have to sit upright or turn up your handlebars when your belly starts to grow? Is it safe to ride the bike at all?

"Well, I've grown fond of exercise in my old age," I begin. I am thirty-four. "I like running, hiking, and cycling. I do a lot of cycling. Will I be able to continue all these?"

He says he thinks they'll be good for me. I'm greatly relieved!

Late December: Two Months

I'm about two months along now. I've kept up my exercise but am battling the "What's-the-Use Blues." It seems there's nothing to look forward to on the bike except getting bigger and maybe so ungainly I won't be able to go at all. Fifteen minutes into every ride I feel a gagging mucus in my throat. I'm afraid I'm going to throw up one of these times but I never do.

January: Three Months

I've conquered the negative feelings by setting some new goals. OK, so I won't be time trialing (at least not seriously), and I may be slowing down, but what a wonderful time to keep concentrating on fitness. After all, there are two of us benefiting from this exercise.

There are centuries coming up in April and May, and I'm considering. It's too early to know how I'll feel . . . I'm due July 12. The only limit I'm placing on myself is all-out sprints. I believe oxygen debt might not be good for the baby.

On one of the Sunday club rides, I'm feeling a bit draggy on the back of our tandem. We excuse ourselves to a fellow riding with us, saying that I'm pregnant.

"You're at your prime!" he congratulates me. With several extra pounds and less than my usual quota of exercise, I do not feel prime.

February: Four Months

The beginning-of-the-ride nausea is all but gone now. I'm developing a distinct ball of baby and it kicks. This baby feels strong. Although I experience uterine contractions almost always when I am bike riding (or running or hiking), I no longer worry about harming the baby. I am concerned for the baby if we don't get our workouts.

March: Five Months

I definitely look pregnant now, at least in my tight cycling shirt. I'm not so afraid of a good workout, knowing that the baby seems to be active and growing well, although I still draw the line at sprints that leave me completely breathless.

But once in a while, on a boring solo ride, I cannot resist chasing down another cyclist just to liven things up. In one particular pursuit I managed to hang on the wheel of a fellow who was young, sleek, and fast—at least compared to me. After several miles he finally slowed to see who was there. I swallowed my gasps, smiled pleasantly, straightened up to reveal my profile and told him it was becoming a bit difficult to keep up in this condition. Actually I felt about ready to die. Not so much from the pregnancy, I think, as for lack of enough good chases like that.

I feel discomforts from time to time, but they're usually minor, intermittent, and seldom a distraction for an entire ride. My growing abdomen is stretching some new muscles, and sometimes I get a stitch in an unusual place, such as the groin. I also feel uterine contractions and stomach aches, probably a little digestive upset. The baby does rearrange your organs inside.

I begin a program of abdomen strengthening exercises: leg lifts, sit-ups, to the best of my ability. That feels so good and seems to help, so I add back and arm exercises. I truly feel wonderful, and the best thing is that I am going to make it on the bicycle. I'm going to ride that century next month. I'm going to ride every day on the Great Western Bike Rally. I'm going to ride the whole nine months!

April: Six Months

Sometimes I do get discouraged on rides lately. So I give myself a pep talk to combat the dark thoughts when they come.

My husband and I ride the Creston Wildflower Century up in beautiful San Luis Obispo County on our tandem. It's a hilly, tough ride. But we don't do badly at all. My husband Jim has really stayed by me and encouraged me. It probably isn't easy for him towing around a pregnant wife on the tandem when he could be doing so much better on his own. But he keeps praising my riding. So how can I quit?

May: Seven Months

On one of my solo rides, I have two flat tires and am delighted to find I can ride the bus to within blocks of home if I remove the front wheel of my bike. I receive some astonished looks, hauling my bike up the steps of the bus in my bulging T-shirt.

I have a definite preference for tandem rides and shorter rides now, although, if anything, I feel better each month rather than worse. I guess I just feel a little safer on the tandem and more equal.

We ride in the Great Western Bike Rally, three days. On the century, Jim chooses a metric option (sixty-two miles) rather than the full 100. (We had just done a tough fifty the day before.) But he announces this choice only after we've ridden about thirty miles. And I was prepared for the 100! He says he thinks the full century would take too much out of me, combined with our rides on the other days. Lest anyone think this an ordeal, mildly competitive riding still seems fun and natural.

When we're home from a ride one day and I'm changing out of my cycling shirt (a nice roomy T-shirt), Jim says, "You know, you really look great." No greater love hath any cycling husband than that compliment at this time.

June: Eight Months

I don't feel particularly ungainly. We haven't even had to turn up the handlebars, and I can still reach the drops.

Jim's knees are inflamed from our constant tandem riding. It's probably a strain with all the starts and stops in traffic near home. So I take to my single, which I can still ride easily. Poor Jim, probably the first husband injured due to exercise when expecting.

July 20: Nine Months

My other two children came exactly one week late. This one was due July 12, so I expected it yesterday. Last Sunday, the fifteenth, we rode our hardest on the club ride since we couldn't possibly have to ride again in this condition. It was fun leaving behind some riders who thought we wouldn't be any competition.

July 22: Nine Months, Ten Days

Another club ride. We once again give it our all. Who cares if it starts me into labor. We hope it does. My poor, dear husband must have taken me out for at least fifteen "last" dinners.

I don't care for rides much longer than thirty miles at this point.

At this week's checkup, my blood pressure had been quite high. I got a reprieve from an induced labor, but was ordered to have bed rest. (I've been given a different doctor. This one doesn't understand about my exercise.)

The bed rest lasted two hours. My husband asked, "What are you going to do?"

"I'm going to shorten my rides, take naps, and let my daughter do the dishes," I answered.

July 29: Nine Months, Seventeen Days

It's not possible! Another Sunday club ride.

I've been losing weight (off of only fifteen pounds I gained). I swear the baby is getting smaller. I can't help worrying now. On almost every ride this week I've felt strong contractions, like the beginning of labor. So it's hard to concentrate.

Jim signs us up for a hilly forty-five-mile ride because that's the one everyone is going on. I feel nearly weepy for the first time instead of glad. I am too tired, too pregnant. And he's going to want to keep up with the rest of them. And what about my "bed rest"?

Once we get going, I feel terrific. But he turns us back after only twenty-five miles. "I wasn't going to let you ride all of it," he says.

"It's just as well," I tell him. "I feel a lot of contractions." We've left many strong riders behind.

July 30: Nine Months, Eighteen Days

I have my weekly checkup in the morning. My doctor is pleased with the results of my "bed rest." She agrees the baby is going to come very soon. By afternoon I'm having real on-and-off labor, so we don't ride today. Twice we start for a movie, and twice it seems unwise.

We leave for the hospital about midnight.

July 31: Nine Months, Nineteen Days

It's an easy labor, a little long but not so hard, not when you're used to these workouts. In fact, I sleep soundly between contractions. At 7:25 A.M. she is born: Penelope Jane, eight pounds, eleven ounces—the poor baby that was getting smaller! She is a beauty from the beginning, so alert, so vigorous, so strong! We are truly blessed. And we thank the exercise for helping.

So that was my final ride, I think to myself drowsily. Not too unlike a century. The months of preparation, the endurance, the excitement, and the pain. A little over seven hours, not a bad time for the ninth month.

May 1

I felt wonderful after Penelope was born. I started jogging after two weeks and cycling after three; gently at first, but soon working up to full steam.

The best news is the baby. She is robust and playful, full of life and good health. Jim and I feel a special closeness to her, having "taken" her on so many physical adventures before she was even born. And we feel a renewed closeness to each other, having done so much together, a great deal right on the same bike. And for our other two children, who were right there cheering us on.

It was a time of life I'll never forget. A pregnancy made unique by exercise, and the exercise the more exhilarating with the pregnancy.

POSTPARTUM PRECAUTIONS

Getting back on your wheels after the baby's birth is something to ease into. Don't be surprised if you just don't feel up to it, and don't feel guilty.

Yes, we hear about elite athletes who make comebacks after pregnancy and even improve their performance. A case in point is Susan Notorangelo, who at thirty-five rewrote the record books in the 1989 Race Across AMerica (RAAM)—that transcontinental megathon for which the race clock ticks twenty-four hours a day until the race ends some eight or nine days later. Susan had won the women's division in 1985 (10:14:25) and bettered her time the following year (10:09:29) while finishing second to Elaine Mariolle's (then-record) 10:02:04. In 1987 Susan took a pass on RAAM and on June 4 gave birth to daughter Rebecca.

Two years later Susan became the only woman finisher in RAAM '89 in a time of 9:09:09. Admittedly, the 2,907-mile course was 127 miles shorter, but she shattered Elaine's record and beat her own previous best by a day. Overall, she placed seventh among thirteen other (male) finishers. Two other women had dropped out. For Notorangelo it was a quantum leap.

As in Susan's case, a return to top-level performance usually takes a couple of years or longer. You too can recapture your level of fitness, perhaps exceed it, but give it time. Before her RAAM victory, Susan Notorangelo told me how it felt getting back into shape after delivery. For the first six weeks she scarcely mounted her bike.

"My first ride was a month later, just around a parking lot, and even doing that I worried about ripping out my stitches," she admitted. "Actually, in those weeks, I had difficulty working up the desire to ride." Her husband Lon (Haldeman, a RAAM winner himself) was out of town for a time. But when he came back, they suspended a baby seat for security and shock absorption in their Burley trailer.

"That way I could pull Rebecca. We started out going ten or fifteen miles about three times a week."

In a few weeks the enjoyment returned, and three months after Rebecca's birth, Susan and Lon rode a century on their tandem, pulling Rebecca in the Burley. "I didn't really feel strong like I do now," Susan amended. "I couldn't go out and ride sixty miles in the morning and then feel fresh and eager for a full day's activities—I'd be pretty exhausted. But the pleasure was back."

At the time of our conversation, fifteen months had passed since Susan delivered. She'd just returned from a demanding seventeen-day, trans-America bike tour she and Lon lead. She'd ridden about seventy-five miles every other day. "I'm just starting to feel good when charging a hill," she said. "I'm about five pounds away from a nice cycling weight, and I'm getting ready to wear a heart rate monitor again and see how I'm really doing."

What's a safe approach for resuming your cycling? The Melpomene Institute for Women's Health Research in St. Paul, Minnesota, encourages women to talk with their doctor/midwife about plans to resume exercise. Women who've had Caesareans may require special instructions. To women with uncomplicated vaginal deliveries, Melpomene recommends these guidelines:

• After an episiotomy you'll probably want to let soreness disappear before vigorous exercise or sitting on a saddle. Besides, you'll be advised against using tampons for about a month, so you may wish to wait for bleeding and secretions to stop.

    (Consider cross-training alternatives. One mountain bike racer I know—Carlotta Cuerdon—donned her in-line skates and put baby Emily in the jog stroller. Pushing Emily around the local outdoor skating park, Carlotta exercised her cycling muscles and strengthened her arms. "Because I still sported stitches from an episiotomy, skating felt more comfortable than the bouncing inherent in jogging," says Carlotta. "And if I needed to slow or stop my skates, I pulled on the stroller's brake.")

• After bleeding has begun to taper off, if exercise brings on heavier bleeding or bright red blood, this can be a sign you're doing too much and that you need to give yourself more recovery time.

• Continue to allow for joint laxity, as the hormonal levels don't even out until several weeks after delivery.

• During this time, let your body tell you what it needs. If you're up feeding the baby every two hours during the night, there may be days when you need a nap more than a bike ride. Make your cycling energizing, not draining, during these months. (On the other hand, a good spin may help you cope better if you suffer postpartum blues.)

• Drink plenty of fluids throughout the day if you are breast-feeding, and wear a bra that gives good support when cycling.

• Now that you're lifting and carrying your baby, keep up those back exercises.

• Maintain healthful eating habits. Let weight loss take place gradually. If you're breast-feeding, weight loss will be slower than if you were not. Cycling will help, and in the meantime, riding has its own calorie requirements. Don't be discouraged.

• Scheduling your riding will challenge the time manager in you, especially during the early months. (Susan suggests letting someone else hold and bottle-feed the baby, even if you normally nurse, so you can get away for a bike ride.)

• Make those rides enjoyable. Even though the new baby creates many demands, provide time for yourself. Your cycling is one way to do it.

Other Feminine Matters

Prior to cycling I was very ill with three surgeries in the female department. Cycling has eliminated most PMS (premenstrual syndrome), and periods are a breeze now. I used to be in pain most of the month. Now I might have some cramping, but nothing to slow me down.

As I recovered from my last surgery, I found I could no longer do aerobics or other exercise that involved bouncing. So I dragged out my old ten-speed and tried riding it. I went maybe three miles and was exhausted. Every night after that I went a little farther and found I could ride without the pain I felt from other exercise. Three months passed, and I worked up to nine miles every night.

Then my friends noticed my weight dropping. So I rode longer and faster each night. My husband bought me a new bike, and from then on I've been hooked. Now I ride twenty to thirty miles every day or use a wind trainer. My weight has dropped twenty-five pounds and I feel great. No more hard menstrual pains and virtually no PMS. –Bobbie J. Pope, Chino Hills, California

Cycling and a woman's sexuality can be a good news/bad news proposition.

Good news? With exercise and fresh air as health promoters, cycling puts you on a natural high. For many women regular exercise lessens menstrual problems and alleviates PMS. Others going through menopause have found both physical and psychological symptoms eased by a conditioning program. In countless ways, being active enhances your body's natural inclination to heal and balance itself. So with confidence and fitness on the rise, you feel good and look great. Usually your sexuality comes out a winner.

But sometimes a problem arises, like sores or swelling or other discomforts we don't normally talk about in polite company. As one bike racer puts it: "You can be behind another rider and see she's walking kinda funny. You say, 'Sore down there?' She says, 'Yeah, I'm so glad I don't have a boyfriend right now.'" Yes, there are times when "Back in the Saddle Again" proves less than a happy theme song. Other conditions such as *amenorrhea* (cessation of menstruation) might not strike us as inconvenient but could cause problems later on.

You may never experience any of these woes, some of which tend to plague cyclists who pile on the miles. Some can be blamed on a badly fitting bicycle or the wrong saddle. Others often relate to poor nutrition. But just in case, this chapter will give you a handle on how to cope and how to prevent a recurrence.

SADDLE SORE

Clitoral numbness, swelling of the *labia* (lips) of the vagina, tiny cuts or blisters—ouch! These things can result from friction against a poorly chosen saddle or improper position on the seat of a bike that doesn't fit (see chapter 5, "So You Want to Buy a Bike?" and chapter 12, "Ouch-less Riding") or from clothing that rubs and binds (see chapter 8, "Clothes With Wheel Appeal"), or a combination of all three. Eliminate those irritants and you may be sitting pretty.

Also, as previously suggested, you might want to try lubricating your short's chamois. Alison Dunlap, a national-class road racer, observes that "on a long day of riding—seventy to eighty miles is long for me—or if riding in the rain, I lube up with a big glob of Bag Balm or Vaseline."

Others swear by Desitin or Noxzema or a product formulated especially for the purpose by a bike racer and physical therapist—Chamois Butt'r.

Lubing is both prevention and remedy for Alison, who notes that when you're racing, you don't have a chance to stop and readjust your shorts if they feel uncomfortable. "I lubricate when I'm stage racing every day; it cuts down on wear and tear. And I lube as my period approaches because sometimes I get saddle sores or a little swollen down there," she adds.

BLADDER BUGS AND YEASTY BEASTIES

"There seem to be two kinds of vulvas," says cyclist/gynecologist Katherine Brubaker, M.D., "those made of leather—and these women can ride twice as many miles as other women, without problems. And then there are women who, as soon as they ride an hour, their tissues break down, they get little fissures, yeast infections, and so on. It doesn't seem to matter how often they wash their shorts. It's seasonal and tends to happen in hot weather."

Yeast are fungi that, under normal conditions, grow harmlessly in the vagina, along with other vaginal flora. These yeast organisms flourish in a warm, moist environment provided, for example, by sweaty, close-fitting bike shorts. Wearing a clean pair on every ride and changing out of them and washing the genital area as soon as possible afterwards make good sense. Choosing the woman's cut-out style of saddle may also help by increasing air flow and reducing pressure on the genitals.

However, if these measures don't alleviate the problem, a woman may need to look for causes beyond her cycling. Did you know, for example, that when you take a course of antibiotics for something—a tooth abscess, a bladder infection, whatever—a yeast infection often follows? The antibiotic has killed off some of the vaginal flora, allowing the yeast to take over. Ever hear that indulging in too many sweets all at once can alter the vaginal pH balance and encourage the growth of yeast? Other factors can also figure in; discuss these with your health-care provider.

To a cyclist with recurring yeast infections, Dr. Brubaker has recommended lubing the shorts chamois with Monistat or Gyne Lotrimin (generic name, chortrimazole), creams that are used in treatment.

Now that these remedies are available over the counter, women can treat themselves for vaginal infection. "And those who have a recurrent problem are more likely to recognize the symptoms," notes Camilla Buchanan, M.D., an obstetrician/gynecologist and a road and criterium racer with many Masters championships to her credit. However, the warning signs—itching, burning, and a white vaginal discharge—can sometimes be confused with certain sexually transmitted diseases. About half the time women think they have a yeast infection, they actually have something else, Dr. Buchanan warns. If you want to go ahead and dose yourself with Monistat, she says, it won't hurt. "But if the problem doesn't get completely better in two or three days, it wasn't a yeast infection and needs diagnosis and treatment."

As for bladder infections, the none-too-subtle symptoms—frequent, painful, maybe even bloody urination—can make life in the saddle mighty uncomfortable. Antibiotics are the cure. Prevention is even better: Pee often, as urine flow interrupts the growth of bacteria. Urinating right after sex helps considerably by clearing the *urethra,* the tube that empties the bladder.

During long days on the bike, drink lots of water and plan for the necessary pit stops. Dehydration contributes to the likelihood of bladder infections. "If you're a good cyclist, you'll drink and drink and drink," says Dr. Brubaker. In addition to plenty of water when riding, cranberry juice and orange juice are excellent to drink at other times because they are acidic, and the harmful bacteria thrive in an alkaline environment.

A bladder infection might be encouraged by irritation of the urethra, rubbing against the shorts, Dr. Brubaker points out. This can be complicated by rectal or vaginal bacteria entering the urethra in this situation. We females with our short urethras—less than an inch long, compared to penis-length in males—are more vulnerable than the guys. If you're prone to these problems, you could put some of the sulfa cream used for treatment on your shorts liner as a preventative measure during a long day of cycling, suggests Dr. Brubaker.

THAT TIME OF THE MONTH

Menstruation can be a nuisance when it comes to bike riding. Tampons protect better in heavy flow times because pads create extra bulk and friction. But even tampons aren't perfect. The string can rub you raw, so cut if off or tuck it inside. Some women find a tampon uncomfortable, and it may need removal at the wrong time—causing an unwanted pit stop during a race, for example.

"Sometimes when my flow isn't heavy," says Estelle Gray, an ultramarathon cyclist and bike builder in Seattle, Washington, "I simply don't wear a tampon or pad, and bleed into my shorts. After all, they're black, and the saddle's black. I always said, the right color for a shorts chamois is black!"

Or you may want to try a feminine hygiene product called Instead, if you find yourself wishing for yet another alternative. That's how Audrey Contente, a triathlete and biomedical researcher, felt. So she developed a pliable, all-plastic, disposable cup intended to contain menstrual flow without leaking. Unlike a contraceptive diaphragm, which must be fitted by a doctor, this one-size-fits-all device is designed to respond to body temperature and mold to each woman's anatomy. You should find Instead on your pharmacy shelves in the feminine hygiene department (or see appendix).

While many women find that exercise seems to help ease discomfort, others aren't so fortunate. Bloating and cramping don't lift anyone's spirits and may interfere with training or competition. Although she prefers the natural approach, Estelle says she knows women who, with their doctors' OK, temporarily go on the pill to shift their cycle so they don't have to deal with their period during a race. If considering this, discuss the pros and cons with your gynecologist.

Another thing to be aware of when planning a major cycling event is cyclical changes in body temperature. According to a study by James Pivarnik, Ph.D., an exercise physiologist at Michigan State University and a triathlete, when our progesterone levels are high—on days fifteen through twenty-six of a twenty-eight-day cycle, say—our body temperatures tend to run higher during exercise. Our heart rates are up, and the same workout feels like more work. At this time we should make an extra effort to stay hydrated and train in the cooler part of the day, advises Dr. Pivarnik.

MISSED YOUR PERIOD?

Some women are relieved—others worry—when menstruation stops for a few months in the cycling season. A skipped period or two isn't unusual, especially if you've dramatically upped the intensity of your training.

But if the disruption of the cycle continues, check with your gynecologist. First off, the cause of this cessation of menstruation, known as *secondary amenorrhea,* may not be your athletic activity. To assume so could be dangerous. Consult your health practitioner to rule out causes unrelated to exercise and to receive appropriate treatment.

Ohio State physiologist Anne Loucks, Ph.D., says her concern over amenorrhea is not meant "as a warning that women should not train at high levels." A former competitive swimmer, Dr. Loucks has studied this condition in athletes whose menses have been disrupted for six months or longer. The women tended to be young, to train rigorously, and to have low body weight and low body fat. "Yet I found women who trained equally hard and who had equally low weight and body fat, who did have periods," she elaborates.

This exercise-associated disturbance of the menses is still not fully understood. According to Dr. Loucks, an energy imbalance caused by eating fewer calories than the body uses "seems to have more impact than exercise per se."

Women who do experience this dysfunction should bear in mind:

•Don't think of amenorrhea as a form of birth control. While evidently ovulation has stopped or become less frequent, it could conceivably start up again.

•Even after the menses resume, periods may be irregular and fertility could be affected.

•As long as amenorrhea continues, estrogen and progesterone levels will remain low. Even among young women, bone thinning can occur; this can translate to greater risk of osteoporosis in later years.

•Treatment for amenorrhea typically includes a recommendation for greater calcium intake and consumption of more calories, sometimes coupled with estrogen and/or progesterone replacement therapy—with or without a decrease in exercise.

To keep from messing up the menses, increase your mileage and training intensity gradually and take in sufficient calories.

WINNING AGAINST BONE-LOSS

Osteoporosis is the loss of bone density associated with decreased estrogen production at menopause. Currently it's estimated that one of every four post-menopausal women has osteoporosis. Fortunately, we can do several things—starting now—to help ensure that our bones are not at risk.

We can take in the necessary calcium for bone building and maintenance (see chapter 11, "Fueling the Engine"). We can inform ourselves about the pros and cons of estrogen replacement therapy, often recommended to help prevent bone thinning, especially for women who have had early hysterectomies or ovarectomies. And we can stay active. Numerous studies have shown a positive relationship between exercise and building stronger bones—at every stage of a woman's life.

What sort of exercise benefits most? Exercise is specific. That is, bones stressed during exercise tend to increase their bone mineral content and mass, while other bones in the same individual may not change. Studies of runners, for example, have shown that they strengthen the bones in their hips and spines but not in their arms.

A research scientist in this fairly new field of study, Everett L. Smith, Ph.D., observes: "In the beginning we assumed that if you exercised and got cardiovascular benefits, you should also get bone benefits." The research, however, seems to show otherwise. Dr. Smith says:

It may be that for the bone to maintain itself, it requires a certain amount of force on the bottom of the foot—which results in a (temporary) bending of the bone. The forces that are applied by a weight-bearing activity like walking are very different from just the muscle pull on the bones in bicycling. So with cycling you may have good muscle tone and help to maintain the bone by good circulation and good nutrition, but that form of exercise may not be of great benefit to maintain the bones of the legs and spine (which are especially at risk of fracture if osteoporosis should develop). I think without some walking or jogging, you won't get the same benefit of exercise for the bone as you would for the cardiovascular system.

Thus Dr. Smith encourages women to be involved in a total fitness program, which would include light weightlifting on a regular basis, "since most women don't do anything with their upper body." He recommends jogging or walking also be included in a fitness program.

Many bike racers and other serious riders already lift weights regularly during the off-season, or sometimes year-round, with strengthening benefits that improve their riding. Many more casual cyclists also do circuit weight training to round out their fitness program. Now here's another reason to recommend it. If you haven't tried weight lifting before, a supervised workout on resistance machines such as Nautilus or Universal is best. These can be adjusted to your current strength level so the exercise is productive but not too difficult.

Want to do your body work outside? Maybe there's a parcourse in a local park where the various exercise stations let you use your body weight as the resistance; usually you walk or jog from one station to the next, perfect for getting in a little weight-bearing exercise.

The triathletes among us are a step ahead with their cross-training. Cyclocross is good, too, as it involves hopping on and off the bike and some running—pretty vigorous stuff. The rest of us can work in other activities we find fun, like racket sports, volleyball, aerobic dance (the high-impact variety), soccer, basketball, or cross-country skiing. And, keeping in mind a British study that showed merely jumping up and down fifty times a day for six months increased young women's hip bone density by 3 to 4 percent, get yourself a jump rope. Or, whenever you have time on your hands (like waiting for friends to arrive for a ride), make like a front suspension. Boing, boing, boing!

The Cycling Gynecologist

I'm an ob-gyn and a cyclist, and I like to decorate my exam rooms to decrease the anxiety associated with the yearly exam. In one room I have many bicycle posters. One is a photograph of me at the top of a long climb on the Solvang century at about mile 80. Needless to say, I look pretty wasted. At the bottom of the poster is written, "Are you sure you want your Pap smear from this person?" —Katherine Brubaker, Irvine, California

Planning Your Own Tour 22

Sometimes finding your own way is the best way. Maybe you want to travel where no organized tour goes. Or you're tempted, as I once was, to tie in a bike trip (four days in the Louisiana bayous) with a visit to friends or relatives (my sister in New Orleans). Perhaps you'd like to stretch your dollars and extend your travel. I know of one couple with more time than money, who managed "an absolutely unforgettable" fourteen-month cycling honeymoon, visiting virtually every country in Europe.

Or just the opposite. Maybe on the spur of the moment you make a brief escape, as did Jane King of Littlehampton, West Sussex, England:

> *I cycled for a few days on a heavy, old rented bike along the lower Loire valley in France. There were tiny, narrow roads along immense blue stretches of river, empty riverside cafes, shops with bread and cheese and little else, fishermen, great suspended nets drying outside ancient farm buildings, stunning chateaux, and friendly cheap hotels. That was magic . . . and no hills!*

Perhaps the freedom of traveling only with the companions you've chosen—or alone if you prefer—is the essence of cycle touring for you. Regardless, you have the added challenge of selecting your own route. Despite your research, you don't quite know what you'll find. You must plan what to take along and anticipate how to deal with whatever mishaps might occur en route. But that's OK. In fact, for some of us these very challenges and the opportunities for discovery (and self-discovery) create much of the appeal.

In the words of Bettina Selby, a British writer and cycle-adventurer, "That's what makes travel real—it leaves room for the unexpected to happen." Bettina has bicycled solo through Pakistan, Kashmir, Turkey, Syria, Egypt, Sudan, Uganda, and you-name-it. When I spoke with her, she was home for a brief respite from some nasty weather during a summer of extensive touring in her own England—a trip she described as "an extensive ramble. I have all the gear, a little tent. I just follow my nose. I'm doing much less mileage and more poking around than on previous travels. It's fascinating. And I keep meeting people who want to haul me off and show me their part of the country." On your own tour, you have the freedom to say yes.

PICKING YOUR ROUTE

You can have as much, or as little, help in selecting a route as you wish. If you've already chosen where you want to go, aside from travel books, you might need nothing more than a sufficiently detailed map. County maps, available at bookstores or county government offices, should show the lightly traveled back roads. If you need more than one map, you can often buy them (in the United States) from the state's Department of Transportation and avoid separate inquiries. For maps of converted rail trails for off-road bike travel, contact the Rails-to-Trails Conservancy, or visit their Web site (see appendix).

In England I've found the Ordnance Survey "Landranger Series" maps (scale of 1¼ inch to 1 mile, or 1: 50,000) excellent. In France I've used Michelin maps, which are less detailed but still very good (scale of 1 cm to 2 km, or 1: 200,000). In the United States topo maps come in a slightly smaller scale (1: 250,000). Maps within this range will serve you well. When possible, choose secondary roads instead of busy highways, and avoid tourist routes to popular attractions. Remember to take elevation changes into account as you estimate travel time.

For a shortcut in planning or to eliminate some of the unknowns, you could try a tour some other cyclist has already taken, adding some "detours" of your own to tailor it to suit. Look at bookshops or the library for books of bicycle tour routes. A local bike club with touring members should have a wealth of mapped trips, suggestions, and enthusiasm to share—good reasons for joining.

Membership also has its privileges in the following national organizations:

- •Adventure Cycling Association, Box 8308, Missoula, MT 59807. Phone: (800) 755-2453; (406) 721-1776; e-mail: acabike@aol.com; Web site: www.adv-cycling.org. Originally called Bikecentennial, and known for developing the TransAmerica Bicycle Trail, a cross-country route using public roads, Adventure Cycling is the biggest bicycle touring organization in the United States and a good source for off-road as well as on-road cycle tourists. It offers tour routing services, as well as a catalog of bicycling books and maps of a network of scenic, lightly traveled roads across America. The Association also develops mountain bike trails, including the partially completed Great Divide Mountain Bike Route, which will stretch from Canada to Mexico along the Continental Divide. Their helpful resource guide, the *Cyclists' Yellow Pages,* plus a subscription to *Adventure Cyclist* magazine are included in membership.
- •League of American Bicyclists, 1612 K. St., Suite 401, Washington, DC 20006. Phone: (202) 822-1333; web site: www.bikeleague.org. Founded as The League of American Wheelmen in 1880, LAB has more than 32,000 member cyclists belonging to over 400 bicycle clubs nationwide. Primarily an advocacy and educational organization, LAB publishes its annual *Tourfinder,* which lists tour operators, state rides, and cycling resources.

North of the border, the Canadian Cycling Association can provide some route information from its headquarters, but more complete information is available from the affiliate provincial districts. Contact the Canadian Cycling Association, 1600 James Naismith Dr., Gloucester, Ontario, Canada K1B 5N4. Phone: (613) 748-5629; e-mail: leisure@canadian-cycling.com; Web site: www.canadian-cycling.com.

For information about touring in the British Isles and for Ordnance Survey maps, contact The CTC, Cotterell House, 69 Meadrow, Godalming, Surrey GU7 3HS England. Phone: 1483 417217; e-mail: cycling@ctc.org.uk; Web site: www.ctc.org.uk.

Many U.S. states and Canadian provinces, eager to lure cycle tourists, will assist you. Write to the state or provincial Department of Tourism and clearly indicate that you seek bicycling route maps and other information. On the lower left of the envelope you might write "Bicycle Touring Info Request."

WHERE TO LAY YOUR WEARY HEAD

You already know there's considerable choice in types of accommodations, from camping to hostels to multistarred hotels, so I'll simply mention a few resources that may prove helpful.

Hosteling is not limited to the under-twenty-one set, though it won't appeal if luxury and privacy concern you most. These inexpensive lodgings may turn out to be quite romantic, however, as Faith Hahn of McAllen, Texas, found on her cycle tour through Germany. In her travel diary, she describes the hostel in Ochsenfurt as

> the smallest, most primitive, and most unusual I've been in. An old tower in the city wall about twenty feet square and six stories high, it really is a seventeenth-century, cold, drafty stone tower! The beds are poor but piled high with German woolen blankets that I think I'll need. There is a bathroom and a cold shower. And there's a fantastic day room at the top, with windows on all four sides and an incredible view of the city. That's where I'm writing and having supper now.

Membership in your country's hosteling organization should net you a handbook with hostel listings plus discount privileges in fifty or so member countries. For information contact:

- American Youth Hostels, National Administration Offices, Box 37613, Washington, DC 20013-7613. Phone: (202) 783-6161.
- Hosteling International/Canada, 400-205 Catherine St., Ottawa, Ontario, Canada K2P 1C3. Phone: (613) 237-7884.
- YHA/England and Wales, Trevalyan House, 8 St. Stevens Hill, St. Albans, Hertsfordshire AL1 2DY, England. Phone: 44 1727 855215.

On an international scale, the organization Servas aims to promote under-standing among peoples through a host program. This should not be looked on as just a freebie: Generally you'd stay two days in someone's home, and in return for a bed and meals you're expected to talk about your country and share your thoughts on world events. No money changes hands. In this fashion, Anita Slomski wrote in *Bicycling* magazine, "I cycl(ed) 3,000 miles over the backroads of Europe away from the tourist traps to find the real people. Countless times I was rewarded with a richness in human warmth and generosity and the pleasure of some truly unforgettable characters." Sometimes, she admits, "telling the same stories every night to a new host and being polite all the time were exhaust-ing. But the rewards were generally worth the effort."

If such cultural exchange appeals, contact Servas to inquire about its screen-ing procedure and membership fee. Lists of hosts (individuals and families, neighborhood centers, ashrams, and communities) are provided, and you may arrange to visit within your own country as well as abroad.

- The United States Servas Committee Inc., 11 John St., Room 407, New York, NY 10038. Phone: (212) 267-0252; e-mail: usservas@.servas.org. (This office can also provide information on Servas in Canada.)
- Servas Canada, Michael Johnson, 229 Hillcrest Ave., Willowdale, Ontario M2N 3P3. Phone: (416) 221-6434.
- The British Servas Committee, Ann Greenhough, 4 Southfield Rd., Burley-in-Wharfedale, Ilkley, West Yorkshire LS29 7PA England. Phone: 44 1943 862965.

Beyond these options, your own reading or a travel agent can lead you to the full spectrum of B&B's, guest houses, pensions, and hotels.

There is also the camping alternative—and the extra gear you must carry to be able to do it. An investment in lightweight, good quality equipment pays off in a lighter, more compact load. It will save your energy and give you more sta-ble bike handling—literally, a lifesaver.

BIKES FOR LOADED TOURING

If you already have a genuine touring bike built for stability under load and a smooth ride, and gearing down in the mid- to low-20s, you're ahead of the game. If you don't, before rushing to the bike shop, consider that just as there are many ways to go touring, there's a range of choices for the bike you might want to transport you. You can also choose between mounting panniers or towing a trailer. Here's one way to look at the options:

- You're credit-card touring. You pack your toothbrush, your credit card, a patch kit, a spare pair of shorts, and a windbreaker in an under-the-saddle bag and off you go. This is perhaps a short trip. Any bike, even a racing bike, could handle that load.

To Trailer or Not to Trailer

Adventure Cycling's Julie Huck (who happens to be this book's cover girl) has led one tour on the Great Divide Mountain Bike Route in Montana and traveled most of the remaining Big Sky Country miles in week-long segments with friends. These wilderness adventures allow her a total escape from "the busyness of life." For these trips, which are mostly on fire roads with occasional technical spots that require walking, Julie uses an all-terrain trailer with a single wheel (the Wheele PacDog) to carry camping gear and clothing. With lots of previous experience using panniers, Julie is well qualified to discuss the pros and cons of using a trailer or panniers for touring.

Besides allowing more options in the type of bike you can ride with a load, Julie notes that a bike with a trailer handles more like an unloaded bike. "You might almost forget it's back there," she says, "until you turn a sharp corner and it sort of tugs on the side you're turning toward. And when you descend, it pushes you even more than panniers." The descents take a little getting used to, she says. A big advantage over panniers, however, is that when you're pulling a trailer and you stand up to climb, you can let the bike sway from side to side with your pedaling strokes because there's a pivot on the trailer. And you have less wind-resistance than with bike bags—"I really cruise on the road," says Julie.

Admittedly, the trailer itself weighs more than a set of panniers and a rack. And "it's another thing that can break"—yet another type of spare tire and tube you need to carry.

Packing a trailer has its pros and cons, too. Unlike some panniers with pockets for dividing up your stuff, a trailer typically has one big packing area, which could trouble the organizationally challenged. Julie keeps track of her gear by packing in different colored, waterproof stuff sacks. To protect from rain, she lines the bottom of the trailer "with a big, ol' garbage bag" and puts another one on top. She likes the way a trailer is always accessible, unlike the main compartments of most panniers if you have a sleeping bag bungeed on top.

Julie warns that when crossing a busy road or passing somebody, you need to remember that you're longer and wider than usual! Especially when touring off-road, check all the "connecting points" each morning and again before heading down something steep, because bolts can shake loose with vibration. As with panniers, expect braking and accelerating to take longer than with an unloaded bike.

- You're hosteling or hoteling for a couple weeks or a weekend. You'll carry a few changes of clothing, your rain gear, a sleeping bag if hosteling, maybe a camera, but no camping or cooking gear, as you'll dine at restaurants. If you don't have a touring bike, you can probably manage fine with a touring/sport bike or a hybrid, provided it has eyelets for mounting a rear rack. Note suggestions further on for apportioning weight on the bike. Or you could pull a trailer.
- You're camping, cooking meals, and packing accordingly. You'll surely be carrying twenty-five pounds, maybe twice that. (Sharon Sommerville, whom

you'll meet in this chapter, toured cross-Canada carrying fifty pounds of gear so she'd have all the comforts. However, every five pounds you can pare off of a burden like that are five pounds less to lug uphill and that much less of a load on your rear wheel spokes.)

If you're in the second or third category and you elect to use bike bags, you'll need at least rear panniers and a rack. (See chapter 7, "Accessories.") Anyone planning to put more than about twenty pounds in a pair of rear panniers should consider adding a low-rider front rack and small front panniers. Dividing the load in this fashion will make for much safer bike handling. The more your total load exceeds about twenty-five pounds, the more likely you'll need a bike with touring geometry.

Or you can opt for a trailer and get acceptable stability with just about any rig but a racing bike. Julie Huck, of Adventure Cycling, has observed increasing trailer use among bike tourists who stop by their office in Missoula, Montana. She attributes it to the much wider selection of bike trailers on the market these days, including a couple designed for off-pavement touring like the B.O.B. and the Wheele PacDog (see appendix).

As for gearing, the triple chainrings on many types of bikes on today's market are the answer to a tourist's prayers, especially if the itinerary includes climbing. But suppose you own a road bike with a double. For unloaded touring, a low gear in the mid- to upper-30s is generally recommended. For carrying up to thirty pounds in your packs, a low down in the low 30s is usually suggested, but many women would appreciate lower. For a heavier load, your low should fall in the mid- to upper-20s.

What about touring on-road with a mountain bike? If it has stable handling without a load, you could add a rack and a moderate load and see how it performs. Or get an off-road trailer, and you'll have the flexibility for dirt touring, too. Certainly you'll possess the gearing for touring.

If you have a knobby-tired MTB, substituting street treads will give you less rolling resistance on the tarmac. You'll still sacrifice some speed compared to a road bike, but if your daily mileage is moderate, and if you find sitting up most comfortable, you probably won't mind.

GETTING LOADED

When packing panniers, distribute weight equally on each side, placing heavy objects low in the bags and close to the bike. This keeps the weightiest part of the load closest to the center of gravity. On the front wheel try to keep weight behind the axle, not in front of it. If your bike handled well without panniers but is now unstable with a load, you probably have the weight too far forward on the front wheel. Before your tour, ride at home with the weight in different positions to see what works best.

Pack so that gear doesn't shift inside your panniers when you take a corner or stop quickly. And don't strap too many things on top of the bags—not only does it make you look like a traveling soup kitchen with a pot bungeed here, a frying pan there, a damp towel flapping in the wind, but it can be dangerous. Extra gear can come loose too readily and catch in the spokes.

If you use bungee cords or straps with an open hook on the end, here's a safety tip: First hook one end down low on your rack and then stretch the free end toward you. Secure your sleeping bag, etc., with it and hook this end high on the rack. This method keeps your face out of firing range if the hook or cord should slip out of your grasp. There are now cords with closed plastic hooks designed to cut down on the hazard of a hook in the eye, but I'd still attach them as described.

Check often to make sure your panniers are mounted securely on the rack, and that nothing is dangling or bending into the spokes. (Many bags have stiffeners to prevent them from bending; if yours don't, improvise a stiffener.) And if you hear a peculiar sound while riding, stop and investigate in case something has come loose. A sudden, unexpected stop because of a wheel jam could send you head over handlebars.

HANDLING A LOADED BIKE

With loaded panniers, your bike will have a whole new feel and will handle differently. But you'll get the hang of it, especially if you anticipate the following:

- Acceleration will be slower. When you start from a standstill to cross a busy street, you'll need extra time to beat oncoming traffic.
- You'll probably need to keep a firmer grip on the bars than normal. The bike may steer a little to one side, despite your attempts to divide the load equally; be on guard to correct it. Lightening the load in your handlebar bag may help. Experiment and see what works best for you.
- On a rough road, the ride will feel rougher. Full bags add to the bounce up and down, or a lateral shimmy. Slow down, if you need to, to keep control.
- Don't forget you're carrying a wide load, even though it's where you can't see it. When passing another cyclist, allow extra room so you don't do the "sleeping bag sideswipe."
- Before a long descent, stop at the top, well off the road—a good place to pause anyway for a snack or to slip into a windbreaker for a cool downhill. Check brakes and wheels, and look over your tires for any debris that should be brushed off. Make sure packs and racks are attached securely.
- A loaded bike gathers more speed on downhills and has startlingly different stopping characteristics. When braking, you'll discover that the bike stops, but the bags and your body want to keep on going. To counteract that momentum, shift your weight quickly but smoothly back on the saddle,

leveling the pedals so you can push against them equally; on drop handle-bars brake from the drops with firm, equal pressure. With or without bike bags, this is a good emergency braking method.

Allow more time to brake to a stop. Keep downhill speed under control, so you have ample reaction time to avoid a gravel patch or pothole. Remember squeeze-and-release braking to minimize heat buildup in your rims. And when you get to one of those delicious, miles-long descents, stop from time to time, off the road. Admire the view (you earned it), and let your rims cool and your hands and arms relax.

•Riding out of the saddle up a hill, you'll find that load on the back wags the entire bike. Don't lean your weight from side to side as you would if unencumbered.

•Walking is OK! Maybe your gears just aren't low enough or it's one hill too many on a long day. It's smarter to walk up than to wobble all over the road. Dismount for gravelly descents; they must be taken slowly. Any effort to brake would end up in a skid on this treacherous stuff.

Enough warnings—the riding technique soon gets to be second nature. If you know how to handle the worst, you'll still be there to relish the good things.

SHOULD I SOLO?

Alison Heine is talking about some of the "good things," when the question of touring alone comes up. Alison, a project officer for the Greater Manchester (England) Cycling Project, tells me she favors Scotland for bicycle touring.

Roads are unfenced, so you can put your tent anywhere. Every village has super bakers' shops and little cafes. There are loads of really cheap B&B's—prices have hardly changed in years. There's lots of daylight, so you can cycle till nine or ten P.M.

Alison bought her bike and camping gear while a student, and she generally camped alone. "I never felt unsafe," she says, "though I'd never have camped on open land, visible from the road, near a city."

She believes, as I do, that many people exaggerate the proportion of troublemakers in this world. "In the Outer Hebrides I met a retired nurse, about eighty, who invited me in for an incredible piece of cake," remembers Alison. "She made me promise to send her a postcard from home to let her know I arrived safely. She was terribly worried about me. I felt sad that she felt so unsafe on her own little island!"

Many cyclists who have toured alone agree that such kindness is typical and intentional harm, rare. One such woman is Sharon Sommerville, of Toronto, who cycled the entire 5,000-mile Trans-Canadian Highway. Except for a few instances when friends had planned to meet her, she rode alone or with cyclists she encountered en route. Sharon doesn't pretend there's no risk in setting off on your own. She prepared for the trip with her personal security in mind.

"But I think if you're prudent and intelligent about touring alone, you're pretty safe," she says. "I felt as confident on the road as I do as a single woman in a medium-size apartment building in downtown Toronto. Because when you're on the road, you're really focused on where you are and what you're doing."

That "focus," Sharon notes, works in well with the attitude a woman takes in self-defense, as she learned in Wen Do, a form of martial arts designed especially for women. Sharon took an intensive two-day course to prepare for the trip. "Part of Wen Do is awareness and extracting yourself from potentially dangerous situations. It's also knowing your limitations." Sharon prepared herself with strategies for physical confrontations, but she would do her best to avoid them.

With that in mind she set "a few cardinal rules": She limited herself to public campgrounds and always made camp before sunset. And she avoided telling anyone she met along the way where she'd be camping. Sharon did admit to inquiring campground owners that she was alone, and they often made a point of looking out for her.

She wore her hair boyishly short in a "brush" cut all summer. Despite a decidedly feminine figure, in a T-shirt, cycling tights, and without makeup, "no kidding, some people mistook me for a guy."

She also established a phone-in system with her parents, who had a large map of Canada with her route marked on it. Every three days she'd telephone to say hello and tell them her whereabouts and where she expected to be in three days. If her parents didn't hear from her by the morning after the third day, they were to call the police to look for her.

That never happened. Along the Trans-Canada, Sharon says,

> There's almost a sense of community, as there's nearly always somebody driving by. And who's going to get out of their car and hurt you? That's not likely. What's more likely is that someone would be aware of you on the road and then try to find you at night. During the day when you're riding, you're as safe as you'd be riding anywhere. And generally people are decent. You get the odd one, and it's the odd one you have to protect yourself against.

As she'd anticipated, Sharon encountered friendly people who went out of their way to be helpful, partly out of fascination with what she was doing. In fact, one of Sharon's reasons for the cross-country trip, aside from seeing Canada, was meeting people.

> And it was fabulous for that. I felt such an incredibly high level of stimulation every day. At home, you fall into patterns in relating to the people you know. But when you're on your bicycle all summer and your "doors" are wide open and your heart is wide open, things come into it—particularly when you travel alone . . .

Sharon admits she had one experience that appeared to be her worst nightmare come true. She was alone one midafternoon on a truly desolate stretch of the highway in Alberta.

It was all sagebrush and cacti, no traffic going by, and I was just trucking along in the heat. Then behind me I heard the sound of motorcycles. Sure enough, two huge Harleys came up and stopped right in front of me on the side of the road. Classic bikers, these guys had long greasy hair, shades, and big beer bellies. It was scary; I felt completely vulnerable.

So what did I do but put on my biggest, brightest smile and cycle by, saying, "Hi, how ya doing?!"

And they said to me, "Where in the hell are you going?"

And the obvious answer was, "Halifax, Nova Scotia."

They said, "What?!"

It turned out they could not believe what they were seeing and they had to stop. They were the nicest guys. They called me "Missy" and said, "Why don't you get a motor for that thing?"

Of the other benefits of touring alone, Sharon observes:

It gives you absolute control of your life. I think if you're a daughter, a mother, a sister, a wife, you have certain roles and responsibilities toward other people. Women, I think, are particularly vulnerable to putting their own needs off. One nice thing about going alone on tour is that you can do what you want. You go where you want to go, at your speed. You can putz around or you can ride hard. You do it your way.

Solo touring will not appeal to every woman (or to every man). The individual who spends little time alone may not feel comfortable with it. The cyclist who can't change a tire, pitch a tent, or use a camp stove has reason to wait until such self-sufficiency is well developed. Moreover, your world view has a great deal to do with whether you'd enjoy even a short tour alone. Women have become aware in recent decades that the protection traditionally given females can fetter us. Yet it's difficult to break the protective bonds. Nor perhaps do we realize to what extent television and newspapers create the sense of a victimizing world.

"If you don't have that attitude about yourself and about the world—that the world is a comfortable place to live in—then you're afraid," observes Sharon. "If you see the world as a scary place and that the world is out to get you, then you'll be fearful.

"Yes, I was a little jittery the first few nights on tour, jumping at every strange little noise," she remembers. "But I'm fairly adventurous. I know I can take care of myself. Experience tells me I can go ahead, push myself a little bit beyond my personal barriers, and I'm going to be OK."

Appendix

GEAR CHARTS

26" Wheels

Number of teeth on sprocket	24	26	28	30	32	34	36	38	39	40	41	42	43	44	45	46	47	48	49	50	51	52	53	
12	52	56	61	65	69	74	78	82	85	87	89	91	83	95	98	100	102	104	106	108	111	113	115	12
13	48	52	56	60	64	68	72	76	78	80	82	84	86	88	90	92	94	96	98	100	102	104	106	13
14	45	48	52	56	60	63	67	70	72	74	76	78	80	82	84	85	87	89	91	93	95	97	98	14
15	42	45	49	52	55	59	62	66	68	69	71	73	75	76	78	80	81	83	85	87	88	90	92	15
16	39	42	45	49	52	55	58	61	63	65	67	68	70	72	73	75	76	78	80	81	83	85	86	16
17	37	40	43	46	49	52	55	58	60	61	63	64	66	67	69	70	72	73	75	76	78	80	81	17
18	35	38	40	43	46	49	52	55	56	58	59	61	62	64	65	66	68	69	71	72	74	75	77	18
19	33	36	38	41	44	47	49	52	53	55	56	57	59	60	62	63	64	66	67	68	70	71	73	19
20	31	34	36	39	42	44	47	49	51	52	53	55	56	57	59	60	61	62	64	65	66	68	69	20
21	30	32	35	37	40	42	45	47	48	50	51	52	53	54	56	57	58	59	61	62	63	64	66	21
22	28	31	33	35	38	40	43	45	46	47	48	50	51	52	53	54	56	57	58	59	60	61	63	22
23	27	29	32	34	36	38	41	43	44	45	46	47	49	50	51	52	53	54	55	57	58	59	60	23
24	26	28	30	32	35	37	39	41	42	43	44	45	47	48	49	50	51	52	53	54	55	56	57	24
25	25	27	29	31	33	35	37	39	41	42	43	44	45	46	47	48	49	50	51	52	53	54	55	25
26	24	26	28	30	32	34	36	38	39	40	41	42	43	44	4	46	47	48	49	50	51	52	53	26
27	23	25	27	29	31	33	35	37	38	39	39	40	41	42	43	44	45	46	47	48	49	50	51	27
28	22	24	26	28	30	32	33	35	36	37	38	39	40	41	42	43	44	45	46	46	47	48	49	28
30	21	23	24	26	28	29	31	33	34	35	36	36	37	38	39	40	41	42	42	43	44	45	46	30
32	20	21	23	24	26	28	29	31	32	33	33	34	35	35	37	37	38	39	40	41	41	42	43	32
34	18	20	21	23	24	26	28	29	30	31	31	32	33	33	34	35	36	37	37	38	39	40	41	34
	24	26	28	30	32	34	36	38	39	40	41	42	43	44	45	46	47	48	49	50	51	52	53	

Number of teeth on chainring

27" Wheels

	24	26	28	29	30	31	32	33	34	35	36	37	38	39	40	41	42	43	44	45	46	47	48	49	50	51	52	53	54
11	59	64	69	71	74	76	79	81	83	86	88	91	93	96	98	101	103	106	108	110	113	115	118	120	123	125	128	130	133
12	54	59	63	65	68	70	72	74	77	79	81	83	86	88	90	92	95	97	99	101	104	106	108	110	113	115	117	119	122
13	50	54	58	60	62	64	66	69	71	73	75	77	79	81	83	85	87	89	91	93	96	98	100	102	104	106	108	110	112
14	46	50	54	56	58	60	62	64	66	68	69	71	73	75	77	79	81	83	85	87	89	91	93	95	96	98	100	102	104
15	43	47	50	52	54	56	58	59	61	63	65	67	68	70	72	74	76	77	79	81	83	85	86	88	90	92	94	95	97
16	41	44	47	49	51	52	54	56	57	59	61	62	64	66	68	69	71	73	74	76	78	79	81	83	84	86	88	89	91
17	38	41	44	46	48	49	51	52	54	56	57	59	60	62	64	65	67	68	70	71	73	75	76	78	79	81	83	84	86
18	36	39	42	44	45	47	48	50	51	53	54	56	57	59	60	62	63	65	66	68	69	71	72	74	75	77	78	80	81
19	34	37	40	41	43	44	45	47	48	50	51	53	54	55	57	58	60	61	63	64	65	67	68	70	71	72	74	75	77
20	31	33	35	37	39	40	41	42	44	45	46	47	49	50	51	53	54	55	57	58	59	61	62	63	65	66	68	70	72
21	31	33	35	37	39	40	41	42	44	45	46	47	49	50	51	53	54	55	57	58	59	60	62	63	64	66	67	68	69
22	29	32	34	36	37	38	39	41	42	43	44	45	47	48	49	50	52	53	54	55	56	58	59	60	61	63	64	65	66
23	28	31	33	34	35	36	38	39	40	41	42	43	45	46	47	48	49	50	52	53	54	55	56	58	59	60	61	62	63
24	27	29	32	33	34	35	36	37	38	39	41	42	43	44	45	46	47	48	50	51	52	53	54	55	56	57	59	60	61
25	26	28	30	31	32	33	35	36	37	38	39	40	41	42	43	44	45	46	48	49	50	51	52	53	54	55	56	57	58
26	25	27	29	30	31	32	33	34	35	36	37	38	39	41	42	43	44	45	46	47	48	49	50	51	52	53	54	55	56
27	24	26	28	29	30	31	32	33	34	35	36	37	38	39	40	41	42	43	44	45	46	47	48	49	50	51	52	53	54
28	23	25	27	28	29	30	31	32	33	34	35	36	37	38	39	40	41	42	43	44	45	46	47	47	48	49	50	51	52
29	22	24	26	27	28	29	30	31	32	33	34	35	36	37	38	39	40	41	42	43	44	45	46	47	47	48	49	49	50
30	22	23	25	26	27	28	29	30	31	332	32	33	34	35	36	37	38	39	40	41	41	42	43	44	45	46	47	48	49
31	21	23	24	25	26	27	28	29	30	30	31	32	33	34	35	36	37	37	38	39	40	41	42	43	44	44	45	46	47
32	20	22	24	24	25	26	27	28	29	30	30	31	32	33	34	35	35	36	37	38	39	40	41	41	42	43	44	45	46
33	20	21	23	24	25	25	26	27	28	29	30	31	32	33	34	34	35	36	37	38	38	39	40	41	42	42	43	43	44
34	19	21	22	23	24	25	25	26	27	28	29	29	30	31	32	33	33	34	35	36	37	37	38	39	40	41	41	42	43

PRODUCT SOURCES AND INFORMATION

ABS Sports, Inc.
129 Johnathan Rd.
Lakehurst, NJ 08733
908/ 323-8773 (phone)
908/ 323-0645 (fax)

Aegis
Champlain St.
P.O. Box 69
Van Buren, ME 04785
207/ 868-3909 (phone)
207/ 868-3499 (fax)

Battle Mountain Bikes
110 E. 4th
Encampment, WY 82325
307/ 327-5952 (phone)
307/ 327-5306 (fax)

B.O.B. Trailers Inc.
3641 Sacramento Dr. #3
San Luis Obispo, CA 93401
805/ 541-2554 (phone)
805/ 543-8464 (fax)
e-mail: bobinc@callamer.com
Web site: www.callamer.com/bobinc

Brompton
C.M. Wasson Co. (U.S. distributor)
423 Chaucer St.
Palo Alto, CA 94301-2202
800/ 783-3447
415/ 321-0808 (phone)
415/ 321-8375 (fax)
e-mail: channel@aol.com
Web site: www.bromptonbike.com

Bullwinkles/Madden Mountaineering
2400 Central Ave.
Boulder, CO 80301
303/ 442-5828 (phone)
303/ 442-5846 (fax)
e-mail: madden@rmi.net
Web site: maddenusa.com

Burley Design Cooperative
4080 Stewart Rd.
Eugene, OR 97402
800/ 311-5294
541/ 687-1644 (phone)
541/ 687-0436 (fax)

Camelbak/FasTrak Systems, Inc.
P.O. Box 1029
Weatherford, TX 76086-1029
800/ 767-8725
817/ 594-1000 (phone)
817/ 594-1030 (fax)
Web site: www.camelbak.com

Cannondale Corporation
16 Trowbridge Dr.
P.O. Box 122
Bethel, CT 06801
800/ BIKE-USA
203/ 749-7000 (phone)
203/ 748-4012 (fax)
e-mail: cdale01@interserv.com
Web site: www.cannondale.com

Chamois Butt'r/Paceline Products
1700 Richfield Rd.
Liberty, MO 64068
816/ 781-0287

Dahon California
833 Meridian St.
Duarte, CA 91010
818/ 305-5264

Fat City Cycles
1049 Pucker St.
Stowe, VT 05672
802/ 253-6998 (phone)
802/ 253-6218 (fax)
e-mail: fatcity011@aol.com

Gaerlan Custom Cycles
838 Grant Ave.
San Francisco, CA 94108
415/ 362-3866 (phone)

Giant Bicycle, Inc.
737 W. Artesia Blvd.
Rancho Dominguez, CA 90220-5515
800/ US-GIANT
Web site: www.giant-bicycle.com

Graber Products/Saris
5253 Verona Rd.
Madison, WI 53711
800/ 783-RAKS
608/ 274-6550 (phone)
608/ 274-1702 (fax)

Granger's/MPI Outdoors
85 Flagship Dr., Suite D
North Andover, MA 01845
800/ 343-5827
Web site: www.grangersusa.com

Green Gear Cycling, Inc.
3364 West 11th Ave.
Eugene, OR 97402
800/ 777-0258
541/ 687-0487 (phone)
541/ 687-0403 (fax)
e-mail: BikeFriday@aol.com

Jamis/G. Joannu Cycle
151 Ludlow Ave.
Northvale, NJ 07647-2398
800/ 222-0570
201/ 768-9050 (phone)

Kona USA
2455 Salashan
Ferndale, WA 98248
800/ KONA-USA
360/ 366-0951 (phone)

Montague Corp.
P.O. Box 381118
Cambridge, MA 02238
800/ 736-5348
617/ 491-7200 (phone)
Web site: www.montagueco.com

Nikwax
P.O. Box 1572
Everett, WA 98206
800/ 577-2700
206/ 303-1410 (phone)
Web site: www.nikwax-usa.com

Ortlieb USA
19030 72nd Ave. S.
Kent, WA 98032
425/ 251-3939 (phone)
425/ 251-0226 (fax)
e-mail: ortliebusa@aol.com

Performance Bicycle Shop
P.O. Box 2741
Chapel Hill, NC 27514
800/ 727-2453

Polar Electro Inc.
99 Seaview Blvd.
Port Washington, NY 11050-4632
800/ 227-1314
516/ 484-2400 (phone)
516/ 484-2789 (fax)

R+E Cycles
5627 University Way, N.E.
Seattle, WA 98105
206/ 527-4822 (phone)
206/ 527-8931 (fax)
e-mail: RodTandem@aol.com
Web site: www.rodcycle.com

REI (Recreational Equipment, Inc.)
P.O. Box 1938
Sumner, WA 98390-0800
800/ 999-4734
Web site: www.rei.com

Recumbent Cyclist News
Box 58755
Renton, WA 98078
206/ 631-5728 (phone)
e-mail: drrecumbnt@aol.com

Swift Folder
Human Powered Machines
455 W. 1st Ave.
Eugene, OR 97401
800/ 343-5568
541/ 344-1197
e-mail: cat@efn.org
Web site: www.efn.org/~cat

Terry Precision Cycling for Women
1704 Wayneport Rd.
Macedon, NY 14502
800/ 289-8379
314/ 986-2104 (fax)
e-mail: www.terrybicycles.com

VAR lever available from:
Terry Precision Cycling for Women (see
above) and
The Third Hand
12225-M Highway 66
Ashland, OR 97520
541/ 488-4800 (phone)
541/ 482-0080 (fax)

Wheele PacDog (Innovations Sports)
7 Chrysler
Irvine, CA 92618
800/ 222-4284
714/ 458-3714 (fax)
e-mail: sales1@isports.com

Z-Creation
2010 8th St.
Boulder, CO 80302
800/ 875-8635
303/ 444-8635 (phone)
303/ 449-1058 (fax)
e-mail: z@zkreation.com

CLOTHING WITH WOMEN'S SIZING

Andiamo!
P.O. Box 1657
Sun Valley, ID 83353
800/ 333-6141
208/ 726-1385 (phone)
208/ 726-1388 (fax)

Bellwether
375 Alabama St.
San Francisco, CA 94110
800/ 321-6198
415/ 863-0436 (phone)
415/ 863-8912 (fax)

Bike Nashbar
4111 Simon Rd.
Youngstown, OH 44512-1343
800/ NASHBAR
Web site: www.nashbar.com

Bouré Sportswear
98 Everett St.
Durango, CO 81301
970/ 247-0339 (phone)
970/ 247-9219 (fax)

Canari
10025 Huennekens St.
San Diego, CA 92121
800/ 929-2925
619/ 455-8245 (phone)
619/ 455-8292 (fax)

Cannondale (see Sources list)

Diadora and Giordana distributed by:
Gita Sporting Goods, Ltd.
12600 Steel Creek Rd.
Charlotte, NC 28273
800-SAY-GITA

Dirt Designs
2805 Wilderness Pl. #1200
Boulder, CO 80301
800/ 269-6641
303/ 541-0662 (phone)
303/ 541-9675 (fax)
e-mail: dirtde@aol.com
Web site: www.dirtdesigns.com

GLD (Girls Love Dirt)/Cantina Apparel Inc.
11545 Sorrento Valley Rd., Suite 311
San Diego, CA 92121
800/ 5-CANTINA
619/ 793-9211 (phone)
619/ 793-9182 (fax)
Web site: www.cantinagear.com

InMotion
7301 Washington Ave. S.
Minneapolis, MN 55439
800/ 552-2976
612/ 829-0144 (phone)
612/ 829-7085 (fax)
Web site: www.inmotion.com

InSport
1870 N.W. 173rd Ave.
Beaverton, OR 97006
800/ 652-5200
503/ 645-3552 (phone)
503/ 629-9455 (fax)

Koulius Zaard
2682 Middlefield Rd., Unit K
Redwood City, CA 94063
800-KOULIUS
415/ 364-9575 (phone)
415/ 364-9573 (fax)
e-mail: KZAARD@aol.com

Lake
805 Greenwood St.
Evanston, IL 60201
800/ 804-7777
847/ 491-9205 (phone)
847/ 491-9269 (fax)
e-mail: phxint@aol.com

Nike, Inc.
One Bowerman Dr.
Beaverton, OR 97005
800/ 344-6453
503/ 671-6453 (phone)
503/ 671-6374 (fax)

Pearl Izumi Technical Wear
2300 Central Ave., Suite G
Boulder, CO 80301
800/ 877-7080
303/ 938-1700 (phone)
303/ 938-8181 (fax)
e-mail: pearlizumi@aol.com
Web site: www.pearlizumi.com/pearl

Performance Bicycle Shop (see Sources list)

Polar Electro Inc. (see Sources list)

Smith Sport Optics, Inc.
P.O. Box 2999
Ketchum, ID 83340
800/ 635-4401
208/ 726-4477 (phone)
208/ 726-6555 (fax)

SporTobin
P.O. Box 115
Hull, MA 02045-0115
800/ 424-3843
617/ 925-5339 (phone)

Sugoi Cycle Clothing
144 E. 7th Ave.
Vancouver, BC
Canada V5T 1M6
800/ 432-1335
800/ 864-7646 (fax)
604/ 875-0887 (phone)
604/ 879-9106 (fax)

Terry Precision Cycling for Women
(see Sources list)

Title Nine Sports
5743 Landregan St.
Emeryville, CA 94608
800/ 609-0092
510/ 655-5999 (phone)
510/ 655-9191 (fax)
e-mail: thefolks@title9sports.com

Zoic Core Clothing
2415 3rd St. #230
San Francisco, CA 94107
800/ 241-WEAR
415/ 241-9898 (fax)
e-mail: www.zoic.com

FAMILY CYCLING SOURCES

Tandem and Family Cycling Magazine
P.O. Box 2939
Eugene, OR 97402
541/ 485-5262 (phone)
541/ 302-1950 (fax)
e-mail: subscriptions@tandemmag.com

Family Cycling Club
Martha and Kreg Ulery
914 Sour Apple Lane, RD #3
Bethlehem, PA 18015
610/ 791-0406 (phone)
e-mail: martha@enter.net

Burley Design Cooperative
4080 Stewart Rd.
Eugene, OR 97402
800/ 311-5294
541/ 687-1644 (phone)
541/ 687-0436 (fax)

Cyclo-Pedia, Inc.
P.O. Box 884
Adrian, MI 49221
800/ 678-1021

Santana Cycles, Inc.
Box 206
LaVerne, CA 91750
909/ 596-7570 (phone)
909/ 596-5853 (fax)
e-mail: santanainc@aol.com

Tandems East
86 Gwynwood Dr.
Pittsgrove, NJ 08318
609/ 451-5104 (phone)
609/ 453-8626 (fax)
e-mail: tandemwiz@aol.com

Tandems Limited
2220 Vanessa Dr.
Birmingham, AL 35242-4430
205/ 991-5519 (phone)
e-mail: tandems@mindspring.com

Totally Tandems, Inc.
P.O. Box 1661
Marshalltown, IA 50158-7661
800/ 255-0576

BIKE TOUR COMPANIES
(A Sampling)

America by Bicycle
603/ 382-1662 (NH)

Arizona Offroad Adventures
800/ 689-2453 (AZ)

Asian Pacific Adventures
800/ 825-1680
213/ 935-3156 (CA)

Backroads
800/ 462-2848
510/ 527-1555 (CA)

Bike & Boat Cycletours Holland and
Cycletours International
31 20 627 40 98 (phone, Netherlands)
Web site: www.cycletours.nl

Bike Vermont
800/ 257-2226
802/ 457-3553 (VT)

Butterfield & Robinson
800/ 678-1147
416/ 864-1354 (Ontario, Canada)

Erickson CycleTours
206/ 524-7731 (WA)

Escape the City Streets
800/ 596-2953
702/ 596-2953 (NV)

Gerhard's Bicycle Odysseys
503/ 223-2402 (OR)

Holiday River & Bike Expeditions
800/ 624-6323
801/ 266-2087 (UT)

La Corsa Tours
800/ LACORSA (NY)

Kaibab Mountain Bike Tours
800/ 451-1133
801/ 259-7423 (UT)

New Mexico Mountain Bike Adventures
505/ 474-0074 (NM)

Nichols Expeditions
800/ 648-8488
801/ 259-3999 (UT)

REI Adventures
800/ 622-2236 (WA)

Rim Tours
800/ 626-7335
801/ 259-5223 (UT)

Roads Less Traveled
800/ 488-8483
303/ 678-8750 (CO)

Velo Echappé
303/ 713-1447 (CO)

Vermont Bicycle Touring
800/ 245-3868
802/ 453-4811 (VT)

Western Spirit
800/ 845-2453
801/ 259-8732 (UT)

CROSS-STATE RIDES

Alabama:
Bicycle Across Magnificent Alabama (BAMA)
538 West Inez Rd.
Dothan, AL 36301-1693

Colorado:
Denver Post Ride the Rockies
Denver Post
1560 Broadway
Denver, CO 80202

Florida:
Bike-Florida
8 Broadway
Kissimmee, FL 34741

Georgia:
Bicycle Ride Across Georgia (BRAG)
P.O. Box 871111
Stone Mountain, GA 30087-0028

Illinois:
Pantagraph Area Cyclists Ride Around Corn
Country (PACRACC)
P.O. Box 2907
Bloomington, IL 61701

Indiana:
Indiana State Parks Touring Ride in Rural
Indiana (TRIRI)
P.O. Box 349
Clear Creek, IN 47426

Iowa:
RAGBRAI
P.O. Box 622
Des Moines, IA 50303-0622

Kansas:
Biking Across Kansas (BAK)
P.O. Box 8648
Wichita, KS 67208

Maine:
Maine's Original Outstanding Super
Adventure (MOOSA)
RR 1, Box 3278
Norway, ME 04268

Maine Wheels Bicycle Club Moose Tour
225 Paris Hill Rd.
South Paris, ME 04281

Trek Across Maine
128 Sewall St.
Augusta, ME 04330

Maine, Nova Scotia, and New Brunswick:
Lighthouse Tour
RR 1, Box 3278
Norway, ME 04268

Maryland:
First National Bank's Cycle Across Maryland
(CAM)
7 Church Ln. #8
Baltimore, MD 21208

Michigan:
Dick Allen Lansing to Mackinaw (DALMAC)
P.O. Box 219
Haslett, MI 48840

Pedal Across Lower Michigan (PALM)
P.O. Box 716
Ann Arbor, MI 48107

Rails-to-Trails Conservancy Detroit Free Press
Michigander
913 W. Holmes, Suite 145
Lansing, MI 48910

Missouri:
Cycle Across Missouri Parks (CAMP)
7187 Manchester Rd.
St. Louis, MO 63143

Montana:
Cycle Montana
Adventure Cycling Association
P.O. Box 8308
Missoula, MT 59807

Nebraska:
Bicycle Ride Across Nebraska (BRAN)
10730 Pacific St., Suite 218
Omaha, NE 68114-4780

New Mexico:
Santa Fe Trail Bicycle Trek
885 Camino Del Este
Santa Fe, NM 87501

North Dakota:
Cycling Around North Dakota In Sacagawea
Country (CANDISC)
Box 459
Garrison, ND 58540
800/ 799-4242

Ohio:
Great Ohio Bicycle Adventure (GOBA)
P.O. Box 14384
Columbus, OH 43214

Oklahoma:
Oklahoma FreeWheel
P.O. Box 21920
Tulsa, OK 74121-1920

Virginia:
Bike Virginia
P.O. Box 203
Williamsburg, VA 23187

Wisconsin:
GReat Annual Bicycle Adventure Along the
Wisconsin River (GRABAAWR)
Box 310
Spring Green, WI 53588-0310

Cross-US or Interstate:
Cycle America
P.O. Box 485
Cannon Falls, MN 55008

Mighty Mississippi Bicycle Adventure
3141 Dean Ct. Suite 107
Minneapolis, MN 55416

Pedal for Power: Across America
190 W. Ostend St., Suite 120
Baltimore, MD 21230

BENEFIT RIDES

MS (Multiple Sclerosis Society) 50, 75, and
150 Rides
Various locations and dates
212/ 476-0461

American AIDS Rides
Various locations and dates
800/ 825-1000

Tour de Cure
(American Diabetes Society)
Various locations and dates
800/ TOUR-888

Bike Aid
(Overseas Development Network)
800/ RIDE-808

MOUNTAIN BIKE FESTIVALS

Canyonlands Fat Tire Festival
Moab, UT
801/ 375-3231

Chequamegon Fat Tire Festival
Hayward, WI
715/ 798-3811 ext. 644

Fat Tire Bike Week
Crested Butte, CO
802/ 484-5737

Kernville Fat Tire Festival
Kernville, CA
800/ 861-6553
619/ 376-6553

New England Mountain Bike Festival
Randolph, VT
802/ 484-5737

West Virginia Fat Tire Festival
Slatyfork, WV
304/ 572-3771

WOMEN'S CAMPS AND CLINICS

Road Biking:

PowerBar Women's Camp
Contact: Carpenter/Phinney Bike Camps
303/ 442-2371 (CO)

Mountain Biking:

Bike Treks International
800/ 338-9445 (CO)

Coyote Hill Mountain Bike Camps
802/ 222-5133 (VT)

DORBA (Dallas Off-Road Bicycling
Association) Women's Weekend
Contact: Barry Montgomery, 972/ 579-5540
(TX)

Elk River Touring
304/ 572-3771 (WV)

MAD (Mature Adventurous Dames)
Contact: Jean Cherouny, 802/ 388-0320 (VT)

Outdoor Experience Mountain Bike Academy
Women's Camp
Contact: Outdoor Experience at Catamount
Family Center, 802/ 879-6001 (VT)

Team Big Bear for Women Only
909/ 866-4565 (CA)

Vail Mountain Bike Camps for Women
970/ 479-9444 (CO)

West Coast Women's Camp
Contact: West Coast School of Mountain
Biking, 604/ 931-6066 (BC, Canada)

West Virginia Women on Wheels
Contact: Elkins BIKEWORKS, 888/ 311-BIKE
(WV)

WOMBATS Camps with Jacquie Phelan
415/ 459-0980 (CA)

ORGANIZATIONS

Canadian Cycling Association
1600 James Naismith Dr.
Gloucester, Ontario K1B 5N4
613/ 748-5629

IMBA (International Mountain Bicycling
Association)
Box 7578
Boulder, CO 80306
303/ 545-9011
303/ 545-9026 (fax)

Rails-to-Trails Conservancy
1100 17th St. N.W., 10th Floor
Washington, DC 20036
202/ 331-9696 (phone)
202/ 466-3742 (fax)
e-mail: rtrails@transact.com
Web site: www.railtrails.org

Tandem Club of America
2220 Vanessa Dr.
Birmingham, AL 35242
205/ 991-7766
e-mail: tandems@mindspring.com

Ultra-Marathon Cycling Association
Box 53
Canyon, TX 79015
806/ 499-3210 (phone)
e-mail: ultra@cycling.org

USA Cycling (USCF and NORBA)
One Olympic Plaza
Colorado Springs, CO 80909
719/ 578-4581 (phone)
719/ 578-4628 (fax)

Selected Bibliography

"The Antioxidant All-Stars," *University of California at Berkeley Wellness Letter,* Vol. 13, No. 6 (March 1997), p. 1.

Beck, John L. and Byron P. Wildermuth, "The Female Athlete's Knee," *Clinics in Sports Medicine,* Vol. 4, No. 2 (April 1985), pp 345–66.

Bernstein, L., B. E. Henderson, R. Hanisch, J. Sullivan-Halley, and R. K. Ross, "Physical Exercise and Reduced Risk of Breast Cancer in Young Women," *Journal of the National Cancer Institute,* Vol. 86 (1994), pp 1403–08.

Blair, Steven N., "Physical Fitness and All-Cause Mortality," *Journal of the American Medical Association,* Vol. 262, No. 17 (3 November, 1989), pp 2395–401.

Brehm, Barbara A., "Hypertension: Does Exercise Have an Effect?", *Fitness Management,* Vol. 1, No. 1 (March–April 1985), pp 11, 56.

Brody, Jane, "Making Sense of Latest Twist on Fat in the Diet," *New York Times,* November 25, 1977, p. F9.

Burros, Marian, "Calcium Tablets Are Not All Created Equal," *New York Times* (27 January, 1988) pp C1, C8.

Butler, Ellen, "The Amenorrheic Athlete," *The Melpomene Report,* June 1985, pp 7–12.

Carpenter, Christine L. "Exercise and Menopause," *Fitness Management* (May–June 1987) pp 20–1.

Carpenter, Marshall W., Stanley P. Sady, Bente Hoegsberg, and others, "Fetal Heart Rate Response to Maternal Exertion," *Journal of the American Medical Association,* Vol. 259, No. 20 (27 May, 1988), pp 3006–9.

Coyle, Edward F. and Andrew R. Coggan, "Glucose Supplementation During Prolonged Cycling," *Sports Mediscope,* Vol. 6, No. 3 (July/August–September/October, 1987), p 4.

Cross, Kenneth D. and Gary Fisher, *A Study of Bicycle/Motor Vehicle Accidents: Identification of Problem Types and Countermeasure Approaches,* Vol. 1, US Department of Transportation, 1977.

Dawson, Alice, "Is Pregnancy a Good Time to Get Fit?" *Women's Sports and Fitness,* April 1986, p. 51.

Driscoll, Charles E., Edward T. Bope, Sue K. Mihalko, and James C. Puffer, "Women in Sports: Guidelines for Patient Fitness," *The Female Patient,* Vol. 13, No. 6 (June 1988), pp 41–51.

Eichner, Edward, "Exercise, Lymphokines, Calories, and Cancer," *The Physician and Sportsmedicine,* Vol. 15, No. 6 (June 1987), pp 109-15.

"Feeling Fat in a Thin Society," *Glamour* (February 1984), pp 198–201, 251–2.

Feldman, W., E. Feldman, and J. T. Goodman, "Culture Versus Biology: Children's Attitudes Toward Thinness and Fitness," *Pediatrics,* Vol. 81, No. 2 (February 1988), pp 190–4.

Freeman, Zelman, "Exercise and Sudden Cardiac Death," *The Medical Journal of Australia,* Vol. 142, No. 7 (1 April 1985), pp 383–4.

Frisch, R. E., G. Wyshak, N. L. Albright and others, "Lower Prevalence of Breast Cancer and Cancers of the Reproductive System Among Former College Athletes Compared to Non-Athletes," *British Journal of Cancer,* Vol. 52 (December 1985), pp 885–91.

Frisch, R. E., G. Wyshak, T. E. Albright, and others, "Lower Prevalence of Diabetes in Female Former College Athletes Compared with Nonathletes," *Diabetes,* Vol. 35 (October 1986), pp 1101–05.

Godin, G. and R. J. Shephard, "Psycho-Social Predictors of Exercise Intentions Among Spouses," *Canadian Journal of Applied Sport Sciences,* Vol. 10, No. 1 (March 1985), pp 36–43.

Gold, J. H. and S. K. Severino (eds.), *Premenstrual Dysphorias: Myths and Realities,* Washington, D. C., American Psychiatric Press, Inc., 1994.

Hales, Dianne and Robert Hales, "Using the Body to Mend the Mind," *American Health,* Vol. 4, No. 5 (June 1985), pp 27–31.

Harnack, Catherine and Valerie Lee, "Maternal Fitness Bibliography," Minneapolis, Melpomene Institute (August 1988).

Hornsby, W. Guyton, *The Fitness Book for People with Diabetes,* Alexandria, Virginia, American Diabetes Association, 1994.

Kaplan, Jerrold A., *Characteristics of the Regular Adult Bicycle User,* Washington, D.C., Federal Highway Administration, 1977.

Kiyonaga, Akira, Kikuo Arakawa, Hiroaki Tanaka, and Munehiro Shindo, "Blood Pressure and Hormonal Responses to Aerobic Exercises," *Hypertension,* Vol. 7, No. 1 (January–February 1985), pp 125–31.

Klein, Donald F. and Paul H. Wender, *Understanding Depression: A Complete Guide to its Diagnosis and Treatment,* New York and Oxford, Oxford University Press, 1993.

Kleiner, Susan M., "Antioxidant Answers," *The Physician and Sportsmedicine,* Vol. 24, No. 8 (August 1996), pp. 21-22.

Krakauer, Lewis J., James L. Anderson, Frank George, and others (eds.), *The Year Book of Sports Medicine, 1984,* Chicago, Year Book Medical Publishers, Inc., 1984.

LaPorte, Ronald E., Stephen Dearwater, Jane A. Cauley, and others, "Physical Activity or Cardiovascular Fitness: Which is More Important for Health?" *The Physician and Sportsmedicine,* Vol. 13, No. 3 (March 1986), pp 145–57.

Lee, Valerie, Laurie Koltes, Bonnie Schultz, and others, "A New Look at Nutrition," *The Melpomene Report* (June 1985), pp 19–24.

Lutter, Judy Mahle, "Mixed Messages About Osteoporosis in Female Athletes," *The Physician and Sportsmedicine,* Vol. 11, No. 9 (September 1983), reprint.

Lutter, Judy Mahle, Susan Merrick, Lyn Steffen, and others, "Physical Activity Through the Life Span: Long-Term Effects of an Active Lifestyle," *The Melpomene Report* (February 1985) pp 4–8.

McKee, Gerald (ed.), "Special Report: The Female Athlete," *Sports Medicine Digest* (1988).

Mellion, Morris B., "Exercise Therapy for Anxiety and Depressions (Parts 1 and 2)," *Postgraduate Medicine,* Vol. 77, No. 3 (15 February, 1986), pp 59–66 and 91–6.

Melpomene Institute for Women's Health Research, "Guidelines for Exercising While Pregnant: Running and Swimming" (unpublished material), revised 1987.

Melpomene, Pregnancy and Exercise Project (unpublished research summaries), Minneapolis (n.d.).

Melpomene, "Post-Partum Exercise Considerations" (unpublished guidelines), (n.d.).

Olsen, Eric, "Exercise, More or Less," *Hippocrates* (January–February 1988) pp 65–72.

Orbach, Susie, *Fat is a Feminist Issue,* New York (Berkeley Books) and London (Paddington Press), 1978.

Orbach, Susie, *Hunger Strike: The Anorectic's Struggle as a Metaphor for Our Age,* New York and London, W. W. Norton & Company, 1986.

Polivy, Janet and C. Peter Herman, *Breaking the Diet Habit,* New York, Basic Books, Inc., 1983.

Riggs, B. Lawrence and L. Joseph Melton III, "Involutional Osteoporosis," *The New England Journal of Medicine,* Vol. 314 (26 June, 1986), pp 1676-84.

Rodgers, Gregory B., Deborah Kale Tinsworth, Curtis Polen and others, *Bicycle Use and Hazard Patterns in the United States,* U.S. Consumer Product Safety Commission, Washington, D.C., June 1994.

Ryan, Monique, "Sports Drinks Can Fuel Short, Hard Efforts," *VeloNews* (May 22, 1995), pp 52–54

Sachs, Jeffrey J., Patricia Holmgreen, Suzanne M. Smith, Daniel M. Sosin, "Bicycle-Associated Head Injuries and Deaths in the United States from 1984 Through 1988," *Journal of the American Medical Association,* Vol. 266 (December 1991), pp 3016–18.

Severino, Sally K., *Premenstrual Syndrome: A Clinician's Guide,* New York, The Guildford Press, Inc., 1989.

Shangold, Mona M., "Gynecologic Concerns in the Woman Athlete," *Clinics in Sports Medicine,* Vol. 3, No. 4 (October 1984), pp 867–78.

Siscovik, David S., Ronald E. LaPorte, and Jeffrey M. Newman, "The Disease-Specific Benefits and Risks of Physical Activity and Exercise," *Public Health Reports,* Vol. 100, No. 2 (March–April 1985), pp 180–8.

Smith, David E., "Diagnostic Treatment and Aftercare Approaches to Cocaine Abuse," *Journal of Substance Abuse Treatment,* Vol. 1 (1984), pp 5–9.

Smith, Everett L., "Exercise for Prevention of Osteoporosis: A Review," *The Physician and Sportsmedicine,* Vol. 10, No. 3 (March 1982), pp 72–83.

Smith, Everett L., (ed.), "Osteoporosis: A Symposium," *The Physician and Sportsmedicine* Vol. 15, No. 11, (November 1987), pp 65-118.

Standing Committee on the Scientific Evaluation of Dietary Reference Intakes, *Dietary Reference Intakes for Calcium, Phosphorus, Magnesium, Vitamin D, and Flouride,* Food and Nutrition Board, Institute of Medicine, National Academy Press, Washington, D.C., (1997).

Subcommittee on the Tenth Edition of the RDAs, Food and Nutrition Board, Commission on Life Sciences, National Research Council, *Recommended Dietary Allowances,* 10th ed., Washington, D. C. National Academy Press (1989).

Thune, Inger, "Physical Activity and Energy Balance—Modifiable Lifestyle Factors for Breast Cancer?," *Irish Medical Journal,* Vol. 90, No. 5 (August/September 1997), pp 168–69.

Thune, I., T. Brenn, E. Lund, and M. Gaard, "Physical Activity and the Risk of Breast Cancer," *The New England Journal of Medicine,* Vol. 336, No. 18 (May 1, 1997), pp 1269–75.

U.S. Department of Agriculture and U.S. Department of Health and Human Services, *Nutrition and Your Health: Dietary Guidelines for Americans,* 4th ed., Washington, D.C., Government Printing Office, (1995).

Weston, Louise C. and Josephine A. Ruggiero, "The Popular Approach to Women's Health Issues: A Content Analysis of Women's Magazines in the 1970's," *Women and Health,* Vol. 10, No. 4 (Winter 1985/86), pp 47–62.

FURTHER READING

Allen, John S. *The Complete Book of Bicycle Commuting,* Emmaus, Pennsylvania, Rodale Press (1981) (out of print).

Bailey, Covert, *The New Fit or Fat,* Boston, Houghton Mifflin (1991).

Bennett, William and Joel Gurin, *The Dieter's Dilemma: Eating Less and Weighing More,* New York, Basic Books, Inc. (1982).

Butler, Joan Marie, *Fit & Pregnant: The Pregnant Woman's Guide to Exercise,* Waverly, New York, Acorn Publishing (1996).

Cuthbertson, Tom, *Anybody's Bike Book,* Berkeley, California, Ten Speed Press (1998).

Epstein, Diane and Kathleen Thompson, *Feeding on Dreams: Why America's Diet Industry Doesn't Work and What Will Work for You,* New York, Macmillan Publishing Company (1994).

Forester, John, *Effective Cycling,* Cambridge, Massachusetts, London MIT Press (1986).

Glowacz, Dave, *Urban Bikers: Tricks & Tips: Low-Tech and No-Tech Ways to Find, Ride, & Keep a Bicycle,* Chicago, Wordspace Press, (1998).

Mountain Biking Skills, by the editors of *Mountain Bike* and *Bicycling,* Emmaus, Rodale Press, Pennsylvania (1996).

Murphy, Dervla, *Full Tilt,* London, John Murray (1965).

Myers, Judy with Maribeth Mellin, *Staying Sober: A Nutrition and Exercise Program for the Recovering Alcoholic,* New York, Pocket Books (1987) (out of print).

Savage, Barbara, *Miles from Nowhere,* Seattle, Washington, Mountaineers Books (1983).

Selby, Bettina, *Riding North One Summer,* London, Chatto and Windus (1990).

Selby, Bettina, *Riding the Desert Trail,* London, Chatto and Windus (1988).

Stuart, Robin and Cathy Jensen, *Mountain Biking for Women,* Waverly, New York, Acorn Publishing (1994).

Index